IBM PC/8088
ASSEMBLY
LANGUAGE
PROGRAMMING

IBM PC/8088 ASSEMBLY LANGUAGE PROGRAMMING

AVTAR SINGH, Ph.D.
Anderson Jacobson, Inc.

WALTER A. TRIEBEL
Intel Corporation

PRENTICE-HALL, INC., *Englewood Cliffs, New Jersey 07632*

Library of Congress Cataloging in Publication Data

Singh, Avtar. (date)
   IBM PC/8088 assembly language programming.

   Bibliography: p.
   Includes index.
   1. Assembler language (Computer program language)
2. IBM Personal Computer--Programming. 3. INTEL
8088 (Microprocessor)--Programming. I. Triebel,
Walter A. II. Title. III. Title: I.B.M. P.C./8088
assembly language programming.
QA76.73.A8S55 1985   001.64'2   84-17991
ISBN 0-13-448358-8 (pbk.)
ISBN 0-13-448317-0 (dsk.)
ISBN 0-13-448309-X (pbk./dsk.)
ISBN 0-13-448127-5 (case)

Editorial/production supervision and interior design: Karen Skrable Fortgang
Cover design: Whitman Studio, Inc.
Manufacturing buyer: Anthony Caruso

If your diskette is defective or damaged in transit, return it directly
to Prentice-Hall at the address below for a no-charge replacement
within 90 days of the date of purchase. Mail the defective diskette
together with your name and address.

               Prentice-Hall, Inc.
               Attention: Ryan Colby
               College Operations
               Englewood Cliffs, New Jersey 07632

The author and publisher of this book have used their best efforts in
preparing this book and software. These efforts include the
development, research, and testing of the theories and programs to
determine their effectiveness. The author and publisher make no
warranty of any kind, expressed or implied, with regard to these
programs or the documentation contained in this book. The author
and publisher shall not be liable in any event for incidental or
consequential damages in connection with, or arising out of, the
furnishing, performance, or use of these programs.

Printed in the United States of America

10 9 8 7 6 5 4 3 2 1

ISBN 0-13-448127-5 {CASE}
ISBN 0-13-448358-8 {PBK}
ISBN 0-13-448309-X {PBK/DSK}   01
ISBN 0-13-448317-0 {DSK}

PRENTICE-HALL INTERNATIONAL, INC., *London*
PRENTICE-HALL OF AUSTRALIA PTY. LIMITED, *Sydney*
EDITORA PRENTICE-HALL DO BRASIL, LTDA., *Rio de Janeiro*
PRENTICE-HALL CANADA INC., *Toronto*
PRENTICE-HALL OF INDIA PRIVATE LIMITED, *New Delhi*
PRENTICE-HALL OF JAPAN, INC., *Tokyo*
PRENTICE-HALL OF SOUTHEAST ASIA PTE. LTD., *Singapore*
WHITEHALL BOOKS LIMITED, *Wellington, New Zealand*

Avtar Singh
To my wife, Jaswant

Walter A. Triebel
To my daughter, Lindsey

CONTENTS

PREFACE

This book, *IBM PC/8088 Assembly Language Programming,* opens to you— the user of an IBM PC—the full power of the 8088 microcomputer in the PC. In this book you will learn 8088 assembly language programming and how to use the software development tools, the macroassembler (MASM), linker (LINK), and debugger (DEBUG) that are available with the PC. The ability to write programs in 8088 assembler permits you to communicate with the 8088 microprocessor directly in its native language—8088 machine language.

You may ask the question, "Why program the PC in assembly language?" There are two key reasons why assembly language programming is very important. The first is that programs written in 8088 assembler operate much faster than those written in a high-level language, such as BASIC or Pascal. In fact, an assembler version of a program may run as much as ten times faster than its equivalent program written in Pascal and as much as one hundred times faster than its equivalent program written in an interpretive BASIC. The second reason for using 8088 assembler is more subtle. It turns out that the general nature of compilers for high-level languages, such as Pascal, produce inefficient machine code. Therefore, programs written in a high-level language need a larger amount of memory. So the second advantage of programming in 8088 assembler is that programs will take up less space in memory.

IBM PC/8088 Assembly Language Programming covers the five things you need to learn to be successful at writing assembly language programs for the IBM PC.

1. Software architecture of the 8088 microprocessor—you learn about its internal registers, flags, memory organization and stack, and how they are used from a software point of view.

2. Software development tools of the PC—you learn how to use the program debugger (DEBUG), the macroassembler (MASM), and the linker (LINK).

3. Instruction set of the 8088—you learn the function of each of the instructions in the instruction set, the allowed operand variations, and how to write statements using the instructions.

4. Programming techniques—you learn basic techniques of programming such as flowcharting, jumps, loops, strings, subroutines, parameter passing, and so on.

5. Applications—you are led step by step through the process of writing programs for many practical applications. Examples are block move routine, ASCII to EBCDIC code conversion, data table search routine, data table sort routine, floating point multiply routine, memory test routine, keyboard and display control routines, time delay routine, and sound generation using the speaker.

In addition to learning these five topics, you will have plenty of hands-on experience as you work your way through the book. This is because you will use the IBM macroassembler, linker, and debugger programs to apply what you learn about 8088 assembly language programming directly on the IBM PC. This is done through examples and assignments that require you to both analyze instructions and programs and then verify your results by performing the same operations on the IBM PC.

USING THIS BOOK

You will learn how to program the IBM PC with 8088 assembler by reading *IBM PC/8088 Assembly Language Programming*. The eight chapters of the book should be read in order. However, Chapter 2 is a review of number systems, information organization, and information coding. Skim through this chapter before reading it; if you are already familiar with this material, the chapter may be skipped.

While reading through the book, perform all examples and assignments that involve operations on your personal computer. The programs for many examples are available on floppy diskette. This diskette is DOS 2.1 compatible.

As you complete the reading of a section of a chapter, do its corresponding assignment section. Check your answers with those provided at the end of the book. Be sure you are able to do all assignments correctly before continuing.

IBM PC/8088
ASSEMBLY
LANGUAGE
PROGRAMMING

1

INTRODUCTION
TO THE IBM PC

1.1 INTRODUCTION

In the last few years we have seen revolutionary changes in the computer industry. During this period there has been a major change in direction of business away from minicomputers to smaller, lower-cost microcomputers. The IBM Personal Computer (the PC, as it has become known), which was introduced in mid-1981, was the first microcomputer introduced with a 16-bit microprocessor, the 8088, as its central processing unit. The PC quickly became the driving force in this evolutionary process, and today it stands as the industry standard in the personal computer marketplace.

In this book we teach you 8088 assembly language programming and how to use the software development tools, the *MASM* (macroassembler), *LINK* (linker), and *DEBUG* (debugger) *programs* that are provided for the PC. This chapter is an introduction to microcomputers and the IBM PC. The topics that follow are discussed:

1. The IBM personal computer—a general-purpose microcomputer
2. General architecture of the IBM PC
3. Software—the computer program
4. Learning to program the PC with assembly language

1.2 THE IBM PERSONAL COMPUTER—
A GENERAL-PURPOSE MICROCOMPUTER

The IBM personal computer (the PC), which is shown in Fig. 1.1, was IBM's first entry into the microcomputer market. Since its introduction in midyear 1981, market acceptance of the PC has grown by leaps and bounds so that today it is the leading personal computer. One of the important keys to its success is that an enormous amount of application software quickly became available for the machine. Today there are more than 3000 off-the-shelf software packages available for use on the PC. They include business applications, software languages, educational programs, games, and even alternate operating systems. The large success of the PC has caused IBM to spawn additional family members. IBM's *PC/XT* is shown in Fig. 1.2 and the *PC Jr.* in Fig. 1.3. Together these three machines offer a wide variety to computing capability, performance, and software base for use in business and at home.

The IBM PC is an example of a *general-purpose digital computer*. By *general-purpose* we mean that it is intended to run programs for a wide variety of applications; by *digital computer* we mean that its intended use is for processing data or information. For instance, one user could use the PC with a standard application package for accounting or inventory control. In this type of application, the primary task of the microcomputer is to analyze and process

Figure 1.1 IBM personal computer. (*Courtesy International Business Machine Corp.*)

Figure 1.2 IBM's PC/XT (*Courtesy International Business Machine Corp.*)

Figure 1.3 IBM's PC Jr. (*Courtesy International Business Machine Corp.*)

a large amount of data, known as the *data base*. Another user could be running a word-processing software package. This is an example of an input/output-intensive task. The user enters text information, this information is reorganized by the microcomputer and then output to a diskette or printer. A third example is where a programmer uses a language, such as FORTRAN, to write programs for scientific applications. Here the primary function of the computer is to solve complex mathematical problems. The point we want to make is that the IBM PC used for each of these applications is the same. The only difference is the software the computer is running.

We have already mentioned that the IBM PC is a *microcomputer*. Let us now look at what a microcomputer is and how it differs from the other classes of computers.

Evolution of the computer marketplace over the last 25 years has taken us from very large *mainframe computers* to smaller *minicomputers* and now even smaller microcomputers. These three classes of computers do not replace each other. They all coexist in the marketplace. Today, computer users have the opportunity to select the computer that best meets their needs. For instance, a large university or institution still would select a mainframe computer for its data processing center. On the other hand, a department or group at a university or in business might select a minicomputer for a multi-user-dedicated need such as application software development. Moreover, managers may select a microcomputer, such as the PC, for their personal needs such as word processing and data base management.

Along the evolutionary path from mainframes to microcomputers, the basic concepts of computer architecture have not changed. Just like the mainframe and minicomputer, the microcomputer is a general-purpose electronic data processing system intended for use in a wide variety of applications. The key difference is that microcomputers, such as the IBM PC, employ the newest *large-scale integrated (LSI) circuit technology* to implement a smaller, reduced-capability computer system, but with a much lower cost than a minicomputer. However, microcomputers such as IBM's PCXT, which are designed for the high-performance end of the microcomputer market, are beginning to capture part of the market that was traditionally supported with lower-performance minicomputers.

1.3 GENERAL ARCHITECTURE OF THE IBM PC

The *hardware* of a microcomputer system can be divided into four functional sections. The block diagram of Fig. 1.4 shows that they are the *input unit, microprocessing unit, memory unit,* and *output unit.* Each of these units has a special function in terms of overall system operation. Let us now look at each of these sections in more detail.

The heart of a microcomputer is its microprocessing unit (MPU). The

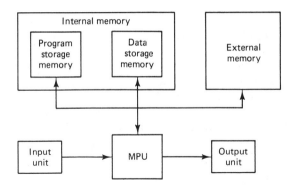

Figure 1.4 General microcomputer system architecture.

MPU of a microcomputer is implemented with an LSI device known as a *microprocessor*. A microprocessor is a general-purpose processing unit built into a single integrated circuit. The microprocessor used in the IBM PC is Intel Corporation's 8088, which is shown in Fig. 1.5.

Earlier we pointed out that the 8088 is a 16-bit microprocessor. To be more accurate, it is the 8-bit external bus version in Intel's 8086 family of 16-bit microprocessors. Even though the 8088 has an 8-bit external bus, its internal architecture is 16 bits in length and it can directly process 16-bit-wide data. For this reason, we consider the 8088 as a 16-bit microprocessor.

The 8088 MPU is the part of the IBM PC that executes instructions of the program and processes data. It is responsible for performing all arithmetic operations and making the logical decisions initiated by the computer's program. In addition to arithmetic and logic functions, the MPU controls overall system operation.

The input and output units are the means by which the MPU com-

Figure 1.5 8088 microprocessor. (*Courtesy Intel Corporation*)

municates with the outside world. Input units, such as the *keyboard* on the
IBM PC, allow the user to input information or commands to the MPU. For instance, a programmer could key in the lines of a BASIC program from the
keyboard. Many other input devices are available for the IBM PC. Two examples are a *mouse* for implementing a more user-friendly input interface and a
joy stick for use when playing video games.

The most widely used output devices on the IBM PC are the *display* and
printer. The output unit in a microcomputer is used to give feedback to the user
and for producing documented results. For instance, key entries from the
keyboard are echoed back to the display. This lets the user confirm that the correct entry was made. Moreover, the results produced by the MPU's processing
can be displayed or printed. Alternate output devices are also available for the
PC; for instance, it can be equipped with a color video display instead of the
standard video display.

The memory unit in a microcomputer is used to store information such as
number or character data. By *store* we mean that memory has the ability to
hold this information for processing or for outputting at a later time. Programs
that define how the computer is to operate and process data also reside in
memory.

In the microcomputer system, memory is divided into two different sections, called *internal memory* and *external memory.* External memory is used
for long-term storage of information that is not currently being used. For example, it can hold programs, files of data, and files of information. In the IBM PC,
the *floppy disk drives* represent the long-term storage memory subsystem. If
the system has 5-1/4-inch double-sided, double-density drives, each floppy
diskette can store up to 320K (three hundred and twenty thousand) bytes of
data. The IBM PC/XT employs a newer form of mass storage device. It has one
of the floppy drives replaced with a 10M (ten million) byte *Winchester hard disk
drive.*

Internal memory is a smaller segment of memory that is used for temporary storage of active information such as the operating system of the computer, the program that is currently being executed, and the data that is being
processed. In Fig. 1.4 we see that internal memory is further subdivided into
program storage memory and *data storage memory.* The program segment of
memory is used to store instructions of the operating system and programs.
The data segment contains data that are to be processed by the programs as
they are executed.

Typically, internal memory is implemented with both *read-only memory*
(ROM) and *random access read/write memory* (RAM) integrated circuits. The
IBM PC has 16K bytes of ROM and can be configured with from 64K bytes to
256K bytes of RAM without adding memory expansion boards. To run the *8088
macroassembler* that is available from IBM on the PC, it must have a minimum
of 96K bytes of RAM.

Data, whether it represents numbers, characters, or instructions, can be stored in either ROM or RAM. In the IBM PC a small part of the operating system and BASIC language are made resident to the computer by supplying them in ROM. By using ROM, this information is made *nonvolatile*—that is, the information is not lost if power is turned off.

On the other hand, data that are to be processed and information that frequently changes must be stored in a type of internal memory from which they can be read by the microprocessor, modified through processing, and written back for storage. For this reason they are stored in RAM instead of ROM. For instance, the *DOS 2.1 operating system* for the PC is provided on a diskette, and to use it we must load it from disk into the RAM of the microcomputer. RAM is a *volatile* memory. That is, when power is turned off, the data that it holds are lost. This is why the DOS operating system must be reloaded into the PC each time power is turned on.

1.4 SOFTWARE—THE COMPUTER PROGRAM

In section 1.3, we described the hardware of a microcomputer system such as the IBM PC. This leads us to the topic of *software*. A computer cannot think about how to process data. It must be told exactly what to do, where to get data, what to do with the data, and where to put the results when it is done. This is the job of software in a microcomputer system.

The sequence of instructions that is used to tell a computer what to do is called a *program*. When the computer is operating, it fetches and executes one instruction of the program after the other. In this way, the instructions of the program guide it step by step through the task that it is to perform.

Software is a general name used to refer to a wide variety of programs that can be run by a microcomputer. Examples are *languages, operating systems, application programs,* and *diagnostics*.

The native language of the IBM PC is 8088 *machine language*. Programs must always be coded in this machine language before they can be executed by the 8088. The 8088 microprocessor understands and performs operations for a group of 117 basic instructions. When expressed in machine code, an instruction is encoded using 0s and 1s. A single machine instruction can take anywhere from one to six bytes of code.

Even though the 8088 only understands machine code, it is almost impossible to write programs directly in machine language. For this reason, programs are normally written in other languages, such as 8088 assembler or a high-level language such as BASIC or Pascal.

In 8088 assembly language each of the basic *instructions* that can be performed by the 8088 microprocessor is described with alphanumeric symbols instead of with zeros and ones. Each instruction is represented by one *assembly language statement* in a program. This statement must specify which operation is to be performed and what data operands are to be processed. For this reason, an instruction can be divided into two parts: its *opcode* (operation code) and its *operands*. The opcode is the part of the instruction that identifies the operation that is to be performed. For example, typical operations are add, subtract, and move. Each opcode is assigned a unique one- through five-letter combination. This letter combination is referred to as the *mnemonic* for the instruction. For example, the mnemonics for the earlier operations are ADD, SUB, and MOV. Operands identify the data that are to be processed as the microprocessor carries out the operation specified by the opcode.

An example of an instruction written in 8088 assembly language is

ADD AX,BX

This instruction says, "Add the contents of BX and AX together and put the sum in AX." AX is called the *destination operand* because it is the place where the result ends up, and BX is called the *source operand.*

Another example of an assembly language statement is

START: MOV AX,BX ;COPY BX INTO AX

This statement begins with the word START:. It is an address identifier for the instruction MOV AX,BX. This type of identifier is called a *label* or *tag*. The instruction is followed by ;COPY BX INTO AX. This part of the statement is called a *comment*. Thus a general format for an assembly language statement is

LABEL INSTRUCTION COMMENT

Programs written in assembly language are referred to as *source code*. An example of a short 8088 assembly language program is shown in Fig. 1.6(a). The assembly language statements are located on the left. Frequently, comments describing the statements are included on the right. This type of documentation makes it easier for a program to be read and debugged.

Assembly language programs cannot be directly executed on the 8088. They must still be converted to equivalent machine code for execution by the 8088. This conversion is automatically done by running the program through what is called an *assembler*. The machine code output produced by the assembler is called *object code*.

Figure 1.6(b) is the *listing* produced by assembling the assembly language source code in Fig. 1.6(a) with IBM's macroassembler for the PC. Reading from left to right, this listing contains addresses of memory locations, the machine language instructions, the original assembly language statements, and comments. Note that for simplicity the machine code instructions are expressed in hexadecimal notation, not in binary.

Use of assembly language makes it much easier to write a program. But notice that there is still a one-to-one relationship between assembly and machine language instructions.

High-level languages make writing programs even easier. In a language like BASIC, high-level commands such as FOR, NEXT, and GO are provided. These commands no longer correspond to a single machine-language state-

```
A>TYPE B:BLOCK.SRC

TITLE   BLOCK-MOVE PROGRAM
        PAGE    ,132
COMMENT *This program moves a block of specified number of bytes
         from one place to another place*

;Define constants used in this program

        N       =       16          ;Bytes to be moved
        BLK1ADDR=       100H        ;Source block offset address
        BLK2ADDR=       120H        ;Destination block offset addr
        DATASEGADDR=    0020H       ;Data segment start address


STACK_SEG       SEGMENT         STACK 'STACK'
                DB              64 DUP(?)
STACK_SEG       ENDS


CODE_SEG        SEGMENT         'CODE'
BLOCK           PROC            FAR
        ASSUME  CS:CODE_SEG,SS:STACK_SEG

;To return to DEBUG program put return address on the stack

        PUSH    DS
        MOV     AX, 0
        PUSH    AX

;Set up the data segment address

        MOV     AX, DATASEGADDR
        MOV     DS, AX

;Set up the source and destination offset adresses

        MOV     SI, BLK1ADDR
        MOV     DI, BLK2ADDR

;Set up the count of bytes to be moved

        MOV     CX, N

;Copy source block to destination block

NXTPT:  MOV     AH, [SI]            ;Move a byte
        MOV     [DI], AH
        INC     SI                  ;Update pointers
        INC     DI
        DEC     CX                  ;Update byte counter
        JNZ     NXTPT               ;Repeat for next byte
        RET                         ;Return to DEBUG program
BLOCK           ENDP
CODE_SEG        ENDS
        END     BLOCK               ;End of program

A>
```

(a)

Figure 1.6 (a) Typical 8088 assembly language program; (b) equivalent assembled machine code.

```
 1
 2
 3                                              TITLE    BLOCK-MOVE PROGRAM
 4
 5                                                       PAGE     ,132
 6
 7                                              COMMENT *This program moves a block of specified number of bytes
 8                                                       from one place to another place*
 9
10
11                                              ;Define constants used in this program
12
13        = 0010                                         N         =         16              ;Bytes to be moved
14        = 0100                                         BLK1ADDR=           100H            ;Source block offset address
15        = 0120                                         BLK2ADDR=           120H            ;Destination block offset addr
16        = 0020                                         DATASEGADDR=        0020H           ;Data segment start address
17
18
19        0000                                  STACK_SEG          SEGMENT            STACK 'STACK'
20        0000      40 [                                           DB                 64 DUP(?)
21                          ??
22                        ]
23
24        0040                                  STACK_SEG          ENDS
25
26
27        0000                                  CODE_SEG           SEGMENT            'CODE'
28        0000                                  BLOCK              PROC               FAR
29                                                        ASSUME  CS:CODE_SEG,SS:STACK_SEG
30
31                                              ;To return to DEBUG program put return address on the stack
32
33        0000  1E                                        PUSH      DS
34        0001  B8 0000                                   MOV       AX, 0
35        0004  50                                        PUSH      AX
36
37                                              ;Set up the data segment address
38
39        0005  B8 0020                                   MOV       AX, DATASEGADDR
40        0008  8E D8                                     MOV       DS, AX
41
42                                              ;Set up the source and destination offset adresses
43
44        000A  BE 0100                                   MOV       SI, BLK1ADDR
45        000D  BF 0120                                   MOV       DI, BLK2ADDR
46
47                                              ;Set up the count of bytes to be moved
48
49        0010  B9 0010                                   MOV       CX, N
50
51                                              ;Copy source block to destination block
52
53        0013  8A 24                           NXTPT:    MOV       AH, [SI]                 ;Move a byte
```

```
54        0015  88 25                                     MOV       [DI], AH
55        0017  46                                        INC       SI                       ;Update pointers
56        0018  47                                        INC       DI
57        0019  49                                        DEC       CX                       ;Update byte counter
58        001A  75 F7                                     JNZ       NXTPT                    ;Repeat for next byte
59        001C  CB                                        RET                                ;Return to DEBUG program
60        001D                                  BLOCK              ENDP
61        001D                                  CODE_SEG           ENDS
62                                                        END       BLOCK                    ;End of program
```

(b)

Figure 1.6 (continued)

```
The IBM Personal Computer Assembler 01-15-84          PAGE    Symbols-1
BLOCK-MOVE PROGRAM


Segments and groups:

                N a m e              Size    align    combine class

    CODE_SEG . . . . . . . . . . .   001D    PARA     NONE    'CODE'
    STACK_SEG. . . . . . . . . . .   0040    PARA     STACK   'STACK'

Symbols:

                N a m e              Type    Value    Attr

    BLK1ADDR . . . . . . . . . . .   Number  0100
    BLK2ADDR . . . . . . . . . . .   Number  0120
    BLOCK. . . . . . . . . . . . .   F PROC  0000     CODE_SEG       Length =001D
    DATASEGADDR. . . . . . . . . .   Number  0020
    N. . . . . . . . . . . . . . .   Number  0010
    NXTPT. . . . . . . . . . . . .   L NEAR  0013     CODE_SEG

    Warning Severe
    Errors  Errors
    0       0

    A>
```

(b)(cont)

Figure 1.6 (continued)

ment. In fact, they may require many statements to be implemented. Again, the program must be converted to machine code before it can be run on the 8088. The program that converts high-level language statements to machine code instructions is called a *compiler*.

Some languages—for instance, BASIC—are not always compiled. Instead, *interpretive* versions of the language are available. When a program written in an interpretive form of BASIC is executed, each line of the program is interpreted just before it is executed and at that moment replaced with a corresponding machine-language routine. It is this machine-code routine that is executed by the 8088.

The question you may be asking yourself right now is that if it is so much easier to write programs with a high-level language, then why is it important to know how to program the 8088 in its assembly language? Let us now answer this question.

We just pointed out that if a program is written in a high-level language, it must be compiled into machine code before it can be run on the 8088. The general nature with which compilers must be designed usually results in inefficient machine code. That is, the quality of the machine code that is produced for the program depends on the quality of the compiler program in use. What is found is that a compiled machine-code implementation of a program that was written in a high-level language results in many more machine-code instructions than an assembled version of an equivalent assembly language program. This leads us to the two key benefits derived from writing programs in assembly language: first, the machine code program that is produced will take up less memory space than the compiled version of the program; second, it will execute much faster.

Now we know the benefits attained by writing programs in assembly language, but we still do not know when these benefits are important. To be important, they must outweigh the additional effort that must be put into writing the program in assembly language instead of a high-level language. One of the major uses of assembly language programming is in *real-time applications.* By *real-time* we mean that the task required by the application must be completed before any other input to the program can occur that will alter its operation.

For example, the *device service routine* that controls the operation of the floppy disk drives of the PC is a good example of a program that is usually written in assembly language. This is because it is a segment of program that must closely control hardware of the microcomputer in real time. In this case, a program that is written in a high-level language probably could not respond quickly enough to control the hardware, and even if it could, operations performed with the disk subsystem would be very slow. Some other examples of hardware-related operations typically performed by routines written in assembler are communication routines such as those that drive the display and printer and the I/O routine that scans the keyboard.

Assembly language is not only important for controlling hardware devices of the microcomputer system. Its use is also important when performing pure software operations. For instance, applications frequently require the microcomputer to search through a large table of data in memory looking for a special string of characters—for instance, a person's name. This type of operation can be easily performed by writing a program in a high-level language; however, for large tables of data the search will take very long. By implementing the search routine through assembly language, the performance of the search operation is greatly improved. Other examples of software operations that may require implementation with high-performance routines derived from assembly language are *code translations,* such as from ASCII to EBCDIC; *table sort* or *search routines,* such as a bubble sort; and *mathematical routines,* such as those for floating-point arithmetic.

Not all parts of an application require real-time performance. For this reason, it is a common practice to mix routines developed through a high-level language and routines developed with assembly language in the same program. That is, assembler is used to code those parts of the application that must perform real-time operations; high-level language is used to write those parts that are not time critical; and the machine-code segments are linked together to form the final application program.

1.5 LEARNING TO PROGRAM THE PC WITH ASSEMBLY LANGUAGE

Now that we have introduced assembly language, machine language, and the importance of programming in assembler, let us look at what you need to learn in order to be able to write programs in 8088 assembly language. As you progress through *IBM PC/8088 Assembly Language Programming,* you will find that to become an effective assembly-language programmer of the IBM PC, you must develop a thorough understanding of the following five topics:

1. Software architecture of the 8088 microprocessor
2. Use of the IBM PC's macroassembler (MASM), linker (LINK), and debugger (DEBUG)
3. Instructions of the 8088's instruction set
4. Programming techniques such as flowcharts, subroutines, and parameter passing
5. Applications such as table sorts, code conversions, and floating-point arithmetic calculations

This is exactly what you will learn in Chapters 3 through 8 of the book.

ASSIGNMENT

Section 1.2

1. What is a *general-purpose* computer?
2. Name the three classes of computers.
3. What are the main similarities and differences between the minicomputer and the microcomputer?

Section 1.3

4. What is the heart of the microcomputer system called?
5. What is an 8088?
6. What is the primary input unit of the PC? Give two other examples of input units available for the PC.
7. What are the primary output devices of the PC?
8. What two sections is the memory of a PC partitioned into?
9. What is the storage capacity of a 5 1/4-inch double-sided, double-density floppy diskette for the PC? What is the storage capacity of the Winchester drive in the PCXT?
10. What do ROM and RAM stand for?
11. How much RAM is needed to run the 8088 macroassembler program on the PC?
12. Why must the operating system be reloaded from the DOS diskette each time power is turned on?

Section 1.4

13. What tells a computer what to do, where to get data, how to process the data, and where to put the results when done?
14. What is the name given to a sequence of instructions that is used to guide a computer through a task?
15. What is the native language of the 8088?
16. How does machine language differ from assembly language?
17. What does *opcode* stand for?
18. What is an *operand*? Give two types.
19. In the assembly language statement

      START: ADD AX,BX ;ADD BX TO AX

    what is the label?
20. What is the function of an assembler? A compiler?
21. What is *object code*?
22. Give two benefits derived from writing programs in assembly language instead of a high-level language.
23. What is meant by the phrase *real-time application*?
24. List two hardware-related applications that require use of assembly language programming. Name two software-related applications.

2

NUMBER SYSTEMS, INFORMATION ORGANIZATION, AND INFORMATION CODING

2.1 INTRODUCTION

In this chapter we shall review some of the basic material that is needed as background in order to study assembly language programming for the 8088 microprocessor in the IBM PC.

In microcomputers such as the PC, data, instructions, and system operations are described using numbers. The types of numbers used are not normally the decimal numbers we are familiar with; instead, binary and hexadecimal numbers are used. For this reason, we shall begin our study of the 8088 and its assembly language with these number systems and a number of other related topics. The topics included in this chapter are as follows:

1. A number system
2. Binary numbers
3. Conversion between decimal and binary numbers
4. Hexadecimal numbers
5. Conversion between hexadecimal and binary numbers
6. Words, bytes, and data organization
7. Addition and subtraction of binary numbers
8. Numeric and alphanumeric codes
9. Parity and the parity bit

2.2 A NUMBER SYSTEM

Here we shall use decimal numbers to develop the general characteristics of a *number system.* A number system is formed by selecting a set of symbols to represent numerical values. When doing this, we can select any group of symbols. The number of symbols used is called the *base* of the number system.

For example, let us look at the decimal number system. It is made by selecting the numerical symbols 0 through 9. These symbols are shown in Fig. 2.1(a). Here we find that 10 different symbols are used, so the base of the decimal number system is 10. Each of these symbols indicates a different numerical quantity. In the decimal system, 0 is the smallest quantity and 9 is the largest quantity.

Digit Notation

With just the 10 basic symbols of the decimal number system, we cannot form every quantity needed in mathematics and science. For this reason, *digit notation* is used. An example of a decimal number written in digit notation is

$$735.23$$

Here the same basic symbols are used to form a larger multidigit number. This number has symbols entered into five different digit locations.

Weight

When digit notation is in use, the value of a symbol depends on its location in the number. The positional value of a digit is known as its *weight.* For instance, in the number 735.23 the symbol 3 occurs in two locations. Because the weights of the digits in which 3 lies are different, each takes on a different positional value.

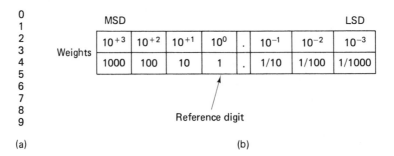

Figure 2.1 (a) Decimal number system symbols; (b) digit notation and weights.

In Fig. 2.1(b) we have shown some digit locations of the decimal number system and the corresponding weights. Here the digit just to the left of the decimal point is used as the reference digit and its weight is 10^0 or 1. This location is called the *units* digit.

Looking at the decimal weights, we find they are formed by raising the base of the number system to a power. For decimal numbers, the base is number 10. The exponent or power of the weight can be + or −. The value of this exponent is found by counting the number of digits to the units location. All digits to the left of the units digit are considered to have a weight with a positive exponent of the power of 10. For the digits to the right of the reference digit, the weights have a negative exponent.

As an example, let us look at the second digit to the left of the units digit in Fig. 2.1(b). This location has a weight of 10^{+2}, or multiplying out, we get 100. For this reason, it is called the *hundreds* digit.

For another example, let us take the second digit to the right of the units location. In Fig. 2.1(b), we find this digit has a weight of 10^{-2} or $\frac{1}{100}$. This location is also known as the *one-hundredths* digit.

Having introduced the weight of a digit, let us now look at how it affects the value of a symbol in that location. The value of a symbol in a digit other than the units digit is found by multiplying the symbol by the weight of the location. In our earlier example, 735.23, the symbol 7 is the hundreds digit. Therefore, it represents the quantity $7 \times 10^{+2}$ or 7(100) equals 700 instead of just 7.

On the other hand, the 3 in the one-hundredths digit stands for 3×10^{-2} and has a value of $\frac{3}{100}$.

Most Significant and Least Significant Digit

Two other terms needed to talk about numbers and number systems are called the *most significant digit* and the *least significant digit*. The leftmost symbol in a number is located in the most significant digit. This location is indicated with the abbreviation MSD. On the other hand, the symbol in the rightmost digit is said to be in the least significant digit location or LSD.

In the number we have been using as an example, the symbol in the MSD location is 7 and its weight is 10^{+2}. Moreover, the LSD has a weight of 10^{-2} and the symbol in this location is 3.

Example 2.1

What are the symbols and weights of the MSD and LSD in the number 4065.066?

Solution:

The leftmost digit is the MSD. Here the symbol and weight are 4 and 10^{+3}, respectively. The LSD is the rightmost digit. Its symbol is 6 and weight 10^{-3}.

2.3 THE BINARY NUMBER SYSTEM

In section 2.2 we introduced the concept of a number system relative to decimal numbers. Earlier we mentioned that binary and hexadecimal numbers are used to describe data, instructions, and operation of microprocessors and microcomputers. Here we will continue our study with the *binary number system.*

The electronic circuits within a microcomputer can operate only in one of two states, ON or OFF. For this reason, binary numbers instead of decimal numbers are used to describe their operation. The base of the binary number system is 2, and just two symbols are used to form all numbers. These symbols are the numbers 0 and 1, as shown in Fig. 2.2(a). From an electronic circuit point of view, binary 0 can represent a circuit input or output that is turned ON. On the other hand, a 1 can be the same input or output when it is turned OFF.

Bits and Weights

To make a large binary number many 0s and 1s are grouped together. The location of a symbol in a binary number is called a *bit* instead of a binary digit. The term *bit* is a contraction of the words "binary digit."

As an example, let us take the binary number

$$1101.001_2$$

Looking at this number, we find it has 7 bits. The number 2 written to the right and slightly below tells that it is a base 2 or binary number.

As with decimal numbers, each bit location in a binary number has a weight. These weights are expressed as the binary base 2 raised to a positive or negative exponent. In Fig. 2.2(b), the weights corresponding to some binary bits are shown. From this diagram, we see the 2^0 bit is the reference bit and its weight is 1.

Bits to the left of the 2^0 bit have weights with positive exponents and those to the right negative exponents. For example, the weight of the third digit left of the point is 2^{+2} or 4. If a 1 occurs in this bit location, as in the number 1101.001, it stands for a decimal value of 4.

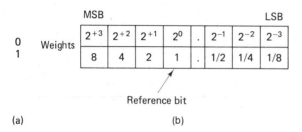

(a)   (b)

Figure 2.2 (a) Binary number system symbols; (b) bit notation and weights.

Most Significant and Least Significant Bits

In a binary number the leftmost bit is called the *most significant bit* and the rightmost the *least significant bit.* These terms are abbreviated as MSB and LSB, respectively. In the number 1101.001, the MSB has a value of 1 and weight 2^{+3} equals 8. On the other hand, the least significant bit is 1 with a weight of 2^{-3} or $\frac{1}{8}$.

Example 2.2

Find the value and weight of the MSB and LSB in the binary number 11.10001.

Solution:

The most significant bit is 1 and has a weight of 2^{+1} equals 2. The LSB is 1 with a weight of 2^{-5} or $\frac{1}{32}$.

2.4 CONVERSION BETWEEN DECIMAL AND BINARY NUMBERS

All numbers can be expressed in both the decimal and binary number systems. In Fig. 2.3 the decimal numbers 0 through 15 are listed along with their equivalent binary numbers. From this list we find that the binary equivalent of decimal number 0 is just binary 0. On the other hand, decimal 15 is written in binary form as 1111. For the study of assembly language programming, it is important to be able to quickly convert between the decimal and binary number forms.

Decimal number	Binary number
0	0
1	1
2	10
3	11
4	100
5	101
6	110
7	111
8	1000
9	1001
10	1010
11	1011
12	1100
13	1101
14	1110
15	1111

Figure 2.3 Equivalent decimal and binary numbers.

Decimal Equivalent of a Binary Number

We begin our study of number system conversions with the method for changing a decimal number to binary form. To find the decimal equivalent of a binary number, we multiply the value in each bit of the number by the weight of the corresponding bit. After this, the products are added to give the decimal number.

As an example, let us find the decimal number for binary 1100_2. Multiplying bit values and weights, we get

$$1100_2 = 1(2^{+3}) + 1(2^{+2}) + 0(2^{+1}) + 0(2^0)$$
$$= 1(8) + 1(4) + 0(2) + 0(1)$$
$$= 8 + 4$$
$$1100_2 = 12_{10}$$

This shows that 1100_2 is the binary equivalent of decimal number 12. Looking in the table of Fig. 2.3, we see that our result is correct.

Example 2.3

Evaluate the decimal equivalent of binary number 101.01.

Solution:

$$101.01 = 1(2^{+2}) + 0(2^{+1}) + 1(2^0) + 0(2^{-1}) + 1(2^{-2})$$
$$= 1(4) + 0(2) + 1(1) + 0(\tfrac{1}{2}) + 1(\tfrac{1}{4})$$
$$= 4 + 1 + .25$$
$$101.01 = 5.25$$

Binary Equivalent of a Decimal Number

The other conversion we must be able to perform is to express a decimal number in binary form. The binary equivalent of a decimal number is found by a method known as the *double dabble process*.

With the double dabble process, the decimal number is repeatedly divided by the base of 2, and the remainders of these divisions are used to form the binary number. When doing this, the decimal number is divided by 2, the quotient brought down, and the remainder written to the right. This procedure is repeated until the quotient is zero. Now we must use the remainders to form the binary number. The least significant bit of the binary number is the remainder of the first division or original number. Each of the remainders that follow gives the bits up to the last remainder, which gives the most significant bit.

To illustrate this method, let us convert the decimal number 12_{10} to binary form. Dividing by 2 gives the results that follow:

```
2 | 12  ——————►  0    LSB
2 |  6  ——————►  0
2 |  3  ——————►  1
2 |  1  ——————►  1    MSB
  |  0
```

$$12_{10} = 1100_2$$

Here we see that dividing 12 by 2 gives a quotient of 6 with 0 remainder. The quotient is brought down and the remainder written on the right. This 0 is the LSB of the binary number for decimal 12. Now the 6 is divided once again by 2 to give a quotient of 3 and a remainder of 0. Dividing twice more, we end up with a quotient of 0 and two more remainders that are both 1. The last remainder is the MSB of the binary answer.

At this point all remainders are known; it remains to form a binary number for 12_{10}. To do this, we start at the MSB remainder and work back toward the LSB to give 1100_2. This binary value is the same as that listed for 12 in the table of Fig. 2.3.

Example 2.4

Convert the decimal number 31 to binary form.

Solution:

```
2 | 31  ——————►  1    LSB
2 | 15  ——————►  1
2 |  7  ——————►  1
2 |  3  ——————►  1
2 |  1  ——————►  1    MSB
  |  0
```

$$31_{10} = 11111_2$$

2.5 THE HEXADECIMAL NUMBER SYSTEM

The *hexadecimal number system* is another number system that is important in the study of microcomputer assembly language programming. In fact, machine language programs for most microcomputers are written using hexadecimal notation.

The base of the hexadecimal number system is 16, and it uses numerical symbols 0 through 9 followed by letters A through F to form numbers. Letters A through F stand for numerical values equal to decimal numbers 10 through 15, respectively. These symbols are listed in Fig. 2.4(a).

To make a useful number, the basic hexadecimal symbols must be written in digit notation. Here the weights of the separate digits are the base 16 raised to a power. An example of hexadecimal weights is given in Fig. 2.4(b). Notice

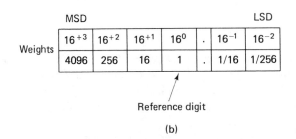

Reference digit

(a)   (b)

Figure 2.4 (a) Hexadecimal symbols;
(b) digit notation and weights.

that the weight of the reference digit is 16^0 equals 1. On the other hand, the most significant digit and least significant digit locations shown have weights of 16^{+3} and 16^{-2}, respectively. Rewriting these weights in decimal form, we get 4096 for the MSD and $\frac{1}{256}$ for the LSD.

Example 2.5

> What are the weights and values of the MSD and LSD in the hexadecimal number $F0A3.B1_{16}$?

Solution:

> The symbol in the MSD of the number is F, and this is the 16^{+3} digit. So its decimal value is 15 and weight 4096. For the LSD, we get a value of 1 and weight of 16^{-2} equals $\frac{1}{256}$.

2.6 CONVERSION BETWEEN HEXADECIMAL AND BINARY NUMBERS

The importance of using hexadecimal numbers in microcomputer programming is that they can be used to rewrite information, such as data or instructions, in a very compact way. For instance, a multibit binary number can be expressed with just a few hexadecimal digits. For this reason, it is important to learn how to directly convert between binary and hexadecimal forms.

In Fig. 2.5(a), we have listed all four-bit binary numbers and their equivalent hexadecimal numbers. Here we see that a four-bit binary zero is the same as a one-digit hexadecimal zero. Moreover, each binary number that follows up through 1111 is the same as one of the hexadecimal numbers from 1 through F. In this way, we find that four binary bits give a single hexadecimal

Binary number	Hexadecimal number
0000	0
0001	1
0010	2
0011	3
0100	4
0101	5
0110	6
0111	7
1000	8
1001	9
1010	A
1011	B
1100	C
1101	D
1110	E
1111	F

(a)

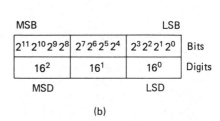

(b)

Figure 2.5 (a) Equivalent binary and hexadecimal numbers; (b) binary bits and hexadecimal digits.

digit. This fact is the basis for converting between binary and hexadecimal number forms.

The diagram in Fig. 2.5(b) shows how bits of a binary number are grouped to make digits of a hexadecimal number. From this illustration we see that the four least significant bits 2^0, 2^1, 2^2, and 2^3 of the binary number give the least significant hexadecimal digit 16^0. This is followed by two more groups of four bits for the 16^1 and 16^2 digits. The MSD 16^2 of the hexadecimal number is formed from the four MSBs, 2^8 through 2^{11}, of the binary number. In this way, a 12-bit binary number is rewritten with just three hexadecimal digits.

Hexadecimal Equivalent of a Binary Number

The first conversion we shall take is to rewrite a binary number in hexadecimal notation. To do this, we start at the rightmost bit of the binary number and separate into groups, each with four bits. After this, we replace each group of bits with its equivalent hexadecimal number.

Example 2.6

Express the binary number 100100001110_2 as a hexadecimal number.

Solution:

$$1001 \vdots 0000 \vdots 1110$$
$$9 \; : \; 0 \; : \; E$$
$$100100001110_2 = 90E_{16}$$

Example 2.7

What is the hexadecimal equivalent of the number 0000011011110001_2?

Solution:

$$0000\!:\!0110\!:\!1111\!:\!0001$$
$$0 \ : \ 6 \ : \ F \ : \ 1$$
$$0000011011110001_2 = 6F1_{16}$$

Binary Equivalent of a Hexadecimal Number

When a hexadecimal number is to be written in binary form, the method we just used must be reversed. In this case, the value in each hexadecimal digit is replaced by its equivalent 4-bit binary number.

Example 2.8

Convert the hexadecimal number A5 to its binary equivalent.

Solution:

$$A \ : \ 5$$
$$1010\!:\!0101$$
$$A5_{16} = 10100101_2$$

Example 2.9

Rewrite the number $C315_{16}$ in binary form.

Solution:

$$C \ : \ 3 \ : \ 1 \ : \ 5$$
$$1100\!:\!0011\!:\!0001\!:\!0101$$
$$C315_{16} = 1100001100010101_2$$

2.7 WORDS, BYTES, AND DATA ORGANIZATION

Having completed our introduction to number systems, we shall turn our interest to how information is organized.

In microcomputers, data, codes, and instructions are represented with binary numbers. The processing of this information is done by electronic circuitry, and the results are described in binary form. However, these results are normally rewritten in hexadecimal notation for compactness.

Words and Word Length

All microcomputers handle information in a fixed-length group of binary bits. A fixed-length group of bits is called a *word*. The number of bits in a word is

Decimal number	Binary number	Hexadecimal number
0	0000	0
1	0001	1
2	0010	2
3	0011	3
4	0100	4
5	0101	5
6	0110	6
7	0111	7
8	1000	8
9	1001	9
10	1010	A
11	1011	B
12	1100	C
13	1101	D
14	1110	E
15	1111	F

Figure 2.6 Four-bit binary words.

known as its *word length*. In general, we find words of various lengths. Some typical lengths are 4 bits, 8 bits, and 16 bits.

In Fig. 2.6 all 16 four-bit binary words are listed. Besides this, equivalent decimal and hexadecimal numbers are provided in this table. Looking under the binary number column, we see that each word must be written with the same number of bits. For instance, the binary number for 2 is written as 0010 instead of just 10. When using word notation, most significant 0s cannot be left out.

Example 2.10

What is the word length of the binary word 1000000011001111? Express the word in hexadecimal form.

Solution:

There are 16 bits in the binary word. Therefore, its word length is 16 bits. Changing the word to hexadecimal form, we get

$$1000 \vdots 0000 \vdots 1100 \vdots 1111$$
$$8 \ : \ 0 \ : \ C \ : \ F$$
$$80CF_{16}$$

The Byte

In some applications, a word of data is processed in 8-bit pieces. The term used to identify an 8-bit piece of a word is called a *byte*. For example, a 16-bit word can be expressed as two bytes, an upper byte consisting of the 8 MSBs and a lower byte consisting of the 8 LSBs.

Example 2.11

Break the word 1111001101000000 into bytes and express in hexadecimal form.

Solution:

Starting with the 8 LSBs, we get the lower byte that follows:

$$01000000_2 = 40_{16}$$

The upper byte is

$$11110011_2 = F3_{16}$$

Signed Number Format

The way in which information is organized in a word is called its *format*. Many different formats are used in microcomputers. A simple 8-bit format is shown in Fig. 2.7. It is the format that is used to describe signed data. In the diagram, we see that the 8-bit data word is divided into two parts. The first part is just the MSB, and it is known as the *sign bit*. When this sign bit is 0, the number is positive, and a 1 in this location means a negative number.

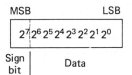

MSB   LSB

$2^7 \ 2^6 \ 2^5 \ 2^4 \ 2^3 \ 2^2 \ 2^1 \ 2^0$

Sign   Data
bit

Figure 2.7 Data word format.

The other 7 bits of the data word can be used to identify the numerical value of the information. With an 8-bit data word length, we can represent plus or minus numbers over the range $0000000_2 = 0_{10}$ to $1111111_2 = 127_{10}$. By using a larger word length, such as 16 bits, we obtain a wider range of numbers.

Example 2.12

Find the sign and value of the 8-bit data word 01110000.

Solution:

$$0\overset{.}{:}1110000$$
$$+\overset{.}{:}1(2^6) + 1(2^5) + 1(2^4) + 0(2^3) + 0(2^2) + 0(2^1) + 0(2^0)$$
$$+\overset{.}{:}64 + 32 + 16$$
$$01110000 = +112$$

The 8088 microprocessor uses a different method to code negative numbers. It represents the negative of a number by replacing the number with its 2's complement. The topic of 2's complements will be discussed shortly.

2.8 ARITHMETIC WITH BINARY NUMBERS

Arithmetic operations, such as addition and subtraction, are performed by the 8088 microprocessor in the IBM PC using numbers expressed in binary form. Let us now look at how addition and subtraction are performed with binary numbers.

Addition of Binary Numbers

When adding binary numbers, we can add the following combinations of 0s and 1s:

$$
\begin{array}{cccc}
0 & 0 & 1 & 1 \\
+0 & +1 & +0 & +1 \\
\hline
0 & 1 & 1 & 0 \ \& \ \text{carry}
\end{array}
$$

Looking at these additions, we see three different results. First, the addition $0+0$ gives a sum of binary 0. On the other hand, combining binary 0 with a 1 by addition results in 1. The last result is obtained by adding 1 to 1. This should give 2, but in binary form 2 is written as 10.

Another way of describing the answer to $1+1$ is to say 0 and a carry of 1 to the next more significant bit. For the first three additions, there is no carry. No carry can be indicated with a binary 0. Therefore, the result of $1+0$ can also be written as 01. This is read as "1 and a carry of 0."

In real addition problems, multibit binary numbers must be used. For instance, the two numbers A and B could each have four bits. In this case, the addition is

$$
\begin{array}{c}
A_3 A_2 A_1 A_0 \\
+ B_3 B_2 B_1 B_0 \\
\hline
S_4 S_3 S_2 S_1 S_0
\end{array}
$$

Here we see that the sum of 2 four-bit binary numbers can have five bits. The fifth bit is marked S_4 and is actually the carry from the fourth bit sum.

Let us give an example of this type of addition:

$$
\begin{array}{ll}
111 & \text{carry} \\
1010 & A \\
+\ \ 1110 & B \\
\hline
11000 & \text{sum}
\end{array}
$$

This problem is the binary addition of the decimal number A equals 10 to B equals 14. The sum we obtained is the binary equivalent of decimal number 24.

Looking at the third bit in the addition example, we see a more general type of addition. In this bit, three binary numbers are added. The carry from the addition in the second bit is added to the sum of the A_2 and B_2 bit values. The result is the sum and a carry to the next bit.

This more general addition includes both a *carry in* C_i and *carry out* C_o. The sum is given by the equation

$$C_i + A + B = S \,\&\, C_o$$

For the 8088 microprocessor, the carry-in and carry-out functions are provided by what is called the *carry flag*.

Example 2.13

What is the sum of the binary numbers $A = 01100101$ and $B = 10010111$? Find the decimal value of the sum.

Solution:

$$
\begin{array}{r l}
111 & C \\
01100101 & A \\
+\,10010111 & B \\
\hline
11111100 & S
\end{array}
$$

The decimal value of $S = 11111100$ is found as follows:

$$S = 128(1) + 64(1) + 32(1) + 16(1) + 8(1) + 4(1)$$

$$S = 252$$

Subtraction of Binary Numbers

Just as we found in our discussion of binary addition, subtractions performed by the 8088 microprocessor are also on numbers expressed in binary form. The basic binary subtractions are as follows:

$$
\begin{array}{cccc}
0 & 0 & 1 & 1 \\
-0 & -1 & -0 & -1 \\
\hline
0 & 1\,\&\,\text{borrow} & 1 & 0
\end{array}
$$

From these subtractions, we find that subtracting binary 1 from 0 requires a borrow of 1 from the next more significant bit. When a 1 is borrowed, it is brought back as $1+1$, and subtracting we get 1. This result is expressed as 1 and a borrow of 1. Looking at the other three subtractions, we find that each can be performed without a borrow. This condition can be indicated as a borrow of 0.

As with addition, subtraction normally involves numbers with more than one bit. For example, we could subtract a four-bit binary number B from another four-bit number A. This results in a four-bit *difference D:*

$$
\begin{array}{r}
A_3 A_2 A_1 A_0 \\
-B_3 B_2 B_1 B_0 \\
\hline
D_3 D_2 D_1 D_0
\end{array}
$$

To illustrate the subtraction process, let us do an example problem:

$$\begin{array}{r} \overset{\overset{11}{\cancel{1}1}}{} \; Br \\ 1\,1\; 1\,0 \quad A \\ -1\,0\;1\,1 \quad B \\ \hline 0\,0\;1\,1 \quad D \end{array}$$

The subtraction in the A_0 bit cannot be performed directly. Instead, 1 must be borrowed from the A_1 bit and brought back as two 1s in the A_0 bit. Now subtraction can be done, and the result is 1.

Moving to the A_1 bit, we find that 1 has already been borrowed to leave a 0. For this reason, the subtraction cannot be done without borrowing. Bringing 1 back from the A_2 bit and subtracting, we obtain a difference of 1. The next two bits can be subtracted without borrowing, and both give binary 0.

Looking at the subtraction of B_1 from A_1, we notice that two borrows have been performed. First, a 1 is borrowed from the A_1 bit and returned to the A_0 bit. This is called a *borrow in* for the A_1 bit. Moreover, a 1 was borrowed from the A_2 bit and returned to the A_1 bit so the subtraction could be performed. This type of borrow is known as a *borrow out* for the A_1 bit. The subtraction in the A_1 bit can be expressed in general as

$$A - B - Br_i = D \,\&\, Br_0$$

The same 8088 flag that is used to represent carry for addition operations is used to indicate the borrow function for subtractions.

Example 2.14

Find the difference $A - B$ for the numbers $A = 10010111$ and $B = 01100101$.

Solution:

$$\begin{array}{r} \overset{\overset{11}{11}}{} \quad Br \\ 10010111 \quad A \\ -01100101 \quad B \\ \hline 00110010 \quad D \end{array}$$

Subtraction by Complements

An alternative approach used in binary subtraction is to use *complement methods*. With complements, we can find the difference of two binary numbers by an addition process instead of directly through subtraction. The most widely used complements are the *1's complement* and *2's complement*.

Before we can begin to subtract binary numbers with the complement methods, we must learn how to form the 1's complement and 2's complement of a binary number.

To form the 1's complement of a binary number, we just change all 1s in the number to 0s and all 0s to 1s. For instance, the 1's complement of the binary number 1010 is 0101.

On the other hand, the 2's complement of a binary number can be formed by first finding its 1's complement and then adding binary 1 to the LSB. As an example, let us continue our example introduced for the 1's complement by forming its 2's complement. We already found the 1's complement to be 0101, and adding 1 results in the 2's complement as 0110.

Example 2.15

What are the 1's complement and 2's complement of the binary number 111000?

Solution:

The 1's complement is obtained by changing all 1s to 0s and 0s to 1s:

$$111000$$
$$000111 \ \text{1's complement}$$

Now to get the 2's complement, 1 is added to the LSB of the 1's complement:

$$000111$$
$$\underline{+1}$$
$$001000 \ \text{2's complement}$$

Subtraction Using the 1's Complement

First we shall show how the 1's complement is used to perform binary subtraction. To do this, the minuend of the subtraction problem is written in its normal binary form. On the other hand, the subtrahend is replaced with its 1's complement. After this, we add the two binary numbers. One more step is needed to complete the 1's complement subtraction. It is called an *end around carry* and is performed by taking the carry from the MSB of the sum and adding it to the LSB of the sum. The number that results after this is the difference between the two binary numbers.

To better understand this procedure, let us take an example problem. As an example, let us subtract the number 0111 from 1010:

$$
\begin{array}{ll}
\text{minuend} & 1010 \\
\text{subtrahend} & -0111
\end{array}
$$

We start the subtraction by replacing the subtrahend with its 1's complement and adding. This gives

$$
\begin{array}{ll}
\text{minuend} & 1010 \\
\text{subtrahend} & \underline{+1000} \\
& 10010
\end{array}
$$

To get the difference, we must still perform the end around carry. The carry from the MSB is 1, and it is added to the LSB of the sum to give the difference:

$$10010$$
$$+1$$
difference 0011

We can check our subtraction by converting the minuend, original subtrahend, and difference to decimal form:

minuend $1010 = 10$
subtrahend $-0111 = -7$
difference $0011 = 3$

This gives 10 minus 7 equal to 3, and the subtraction is correct.

Example 2.16

Find the difference $111100 - 010101$ using the 1's complement subtraction method.

Solution:

$$111100$$
$$-010101$$

Changing the subtrahend to 1's complement form and adding results in

$$111100$$
$$+101010$$
$$1100110$$

Performing the end around carry, we get

$$1100110$$
$$+1$$
$$100111$$

The difference is equal to 100111.

The 2's complement of the subtrahend can be used instead of the 1's complement in the subtraction of binary numbers. In this case, we just replace the subtrahend with its 2's complement, add the two numbers, and then discard the carry from the MSB.

To illustrate the 2's complement procedure, let us repeat the subtraction $1010 - 0111$ that we did with the 1's complement method:

minuend 1010
subtrahend -0111

The 2's complement of the subtrahend is found by changing all 1s to 0s and 0s to 1s to give the 1's complement and then adding 1. For the subtrahend 0111, we get

$$1000 + 1 = 1001$$

By substituting the 2's complement into the subtrahend and adding, the result is

$$
\begin{array}{ll}
\text{minuend} & 1010 \\
\text{subtrahend} & +\,1001 \\
\hline
\text{difference} & \cancel{1}\,0011
\end{array}
$$

Eliminating the carry from the MSB, we get the difference as 0011. Comparing this answer to that found by the 1's complement method, we see that both results are the same.

Example 2.17

Use the 2's complement method of subtraction to find the difference 101010 − 000111.

Solution:

$$
\begin{array}{r}
101010 \\
-\,000111 \\
\end{array}
$$

The 2's complement of the subtrahend is found to be

$$111000 + 1 = 111001$$

By replacing the subtrahend with the 2's complement, the difference is obtained by adding:

$$
\begin{array}{r}
101010 \\
+\,111001 \\
\hline
\cancel{1}100011 \\
\end{array}
$$

The difference is 100011.

The 8088 microprocessor in the IBM PC employs the 2's complement subtraction method to subtract binary numbers.

2.9 STANDARD NUMERIC AND ALPHANUMERIC CODES

In microcomputer systems, numerical data and other information are sometimes expressed in binary codes. For instance, the *binary-coded decimal* (BCD) code and *American Standard Code for Information Interchange* (ASCII) code are widely used in coding of numeric data (numbers 0 through 9) and alphanumeric data (letters A through Z, numbers 0 through 9, and control characters such as NUL, SOH, and EOT), respectively. The 8088 microprocessor is equipped with special instructions to perform addition and subtraction with numbers expressed in BCD or ASCII code. However, to perform other types of operations on coded information a code conversion may need to be performed through software. Let us now look at a few of the most popular numeric and alphanumeric codes and how they are used to code information.

Binary-Coded Decimal Code

One of the most widely used codes in microcomputer equipment is the *binary-coded decimal*. This code is also called the *BCD code*.

To form the BCD code, the first 10 four-bit binary numbers are selected to represent decimal numbers 0 through 9, respectively. The BCD code is shown in the table of Fig. 2.8. Looking at this table, we see that decimal number 0 is written as 0000 in BCD.

Decimal	BCD
0	0000
1	0001
2	0010
3	0011
4	0100
5	0101
6	0110
7	0111
8	1000
9	1001

Figure 2.8 BCD code.

Example 2.18

Write the decimal number 84 in BCD code.

Solution:

To write this two-digit number in BCD code, the value in each digit must be replaced with its 4-bit equivalent from the BCD code. Using the table of Fig. 2.8, we get

$$8 = 1000$$

$$4 = 0100$$

Combining these two codes, we find that

$$84_{10} = 10000100_{BCD}$$

Example 2.19

Find the decimal value for the BCD-coded number 00010010.

Solution:

Starting from the LSB, the number is divided into two groups, each with four bits. These groups represent BCD digits and are to be replaced with their equivalent decimal numbers:

$$00010010 = 0001 \quad 0010$$

$$00010010 = 12$$

Example 2.20

Rewrite the binary number 11000000_2 using BCD code.

Solution:

To express this binary number in BCD code, we must first find its decimal value. This value is obtained as follows:

$$11000000 = 1(2^7) + 1(2^6)$$

$$= 1(128) + 1(64)$$

$$11000000_2 = 192_{10}$$

Next, each decimal digit is replaced with its equivalent four-bit BCD code:

$$192_{10} = 000110010010_{BCD}$$

American Standard Code for Information Interchange

The *American Standard Code for Information Interchange* is the most widely utilized alphanumeric code today. The name of this code is abbreviated as *ASCII*. This code is widely used for the input and output of data for peripheral devices in microcomputer systems as well as for the communication of data.

Each word in the ASCII contains seven bits. They are identified as

$$b_7 b_6 b_5 b_4 b_3 b_2 b_1$$

Here bit b_7 is the MSB and b_1 the LSB. A table of the ASCII is given in Fig. 2.9(a) and the meaning of each of its control characters is identified in Fig. 2.9(b).

In the table, we see that the four LSBs $b_4 b_3 b_2 b_1$ of the word identify the rows of characters. Notice in Fig. 2.9(a) that their binary and hexadecimal values are listed in the two columns at the left-hand side of the table. On the other hand, the three MSBs $b_7b_6b_5$ identify the columns of characters. Their binary and hexadecimal values are written across the top of the table.

Let us use the table in Fig. 2.9(a) to set up the ASCII word for the carriage return (CR) control character. CR is located toward the bottom in the left of the two columns of control characters. Going to the top of this column, we get $b_7b_6b_5$ equal 000_2.

$$b_7b_6b_5 = 000_2 = 0_{16}$$

Now going to the left across the row for CR, we get

$$b_4b_3b_2b_1 = 1101_2 = D_{16}$$

Therefore, the complete word for CR is:

$$CR = 0001101_2 = 0D_{16}$$

$b_4 b_3 b_2 b_1$	H_1 / H_0	0	1	2	3	4	5	6	7
	b_7	0	0	0	0	1	1	1	1
	b_6	0	0	1	1	0	0	1	1
	b_5	0	1	0	1	0	1	0	1
0 0 0 0	0	NUL	DLE	SP	0	@	P	'	p
0 0 0 1	1	SOH	DC1	!	1	A	Q	a	q
0 0 1 0	2	STX	DC2	''	2	B	R	b	r
0 0 1 1	3	ETX	DC3	#	3	C	S	c	s
0 1 0 0	4	EOT	DC4	$	4	D	T	d	t
0 1 0 1	5	ENQ	NAK	%	5	E	U	e	u
0 1 1 0	6	ACK	SYN	&	6	F	V	f	v
0 1 1 1	7	BEL	ETB	'	7	G	W	g	w
1 0 0 0	8	BS	CAN	(	8	H	X	h	x
1 0 0 1	9	HT	EM	)	9	I	Y	i	y
1 0 1 0	A	LF	SUB	*	:	J	Z	j	z
1 0 1 1	B	$\vee$	ESC	+	;	K	[	k	{
1 1 0 0	C	FF	FS	,	<	L	\	l	|
1 1 0 1	D	CR	GS	−	=	M	]	m	}
1 1 1 0	E	SO	RS	.	>	N	$\wedge$	n	~
1 1 1 1	F	SI	US	/	?	O	−	o	DEL

(a)

Figure 2.9 (a) ASCII; (b) ASCII control characters.

Character	Meaning
NUL	Null
SOH	Start of header
STX	Start of text
ETX	End of text
EOT	End of tape
ENQ	Enquiry
ACK	Acknowledge
BEL	Bell
BS	Backspace
HT	Horizontal tabulation
LF	Line-feed
VT	Vertical tabulation
FF	Form feed
CR	Carriage return
SO	Shift-out
SI	Shift-in
DLE	Data link escape
DC1	Device control 1
DC2	Device control 2
DC3	Device control 3
DC4	Device control 4
NAK	Negative acknowledge
SYN	Synchronous idle
ETB	End of transmission block
CAN	Cancel
EM	End of medium
SUB	Subroutine
ESC	Escape
FS	File separator
GS	Group separator
RS	Record separator
US	Unit separator
SPACE	Blank space
DEL	Delete

(b)

Figure 2.9 (continued)

Example 2.21

Write the statement LET Y = X + 1 in ASCII.

Solution:

$$L = 1001100_2 = 4C_{16}$$
$$E = 1000101_2 = 45_{16}$$
$$T = 1010100_2 = 54_{16}$$
$$SP = 0100000_2 = 20_{16}$$
$$Y = 1011001_2 = 59_{16}$$
$$= \; = 0111101_2 = 3D_{16}$$
$$X = 1011000_2 = 58_{16}$$
$$+ \; = 0101011_2 = 2B_{16}$$
$$1 = 0110001_2 = 31_{16}$$

Extended Binary-Coded Decimal Interchange Code

The other alphanumeric code to be introduced, the *Extended Binary-Coded Decimal Interchange Code (EBCDIC)*, is formed with eight-bit words. The format of its word is

$$b_8b_7b_6b_5b_4b_3b_2b_1$$

The addition of the eighth bit permits up to 256 characters. The standard characters and their binary words are identified by the table in Fig. 2.10(a).

Using this table in the same way as we did for the earlier ASCII example, we can form the EBCDIC word for specific characters. Here are some examples:

$$DEL \, (delete) = 00000111_2 = 07_{16}$$
$$1 = 11110001_2 = F1_{16}$$
$$t = 10100011_2 = A3_{16}$$

Unused words of the code can be assigned special characters in the design of the microcomputer. The meanings of the control characters are given in Fig. 2.10(b).

Example 2.22

Express the statement PRINT Y/X as EBCDIC words.

Solution:

$$P = 11010111_2 = D7_{16}$$
$$R = 11011001_2 = D9_{16}$$

Figure 2.10 (a) EBCDIC; (b) EBCDIC control characters.

b8 b7 b6 b5 → b4 b3 b2 b1 ↓ / H	0 0000	1 0001	2 0010	3 0011	4 0100	5 0101	6 0110	7 0111	8 1000	9 1001	A 1010	B 1011	C 1100	D 1101	E 1110	F 1111
0 0000	NUL				SP	&	-									0
1 0001		RES	BYP	PN			/		a	j			A	J		1
2 0010		NL	EF	RS					b	k	s		B	K	S	2
3 0011									c	l	t		C	L	T	3
4 0100	PF	RES	BYP	PN					d	m	u		D	M	U	4
5 0101	HT	NL	EF	RS					e	n	v		E	N	V	5
6 0110	LC	BS	EOB	UC					f	o	w		F	O	W	6
7 0111	DEL	IDL	PRE	EOT					g	p	x		G	P	X	7
8 1000									h	q	y		H	Q	Y	8
9 1001									i	r	z		I	R	Z	9
A 1010					¢	!	|	:								
B 1011					.	$	,	#								
C 1100					<	*	%	@								
D 1101					(	)	_	'								
E 1110					+	;	>	=								
F 1111					|	¬	?	"								

(Control character rows, columns 0–3): PF, RES, BYP, PN (row 4); HT, NL, EF, RS (row 5); LC, BS, EOB, UC (row 6); DEL, IDL, PRE, EOT (row 7); NUL (row 0, column 0).

(a)

Character	Meaning
NUL	Null
PF	Punch off
HT	Horizontal tab
LC	Lower case
DEL	Delete
RES	Restore
HL	New line
BS	Backspace
IDL	Idle
BYP	Bypass
LF	Line feed
EOB	End of block
PRE	Prefix
SM	Set mode
PN	Punch on
RS	Reader stop
UC	Upper case
EOT	End of transmission
SP	Blank space

(b)   **Figure 2.10** (continued)

$$I = 11001001_2 = C9_{16}$$
$$N = 11010101_2 = D5_{16}$$
$$T = 11100011_2 = E3_{16}$$
$$SP = 01000000_2 = 40_{16}$$
$$Y = 11101000_2 = E8_{16}$$
$$/ = 01100001_2 = 61_{16}$$
$$X = 11100111_2 = E7_{16}$$

2.10 PARITY AND THE PARITY BIT

Coded information is frequently transferred between the microcomputer and peripherals such as the display or printer. For instance, whenever data are to be printed, the microcomputer may output the data in ASCII form to the printer unit. This transfer of data from microcomputer to printer must be done without error. However, a problem found in some environments is that noise can occur that causes errors in the transfer of data. For instance, noise on the cable between the microcomputer and printer could cause a zero transmitted by the microcomputer to be received by the printer as a 1. In a similar way, a logic 1 can be changed to a zero. In either case, the printer would print the wrong character. To improve reliability of information transfer, codes with *parity* are often used. When parity is used, circuits or software can be used to test the input data for correct transmission.

Odd and Even Parity

Coded information can have one of two types of parity. They are called *odd parity* and *even parity*. For a code to have parity, each word must have an odd number of bits at the 1 logic level. On the other hand, even parity means that each word in the code has an even number of bits that are 1.

Parity Bit

A code without parity such as the BCD or ASCII can be made to have parity by adding another bit. This additional bit is called the *parity bit,* and its logic level can be set to give even or odd parity.

For example, in Fig. 2.11 the BCD code is shown with a parity bit set for even parity. Here we see that the parity bit P is made 1 when there is an odd number of bits at logic 1 and left 0 when an even number of bits are already 1. From this table, we see that the word 0000 is considered to have even parity.

Alphanumeric Codes With Parity

In the same way that parity was just added to the BCD code, a parity bit can be added to the ASCII or EBCDIC alphanumeric codes to produce parity. Figure 2.12 is an example of the ASCII code with parity. For simplicity, only the words for numbers 0 through 9 and letters A through Z are shown. Here we see that an eighth bit P is added to the seven-bit ASCII code. Its logic level has been set to produce odd parity.

P	A	B	C	D
0	0	0	0	0
1	0	0	0	1
1	0	0	1	0
0	0	0	1	1
1	0	1	0	0
0	0	1	0	1
0	0	1	1	0
1	0	1	1	1
1	1	0	0	0
0	1	0	0	1

Figure 2.11 BCD code with even parity.

ASCII character	Code							
	P	b_7	b_6	b_5	b_4	b_3	b_2	b_1
0	1	0	1	1	0	0	0	0
1	0	0	1	1	0	0	0	1
2	0	0	1	1	0	0	1	0
3	1	0	1	1	0	0	1	1
4	0	0	1	1	0	0	1	1
5	1	0	1	1	0	1	0	0
6	1	0	1	1	0	1	1	0
7	0	0	1	1	0	1	1	1
8	0	0	1	1	1	0	0	0
9	1	0	1	1	1	0	0	1
A	1	1	0	0	0	0	0	1
B	1	1	0	0	0	0	1	0
C	0	1	0	0	0	0	1	1
D	1	1	0	0	0	1	0	0
E	0	1	0	0	0	1	0	1
F	0	1	0	0	0	1	1	0
G	1	1	0	0	0	1	1	1
H	1	1	0	0	1	0	0	0
I	0	1	0	0	1	0	0	1
J	0	1	0	0	1	0	1	0
K	1	1	0	0	1	0	1	1
L	0	1	0	0	1	1	0	0
M	1	1	0	0	1	1	0	1
N	1	1	0	0	1	1	1	0
O	1	1	0	0	1	1	1	0
P	1	1	0	1	0	0	0	0
Q	0	1	0	1	0	0	0	1
R	0	1	0	1	0	0	1	0
S	1	1	0	1	0	0	1	1
T	0	1	0	1	0	1	0	0
U	1	1	0	1	0	1	0	1
V	1	1	0	1	0	1	1	0
W	1	1	0	1	0	1	1	0
X	0	1	0	1	1	0	0	0
Y	1	1	0	1	1	0	0	1
Z	1	1	0	1	1	0	1	0

(b)

Figure 2.12 ASCII letters and numbers expressed with odd parity bit.

ASSIGNMENTS

Section 2.2

1. What is the base of the decimal number system?
2. Write the symbols used to represent numerical values in the decimal system.
3. What term is used to refer to the positional value of a digit?
4. What do the abbreviations MSD and LSD stand for?
5. What are the symbols and weights of the MSD and LSD in the decimal number 9057.238?

Section 2.3

6. Write the two basic symbols used in the binary number system.
7. What is the name given to a binary digit?
8. How are most significant bit and least significant bit abbreviated?
9. What is the weight of the second bit to the left of the binary point?
10. Find the symbols and weights of the most significant bit and least significant bit in the number 100111.0101_2.

Section 2.4

11. Make a list of the binary equivalents of decimal numbers from 0 through 9.
12. Evaluate the decimal equivalent for each of the following binary numbers.
    (a) 110   (b) 1011   (c) 010101   (d) 1111111
13. Find the decimal value of the number 1000111_2.
14. Convert the decimal numbers that follow to binary form.
    (a) 5   (b) 9   (c) 42   (d) 100
15. What is the binary number for decimal 500?

Section 2.5

16. Write the 16 basic symbols of the hexadecimal number system.
17. What is the weight of the second hexadecimal digit to the left of the point?
18. Find the symbol and weight of the MSD in the hexadecimal number C8B.

Section 2.6

19. Convert the binary numbers that follow to hexadecimal form.
    (a) 00111001   (b) 11100010   (c) 10011010   (d) 001110100000
20. What is the hexadecimal equivalent of the number 11110000_2?
21. Evaluate the binary equivalent of each hexadecimal number that follows.
    (a) 6B   (b) F3   (c) 45   (d) 2B0

22. Write the binary number for $A1B_{16}$.
23. Make a list of the hexadecimal numbers for the decimal numbers 0 through 20.

Section 2.7

24. What is the word length for each of the following binary words?
    (a) 000111   (b) 11000101   (c) 0001111000000000
25. Break the word in problem 24(b) into 4-bit digits and express in hexadecimal form.
26. Divide the word in problem 24(c) into 4-bit digits and write in hexadecimal form.
27. Each of the following binary data words has the format shown in Fig. 2.7. What is the sign and value of the data word?
    (a) 00010101   (b) 11100000

Section 2.8

28. Find the binary sum in each of the following problems.
    (a) $10101 + 11000 =$ (b) $01001111 + 11011100 =$
29. Add the binary number 11000 to 11011. Convert the binary answer to decimal form.
30. Perform the binary subtractions that follow.
    (a) $11000 - 10101 =$ (b) $11011100 - 01001111 =$
31. Find the 1's complement of each number that follows.
    (a) 0010111   (b) 101000000
32. What is the 2's complement of each number that follows?
    (a) 1110111   (b) 011101101
33. Do the subtractions that follow by the 1's complement method.
    (a) $11100 - 01010 =$ (b) $101011100 - 011111111 =$
34. Use the 2's complement method to subtract the numbers that follow.
    (a) $10000 - 00111 =$ (b) $1111000 - 0001111 =$
35. Subtract $B = 1001$ from $A = 1010$ with the 1's complement method.
36. Using the 2's complement method, subtract $B = 010001$ from $A = 100000$.

Section 2.9

37. Find the decimal value for the binary-coded decimal numbers that follow.
    (a) 1001   (b) 00111001   (c) 100001110000
38. Write the decimal numbers that follow in BCD code.
    (a) 29   (b) 99   (c) 106
39. Convert the binary numbers that follow to decimal form and then express in BCD code.
    (a) 11010110   (b) 1000011
40. Express each of the following alphanumerics in ASCII.
    (a) 7   (b) Y   (c) $
41. How would the statement FOR I=1 TO 10 be written in ASCII?

42. What is the statement if it is coded in ASCII as

    1001110
    1000101
    1011000
    1010100
    0100000
    1001001

43. How is each of the alphanumerics in problem 40 expressed in EBCDIC?
44. Express the statement GOTO 100 in EBCDIC.
45. What is this EBCDIC statement?

    11011001
    11000101
    11100011
    11100100
    11011001
    11010101

Section 2.10

46. Describe a code with even parity and a code with odd parity.
47. What is the term used to refer to an extra bit added to a code to give even or odd parity?
48. Make a table of the numbers of the EBCDIC with a parity bit (P) set for odd parity.

3

SOFTWARE
ARCHITECTURE
OF THE 8088
MICROPROCESSOR

3.1 INTRODUCTION

Chapter 2 was a review of the topics of number systems, information organization, and information coding. In this chapter we shall begin our study of the 8088 microprocessor and assembly language programming for the IBM PC.

In order to program the 8088 with assembly language, we must understand how the 8088 microprocessor and its memory subsystem operate from a software point of view. For this reason, here we will examine the *software architecture* of the 8088 microprocessor. The following topics are covered in the chapter:

1. Software model of the 8088 microprocessor
2. Memory address space and data organization
3. Segment registers and memory segmentation
4. Dedicated and general use of memory
5. Instruction pointer
6. Data registers
7. Pointer and index registers
8. Flag register
9. Generating a memory address
10. The stack
11. Input/output address space
12. Addressing modes of the 8088 microprocessor

3.2 SOFTWARE MODEL OF THE 8088 MICROPROCESSOR

The purpose of developing a *software model* is to aid the programmer in understanding the operation of the microcomputer system from a software point of view. To be able to program a microprocessor, one does not need to know all of its hardware features. For instance, we do not necessarily need to know the function of the signals at its various pins, their electrical connections, or their switching characteristics. Moreover, the function, interconnection, and operation of the internal circuits of the microprocessor also need not normally be considered.

What is important to the programmer is to know the various registers within the device and to understand their purpose, functions, operating

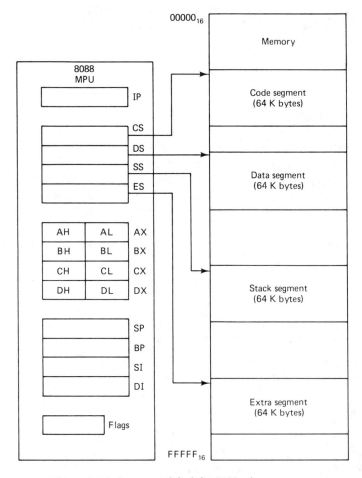

Figure 3.1 Software model of the 8088 microprocessor.

capabilities, and limitations. Furthermore, it is essential to know how external memory is organized and how it is addressed to obtain instructions and data.

The software architecture of the 8088 microprocessor is illustrated with the software model shown in Fig. 3.1. Looking at this diagram, we see that it includes 13 16-bit internal registers: the *instruction pointer* (IP), *four data registers* (AX, BX, CX, and DX), *two pointer registers* (BP and SP), *two index registers* (SI and DI), and *four segment registers* (CS, DS, SS, and ES). In addition to these registers, there is another register called the *status register* (SR), with nine of its bits implemented for status and control flags. The model also includes a *1,048,576* (1M) *byte address space* for implementation of external memory. Our concern here is with what can be done with this architecture and how to do it through software. For this purpose, we will now begin a detailed study of the elements of the model and their relationship to software.

3.3 THE MEMORY ADDRESS SPACE AND DATA ORGANIZATION

Now that we have introduced the idea of a software model, let us look at how information such as numbers, characters, and instructions are stored in memory.

As shown in Fig. 3.2, the 8088 microprocessor supports 1M bytes of external memory. This memory space is organized as bytes of data stored at consecutive addresses over the address range 00000_{16} to $FFFFF_{16}$. From an addressing point of view, *even-* or *odd-addressed bytes of data* can be independently accessed. In this way, we see that the memory in an 8088-based microcomputer is actually organized as eight-bit bytes, not as 16-bit words. However, the 8088 can access any two consecutive bytes as a *word*. In this case, the *lower-addressed byte is the least significant byte* of the word and the *higher-addressed byte is its most significant byte.*

Figure 3.3(a) demonstrates how a word of data is stored in memory. Notice that the storage location at the lower address, 00724_{16}, contains the value $00000010_2 = 02_{16}$. Moreover, the contents of the next-higher-addressed storage location 00725_{16} are $01010101_2 = 55_{16}$. These two bytes represent the word $0101010100000010_2 = 5502_{16}$.

Figure 3.2 Address space of the 8088. (*Courtesy Intel Corporation*)

To permit efficient use of memory, words of data can be stored at even- or odd-address boundaries. The LSB of the address determines the type of *word boundary*. If this bit is 0, the word is said to be held at an *even-address boundary*. That is, a word at an even-address boundary corresponds to two consecutive bytes, with the least significant byte located at an even address. For example, the word in Fig. 3.3(a) has its least significant byte at address 00724_{16}. Therefore, it is stored at an even-address boundary.

Example 3.1

What is the data word shown in Fig. 3.3(b)? Express the result in hexadecimal form. Is it stored at an even- or an odd-address boundary?

Solution:

The most significant byte of the word is stored at address $0072C_{16}$ and equals

$$11111101_2 = FD_{16}$$

Its least significant byte is stored at address $0072B_{16}$ and is

$$10101010_2 = AA_{16}$$

Together these two bytes give the word

$$1111110110101010_2 = FDAA_{16}$$

Expressing the address of the least significant byte in binary form gives

$$0072B_{16} = 0000000011100101011_2$$

Since the rightmost bit is logic 1, the word is stored at an odd-address boundary in memory.

The *double word* is another data form that can be processed by the 8088 microcomputer. A double word corresponds to four consecutive bytes of data stored in memory. An example of double-word data is a *pointer* that is used to address data or code outside the current segment. The word of this pointer that is stored at the higher address is called the *segment base address* and the word at the lower address is called the *offset value*.

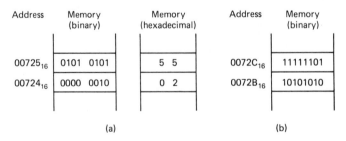

(a)   (b)

Figure 3.3 (a) Storing a word of data in memory; (b) example.

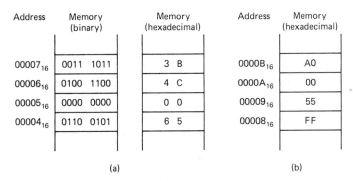

Address	Memory (binary)	Memory (hexadecimal)
00007_{16}	0011 1011	3 B
00006_{16}	0100 1100	4 C
00005_{16}	0000 0000	0 0
00004_{16}	0110 0101	6 5

(a)

Address	Memory (hexadecimal)
$0000B_{16}$	A0
$0000A_{16}$	00
00009_{16}	55
00008_{16}	FF

(b)

Figure 3.4 (a) Storing a 32-bit pointer in memory; (b) example.

An example showing storage of a pointer in memory is given in Fig. 3.4(a). Here we find that the higher-addressed word, which represents the segment address, is stored starting at even-address boundary 00006_{16}. The most significant byte of this word is at address 00007_{16} and equals $00111011_2 = 3B_{16}$. Its least significant byte is at address 00006_{16} and equals $01001100_2 = 4C_{16}$. Combining these two values, we get the segment base address, which equals $0011101101001100_2 = 3B4C_{16}$.

The offset part of the pointer is the lower-addressed word. Its least significant byte is stored at address 00004_{16}. This location contains $01100101_2 = 65_{16}$. The most significant byte is at address 00005_{16}, which contains $00000000_2 = 00_{16}$. The resulting offset is $0000000001100101_2 = 0065_{16}$.

Example 3.2

How should the pointer with segment-base address equal to $A000_{16}$ and offset address $55FF_{16}$ be stored at an even-address boundary starting at 00008_{16}?

Solution:

Storage of the two-word pointer requires four consecutive byte locations in memory starting at address 00008_{16}. The least significant byte of the offset is stored at address 00008_{16}. This value is shown as $11111111_2 = FF_{16}$ in Fig. 3.4(b). The most significant byte of the offset, which is 55_{16}, is stored at address 00009_{16}. These two bytes are followed by the least significant byte of the segment-base address, 00_{16}, at address $0000A_{16}$, and its most significant byte, $A0_{16}$, at address $0000B_{16}$.

3.4 SEGMENT REGISTERS AND MEMORY SEGMENTATION

Even though the 8088 has a 1M-byte memory address space, not all of this memory can be active at one time. Actually, the 1M byte of memory can be partitioned into sixteen 64K (65,536) byte *segments*. Each of these segments represents an independently addressable unit of memory consisting of 64K consecutive byte-wide storage locations. Each segment is assigned a *base address* that identifies its starting point, that is, its lowest-addressed byte storage location.

Only four of these 64K-byte segments can be active at a time. They are called the *code segment, stack segment, data segment,* and *extra segment.* The locations of the segments of memory that are active, as shown in Fig. 3.5, are identified by the value of address held in the 8088's four internal segment registers: CS (*code segment*), SS (*stack segment*), DS (*data segment*), and ES (*extra segment*). These four registers are shown in Fig. 3.5. Each contains a 16-bit base address that points to the lowest-addressed byte of the segment in memory. These four segments give a maximum of 256K bytes of active memory. Of this, 64K bytes are allocated for code (*program storage*), 64K bytes for a *stack,* and 128K bytes for *data storage.*

The values held in these registers are usually referred to as the *current segment register values.* For example, the word in CS points to the first byte-wide storage location in the current code segment.

Figure 3.6 illustrates the *segmentation of memory.* In this diagram, we have identified 64K-byte segments with letters such as A, B, and C. The data segment (DS) register contains the value B. Therefore, the second 64K-byte segment of memory, which is labeled B, acts as the current data storage segment. This is the segment in which data that are to be processed by the microcomputer are stored. Therefore, this part of the microcomputer's memory must contain read/write storage locations that can be accessed by instructions as storage locations for source and destination operands. Segment E is selected for the code segment. It is this segment of memory from which instructions of the program are currently being fetched for execution. The stack segment (SS) register contains H, thereby selecting the 64K-byte segment labeled as H for use as a stack. Finally, the extra segment register ES is loaded with J such that segment J of memory can function as a second 64K-byte data storage segment.

The segment registers are said to be *user accessible.* This means that the programmer can change the value they hold through software. Therefore, for a program to gain access to another part of memory, it just has to change the value of the appropriate register or registers. For instance, a new 128K-byte data space can be brought in by simply changing the values in DS and ES. This can be done by executing just two instructions: *load data segment* (LDS) to change the value in DS and *load extra segment* (LES) to change the value in ES.

There is one restriction on the value that can be assigned to a segment as a base address: this is that it must reside on a 16-byte address boundary. Valid examples are 00000_{16}, 00010_{16}, and 00020_{16}. Other than this restriction, segments can be *contiguous, adjacent, disjointed,* or even *overlapping.* For example, in Fig. 3.6, segments A and B are contiguous, whereas segments B and C are overlapping.

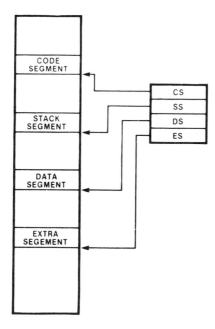

Figure 3.5 Active segments of memory. (*Courtesy Intel Corporation*)

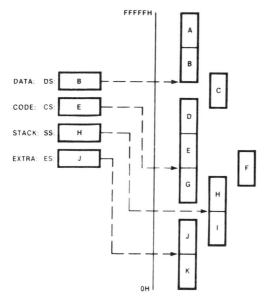

Figure 3.6 Contiguous, adjacent, disjointed, and overlapping segments. (*Courtesy Intel Corporation*)

3.5 DEDICATED AND GENERAL USE OF MEMORY

Any part of the 8088 microcomputer's 1M-byte address space can be implemented; however, some address locations have *dedicated functions*. These locations should not be used as general memory where data or instructions of the program are stored. Let us now look at these reserved and general-use parts of memory.

Figure 3.7 shows the *reserved* and *general-use (open) parts* of the 8088's *address space*. Notice that storage locations from address 00000_{16} to $0007F_{16}$ are dedicated. These 128 bytes of memory are reserved for storage of pointers to service routines. As indicated earlier, each pointer requires four bytes of memory. Two bytes hold the 16-bit segment address and the other two hold the 16-bit offset.

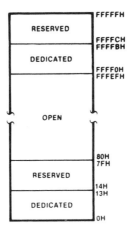

Figure 3.7 Dedicated and general use of memory. (*Courtesy Intel Corporation*)

At the high end of the memory address space is another reserved pointer area. It is located from address $FFFFC_{16}$ through $FFFFF_{16}$. These four memory locations are reserved for storage of the address that points to the start of the *power-up initialization service routine.* Moreover, Intel Corporation, the manufacturer of the 8088, has identified the twelve storage locations from address $FFFF0_{16}$ through $FFFFB_{16}$ as dedicated for use with future products; therefore, they should not be used.

3.6 INSTRUCTION POINTER

The next register from the 8088's software model of Fig. 3.1 that we will consider is the *instruction pointer* (IP). It is also 16-bits in length and identifies the location of the next instruction to be executed in the current code segment. It is similar to a *program counter;* however, IP contains an offset instead of the actual address of the next instruction. This is because the 8088 contains 16-bit registers, but requires a 20-bit address for addressing memory. Internal to the 8088, the offset in IP is combined with the contents of CS to generate the address of the instruction.

During normal operation, the 8088 fetches instructions one after the other from the code segment of memory and executes them. After an instruction is fetched it must be decoded within the 8088 and, if necessary, it reads operands from either the data segment of memory or internal registers. Next the operation specified in the instruction is performed on the operands and the results written back to either an internal register or a storage location in memory. The 8088 is now ready to execute the next instruction.

Every time an instruction is fetched from memory, the 8088 updates the value in IP such that it points to the first byte of the next sequential instruction. In this way, it is always ready to fetch the next instruction of the program. Actually, the 8088 has an internal *code queue* and *prefetches* up to six bytes of instruction code and holds them internal for execution.

The active code segment can be changed by simply executing an instruction that loads a new value into the CS register. For this reason, we can use any of the 16 independent 64K-byte segments of memory for storage of code.

3.7 DATA REGISTERS

As shown in Fig. 3.1, there are four *general-purpose data registers* that are located within the 8088. During program execution, they are used for temporary storage of frequently used intermediate results. The advantage of storing these data in internal registers instead of memory is that they can be accessed much faster.

The data registers are shown in more detail in Fig. 3.8(a). Here we see that the four data registers are referred to as the *accumulator register* (A), the *base register* (B), the *count register* (C), and the *data register* (D). These names imply special functions that are performed by each register. Each of these registers can be accessed either as a whole for 16-bit data operations or as two 8-bit registers for byte-wide data operations. References to a register as a word are identified by an X after the register letter. For instance, the accumulator is referenced as AX. In a similar way, the other three registers are referred to as BX, CX, and DX.

On the other hand, when referencing one of these registers on a byte-wide basis, its high byte and low byte are identified by following the register name with the letter H or L, respectively. For the A register, the most significant byte is referred to as AH and the least significant byte as AL. The other byte-wide register pairs are BH and BL, CH and CL, and DH and DL.

Any of the general-purpose data registers can be used as the source or destination of an operand during arithmetic or logic operations, such as add or

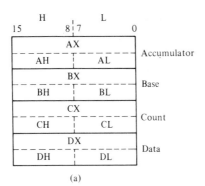

Register	Operations
AX	Word multiply, word divide, word I/O
AL	Byte multiply, byte divide, byte I/O, translate, decimal arithmetic
AH	Byte multiply, byte divide
BX	Translate
CX	String operations, loops
CL	Variable shift and rotate
DX	Word multiply, word divide, indirect I/O

(a)   (b)

Figure 3.8 (a) General purpose data registers; (*Courtesy Intel Corporation*) (b) dedicated register functions. (*Courtesy Intel Corporation*)

AND. However, for some operations, such as those performed by string instructions, specific registers are used. In the case of a string instruction, register C is used to store a count representing the number of bytes to be processed. This is the reason it is given the name *count register.* Another use of C is for the count of the number of bits by which the contents of an operand must be shifted or rotated during the execution of the multibit shift or rotate instructions.

Another example of dedicated use of data registers is that all I/O operations require the data that are to be input or output to be in the A register, while register D holds the address of the I/O port. Figure 3.8(b) summarizes the dedicated functions of the general-purpose data registers.

3.8 POINTER AND INDEX REGISTERS

There are four other general-purpose registers shown in Fig. 3.1: two *pointer registers* and two *index registers.* They are used to store offset addresses of memory locations relative to the segment registers. The values held in these registers can be read, loaded, or modified through software. This is done prior to executing the instruction that references the register for address offset. In this way, the instruction simply specifies which register contains the offset address.

Figure 3.9 shows that the two pointer registers are the *stack pointer* (SP) and *base pointer* (BP). The contents of SP and BP are used as offsets from the current value of SS during the execution of instructions that involve the stack segment of memory. In this way, they permit easy access to locations in the stack part of memory. The value in SP always represents the offset of the next

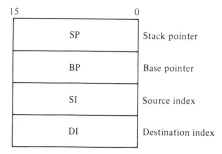

Figure 3.9 Pointer and index registers. (*Courtesy Intel Corporation*)

stack location that can be accessed. That is, when combined with SS, it results in a 20-bit address that points to the *top of the stack.*

BP also represents an offset from the pointer in the SS register. However, its intended use is for access to data within the stack segment of memory. BP is employed as the offset whenever the based addressing mode is used for an operand. One common use is within a subroutine that must reference parameters that were passed to the subroutine by way of the stack. In this case, instructions are written that use based addressing to examine the value of parameters held in the stack.

The index registers are used to hold offset addresses for instructions that access data stored in the data segment of memory. For this reason, they are always combined with the value in the DS register. In instructions that use indexed type of addressing, the *source index* (SI) register is used to store an offset address for a source operand, and the *destination index* (DI) register is used for storage of an offset that identifies the location of a destination operand. For example, a string instruction that requires an offset to the location of a source or destination operand would use these registers.

The index registers can also be used as source or destination registers in arithmetic and logical operations. Unlike the general-purpose registers, these registers must always be used for 16-bit operations and cannot be accessed as two separate bytes.

3.9 FLAG REGISTER

The *flag register* is another 16-bit register within the 8088. However, as shown in Fig. 3.10, just nine of its bits are implemented. Six of these bits represent status flags. They are the *carry flag* (CF), the *parity flag* (PF), the *auxiliary carry flag* (AF), the *zero flag* (ZF), the *sign flag* (SF), and the *overflow flag* (OF). The logic state of these *status flags* indicates conditions that are produced as the result of executing an arithmetic or logic instruction. That is, specific flag bits are reset (logic 0) or set (logic 1) at the completion of execution of the instruction.

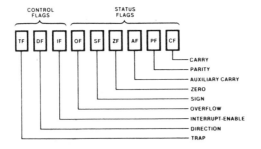

Figure 3.10 Status flags. (*Courtesy Intel Corporation*)

Let us first summarize the operation of these status flags:

1. The carry flag (CF): CF is set if there is a carry-out or a borrow-in for the most significant bit of the result during the execution of an arithmetic instruction. Otherwise, CF is reset.

2. The parity flag (PF): PF is set if the result produced by the instruction has even parity, that is, if it contains an even number of bits at the 1 logic level. If parity is odd, PF is reset.

3. The auxiliary carry flag (AF): AF is set if there is a carry-out from the low nibble into the high nibble or a borrow-in from the high nibble into the low nibble of the lower byte in a 16-bit word. Otherwise, AF is reset.

4. The zero flag (ZF): ZF is set if the result of an arithmetic or logic operation is zero. Otherwise, ZF is reset.

5. The sign flag (SF): The MSB of the result is copied into SF. Thus SF is set if the result is a negative number or reset if it is positive.

6. The overflow flag (OF): When OF is set, it indicates that the signed result is out of range. If the result is not out of range, OF remains reset.

For example, at the completion of execution of a byte-addition instruction, the carry flag (CF) could be set to indicate that the sum of the operands caused a carry-out condition. The auxiliary carry flag (AF) could also set due to the execution of the instruction. This depends on whether or not a carry-out occurred from the least significant nibble to the most significant nibble when the byte operands are added. The sign flag (SF) is also affected and it will reflect the logic level of the MSB of the result.

The 8088 provides instructions within its instruction set which are able to use these flags to alter the sequence in which the program is executed. For instance, ZF equal to logic 1 could be tested as the condition that would initiate a jump to another part of the program.

The other three implemented flag bits are *control flags*. They are the *direction flag* (DF), the *interrupt enable flag* (IF), and the *trap flag* (TF). These three flags are provided to control functions of the 8088 as follows:

1. The trap flag (TF): If TF is set, the 8088 goes into the *single-step mode*. When in the single-step mode, it executes one instruction at a time. This type of operation is very useful for debugging programs.

2. The interrupt flag (IF): For the 8088 to recognize *maskable interrupt requests* at its INT input, the IF flag must be set. When IF is reset, requests at INT are ignored and the maskable interrupt interface is disabled.

3. The direction flag (DF): The logic level of DF determines the direction in which string operations will occur. When it is reset, the string instruction automatically decrements the address. Therefore, the string data transfers proceed from high address to low address. On the other hand, setting DF causes the string address to be incremented. In this way, transfers proceed from low address to high address.

The instruction set of the 8088 includes instructions for saving, loading, or manipulating specific bits of the status register. For instance, special instructions are provided to permit user software to set or reset CF, DF, and IF at any point in the program. For instance, just prior to the beginning of a string operation DF could be reset so that the string address automatically decrements.

3.10 GENERATING A MEMORY ADDRESS

The *logical addresses* that occur in the program of the 8088 are always 16 bits in length. This is because all registers and memory locations are 16 bits long. However, the *physical addresses* that are used to access memory are 20 bits in length. The generation of the physical address involves combining a 16-bit offset value that is located in either an index register or pointer register and a 16-bit base value that is located in one of the segment registers.

The source of the offset address depends on which type of memory reference is taking place. It can be the base pointer (BP) register, base (BX) register, source index (SI) register, destination index (DI) register, or instruction pointer (IP). On the other hand, the base value always resides in one of the segment registers: CS, DS, SS, or ES.

For instance, when an instruction acquisition takes place, the source of the base address is always the code segment (CS) register and the source of the offset is always the instruction pointer (IP). On the other hand, if the value of a variable is being written to memory during the execution of an instruction, typically, the base address will be in the data-segment (DS) register and the offset will be in the destination index (DI) register. Segment override prefixes can be used to change the segment from which the variable is accessed.

Another example is the stack address that is needed when pushing parameters onto the stack. This address is formed from the contents of the stack segment (SS) register and stack pointer (SP).

Remember that the segment-base address represents the starting location of the 64K-byte segment in memory: that is, the lowest-addressed byte in the segment. The offset identifies the distance in bytes that the storage location of interest resides from this starting address. Therefore, the lowest-addressed byte in a segment has an offset of 0000_{16} and the highest-addressed byte has an offset of $FFFF_{16}$.

Figure 3.11 shows how a segment address and offset value are combined to give a physical address. What happens is that the value in the segment register is shifted left by four bits with its LSBs being filled with 0s. Then the offset value is added to the 16 LSBs of the shifted segment address. The result of this addition is the 20-bit physical address.

The example in Fig. 3.11 represents a segment address of 1234_{16} and an offset address of 0022_{16}. First let us express the base address in binary form. This gives

$$1234_{16} = 0001001000110100_2$$

Shifting left four times and filling with zeros results in

$$00010010001101000000_2 = 12340_{16}$$

The offset in binary form is

$$0022_{16} = 0000000000100010_2$$

Adding the shifted segment address and offset, we get

$$00010010001101000000_2 + 0000000000100010_2 = 00010010001101100010_2$$
$$= 123642_{16}$$

This address calculation is automatically done within the 8088 each time a memory access is initiated.

Example 3.3

What would be the offset required to map to address location $002C3_{16}$ if the segment base address is $002A_{16}$?

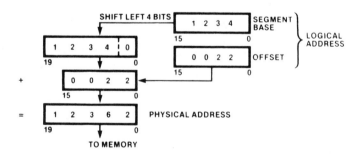

Figure 3.11 Generating a physical address. (*Courtesy Intel Corporation*)

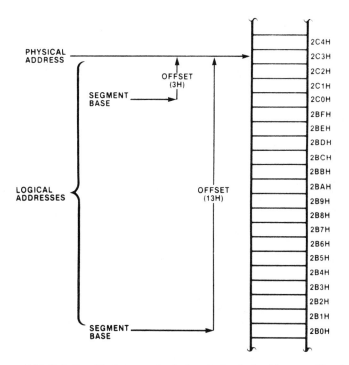

Figure 3.12 Relationship between logical and physical addresses. (*Courtesy Intel Corporation*)

Solution:

The offset value can be obtained by shifting the segment base address left four bits and then subtracting it from the physical address. Shifting left gives

$$002A0_{16}$$

Now subtracting, we get the value of the offset:

$$002C3_{16} - 002A0_{16} = 0023_{16}$$

Actually, many different logical addresses can be mapped to the same physical address location in memory. This is done by simply changing the values of the base address in the segment register and its corresponding offset. The diagram in Fig. 3.12 demonstrates this idea. Notice that base $002B_{16}$ with offset 0013_{16} maps to physical address $002C3_{16}$ in memory. However, if the segment base address is changed to $002C_{16}$ with a new offset of 0003_{16}, the physical address is still $002C3_{16}$.

3.11 THE STACK

As indicated earlier, *stack* is implemented in the memory of the 8088 microcomputer. It is 64K bytes long and is organized as 32K words. Moreover, we found that the lowest-addressed byte in the current stack is pointed to by the base address in the SS register.

During a *subroutine call* the contents of specific internal registers of the 8088 and other parameters are pushed to this special stack part of memory. Here they are maintained temporarily. At completion of the subroutine, these values are popped off the stack and put back into the same internal registers where they originally resided.

For instance, when a *call* instruction is executed, the 8088 automatically pushes the current values in CS and IP onto the stack. As part of the subroutine, the contents of other registers can also be saved on the stack by executing *push* instructions. An example is the instruction PUSH SI. When executed, it causes the contents of the source index register to be pushed onto the stack.

At the end of the subroutine, *pop* instructions can be included to pop values from the stack back into their corresponding internal registers. For example, POP SI causes the value at the top of the stack to be popped back into the source index register.

Any number of stacks may exist in an 8088 microcomputer. A new stack can be brought in by simply changing the value in the SS register. For instance, executing the instruction MOV SS,DX loads a new value from DX into SS. Even though many stacks can exist, only one can be active at a time.

Another register, the stack pointer (SP), contains an offset from the value in SS. The address obtained from the contents of SS and SP is the physical address of the last storage location in the stack to which data were pushed. This is known as the *top of the stack.* The value in the stack pointer is initialized to $FFFF_{16}$ upon start-up of the microcomputer. Combining this value with the current value in SS gives the highest-addressed location in the stack: that is, the *bottom of the stack.*

The 8088 pushes data and addresses to the stack one word at a time. Each time the contents of a register are to be pushed onto the top of the stack, the value in the stack pointer is first automatically decremented by two and then the contents of the register are written into memory. In this way we see that the stack grows down in memory from the bottom of the stack, which corresponds to the physical address derived from SS and $FFFF_{16}$, toward the *end of the stack,* which corresponds to the physical address obtained from SS and offset 0000_{16}.

When a value is popped from the top of the stack, the reverse of this sequence occurs. The physical address defined by SS and SP points to the location of the last value pushed onto the stack. Its contents are first popped off the stack and put into the specific register within the 8088; then SP is automatically incremented by two. The top of the stack now corresponds to the previous value pushed onto the stack.

An example that shows how the contents of a register are pushed onto the stack is shown in Fig. 3.13(a). Here we find the state of the stack prior to execu-

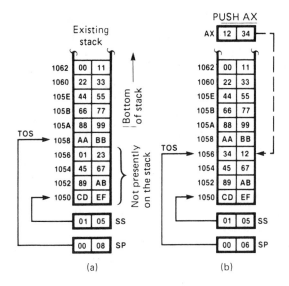

Figure 3.13 (a) Stack just prior to push operation; (*Courtesy Intel Corporation*) (b) stack after execution of the PUSH AX instruction. (*Courtesy Intel Corporation*)

tion of the PUSH instruction. Notice that the stack segment register contains 105_{16}. As indicated, the bottom of the stack resides at the physical address derived from SS with offset $FFFF_{16}$. This gives the bottom of stack address A_{BOS}

$$A_{BOS} = 1050_{16} + FFFF_{16}$$

$$= 1104F_{16}$$

Furthermore, the stack pointer, which represents the offset from the bottom of the stack to the top of the stack, equals 0008_{16}. Therefore, the current top of the stack is at physical address A_{TOS} equals

$$A_{TOS} = 1050_{16} + 0008_{16}$$

$$= 1058_{16}$$

Addresses with higher values than that of the top of stack, 1058_{16}, contain valid stack data. Those with lower addresses do not yet contain valid stack data. Notice that the last value pushed to the stack in Fig. 3.13(a) was $BBAA_{16}$.

Figure 3.13(b) demonstrates what happens when the PUSH AX instruction is executed. Here we see that AX contains the value 1234_{16}. Notice that execution of the PUSH instruction causes the stack pointer to be decremented by two but does not affect the contents of the stack segment register. Therefore, the next location to be accessed in the stack corresponds to address 1056_{16}. It is to this location that the value in AX is pushed. Notice that the most significant byte of AX, which equals 12_{16}, now resides in the least significant byte of the word in stack, and the least significant byte 34_{16} is held in the most significant byte.

Now let us look at an example in which stack data are popped back into the register from which they were pushed. Figure 3.14 illustrates this operation. In Fig. 3.14(a), the stack is shown to be in the state that resulted due to our prior PUSH AX example. That is, SP equals 0006_{16}, SS equals 105_{16}, the address of the top of the stack equals 1056_{16}, and the word at the top of the stack equals 1234_{16}.

Looking at Fig. 3.14(b), we see what happens when the instructions POP AX and POP BX are executed in that order. Here we see that execution of the first instruction causes the 8088 to read the value from the top of the stack and put it into the AX register as 1234_{16}. Next, SP is incremented to give 0008_{16} and another read cycle is initiated from the stack. This second read corresponds to the POP BX instruction and it causes the value $BBAA_{16}$ to be loaded into the BX register. SP is incremented once more and now equals $000A_{16}$. Therefore, the new top of stack is at address $105A_{16}$.

From Fig. 3.14(b) we see that the values read out of 1056_{16} and 1058_{16} still remain at these addresses. But now they reside at locations that are considered

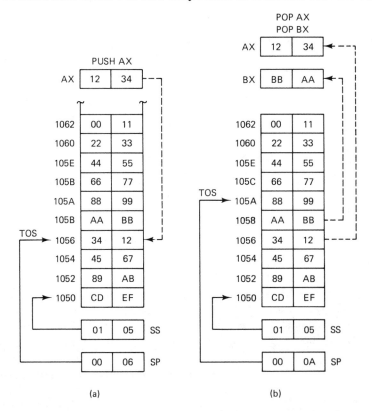

Figure 3.14 (a) Stack just prior to POP operation; (*Courtesy Intel Corporation*) (b) stack after execution of the POP AX and POP BX instructions. (*Courtesy Intel Corporation*)

to be above the top of the stack. Therefore, they no longer represent valid stack data.

3.12 INPUT/OUTPUT ADDRESS SPACE

The 8088 has separate memory and input/output (I/O) address spaces. The *I/O address space* is the place where I/O interfaces such as printer and terminal ports are to be implemented. Figure 3.15 shows a map of the 8088's I/O address space. Notice that the address range is from 0000_{16} to $FFFF_{16}$. This represents just 64K byte-addresses; therefore, unlike memory, I/O addresses are just 16 bits long.

The part of the map from address 0000_{16} through FF_{16} is referred to as *page 0*. Certain of the 8088's I/O instructions can only perform operations to I/O devices located in this part of the I/O address space. Other I/O instructions can input or output data from devices located anywhere in the I/O address space. Notice that the eight locations from address $00F8_{16}$ through $00FF_{16}$ are specified as reserved by Intel Corporation and should not be used.

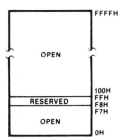

Figure 3.15 I/O address space. (*Courtesy Intel Corporation*)

3.13 THE 8088'S ADDRESSING MODES

When the 8088 executes an instruction, it performs the specified function on data. These data are called its *operands* and may be part of the instruction, reside in one of the internal registers of the 8088, stored at an address in memory, or held at an I/O port. To access these different types of operands, the 8088 is provided with various *addressing modes*. Here are the modes available on the 8088: *register addressing, immediate addressing, direct addressing, register indirect addressing, based addressing, indexed addressing, based indexed addressing, string addressing,* and *port addressing.*

Of these nine modes, all but register addressing, port addressing, and immediate addressing make reference to an operand stored in memory. Therefore, they require the 8088 to initiate a read or write of memory. The addressing modes provide different ways of computing the address of an operand. Let us now consider in detail each of these addressing modes.

Register Addressing Mode

With the register addressing mode, the operand to be accessed is specified as residing in an internal register of the 8088. An example of an instruction that uses this addressing mode is

MOV AX,BX

This stands for move the contents of BX, the *source operand*, to AX, the *destination operand*. Both the source and destination operands have been specified as the contents of internal registers of the 8088.

Let us now look at the effect of executing the register addressing mode MOV instruction. In Fig. 3.16(a) we see the state of the 8088 just prior to fetch-

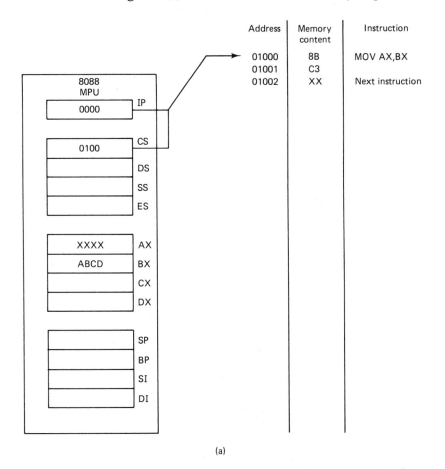

(a)

Figure 3.16 (a) Register addressing mode instruction before execution; (b) after execution.

ing the instruction. Notice that IP and CS point to the MOV AX,BX instruction at address 01000_{16}. Prior to execution of this instruction, the contents of BX are $ABCD_{16}$ and the contents of AX represent a don't-care state. As shown in Fig. 3.16(b), the result of executing the instruction is that $ABCD_{16}$ is copied into AX.

Immediate Addressing Mode

If a source operand is part of the instruction instead of the contents of a register or memory location, it represents what is called an *immediate operand* and is accessed using the immediate addressing mode. Typically, immediate operands represent constant data.

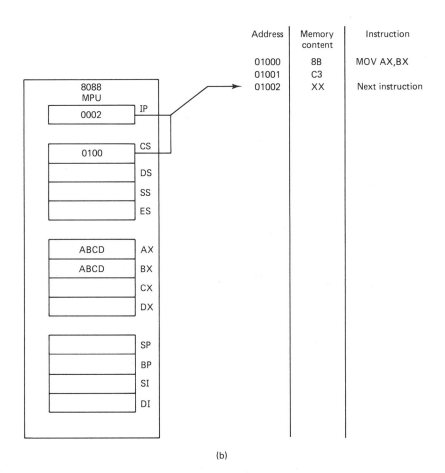

(b)

Figure 3.16 (continued)

Immediate operands can be either a byte or word of data. In the instruction

MOV AL,15H

the source operand 15_{16} is an example of a byte-wide immediate source operand. Note that the value of the immediate operand must always begin with one of the numbers 0 through 9. For example, if the immediate operand is to be $A5_{16}$, it must be written as 0A5H. The destination operand, which is the contents of AL, uses register addressing. Thus this instruction employs both the immediate and register addressing modes.

Figure 3.17(a) and (b) illustrates execution of this instruction. Here we find that the immediate operand 15_{16} is stored in the code segment of memory

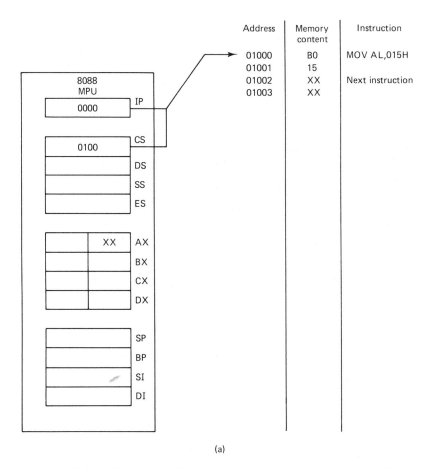

(a)

Figure 3.17 (a) Immediate addressing mode instruction before execution; (b) after execution.

in the byte location immediately following the opcode of the instruction. This value is fetched, along with the opcode for MOV, into the instruction queue within the 8088. When it performs the move operation, the source operand is fetched from the instruction queue and not from the memory, and no external memory operations are performed. Notice that the result produced by executing this instruction is that the immediate operand is loaded into the lower-byte part of the accumulator (AL).

Direct Addressing Mode

Direct addressing differs from immediate addressing in that the locations following the instruction opcode hold an *effective memory address* (EA) instead of data. This effective address is the 16-bit offset of the storage location of the

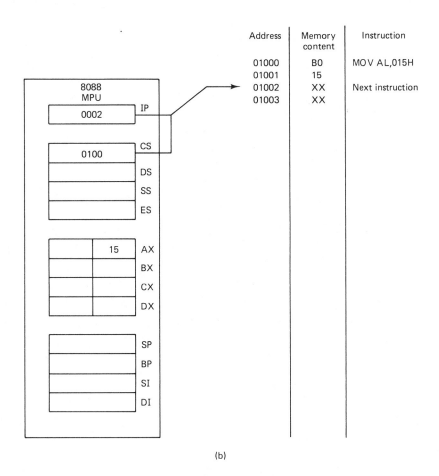

(b)

Figure 3.17 (continued)

operand from the current value in the DS register. EA is combined with the contents of DS in the 8088 to produce the physical address of the operand.

An example of an instruction that uses direct addressing for its source operand is

MOV CX,BETA

This stands for "move the contents of the memory location, which is labeled as BETA in the current data segment, into the internal register CX." The assembler computes the offset of BETA from the beginning of the data segment and encodes it as part of the instruction's machine code.

In Fig. 3.18(a) we find that the value of the offset is stored in the two byte locations that follow the instruction. This value is also known as the *displace-*

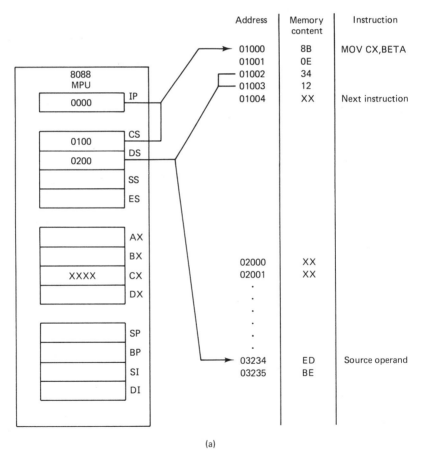

(a)

Figure 3.18 (a) Direct addressing mode instruction before execution; (b) after execution.

ment. Notice that the value assigned to constant BETA is 1234_{16}. As the instruction is executed, the 8088 combines 1234_{16} with 0200_{16} to get the physical address of the source operand. This gives

$$PA = 02000_{16} + 1234_{16}$$

$$= 03234_{16}$$

Then it reads the word of data starting at this address, which is $BEED_{16}$, and loads it into the CX register. This result is illustrated in Fig. 3.18(b).

Register Indirect Addressing Mode

Register indirect addressing is similar to the direct addressing we just described in that an effective address is combined with the contents of DS to ob-

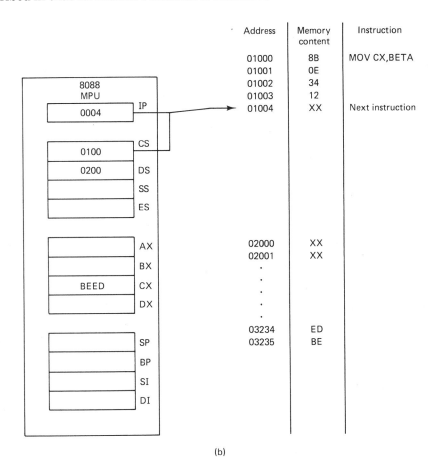

(b)

Figure 3.18 (continued)

tain a physical address. However, it differs in the way the offset is specified. This time EA resides in either a pointer register or an index register within the 8088. The pointer register can be either base register BX or base pointer register BP, and the index register can be source index register SI or destination index register DI.

An example of an instruction that uses register indirect addressing is

MOV AX,[SI]

This instruction moves the contents of the memory location offset by the value of EA in SI from the beginning of the current data segment to the AX register.

For instance, as shown in Fig. 3.19(a) and (b), if SI contains 1234_{16} and DS

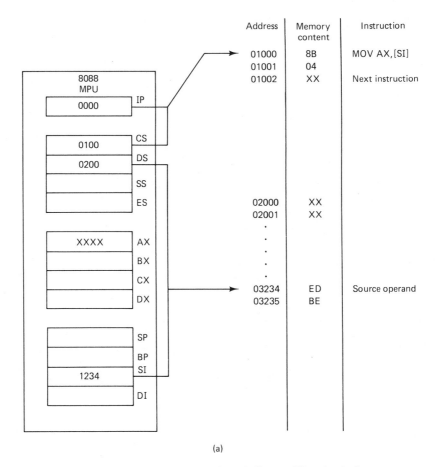

(a)

Figure 3.19 (a) Instruction using register indirect addressing before execution; (b) after execution.

contains 0200_{16}, the result produced by executing the instruction is that the contents of memory location

$$PA = 02000_{16} + 1234_{16}$$

$$= 03234_{16}$$

are moved to the AX register. Notice in Fig. 3.19(b) that this value is $BEED_{16}$. In this example, the value 1234_{16} that was found in the SI register must have been loaded with another instruction prior to executing the MOV instruction.

Notice that the result produced by executing this instruction and the example for the direct addressing mode are the same. However, they differ in the way in which the physical address was generated. The direct addressing method lends itself to applications where the value of EA is a constant. On the other hand, register indirect addressing can be used when the value of EA is

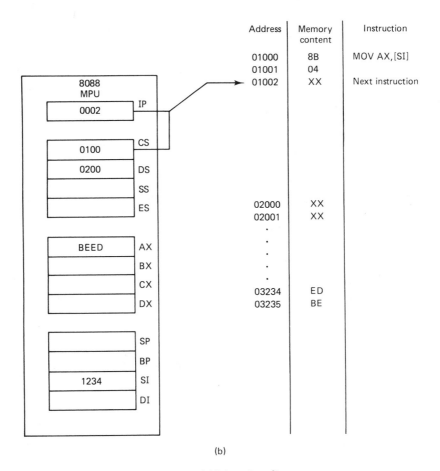

(b)

Figure 3.19 (continued)

calculated and stored, for example, in SI by a previous instruction. That is, EA is a variable.

Based Addressing Mode

In the based addressing mode, the physical address of the operand is obtained by adding a direct or indirect displacement to the contents of either base register BX or base pointer register BP and the current value in DS or SS, respectively. A MOV instruction that uses based addressing to specify the location of its destination operand is as follows:

MOV [BX]+BETA,AL

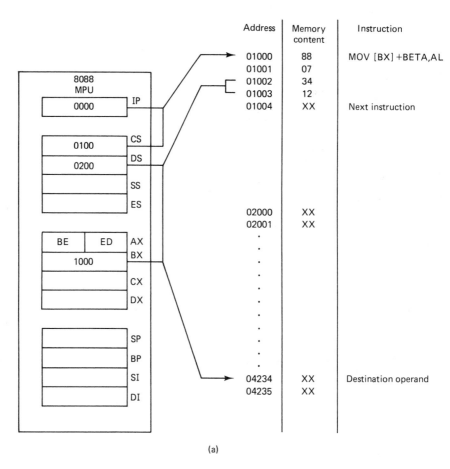

(a)

Figure 3.20 (a) Instruction using direct base pointer addressing before execution; (b) after execution.

This instruction uses base register BX and direct displacement BETA to derive the EA of the destination operand. The based addressing mode is implemented by specifying the base register in brackets followed by a + sign and the direct displacement. The source operand in this example is located in byte accumulator AL.

As shown in Fig. 3.20(a) and (b), the fetch and execution of this instruction causes the 8088 to calculate the physical address of the destination operand from the contents of DS, BX, and the direct displacement. The result is

$$PA = 02000_{16} + 1000_{16} + 1234_{16}$$

$$= 04234_{16}$$

Then it writes the contents of source operand AL into the storage location at 04234_{16}. The result is that ED_{16} is copied into the destination memory location.

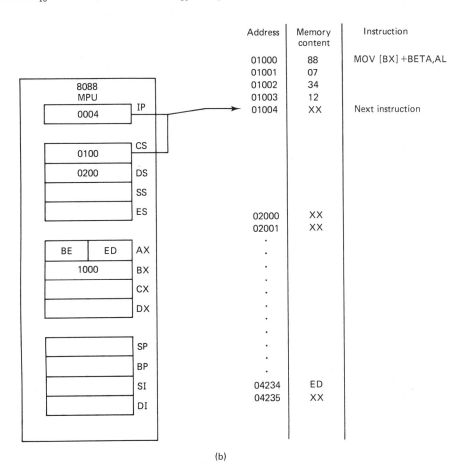

(b)

Figure 3.20 (continued)

If BP is used instead of BX, the calculation of the physical address is performed using the contents of the stack segment (SS) register instead of DS. This permits access to data in the stack segment of memory.

Indexed Addressing Mode

Indexed addressing works identically to the based addressing we just described; however, it uses the contents of one of the index registers, instead of BX or BP, in the generation of the physical address. Here is an example:

MOV AL,[SI]+ARRAY

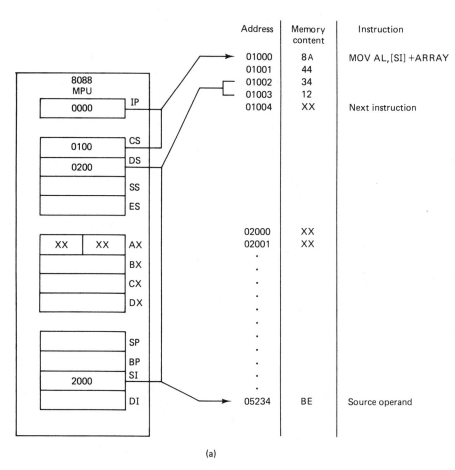

(a)

Figure 3.21 (a) Instruction using direct indexed addressing before execution; (b) after execution.

The source operand has been specified using direct indexed addressing. Notice that the notation this time is such that ARRAY, which is a *direct displacement*, is added to the selected index register, SI. Just like for the base register in based addressing, the index register is enclosed in brackets.

The effective address is calculated as

$$EA = (SI) + ARRAY$$

and the physical address is obtained by combining the contents of DS with EA.

The example in Fig. 3.21(a) and (b) shows the result of executing the MOV instruction. First the physical address of the source operand is calculated from DS, SI, and the direct displacement.

$$PA = 02000_{16} + 2000_{16} + 1234_{16}$$

$$= 05234_{16}$$

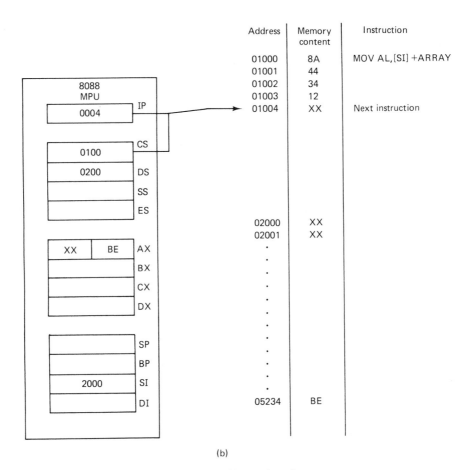

(b)

Figure 3.21 (continued)

Then the byte of data stored at this location, which is BE_{16}, is read into the lower byte AL of the accumulator register.

Based Indexed Addressing Mode

Combining the based addressing mode and the indexed addressing mode together results in a new, more powerful mode known as based indexed addressing. Let us consider an example of a MOV instruction using this type of addressing.

MOV AH,[BX][SI]+BETA

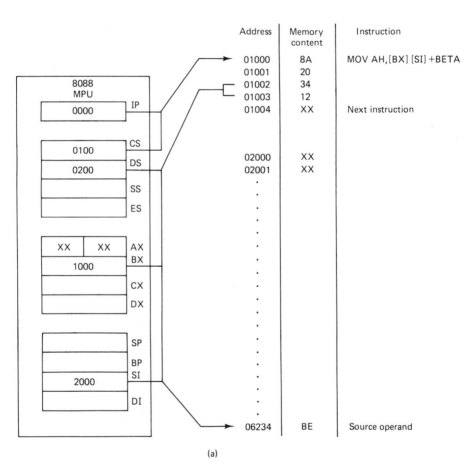

(a)

Figure 3.22 (a) Instruction using based indexed addressing before execution; (b) after execution.

Notice that the source operand is accessed using based indexed addressing mode. Therefore, the effective address of the source operand is obtained as

$$EA = (BX) + (SI) + BETA$$

and the physical address of the operand from the current DS and the calculated EA.

   An example of executing this instruction is illustrated in Fig. 3.22(a) and (b). The address of the source operand is calculated as

$$PA = 02000_{16} + 1000_{16} + 2000_{16} + 1234_{16}$$

$$= 6234_{16}$$

Execution of the instruction causes the value stored at this location to be written into AH.

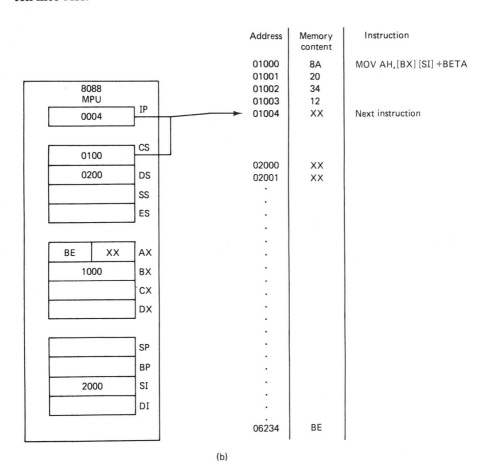

(b)

Figure 3.22 (continued)

String Addressing Mode

The string instructions of the 8088's instruction set automatically use the source and destination index registers to specify the effective addresses of the source and destination operands, respectively. The move string instruction

MOVS

is an example. Notice that neither SI nor DI appears in the string instruction, but both are used during its execution.

Port Addressing Mode

Port addressing is used in conjunction with the IN and OUT instructions to access input and output ports. For ports in the I/O address space, only the direct addressing mode and an indirect addressing mode using DX are available. For example, direct addressing of an input port is used in the instruction

IN AL,15H

This stands for "input the data from the byte-wide input port at address 15_{16} of the I/O address space to register AL."

Next, let us consider another example. Using indirect port addressing for the source operand in an IN instruction, we get

IN AL,DX

It means "input the data from the byte-wide input port whose address is specified by the contents of register DX." For instance, if (DX) equals 1234_{16}, the contents of the port at this I/O address are loaded into AL.

ASSIGNMENTS

Section 3.2

1. What is the purpose of a software model of the 8088 microprocessor?
2. What must an assembly language programmer know about the registers within the 8088 microprocessor?
3. How many registers are located within the 8088?
4. How large is the 8088's memory address space?

Section 3.3

5. What is the highest address in the 8088's memory address space? Lowest address?

6. Is memory in the 8088 microcomputer organized as bytes, words, or double words?

7. The contents of memory location $B0000_{16}$ are FF_{16}, and that at $B0001_{16}$ are 00_{16}. What is the even-addressed data word stored starting at address $B0000_{16}$?

8. Show how the double word 12345678_{16} will be stored in memory starting at address $A001_{16}$.

Section 3.4

9. How much memory can be active at a given time in the 8088 microcomputer?

10. Which of the 8088's internal registers are to be used for memory segmentation?

11. How much of the 8088's active memory is available as general-purpose data storage memory?

12. Which range of the 8088's memory address space can be used to store instructions of a program?

Section 3.5

13. What is the dedicated use of the part of the 8088's address space from 00000_{16} through $0007F_{16}$?

14. What is stored at addresses $FFFFC_{16}$ through $FFFFF_{16}$?

Section 3.6

15. What is the function of the instruction pointer register?

16. Overview the fetch and execution of an instruction by the 8088.

17. What happens to the value in IP each time the 8088 fetches an instruction?

Section 3.7

18. Make a list of the general-purpose data registers of the 8088.

19. How is the word value of the base register labeled?

20. How are the upper and lower bytes of the data register denoted?

21. What dedicated operations are assigned to the CX register?

Section 3.8

22. What kind of information is stored in the pointer and index registers?

23. Name the two pointer registers.

24. For which segment register are the contents of the pointer registers used as an offset?

25. For which segment register are the contents of the index registers used as an offset?
26. What is the difference between SI and DI?

Section 3.9

27. Categorize each flag bit of the 8088 as either a control flag or a flag that monitors the status due to execution of an instruction.
28. Describe the function of each of the status flags.
29. How are the status flags used by software?
30. Which flag determines whether the address for a string operation is incremented or decremented?
31. Can the state of the flags be modified through software?

Section 3.10

32. What are the word lengths of the 8088's logical and physical addresses?
33. What two address elements are combined to form a physical address?
34. If the current values in the code segment register and the instruction pointer are 0200_{16} and $01AC_{16}$, respectively, what is the physical address of the next instruction?
35. A data segment is to be located from address $A0000_{16}$ to $AFFFF_{16}$; what value must be loaded into DS?
36. If the data-segment register contains the value found in problem 35, what value must be loaded into DI if it is to point to a destination operand stored at address $A1234_{16}$ in memory?

Section 3.11

37. What is the function of the stack?
38. If the current values in the stack segment register and stack pointer are $0C00_{16}$ and $FF00_{16}$, respectively, what is the address of the top of the stack?
39. For the base and offset addresses in problem 38, how many words of data are currently held in the stack?
40. Show how the value $EE11_{16}$ from register AX would be pushed onto the top of the stack as it exists in problem 38.

Section 3.12

41. In the 8088 are the input/output and memory address spaces common or separate?
42. How large is the 8088's I/O address space?
43. What is the name given to the part of the I/O address space from 0000_{16} through $00FF_{16}$?

Section 3.13

44. Make a list of the addressing modes available on the 8088.

45. Identify the addressing modes used for the source and the destination operands in the instructions that follow.

    (a) MOV AL,BL
    (b) MOV AX,0FFH
    (c) MOV [DI],AX
    (d) MOV DI,[SI]
    (e) MOV [BX]+XYZ,CX
    (f) MOV [DI]+XYZ,AH
    (g) MOV [BX][DI]+XYZ,AL

46. Compute the physical address for the specified operand in each of the following instructions. The register contents are as follows: $CS = 0A00_{16}$, $DS = 0B00_{16}$, $SI = 0100_{16}$, $DI = 0200_{16}$, $BX = 0300_{16}$, and $XYZ = 0400_{16}$.

    (a) Destination operand of the instruction in (c) of problem 45.
    (b) Source operand of the instruction in (d) of problem 45.
    (c) Destination operand of the instruction in (e) of problem 45.
    (d) Destination operand of the instruction in (f) of problem 45.
    (e) Destination operand of the instruction in (g) of problem 45.

4

MACHINE LANGUAGE CODING AND THE SOFTWARE DEVELOPMENT TOOLS OF THE IBM PC

4.1 INTRODUCTION

In Chapter 3 we examined the software architecture of the 8088 microprocessor. This chapter describes how the 8088 assembly language instructions are encoded in machine language and how to use the DEBUG program on the IBM PC to load, assemble, execute, and debug programs. The topics discussed are as follows:

1. Converting assembly language instructions to machine language
2. Encoding a complete source program in machine code
3. The IBM PC and its DEBUG program
4. Examining and modifying the contents of memory
5. Loading, verifying, and saving machine code programs
6. Assembling instructions with the ASSEMBLE command
7. Executing instructions and programs with the TRACE and GO commands
8. Debugging a program

4.2 CONVERTING ASSEMBLY LANGUAGE INSTRUCTIONS TO MACHINE CODE

To convert an assembly language program to machine code, we must convert each assembly language instruction to its equivalent machine-code instruction. In general, for an instruction, the machine code specifies things like what operation is to be performed, what operand or operands are to be used, whether the operation is performed on byte or word data, whether the operation involves operands that are located in registers or a register and a storage location in memory, and, if one of the operands is in memory, how its address is to be generated. All of this information is encoded into the bits of the machine-code instruction.

The machine-code instructions of the 8088 vary in the number of bytes used to encode them. Some instructions can be encoded with just one byte, others in two bytes, and many require more. The maximum number of bytes an instruction might take is six. Single-byte instructions generally specify a simpler operation with a register or a flag bit. For instance, *complement carry* (CMC) is an example of a single-byte instruction. It is specified by the machine-code byte 11110101_2, which equals $F5_{16}$.

$$CMC = 11110101_2 = F5_{16}$$

The machine code for instructions can be obtained by following the formats that are used in encoding the instructions of the 8088 microprocessor. Most multibyte instructions use the *general instruction format* shown in Fig. 4.1. Exceptions to this format will be considered separately later. For now, let us describe the functions of the various bits and fields (groups of bits) in each byte of this format.

Looking at Fig. 4.1, we see that byte 1 contains three kinds of information: the *operation code* (opcode), the *register direction bit* (D), and the *data size bit* (W). Let us summarize the function of each of these pieces of information.

1. Opcode field (6 bits) specifies the operation, such as add, subtract, or move, that is to be performed.

2. Register direction bit (D bit) specifies whether the register operand that is specified in byte 2 is the source or destination operand. A logic 1 at this bit

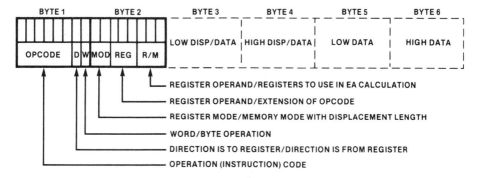

Figure 4.1 General instruction format. (*Courtesy Intel Corporation*)

position indicates that the register operand is a destination operand; a logic 0 indicates that it is a source operand.

3. Data size bit (W bit) specifies whether the operation will be performed on eight-bit or 16-bit data. Logic 0 selects eight bits and 1 selects 16 bits.

For instance, if a 16-bit value is to be added to register AX, the six most significant bits specify the add register operation. This opcode is 000000_2. The next bit, D, will be at logic 1 to specify that a register, AX in this case, holds the destination operand. Finally, the least significant bit, W, will be logic 1 to specify a 16-bit data operation.

The second byte in Fig. 4.1 has three fields. They are the *mode* (MOD) *field*, the *register* (REG) *field*, and the *register/memory* (R/M) *field*. These fields are used to specify which register is used for the first operand and where the second operand is stored. The second operand can be in either a register or a memory location.

The three-bit REG field is used to identify the register for the first operand. This is the operand that was defined as the source or destination by the D bit in byte 1. The encoding for each of the 8088's registers is shown in Fig. 4.2. Here we find that the 16-bit register AX and the eight-bit register AL are specified by the same binary code. Notice that the decision whether to use AX or AL is made based on the setting of the operation size (W) bit in byte 1.

For instance, in our earlier example, we said that the first operand, which is the destination operand, is register AX. For this case, the REG field is set to 000.

The two-bit MOD field and three-bit R/M field together specify the second operand. Encoding for these two fields are shown in Fig. 4.3(a) and (b), respectively. MOD indicates whether the operand is in a register or memory. Notice that in the case of a second operand that is in a register, the MOD field is always 11. The R/M field along with the W bit from byte 1 selects the register.

For example, if the second operand, the source operand, in our earlier addition example is to be in BX, the MOD and R/M fields will be made MOD = 11 and R/M = 011, respectively.

REG	W = 0	W = 1
000	AL	AX
001	CL	CX
010	DL	DX
011	BL	BX
100	AH	SP
101	CH	BP
110	DH	SI
111	BH	DI

Figure 4.2 Register (REG) field encoding. (*Courtesy Intel Corporation*)

CODE	EXPLANATION
00	Memory Mode, no displacement follows*
01	Memory Mode, 8-bit displacement follows
10	Memory Mode, 16-bit displacement follows
11	Register Mode (no displacement)

*Except when R/M = 110, then 16-bit displacement follows

(a)

MOD = 11			EFFECTIVE ADDRESS CALCULATION			
R/M	W = 0	W = 1	R/M	MOD = 00	MOD = 01	MOD = 10
000	AL	AX	000	(BX) + (SI)	(BX) + (SI) + D8	(BX) + (SI) + D16
001	CL	CX	001	(BX) + (DI)	(BX) + (DI) + D8	(BX) + (DI) + D16
010	DL	DX	010	(BP) + (SI)	(BP) + (SI) + D8	(BP) + (SI) + D16
011	BL	BX	011	(BP) + (DI)	(BP) + (DI) + D8	(BP) + (DI) + D16
100	AH	SP	100	(SI)	(SI) + D8	(SI) + D16
101	CH	BP	101	(DI)	(DI) + D8	(DI) + D16
110	DH	SI	110	DIRECT ADDRESS	(BP) + D8	(BP) + D16
111	BH	DI	111	(BX)	(BX) + D8	(BX) + D16

(b)

Figure 4.3 (a) Mode (MOD) field encoding (*Courtesy of Intel Corporation*); (b) register/ memory (R/M) field encoding. (*Courtesy Intel Corporation*)

Example 4.1

The instruction

MOV BL,AL

stands for "move the byte contents from source register AL to destination register BL." Using the general format in Fig. 4.1, show how to encode the instruction in machine code. Assume that the six-bit opcode for the move operation is 100010.

Solution:

In byte 1 the first six bits specify the move operation and thus must be 100010.

$$\text{OPCODE} = 100010_2$$

The next bit, which is D, indicates whether the register that is specified by the REG part of byte 2 is a source or destination operand. Let us say that we will encode AL in the REG field of byte 2; therefore, D is set equal to 0 for source operand.

$$D = 0$$

The last bit (W) in byte 1 must specify a byte operation. For this reason, it is also set to 0.

$$W = 0$$

This leads to

$$\text{BYTE } 1 = 10001000_2 = 88_{16}$$

In byte 2 the source operand, which is specified by the REG field, is AL. The corresponding code from Fig. 4.2 is:

$$\text{REG} = 000$$

Since the second operand is also a register, the MOD field is made 11. The R/M field specifies that the destination register is BL and the code from Fig. 4.3(b) is 011. This gives

$$\text{MOD} = 11$$

$$\text{R/M} = 011$$

Therefore, byte 2 is

$$\text{BYTE } 2 = 11000011_2 = \text{C3}_{16}$$

The entire hexadecimal code for the instruction is

MOV BL,AL = 88C3H

For a second operand that is located in memory, there are a number of different ways its location can be specified. That is, any of the addressing modes supported by the 8088 microprocessor can be used to generate its address. The addressing mode is also selected with the MOD and R/M fields.

Notice in Fig. 4.3(b) that the addressing mode for an operand in memory is indicated by one of the other three values (00, 01, and 10) in the MOD field and an appropriate R/M code. The different ways in which the operand's address can be generated are shown in the effective address calculation part of the table in Fig. 4.3(b). These different address calculation expressions correspond to the addressing modes we introduced in Chapter 3. For instance, if the base (BX) register contains the memory address, this fact is encoded into the instruction by making MOD = 00 and R/M = 111.

Example 4.2

The instruction

ADD AX,[SI]

stands for "add the 16 bit contents of the memory location indirectly specified by SI to the contents of AX." Encode the instruction in machine code. The opcode for this add operation is 000000_2.

Solution:

To specify a 16-bit add operation with a register as the destination, the first byte of machine code will be

$$\text{BYTE } 1 = 00000011_2 = 03_{16}$$

The REG field bits in byte 2 are 000 to select AX as the destination register. The other operand is in memory and its address is specified by the contents of SI with no displacement. In Figs. 4.3(a) and (b), we find that for indirect addressing using SI with no displacement, MOD equals 00 and R/M equals 100.

$$\text{MOD} = 00$$

$$\text{R/M} = 100$$

This gives

$$\text{BYTE } 2 = 00000100_2 = 04_{16}$$

Thus the machine code for the instruction is

$$\text{ADD AX,[SI]} = 0304\text{H}$$

Some of the addressing modes of the 8088 need either data or an address displacement to be coded into the instruction. These types of information are encoded using additional bytes. For instance, looking at Fig. 4.1, we see that byte 3 is needed in the encoding of an instruction if it uses a byte-size address displacement, and both byte 3 and byte 4 are needed if the instruction uses a word-size displacement.

The size of the displacement is encoded into the MOD field. For example, if the effective address is to be generated by the expression

$$(\text{BX}) + \text{D8}$$

where D8 stands for *eight-bit displacement,* MOD is set to 01 to specify memory mode with an eight-bit displacement and R/M is set to 111 to select BX.

Bytes 3 and 4 are also used to encode byte-wide immediate operands, word-wide immediate operands, and direct addresses. For example, in an instruction where direct addressing is used to identify the location of an operand in memory, the MOD field must be 00 and the R/M field 110. The offset value of the operand's address is coded into the bytes that follow.

If both a 16-bit displacement and a 16-bit immediate operand are used in the same instruction, the displacement is encoded into bytes 3 and 4 and the immediate operand into bytes 5 and 6.

Example 4.3

What is the machine code for the instruction

$$\text{XOR} \quad \text{CL,[1234H]}$$

This instruction stands for exclusive-OR the byte of data at memory address 1234_{16} with the byte contents of CL. The opcode for exclusive-OR is 001100_2.

Solution:

Using the XOR opcode 001100_2, 1 for destination operand, and 0 for byte data, we get

$$\text{BYTE} \; 1 = 00110010_2 = 32_{16}$$

The REG field has to specify CL, which makes it equal to 001. In this case a direct address has been specified for operand 2. This requires $\text{MOD} = 00$ and $\text{R/M} = 110$. Thus

$$\text{BYTE} \; 2 = 00001110_2 = 0E_{16}$$

To specify the address 1234_{16}, we must use byte 3 and byte 4. The least significant byte of the address is encoded first, followed by the most significant byte. This gives

$$\text{BYTE} \; 3 = 34_{16}$$

and

$$\text{BYTE} \; 4 = 12_{16}$$

The entire machine code form of the instruction is

$$\text{XOR} \quad \text{CL,[1234H]} = 320E3412H$$

Example 4.4

The instruction

$$\text{ADD} \quad \text{[BX][DI]} + \text{DISP,AX}$$

means "add the word contents of AX to the contents of the memory location specified by based indexed addressing mode." The opcode for the add operation is 000000_2 and assume that DISP equals 1234_{16}.

Solution:

The add opcode, which is 000000_2, a 0 for source operand, and a 1 for word data, gives

$$\text{BYTE } 1 = 00000001_2 = 01_{16}$$

The REG field in byte 2 is 000 to specify AX as the source register. Since there is a displacement and it needs 16 bits for encoding, the MOD field obtained from Fig. 4.3(a) is 10. The R/M field, which is also obtained from Fig. 4.3(b), is set to 001 for an effective address generated from SI and BX. This gives the second byte as

$$\text{BYTE } 2 = 10000001_2 = 81_{16}$$

The displacement 1234_{16} is encoded in the next two bytes with the least significant byte first. Therefore, the machine code that results is

$$\text{ADD } [BX][DI] + \text{DISP,AX} = 01813412H$$

As we indicated earlier, the general format in Fig. 4.1 cannot be used to encode all the instructions that can be executed by the 8088. There are minor modifications that must be made to this general format to encode a few instructions. In some instructions one or more single-bit fields are needed. These one-bit fields and their functions are shown in Fig. 4.4.

For instance, the general format of the *repeat* (REP) instruction is

$$\text{REP} = 1111001Z$$

Here bit Z is made 1 or 0 depending upon whether the repeat operation is to be done when the zero flag is set or when it is reset. Similarly, the other two bits S and V in Fig. 4.4 are used to encode sign extension for arithmetic instructions and to specify the source of the count for shift or rotate instructions, respectively.

The formats for all of the instructions in the 8088's instruction set are shown in Fig. 4.5. This is the information that can be used to encode any 8088 program.

Field	Value	Function
S	0 1	No sign extension Sign extend 8-bit immediate data to 16 bits if W=1
V	0 1	Shift/rotate count is one Shift/rotate count is specified in CL register
Z	0 1	Repeat/loop while zero flag is clear Repeat/loop while zero flag is set

Figure 4.4 Additional one bit fields and their functions. (*Courtesy Intel Corporation*)

MOV = Move:

	7 6 5 4 3 2 1 0	7 6 5 4 3 2 1 0	7 6 5 4 3 2 1 0	7 6 5 4 3 2 1 0	7 6 5 4 3 2 1 0	7 6 5 4 3 2 1 0
Register/memory to/from register	1 0 0 0 1 0 d w	mod reg r/m	(DISP-LO)	(DISP-HI)		
Immediate to register/memory	1 1 0 0 0 1 1 w	mod 0 0 0 r/m	(DISP-LO)	(DISP-HI)	data	data if w = 1
Immediate to register	1 0 1 1 w reg	data	data if w = 1			
Memory to accumulator	1 0 1 0 0 0 0 w	addr-lo	addr-hi			
Accumulator to memory	1 0 1 0 0 0 1 w	addr-lo	addr-hi			
Register/memory to segment register	1 0 0 0 1 1 1 0	mod 0 SR r/m	(DISP-LO)	(DISP-HI)		
Segment register to register/memory	1 0 0 0 1 1 0 0	mod 0 SR r/m	(DISP-LO)	(DISP-HI)		

PUSH = Push:

Register/memory	1 1 1 1 1 1 1 1	mod 1 1 0 r/m	(DISP-LO)	(DISP-HI)
Register	0 1 0 1 0 reg			
Segment register	0 0 0 reg 1 1 0			

POP = Pop:

Register/memory	1 0 0 0 1 1 1 1	mod 0 0 0 r/m	(DISP-LO)	(DISP-HI)
Register	0 1 0 1 1 reg			
Segment register	0 0 0 reg 1 1 1			

XCHG = Exchange:

Register/memory with register	1 0 0 0 0 1 1 w	mod reg r/m	(DISP-LO)	(DISP-HI)
Register with accumulator	1 0 0 1 0 reg			

IN = Input from:

Fixed port	1 1 1 0 0 1 0 w	DATA-8
Variable port	1 1 1 0 1 1 0 w	

OUT = Output to:

Fixed port	1 1 1 0 0 1 1 w	DATA-8		
Variable port	1 1 1 0 1 1 1 w			
XLAT = Translate byte to AL	1 1 0 1 0 1 1 1			
LEA = Load EA to register	1 0 0 0 1 1 0 1	mod reg r/m	(DISP-LO)	(DISP-HI)
LDS = Load pointer to DS	1 1 0 0 0 1 0 1	mod reg r/m	(DISP-LO)	(DISP-HI)
LES = Load pointer to ES	1 1 0 0 0 1 0 0	mod reg r/m	(DISP-LO)	(DISP-HI)
LAHF = Load AH with flags	1 0 0 1 1 1 1 1			
SAHF = Store AH into flags	1 0 0 1 1 1 1 0			
PUSHF = Push flags	1 0 0 1 1 1 0 0			
POPF = Pop flags	1 0 0 1 1 1 0 1			

Figure 4.5 8086 instruction encoding tables. (*Courtesy Intel Corporation*)

ARITHMETIC

ADD = Add:

	7 6 5 4 3 2 1 0	7 6 5 4 3 2 1 0	7 6 5 4 3 2 1 0	7 6 5 4 3 2 1 0	7 6 5 4 3 2 1 0	7 6 5 4 3 2 1 0
Reg/memory with register to either	0 0 0 0 0 0 d w	mod reg r/m	(DISP-LO)	(DISP-HI)		
Immediate to register/memory	1 0 0 0 0 0 s w	mod 0 0 0 r/m	(DISP-LO)	(DISP-HI)	data	data if s: w=01
Immediate to accumulator	0 0 0 0 0 1 0 w	data	data if w=1			

ADC = Add with carry:

Reg/memory with register to either	0 0 0 1 0 0 d w	mod reg r/m	(DISP-LO)	(DISP-HI)		
Immediate to register/memory	1 0 0 0 0 0 s w	mod 0 1 0 r/m	(DISP-LO)	(DISP-HI)	data	data if s: w=01
Immediate to accumulator	0 0 0 1 0 1 0 w	data	data if w=1			

INC = Increment:

Register/memory	1 1 1 1 1 1 1 w	mod 0 0 0 r/m	(DISP-LO)	(DISP-HI)
Register	0 1 0 0 0 reg			
AAA = ASCII adjust for add	0 0 1 1 0 1 1 1			
DAA = Decimal adjust for add	0 0 1 0 0 1 1 1			

SUB = Subtract:

Reg/memory and register to either	0 0 1 0 1 0 d w	mod reg r/m	(DISP-LO)	(DISP-HI)		
Immediate from register/memory	1 0 0 0 0 0 s w	mod 1 0 1 r/m	(DISP-LO)	(DISP-HI)	data	data if s: w=01
Immediate from accumulator	0 0 1 0 1 1 0 w	data	data if w=1			

SBB = Subtract with borrow:

Reg/memory and register to either	0 0 0 1 1 0 d w	mod reg r/m	(DISP-LO)	(DISP-HI)		
Immediate from register/memory	1 0 0 0 0 0 s w	mod 0 1 1 r/m	(DISP-LO)	(DISP-HI)	data	data if s: w=01
Immediate from accumulator	0 0 0 1 1 1 0 w	data	data if w=1			

DEC Decrement:

Register/memory	1 1 1 1 1 1 1 w	mod 0 0 1 r/m	(DISP-LO)	(DISP-HI)
Register	0 1 0 0 1 reg			
NEG Change sign	1 1 1 1 0 1 1 w	mod 0 1 1 r/m	(DISP-LO)	(DISP-HI)

CMP = Compare:

Register/memory and register	0 0 1 1 1 0 d w	mod reg r/m	(DISP-LO)	(DISP-HI)		
Immediate with register/memory	1 0 0 0 0 0 s w	mod 1 1 1 r/m	(DISP-LO)	(DISP-HI)	data	data if s: w=1
Immediate with accumulator	0 0 1 1 1 1 0 w	data				
AAS ASCII adjust for subtract	0 0 1 1 1 1 1 1					
DAS Decimal adjust for subtract	0 0 1 0 1 1 1 1					
MUL Multiply (unsigned)	1 1 1 1 0 1 1 w	mod 1 0 0 r/m	(DISP-LO)	(DISP-HI)		

Figure 4.5 (continued)

ARITHMETIC	7 6 5 4 3 2 1 0	7 6 5 4 3 2 1 0	7 6 5 4 3 2 1 0	7 6 5 4 3 2 1 0	7 6 5 4 3 2 1 0	7 6 5 4 3 2 1 0
IMUL Integer multiply (signed)	1 1 1 1 0 1 1 w	mod 1 0 1 r/m	(DISP-LO)	(DISP-HI)		
AAM ASCII adjust for multiply	1 1 0 1 0 1 0 0	0 0 0 0 1 0 1 0	(DISP-LO)	(DISP-HI)		
DIV Divide (unsigned)	1 1 1 1 0 1 1 w	mod 1 1 0 r/m	(DISP-LO)	(DISP-HI)		
IDIV Integer divide (signed)	1 1 1 1 0 1 1 w	mod 1 1 1 r/m	(DISP-LO)	(DISP-HI)		
AAD ASCII adjust for divide	1 1 0 1 0 1 0 1	0 0 0 0 1 0 1 0	(DISP-LO)	(DISP-HI)		
CBW Convert byte to word	1 0 0 1 1 0 0 0					
CWD Convert word to double word	1 0 0 1 1 0 0 1					

LOGIC						
NOT Invert	1 1 1 1 0 1 1 w	mod 0 1 0 r/m	(DISP-LO)	(DISP-HI)		
SHL/SAL Shift logical/arithmetic left	1 1 0 1 0 0 v w	mod 1 0 0 r/m	(DISP-LO)	(DISP-HI)		
SHR Shift logical right	1 1 0 1 0 0 v w	mod 1 0 1 r/m	(DISP-LO)	(DISP-HI)		
SAR Shift arithmetic right	1 1 0 1 0 0 v w	mod 1 1 1 r/m	(DISP-LO)	(DISP-HI)		
ROL Rotate left	1 1 0 1 0 0 v w	mod 0 0 0 r/m	(DISP-LO)	(DISP-HI)		
ROR Rotate right	1 1 0 1 0 0 v w	mod 0 0 1 r/m	(DISP-LO)	(DISP-HI)		
RCL Rotate through carry flag left	1 1 0 1 0 0 v w	mod 0 1 0 r/m	(DISP-LO)	(DISP-HI)		
RCR Rotate through carry right	1 1 0 1 0 0 v w	mod 0 1 1 r/m	(DISP-LO)	(DISP-HI)		

AND = And:

	7 6 5 4 3 2 1 0	7 6 5 4 3 2 1 0	7 6 5 4 3 2 1 0	7 6 5 4 3 2 1 0	7 6 5 4 3 2 1 0	7 6 5 4 3 2 1 0
Reg/memory with register to either	0 0 1 0 0 0 d w	mod reg r/m	(DISP-LO)	(DISP-HI)		
Immediate to register/memory	1 0 0 0 0 0 0 w	mod 1 0 0 r/m	(DISP-LO)	(DISP-HI)	data	data if w=1
Immediate to accumulator	0 0 1 0 0 1 0 w	data	data if w=1			

TEST = And function to flags no result:

Register/memory and register	0 0 0 1 0 0 d w	mod reg r/m	(DISP-LO)	(DISP-HI)		
Immediate data and register/memory	1 1 1 1 0 1 1 w	mod 0 0 0 r/m	(DISP-LO)	(DISP-HI)	data	data if w=1
Immediate data and accumulator	1 0 1 0 1 0 0 w	data				

OR = Or:

Reg/memory and register to either	0 0 0 0 1 0 d w	mod reg r/m	(DISP-LO)	(DISP-HI)		
Immediate to register/memory	1 0 0 0 0 0 0 w	mod 0 0 1 r/m	(DISP-LO)	(DISP-HI)	data	data if w=1
Immediate to accumulator	0 0 0 0 1 1 0 w	data	data if w=1			

XOR = Exclusive or:

Reg/memory and register to either	0 0 1 1 0 0 d w	mod reg r/m	(DISP-LO)	(DISP-HI)		
Immediate to register/memory	0 0 1 1 0 1 0 w	data	(DISP-LO)	(DISP-HI)	data	data if w=1
Immediate to accumulator	0 0 1 1 0 1 0 w	data	data if w=1			

Figure 4.5 (continued)

STRING MANIPULATION

	76543210
REP = Repeat	1 1 1 1 0 0 1 z
MOVS = Move byte/word	1 0 1 0 0 1 0 w
CMPS = Compare byte/word	1 0 1 0 0 1 1 w
SCAS = Scan byte/word	1 0 1 0 1 1 1 w
LODS = Load byte/wd to AL/AX	1 0 1 0 1 1 0 w
STDS = Stor byte/wd from AL/A	1 0 1 0 1 0 1 w

CONTROL TRANSFER

CALL = Call:

	76543210	76543210	76543210	76543210
Direct within segment	1 1 1 0 1 0 0 0	IP-INC-LO	IP-INC-HI	
Indirect within segment	1 1 1 1 1 1 1 1	mod 0 1 0 r/m	(DISP-LO)	(DISP-HI)
Direct intersegment	1 0 0 1 1 0 1 0	IP-lo	IP-hi	
		CS-lo	CS-hi	
Indirect intersegment	1 1 1 1 1 1 1 1	mod 0 1 1 r/m	(DISP-LO)	(DISP-HI)

JMP = Unconditional Jump:

	76543210	76543210	76543210	76543210
Direct within segment	1 1 1 0 1 0 0 1	IP-INC-LO	IP-INC-HI	
Direct within segment-short	1 1 1 0 1 0 1 1	IP-INC8		
Indirect within segment	1 1 1 1 1 1 1 1	mod 1 0 0 r/m	(DISP-LO)	(DISP-HI)
Direct intersegment	1 1 1 0 1 0 1 0	IP-lo	IP-hi	
		CS-lo	CS-hi	
Indirect intersegment	1 1 1 1 1 1 1 1	mod 1 0 1 r/m	(DISP-LO)	(DISP-HI)

RET = Return from CALL:

	76543210	76543210	76543210
Within segment	1 1 0 0 0 0 1 1		
Within seg adding immed to SP	1 1 0 0 0 0 1 0	data-lo	data-hi
Intersegment	1 1 0 0 1 0 1 1		
Intersegment adding immediate to SP	1 1 0 0 1 0 1 0	data-lo	data-hi
JE/JZ = Jump on equal/zero	0 1 1 1 0 1 0 0	IP-INC8	
JL/JNGE = Jump on less/not greater or equal	0 1 1 1 1 1 0 0	IP-INC8	
JLE/JNG = Jump on less or equal/not greater	0 1 1 1 1 1 1 0	IP-INC8	
JB/JNAE = Jump on below/not above or equal	0 1 1 1 0 0 1 0	IP-INC8	
JBE/JNA = Jump on below or equal/not above	0 1 1 1 0 1 1 0	IP-INC8	
JP/JPE = Jump on parity/parity even	0 1 1 1 1 0 1 0	IP-INC8	
JO = Jump on overflow	0 1 1 1 0 0 0 0	IP-INC8	
JS = Jump on sign	0 1 1 1 1 0 0 0	IP-INC8	
JNE/JNZ = Jump on not equal/not zer0	0 1 1 1 0 1 0 1	IP-INC8	

Figure 4.5 (continued)

CONTROL TRANSFER (Cont'd.)

	7 6 5 4 3 2 1 0	7 6 5 4 3 2 1 0
JNL/JGE = Jump on not less/greater or equal	0 1 1 1 1 1 0 1	IP-INC8
JNLE/JG = Jump on not less or equal/greater	0 1 1 1 1 1 1 1	IP-INC8
JNB/JAE = Jump on not below/above or equal	0 1 1 1 0 0 1 1	IP-INC8
JNBE/JA = Jump on not below or equal/above	0 1 1 1 0 1 1 1	IP-INC8
JNP/JPO = Jump on not par/par odd	0 1 1 1 1 0 1 1	IP-INC8
JNO = Jump on not overflow	0 1 1 1 0 0 0 1	IP-INC8
JNS = Jump on not sign	0 1 1 1 1 0 0 1	IP-INC8
LOOP = Loop CX times	1 1 1 0 0 0 1 0	IP-INC8
LOOPZ/LOOPE = Loop while zero/equal	1 1 1 0 0 0 0 1	IP-INC8
LOOPNZ/LOOPNE = Loop while not zero/equal	1 1 1 0 0 0 0 0	IP-INC8
JCXZ = Jump on CX zero	1 1 1 0 0 0 1 1	IP-INC8

INT = Interrupt:

	7 6 5 4 3 2 1 0	
Type specified	1 1 0 0 1 1 0 1	DATA-8
Type 3	1 1 0 0 1 1 0 0	
INTO = Interrupt on overflow	1 1 0 0 1 1 1 0	
IRET = Interrupt return	1 1 0 0 1 1 1 1	

PROCESSOR CONTROL

	7 6 5 4 3 2 1 0			
CLC = Clear carry	1 1 1 1 1 0 0 0			
CMC = Complement carry	1 1 1 1 0 1 0 1			
STC = Set carry	1 1 1 1 1 0 0 1			
CLD = Clear direction	1 1 1 1 1 1 0 0			
STD = Set direction	1 1 1 1 1 1 0 1			
CLI = Clear interrupt	1 1 1 1 1 0 1 0			
STI = Set interrupt	1 1 1 1 1 0 1 1			
HLT = Halt	1 1 1 1 0 1 0 0			
WAIT = Wait	1 0 0 1 1 0 1 1			
ESC = Escape (to external device)	1 1 0 1 1 x x x	m o d y y y r/m	(DISP-LO)	(DISP-HI)
LOCK = Bus lock prefix	1 1 1 1 0 0 0 0			
SEGMENT = Override prefix	0 0 1 reg 1 1 0			

Figure 4.5 (continued)

Example 4.5

The instruction

MOV WORD PTR [BP][DI] + 1234H,0ABCDH

stands for "move the immediate data word $ABCD_{16}$ into the memory location specified by based indexed addressing mode." Express the instruction in machine code.

Solution:

Since this instruction does not involve one of the registers as an operand, it does not follow the general format we have been using. From Fig. 4.5 we find that the format of byte 1 in an immediate data-to-memory move is

1100011W

In our case, we are moving word-size data; therefore, W equals 1. This gives

$$BYTE \ 1 = 11000111_2 = C7_{16}$$

Again from Fig. 4.5, we find that byte 2 has the form

$$BYTE \ 2 = (MOD)000(R/M)$$

For a memory operand using a 16-bit displacement, Fig. 4.3(a) shows that MOD equals 10, and for based indexed addressing using BP and DI with a 16-bit displacement, Fig. 4.3(b) shows that R/M equals 011. This gives

$$BYTE \ 2 = 10000011_2 = 83_{16}$$

Bytes 3 and 4 encode the displacement with its low byte first. Thus for a displacement of 1234_{16}, we get

$$BYTE \ 3 = 34_{16}$$

and

$$BYTE \ 4 = 12_{16}$$

Lastly, bytes 5 and 6 encode the immediate data also with the least significant byte first. For data word $ABCD_{16}$, we get

$$BYTE \ 5 = CD_{16}$$

and

$$BYTE \ 6 = AB_{16}$$

The entire instruction in machine code is

MOV WORD PTR [BP][DI] + 1234H,0ABCDH = C7833412CDABH

Instructions that involve a segment register need a two-bit field to encode which register is to be affected. This field is called the *SR field*. The four segment registers ES, CS, SS, and DS are encoded according to the table in Fig. 4.6.

Register	SR
ES	00
CS	01
SS	10
DS	11

Figure 4.6 Segment register codes.

Example 4.6

The instruction

MOV [BP][DI] + 1234H,DS

stands for "move the contents of the data segment register to the memory location specified by based indexed addressing mode." Express the instruction in machine code.

Solution:

From Fig. 4.5 we see that this instruction is encoded as

10001100(MOD)0(SR)(R/M)(DISP)

The MOD and R/M fields are the same as in Example 4.5. That is,

$$MOD = 10$$

and

$$R/M = 011$$

Moreover, the value of DISP is given as 1234_{16}. Finally, from Fig. 4.6 we find that to specify DS the SR field is

$$SR = 11$$

Therefore, the instruction is coded as

$$1000110010011011001101000010010_2 = 8C9B3412_{16}$$

4.3 ENCODING A COMPLETE PROGRAM IN MACHINE CODE

To encode a complete assembly language program in machine code, we must individually encode each of its instructions. This can be done by using the instruction formats shown in Fig. 4.5 and the information in the tables of Figs. 4.2, 4.3, 4.4, and 4.6. We first identify the general machine-code format for the instruction in Fig. 4.5. After determining the format, the bit fields can be evaluated using the tables of Figs. 4.2, 4.3, 4.4, and 4.6. Finally, the binary-coded instruction can be expressed in hexadecimal form.

To execute a program on the PC, we must first store the machine code of the program in the code segment of memory. The bytes of machine code are stored in sequentially addressed locations in memory. The first byte of the program is stored at the lowest-value address; it is followed by the other bytes in the order in which they are encoded. That is, the address is incremented by one after storing each byte of machine code in memory.

Example 4.7

Encode the "block move" program shown in Fig. 4.7(a) and show how it would be stored in memory starting at address 200_{16}.

Solution:

To encode this program into its equivalent machine code, we will use the instruction set table in Fig. 4.5. The first instruction

$$\text{MOV AX,020H}$$

is a "move immediate data to register" instruction. In Fig. 4.5 we find it has the form

$$1011(W)(REG)(DATA) \qquad DATA \ IF \ W = 1$$

Since the move is to register AX, Fig. 4.2 shows that the W bit is 1 and REG is 000. The immediate data 020_{16} follows this byte with the least significant byte coded first. This gives the machine code for the instruction as

$$1011100000010000000000000_2 = B82000_{16}$$

The second instruction

$$\text{MOV DS,AX}$$

represents a "move register to segment register" operation. This instruction has the general format

$$10001110(MOD)0(SR)(R/M)$$

From Fig. 4.3(a) and (b), we find that for this instruction MOD = 11 and R/M is 000 for AX. Furthermore, from Fig. 4.6, we find that SR = 11 for data segment. This results in the code

$$1000111011011000_2 = 8ED8_{16}$$

for the second instruction.

The next three instructions have the same format as the first instruction. In the third instruction, REG is 110 for SI and the data is 0100_{16}. This gives

$$1011111000000000000000001_2 = BE0001_{16}$$

The fourth instruction has REG coded as 111 (DI) and the data as 0120_{16}. This results in

$$1011111100100000000000001_2 = BF2001_{16}$$

And in the fifth instruction REG is 001 for CX with 0010_{16} as the data. This gives

$$1011100100010000000000000_2 = B91000_{16}$$

Instruction six changes. It is a move of byte data from memory to a register. From Fig. 4.5 we find that its general format is

$$100010(D)(W)(MOD)(REG)(R/M)$$

```
           MOV AX,020H    ;LOAD AX REGISTER
           MOV DS,AX      ;LOAD DATA SEGMENT ADDRESS
           MOV SI,0100H   ;LOAD SOURCE BLOCK POINTER
           MOV DI,0120H   ;LOAD DESTINATION BLOCK POINTER
           MOV CX,010H    ;LOAD REPEAT COUNTER
  NXTPT:   MOV AH,[SI]    ;MOVE SOURCE BLOCK ELEMENT TO AX
           MOV [DI],AH    ;MOVE ELEMENT FROM AX TO DESTINATION BLOCK
           INC SI         ;INCREMENT SOURCE BLOCK POINTER
           INC DI         ;INCREMENT DESTINATION BLOCK POINTER
           DEC CX         ;DECREMENT REPEAT COUNTER
           JNZ NXTPT      ;JUMP TO NXTPT IF CX NOT EQUAL TO ZERO
           NOP            ;NO OPERATION
```

(a)

Instruction	Type of instruction	Machine code
MOV AX,020H	Move immediate data to register	$1011100000010000000000000_2 = B82000_{16}$
MOV DS,AX	Move register to segment register	$1000111011011000_2 = 8ED8_{16}$
MOV SI,0100H	Move immediate data to register	$1011111000000000000000001_2 = BE0001_{16}$
MOV DI,0120H	Move immediate data to register	$1011111100100000000000001_2 = BF2001_{16}$
MOV CX,010H	Move immediate data to register	$1011100100010000000000000_2 = B91000_{16}$
MOV AH,[SI]	Move memory data to register	$1000101000100100_2 = 8A24_{16}$
MOV [DI],AH	Move register data to memory	$1000100000100101_2 = 8825_{16}$
INC SI	Increment register	$01000110_2 = 46_{16}$
INC DI	Increment register	$01000111_2 = 47_{16}$
DEC CX	Decrement register	$01001001_2 = 49_{16}$
JNZ NXTPT	Jump on not equal to zero	$0111010111110111_2 = 75F7_{16}$
NOP	No operation	$10010000_2 = 90_{16}$

(b)

Figure 4.7 (a) Block move program; (b) machine coding of the block move program; (c) storing the machine code in memory.

Memory address	Contents	Instruction
200H	B8H	MOV AX,020H
201H	20H	
202H	00H	
203H	8EH	MOV DS,AX
204H	D8H	
205H	BEH	MOV SI,0100H
206H	00H	
207H	01H	
208H	BFH	MOV DI,0120H
209H	20H	
20AH	01H	
20BH	B9H	MOV CX,010H
20CH	10H	
20DH	00H	
20EH	8AH	MOV AH,[SI]
20FH	24H	
210H	88H	MOV [DI],AH
211H	25H	
212H	46H	INC SI
213H	47H	INC DI
214H	49H	DEC CX
215H	75H	JNZ $−9
216H	F7H	
217H	90H	NOP

(c)

Figure 4.7 (continued)

Since AH is the destination and the instruction operates on bytes of data, the D and W bits are 1 and 0, respectively, and the REG field is 100. The contents of SI are used as a pointer to the source operand; therefore, MOD is 00 and R/M is 100. This gives

$$1000101000100100_2 = 8A24_{16}$$

The last MOV instruction has the same form. However, in this case, AH is the destination and DI is the address pointer. This makes D equal 0 and R/M equal 101. Therefore, we get

$$1000100000100101_2 = 8825_{16}$$

The next two instructions increment registers and have the general form

$$01000(REG)$$

For the first one, register SI is incremented. Therefore, REG equals 110. This results in

$$01000110_2 = 46_{16}$$

In the second, DI (REG = 111) is incremented and this gives

$$01000111_2 = 47_{16}$$

The two INC instructions are followed by a DEC instruction. Its general form is

$$01001(REG)$$

To decrement CX (REG = 001), we get

$$01001001_2 = 49_{16}$$

The next instruction is a jump to the location NXTPT. Its form is

$$01110101(IP{-}INC8)$$

We will not yet complete this instruction because it will be easier to determine the number of bytes to be jumped after the data has been coded for storage in memory. The final instruction is NOP and it is coded as

$$10010000_2 = 90_{16}$$

The entire machine code program is shown in Fig. 4.7(b). As shown in Fig. 4.7(c), our encoded program will be stored in memory starting from memory address 200_{16}. The choice of program beginning address establishes the address for the NXTPT label. Notice that the MOV AH,[SI] instruction, which has this label, starts at address $20E_{16}$. This is nine bytes back from the value in IP after fetching the JNZ instruction. Therefore, the displacement (IP − INC8) in the JNZ instruction is −9 and it is encoded as

$$0111010111110111_2 = 75F7_{16}$$

4.4 THE IBM PC AND ITS DEBUG PROGRAM

Now that we know how to convert an assembly language program to machine code and how this machine code is stored in memory, we are ready to enter the program into the PC; execute it; examine the results that it produces; and, if necessary, debug any errors in its operation. It is the *DEBUG program*, which is part of the PC's *DOS 2.1 operating system*, that permits us to initiate these types of operations from the keyboard of the PC. In this section we will show how to load the DEBUG program from DOS, use it to examine or modify the contents of the 8088's internal registers, and how to return back to DOS from DEBUG.

Using DEBUG, the programmer can issue commands to the 8088 microcomputer in the PC. DEBUG resides on the *DOS supplemental programs diskette*. Assuming that the DOS operating system has already been loaded and the supplemental programs diskette is in drive A, we load DEBUG by simply issuing the command

```
A>  DEBUG  (↵)
```

Actually, "DEBUG" can be typed in using either uppercase or lowercase characters.

Example 4.8

Initiate the DEBUG program from the keyboard of the PC. What prompt for command entry is displayed when in the debugger?

Solution:

When the DOS operating system has been loaded and the DOS supplemental programs diskette resides in drive A, DEBUG is brought up by entering

$$A > \quad DEBUG \quad (\hookleftarrow)$$

Drive A is accessed to load the DEBUG program from the DOS diskette, DEBUG is then executed and its prompt—which is a "_"—is displayed. DEBUG is now waiting to accept a command. Figure 4.8 shows what will be displayed on the screen.

```
A>DEBUG
_
```

Figure 4.8 Loading the DEBUG program.

The keyboard is the input unit of the debugger and permits the user to enter commands that will load data, such as the machine code of a program; examine or modify the state of the 8088's internal registers; or execute a program. All we need to do is type in the command and then depress the ($\hookleftarrow$) key. These debug commands are the tools a programmer needs to enter, execute, and debug programs.

When the command-entry sequence is completed, the DEBUG program decodes the entry to determine which operation is to be performed, verifies that it is a valid command, and if valid, passes control to a routine that performs the operation. At the completion of the operation, results are displayed on the screen and the DEBUG prompt is reissued. The PC remains in this state until new entries are made from the keyboard.

There are six kinds of information that are typically entered as part of a command: *a command letter, an address, a register name, a file name, a drive name, and data.* The entire command set of DEBUG is shown in Fig. 4.9. This table gives the name for each command, its function, and illustrates its general *syntax.* By syntax, we mean the order in which key entries must be made to initiate the command.

With the loading of DEBUG, the state of the 8088 microprocessor is initialized. This *initial state* is illustrated with the software model in Fig. 4.10. Notice that registers AX, BX, CX, DX, BP, SI, DI, and all of the flags are reset to zero; IP is initialized to 0100_{16}; CS, DS, SS, and ES are all loaded with $08F1_{16}$; and SP is loaded with $FFEE_{16}$. We can use the register command to verify this initial state.

Command	Syntax	Function
Register	R [REGISTER NAME]	Examine or modify the contents of an internal register
Quit	Q	End use of the DEBUG program
Dump	D [ADDRESS]	Dump the contents of memory to the display
Enter	E [ADDRESS] [LIST]	Examine or modify the contents of memory
Fill	F [STARTING ADDRESS] [ENDING ADDRESS] [LIST]	Fill a block in memory with the data in list
Move	M [STARTING ADDRESS] [ENDING ADDRESS] [DESTINATION ADDRESS]	Move a block of data from a source location in memory to a destination location
Compare	C [STARTING ADDRESS] [ENDING ADDRESS] [DESTINATION ADDRESS]	Compare two blocks of data in memory and display the locations that contain different data
Search	S [STARTING ADDRESS] [ENDING ADDRESS] [LIST]	Search through a block of data in memory and display all locations that match the data in list
Unassemble	U [STARTING ADDRESS] [ENDING ADDRESS]	Unassemble the machine code into its equivalent assembler instructions
Write	W [STARTING ADDRESS] [DRIVE] [STARTING SECTOR] [NUMBER OF SECTORS]	Save the contents of memory in a file on a diskette
Load	L [STARTING ADDRESS] [DRIVE] [STARTING SECTOR] [NUMBER OF SECTORS]	Load memory with the contents of a file on a diskette
Assemble	A [STARTING ADDRESS]	Assemble the instruction into machine code and store in memory
Trace	T = [ADDRESS] [NUMBER]	Trace the execution of the specified number of instructions
Go	G [STARTING ADDRESS] [BREAKPOINT ADDRESS]	Execute the instructions down through the breakpoint address

Figure 4.9 DEBUG program command set.

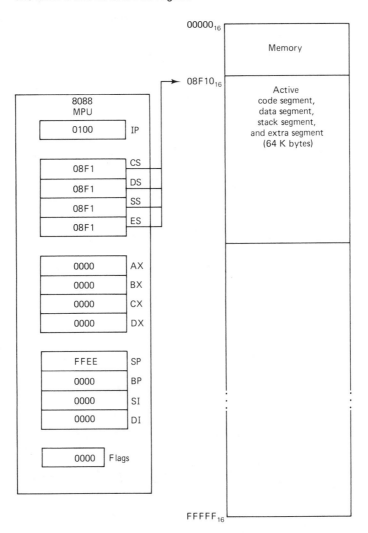

Figure 4.10 Software model of the 8088 microprocessor.

Let us now look at the syntax for the *REGISTER* (R) *command* in more detail. This is the debugger command that allows us to examine or modify the internal registers of the 8088. Notice that the general syntax for this command is given in Fig. 4.9 as

R [REGISTER NAME] (↵)

Here the command letter is R. It is followed by the register name and the return key. Figure 4.11 shows what must be entered as the register name for each of the 8088's registers.

Symbol	Register
AX	Accumulator register
BX	Base register
CX	Count register
DX	Data register
SI	Source index register
DI	Destination index register
SP	Stack pointer register
BP	Base pointer register
CS	Code segment register
DS	Data segment register
SS	Stack segment register
ES	Extra segment register
F	Flag register

Figure 4.11 Register mnemonics for the R command.

An example of the command sequence needed to examine or modify the value in register AX is

$$\_R \ AX \ (\hookleftarrow)$$

Its execution causes the current value in AX to be displayed as

$$AX \ 0000$$
$$:\_$$

Here we see that AX contains 0000_{16}. The examine register command is not yet complete. Notice that a ":" followed by the cursor is also displayed. We can now either depress ($\hookleftarrow$) to complete the command or enter a new value for AX following the colon and then depress ($\hookleftarrow$). Let us load AX with a new value of $00FF_{16}$. This is done by the entry

$$:00FF \ (\hookleftarrow)$$
$$\_$$

Example 4.9

Verify the initialization of the 8088 by examining the contents of its registers with the register command.

Solution:

If we enter the register command without a specific register name, the debugger causes the state of all registers and flags to be displayed. That is, if we enter

$$\_R \ (\hookleftarrow)$$

```
-R
AX=0000  BX=0000  CX=0000  DX=0000  SP=70EE  BP=0000  SI=0000  DI=0000
DS=08F1  ES=08F1  SS=08F1  CS=08F1  IP=0100   NV UP DI PL NZ NA PO NC
08F1:0100 0000          ADD      [BX+SI],AL                    DS:0000=CD
-
```

Figure 4.12 Displaying the initialized state of the 8088.

the information displayed is that shown in Fig. 4.12. Looking at Fig. 4.12, we see that all registers were initialized as expected. To verify that all flags were reset, we must compare the flag settings that are listed to the right of the value for IP, note that the displayed flag settings are NV, UP, DI, PL, NZ, NA, PO, and NC, with the table of Fig. 4.13. They all correspond to the reset flag state.

Flag	Meaning	Set	Reset
OF	Overflow	OV	NV
DF	Direction	DN	UP
IF	Interrupt	EI	DI
SF	Sign	NG	PL
ZF	Zero	ZR	NZ
AF	Auxiliary carry	AC	NA
PF	Parity	PE	PO
CF	Carry	CY	NC

Figure 4.13 Notations used for displaying flag status.

Example 4.10

Issue commands to the debugger on the PC that will cause the value in BX to be modified to $FF00_{16}$ and then verify that this new value exists in BX.

Solution:

To modify the value in BX, all we need to do is issue the register command with BX and then respond to the :_ by entering the value $FF00_{16}$. This is done with the command sequence

```
_R  BX  (↵)
BX  0000
:FF00     (↵)
-
```

We can verify that $FF00_{16}$ has been loaded into BX by issuing another register command as follows

```
_R  BX  (↵)
BX  FF00
:_        (↵)
-
```

```
-R BX
BX 0000
:FF00
-R BX
BX FF00
:
```

Figure 4.14 Displayed information for Example 4.10.

The displayed information for this command sequence is shown in Fig. 4.14.

The way in which the register command is used to modify flags is different than how it is used to modify the contents of a register. If we enter the command

$$\_R\ F\ (\leftarrow)$$

the states of the flags are displayed as

$$NV\ UP\ DI\ PL\ NZ\ NA\ PO\ NC\!-\!\_$$

To modify one or more flags, just type in their new states (using the notations shown in Fig. 4.13) and depress the return key. For instance, to set the carry and zero flags, we enter

$$NV\ UP\ DI\ PL\ NZ\ NA\ PO\ NC\_\ CY\ ZR\ (\leftarrow)$$

Note that the new flag states can be entered in any order.

Example 4.11

Use the register command to set the parity flag to even parity. Verify that the flag has been changed.

Solution:

To set PF for even parity, we can issue the register command for the flag register and then enter PE as the new flag data. This is done with the command sequence

$$\_R\ F\ (\leftarrow)$$
$$NV\ UP\ DI\ PL\ NZ\ NA\ PO\ NC\_\ PE\ (\leftarrow)$$

To verify that PO has been changed to its PE state, just initiate another register command for the flag register, but this time no new flag states are entered. This command is issued as follows:

$$\_R\ F\ (\leftarrow)$$
$$NV\ UP\ DI\ PL\ NZ\ NA\ PE\ NC\!-\!\_\ (\leftarrow)$$

Notice that the state of the parity flag has changed from PO to PE. Figure 4.15 shows these commands and the displayed flag status that results.

```
-R F
NV UP DI PL NZ NA PO NC -PE
-
```

Figure 4.15 Displayed information for Example 4.11.

The REGISTER command is very important for debugging of programs. For instance, it can be used to check the contents of a register or flag prior to and again just after execution of an instruction. In this way, we can tell whether or not the instruction correctly performed the required operation.

If the command that was entered is identified as being invalid, an *error message* is displayed. Let us look at an example of an invalid command entry. To do this, we will repeat our earlier example in which AX was loaded with $00FF_{16}$, but in the entry of $00FF_{16}$ the uppercase letter O is keyed in instead of zeros. The result produced by issuing this command is shown in Fig. 4.16. Here we see that a warning "ERROR" is displayed and the symbol "^" is used to mark the starting location of the error in the command.

```
-R AX
AX 0000
:OOFF
   ^ Error
-
```

Figure 4.16 Invalid entry.

We will examine one more command before going on. We now know how to call up the DEBUG program from DOS, but we must also know how to return to DOS once in DEBUG. The debugger contains a special command to do this. It is called *QUIT* (Q). Therefore, to return to DOS we simply respond to the debug prompt with

```
-Q (⏎)
```

4.5 EXAMINING AND MODIFYING THE CONTENTS OF MEMORY

In section 4.4 we studied the command that permitted us to examine or modify the contents of the 8088's internal registers. Here we will continue our study of DEBUG's commands with those that can be used to examine and modify the contents of memory. The ability to do this is essential for debugging programs. For instance, the contents of a memory address can be examined just before and just after the execution of an instruction. In this way, we can verify that the instruction performs the operation correctly. Another use of this type of command is to load a program into the code segment of the 8088's memory. The complete command set of DEBUG was shown in Fig. 4.9. Six of these commands, DUMP, ENTER, FILL, MOVE, COMPARE, and SEARCH, are provided for use in examining or modifying the contents of storage locations in memory.

DUMP Command

The *DUMP* (D) *command* allows us to examine the contents of a memory location or a block of consecutive memory locations. Looking at Fig. 4.9, we see that the general syntax for DUMP is

D [ADDRESS]

The value of address entered is automatically referenced to the current value in the data segment (DS) register. For instance, issuing the command

D (↵)

causes the 128 consecutive bytes offset by 0100_{16} from the current value in DS to be displayed. Remember that when DEBUG is loaded, DS is initialized as $08F1_{16}$. Therefore, issuing this command gives the memory dump shown in Fig. 4.17.

Notice that 16 bytes of data are displayed per line and only the address of the first byte is shown at the left. From Fig. 4.17 we see that this is denoted as 08F1:0100. This stands for physical address 09010_{16}. The second byte of data displayed in the first line corresponds to the memory address 08F1:0101 equals 09011_{16} and the last byte corresponds to the memory address 08F1:010F equals $0901F_{16}$.

For all memory dumps, an ASCII version of the memory data is also displayed. It is displayed to the right of the hexadecimal data. In Fig. 4.17 this results in a series of "." because all bytes that result in an unprintable ASCII character are displayed as the symbol ".". In ASCII 00_{16} is the NUL character, which does not print as a symbol.

The results shown in Fig. 4.17 could be obtained with several other forms

```
-D
08F1:0100  00 00 00 00 00 00 00 00-00 00 00 00 00 00 00 00   ................
08F1:0110  00 00 00 00 00 00 00 00-00 00 00 00 00 00 00 00   ................
08F1:0120  00 00 00 00 00 00 00 00-00 00 00 00 00 00 00 00   ................
08F1:0130  00 00 00 00 00 00 00 00-00 00 00 00 00 00 00 00   ................
08F1:0140  00 00 00 00 00 00 00 00-00 00 00 00 00 00 00 00   ................
08F1:0150  00 00 00 00 00 00 00 00-00 00 00 00 00 00 00 00   ................
08F1:0160  00 00 00 00 00 00 00 00-00 00 00 00 00 00 00 00   ................
08F1:0170  00 00 00 00 00 00 00 00-00 00 00 00 00 00 00 00   ................
-
```

Figure 4.17 Examining the contents of 128 consecutive bytes in memory.

of the DUMP command. One way is to enter the current value of DS, which is $08F1_{16}$, and an offset of 0100_{16} in the address field. This results in the command

$$D\ \ 08F1:100\ \ (\dashv)$$

Another way is to enter DS instead of its value with the offset. This gives

$$D\ \ DS:100\ \ (\dashv)$$

In fact, the same results can be obtained by issuing the command

$$D\ \ 100\ \ (\dashv)$$

Example 4.12

What is the physical address range of the bytes of data in the last line of data shown in Fig. 4.17?

Solution:

In Fig. 4.17 we see that the first byte is at address 08F1:0170. This is the physical address

$$PA = 08F10_{16} + 0170_{16} = 09080_{16}$$

The last byte is at address 08F1:017F and its physical address is

$$PA = 08F10_{16} + 017F_{16} = 0908F_{16}$$

Example 4.13

What happens if we repeat the entry D $(\dashv)$ after obtaining the memory dump shown in Fig. 4.17?

Solution:

The contents of the next 128 consecutive bytes of memory are dumped to the display. The displayed information is shown in Fig. 4.18.

```
-D
08F1:0180   00 00 00 00 00 00 00 00-00 00 00 00 00 00 00 00    ................
08F1:0190   00 00 00 00 00 00 00 00-00 00 00 00 00 00 00 00    ................
08F1:01A0   00 00 00 00 00 00 00 00-00 00 00 00 00 00 00 00    ................
08F1:01B0   00 00 00 00 00 00 00 00-00 00 00 00 00 00 00 00    ................
08F1:01C0   00 00 00 00 00 00 00 00-00 00 00 00 00 00 00 00    ................
08F1:01D0   00 00 00 00 00 00 00 00-00 00 00 00 00 00 00 00    ................
08F1:01E0   00 00 00 00 00 00 00 00-00 00 00 00 00 00 00 00    ................
08F1:01F0   00 00 00 00 00 00 00 00-00 00 00 00 00 00 00 00    ................
```

Figure 4.18 Displayed information for repeat of 128 byte memory dump command.

Frequently, we do not want to examine such a large block of memory. Instead we may want to look at just a few bytes or a specific-size block. The DUMP command can also do this. This time we enter two addresses. The first address defines the starting point of the block and the second address defines the end of the block. For instance, if we want to examine the two bytes of data that are at offsets equal to 200_{16} and 201_{16} in the current data segment, we enter the command

D DS:200 201 (↵)

The result obtained by executing this command is given in Fig. 4.19.

```
-D DS:200 201
08F1:0200   00 00
 _
```

Figure 4.19 Displaying just two bytes of data.

Example 4.14

Issue a dump command that will display the 32 bytes of memory that are located at offsets 0300_{16} through $031F_{16}$ in the current data segment.

Solution:

The command needed to display the contents of this part of memory is

D 300 31F (↵)

and the information that is displayed is shown in Fig. 4.20.

Up to now, all the data displayed with the DUMP command was contained in the data segment of memory. It is also possible to examine data that is stored in the code segment, stack segment, or extra segment. To do this, we simply use the appropriate segment-register description in the command. For instance, the commands needed to dump the values in the first 16 bytes of the current code segment and extra segment are

D CS:0 F (↵)
D ES:0 F (↵)

```
-D 300 31F
08F1:0300   00 00 00 00 00 00 00 00-00 00 00 00 00 00 00 00   ................
08F1:0310   00 00 00 00 00 00 00 00-00 00 00 00 00 00 00 00   ................
 _
```

Figure 4.20 Displayed information for Example 4.14.

Example 4.15

Use the DUMP command to examine the 16 bytes of memory just below the top of the stack.

Solution:

The top of the stack is defined by the contents of the SS and SP registers. Earlier we found that SP was initialized to $FFEE_{16}$ when debug was loaded. Therefore, the 16 bytes we are interested in reside at offset $FFEE_{16}$ through $FFFD_{16}$ from the current value in SS. This part of the stack is examined with the command

D SS:FFEE FFFD (↵)

The results displayed by executing this command are shown in Fig. 4.21.

```
-D SS:FFEE  FFFD
0BF1:FFEE    FF FF                                                        . .
0BF1:FFF0    FF FF FF FF FF FF FF FF-FF FF FF FF FF FF          . . . . . . . . . . . . . .
-
```

Figure 4.21 Displayed information for Example 4.15.

ENTER Command

The DUMP command allowed us to examine the contents of memory, but we also need to be able to modify the data stored in memory—for instance, to load a machine-code program. It is for this purpose that the *ENTER* (E) *command* is provided in the DEBUG program.

In Fig. 4.9 we find that the syntax of the ENTER command is

E [ADDRESS] [LIST]

The address part of the command is entered the same way we just described for the DUMP command. The list that follows the address is the data that gets loaded into memory.

As an example, let us write a command that will load five consecutive byte-wide memory locations that start at address DS:100 with the value FF_{16}. This is done with the command

E DS:100 FF FF FF FF FF (↵)

Now to verify that the new values of data have been stored in memory, let us dump the contents of these locations to the display. To do this, we issue the command

D DS:100 104 (↵)

This series of commands and the displayed results are illustrated in Fig. 4.22.

```
-E DS:100 FF FF FF FF FF
-D DS:100 104
08F1:0100  FF FF FF FF FF                                    . . . . .
-
```

Figure 4.22 Modifying five consecutive bytes of memory and verifying the change of data.

The ENTER command can also be used in a way in which it either examines or modifies the contents of memory. If we issue the command with an address but no data, what happens is that the contents of the addressed storage location are displayed. For instance, the command

$$E \ DS:100 \ (\lrcorner)$$

causes the value at this address to be displayed as follows:

$$08F1:0100 \ FF.\_$$

Notice that the value at address 08F1:0100 is FF$_{16}$.

At this point we have several options—for one, the return key could be depressed. This terminates the ENTER command without changing the contents of the displayed memory location and causes the debug prompt to be displayed. Instead of depressing return, we could depress the space bar. Again, this would cause the display contents not to be changed. Instead, it causes the contents of the next memory address to be displayed. Let us assume that this was done. Then the display would read

$$08F1:0100 \ FF. \ FF.\_$$

Here we see that the data stored at address 08F1:0101 is also FF$_{16}$. A third type of entry that could be made is to enter a new value of data and then depress the space bar or return key. For example, we could enter 11 and then depress space. This gives the display

$$08F1:0100 \ FF. \ FF.11 \ FF.\_$$

The value pointed to by address 08F1:101 has been changed to 11 and the contents of address 08F1:0102, which are FF$_{16}$ displayed. Now depress the return key to finalize the data-entry sequence.

Example 4.16

Start a data-entry sequence by examining the contents of address DS:100 and then, without entering new data, depress the " − " key. What happens?

Solution:

The data-entry sequence is initiated as

E DS:100 (↵)
08F1:0100 FF._

Now entering " − " causes the address and data that follow to be displayed.

08F1:00FF 00._

Notice that the address of the previous storage location was displayed by entering minus (−). This result is illustrated in Fig. 4.23.

```
-E DS:100
08F1:0100  FF.-
08F1:00FF  00.
-
```

Figure 4.23 Using the " − " key to examine the contents of the previous memory location.

The ENTER command can also be used to enter ASCII data. This is done by simply enclosing the data entered in quotation marks. An example is the command

E DS:200 "ASCII" (↵)

This command causes the ASCII data for letters A, S, C, I, and I to be stored in memory at addresses DS:200, DS:201, DS:202, DS:203, and DS:204, respectively. This character data entry can be verified with the command

D DS:200 204 (↵)

Looking at the ASCII field of the data dump shown in Fig. 4.24, we see that the correct ASCII data was stored into memory.

```
-E DS:200 "ASCII"
-D DS:200 204
08F1:0200  41 53 43 49 49                                ASCII
-
```

Figure 4.24 Loading ASCII data into memory with the ENTER command.

FILL Command

Frequently we want to fill a block of consecutive memory locations all with the same data. For example, we may need to initialize all storage locations in an area of memory that will store data with zeros. To do this address by address with the ENTER command would be very time-consuming. It is to simplify this type of operation that the *FILL* (F) *command* is provided in the DEBUG program.

From Fig. 4.9, we find that the general form of the FILL command is

```
F [STARTING ADDRESS] [ENDING ADDRESS] [LIST]
```

Here *starting address* and *ending address* locate the block of data in memory. They are followed by a *list* of data. An example is the command

```
F 100 11F 22 (↵)
```

Execution of this command causes the 32 byte locations in the range 08F1:100 through 08F1:11F to be loaded with 22_{16}. The fact that this change in memory contents has happened can be verified with the command

```
D 100 11F (↵)
```

Figure 4.25 shows the result of executing these two commands.

```
-F 100 11F 22
-D 100 11F
08F1:0100   22 22 22 22 22 22 22 22-22 22 22 22 22 22 22 22    """"""""""""""""""
08F1:0110   22 22 22 22 22 22 22 22-22 22 22 22 22 22 22 22    """"""""""""""""""
-
```

Figure 4.25 Initializing a block of memory with the FILL command.

Example 4.17

Initialize all storage locations in the block of memory from DS:120 through DS:13F with the value 33_{16} and the block of storage locations from DS:140 through DS:15F with the value 44_{16}. Verify that the contents of these ranges of memory were correctly modified.

Solution:

The initialization operations can be done with the FILL commands that follow:

```
F 120 13F 33 (↵)
F 140 15F 44 (↵)
```

and verified with the DUMP command

D 120 15F (⏎)

The information displayed by the DUMP command is shown in Fig. 4.26.

```
-F  120  13F  33
-F  140  15F  44
-D  120  15F
08F1:0120    33 33 33 33 33 33 33 33-33 33 33 33 33 33 33 33    3333333333333333
08F1:0130    33 33 33 33 33 33 33 33-33 33 33 33 33 33 33 33    3333333333333333
08F1:0140    44 44 44 44 44 44 44 44-44 44 44 44 44 44 44 44    DDDDDDDDDDDDDDDD
08F1:0150    44 44 44 44 44 44 44 44-44 44 44 44 44 44 44 44    DDDDDDDDDDDDDDDD
-
```

Figure 4.26 Displayed information for Example 4.17.

MOVE Command

The *MOVE* (M) *command* allows us to move a block of data from one part of memory to another part. For instance, using this command, a 32-byte block of data that resides in memory from address DS:100 to DS:11F can be moved to the address range DS:200 through DS:21F with a single command.

The general form of the command is given in Fig. 4.9 as

M [STARTING ADDRESS] [ENDING ADDRESS] [DESTINATION ADDRESS]

Notice that it is initiated by depressing the M key. After this, we must enter three addresses. The first two addresses are the starting address and ending address of the source block of data—that is, the block of data that is to be moved. The third address is the *destination starting address*—that is, the starting address of the segment of memory to which the block of data is to be moved.

The command for our earlier example is written as

M 100 11F 200 (⏎)

Example 4.18

Fill each storage location in the block of memory from address DS:100 through DS:11F with the value 11. Then copy this block of data to a destination block starting at DS:160. Verify that the block move was correctly done.

Solution:

First we will fill the source block with 11_{16} using the command

F 100 11F 11 (⏎)

Next it is copied to the destination with the command

M 100 11F 160 (⏎)

Finally, we dump the complete range from DS:100 to DS:17F by issuing the command

D 100 17F (⏎)

The result of this memory dump is given in Fig. 4.27. It verifies that the block move was successfully performed.

```
-F 100 11F 11
-M 100 11F 160
-D 100 17F
08F1:0100  11 11 11 11 11 11 11 11-11 11 11 11 11 11 11 11   ................
08F1:0110  11 11 11 11 11 11 11 11-11 11 11 11 11 11 11 11   ................
08F1:0120  33 33 33 33 33 33 33 33-33 33 33 33 33 33 33 33   3333333333333333
08F1:0130  33 33 33 33 33 33 33 33-33 33 33 33 33 33 33 33   3333333333333333
08F1:0140  44 44 44 44 44 44 44 44-44 44 44 44 44 44 44 44   DDDDDDDDDDDDDDDD
08F1:0150  44 44 44 44 44 44 44 44-44 44 44 44 44 44 44 44   DDDDDDDDDDDDDDDD
08F1:0160  11 11 11 11 11 11 11 11-11 11 11 11 11 11 11 11   ................
08F1:0170  11 11 11 11 11 11 11 11-11 11 11 11 11 11 11 11   ................
-
```

Figure 4.27 Displayed information for Example 4.18.

COMPARE Command

Another type of memory operation we sometimes need to perform is to compare the contents of two blocks of data to determine if they are equal or unequal. This operation can be easily done with the *COMPARE* (C) *command* of the DEBUG program. Figure 4.9 shows that the general form of this command is

C [STARTING ADDRESS] [ENDING ADDRESS] [DESTINATION ADDRESS]

For example, to compare a block of data located from address DS:100 through DS:10F to an equal-size block of data starting at address DS:160, we issue the command

C 100 10F 160 (⏎)

This command causes the contents of corresponding address locations in each block to be compared to each other. That is, the contents of address DS:100 are compared to that at address DS:160, that at address DS:101 are compared to that at address DS:161, and so on. Each time unequal elements are found, the address and contents of that byte in both blocks are displayed.

Since both of these blocks contain the same information, no data are displayed. However, if this source block is next compared to the destination block starting at address DS:120 by entering the command

C 100 10F 120 (⏎)

```
-C 100 10F 120
08F1:0100   11   33   08F1:0120
08F1:0101   11   33   08F1:0121
08F1:0102   11   33   08F1:0122
08F1:0103   11   33   08F1:0123
08F1:0104   11   33   08F1:0124
08F1:0105   11   33   08F1:0125
08F1:0106   11   33   08F1:0126
08F1:0107   11   33   08F1:0127
08F1:0108   11   33   08F1:0128
08F1:0109   11   33   08F1:0129
08F1:010A   11   33   08F1:012A
08F1:010B   11   33   08F1:012B
08F1:010C   11   33   08F1:012C
08F1:010D   11   33   08F1:012D
08F1:010E   11   33   08F1:012E
08F1:010F   11   33   08F1:012F
---
```

Figure 4.28 Results produced when unequal data are found in a COMPARE command.

All elements in both blocks are unequal; therefore, the information shown in Fig. 4.28 is displayed.

SEARCH Command

The *SEARCH* (S) *command* can be used to scan through a block of data in memory to determine whether or not it contains certain data. The general form of this command is given in Fig. 4.9 as

S [STARTING ADDRESS] [ENDING ADDRESS] [LIST]

When the command is issued, the contents of each storage location in the block of memory between the starting address and the ending address are compared to the data in list. The address is displayed for each memory location where a match is found.

Example 4.19

Perform a search of the block of data from address DS:100 through DS:17F to determine which memory locations contain 33_{16}.

Solution:

The search command that must be issued is as follows:

S 100 17F 33 (↵)

Figure 4.29 shows that all addresses in the range 120_{16} through 137_{16} contain this value of data.

```
-S 100 17F 33
08F1:0120
08F1:0121
08F1:0122
08F1:0123
08F1:0124
08F1:0125
08F1:0126
08F1:0127
08F1:0128
08F1:0129
08F1:012A
08F1:012B
08F1:012C
08F1:012D
08F1:012E
08F1:012F
08F1:0130
08F1:0131
08F1:0132
08F1:0133
08F1:0134
08F1:0135
08F1:0136
08F1:0137
08F1:0138
08F1:0139
08F1:013A
08F1:013B
08F1:013C
08F1:013D
08F1:013E
08F1:013F
_
```

Figure 4.29 Displayed information for Example 4.29.

4.6 LOADING, VERIFYING, AND SAVING MACHINE–CODE PROGRAMS

Up to this point in the chapter we have learned how to encode instructions and programs in machine code and how to use the register and memory commands of DEBUG to examine or modify the contents of the 8088's internal registers or data stored in external memory. Let us now look at how we can load machine-code instructions and programs into the memory of the PC.

In section 4.5 we found that the ENTER command can be used to load either a single or a group of memory locations with data, such as the machine code for instructions. As an example, let us load the machine code $88C3_{16}$ that was found for the instruction MOV BL,AL in Example 4.1. This instruction is loaded into memory starting at address CS:100 with the ENTER command

E CS:100 88 C3 (⏎)

Moreover, we can verify that it has loaded correctly with the DUMP command

D CS:100 101 (⏎)

This displays the data

08F1:0100 88 C3

Let us now introduce another command that is important for loading and debugging machine code on the PC. It is the *UNASSEMBLE* (U) *command.* By *unassemble* we mean the process of converting machine-code instructions to their equivalent assembly language source statement. Therefore, the U command lets us specify a range in memory, and execution of the command causes the equivalent source statements to be displayed on the screen.

Looking at Fig. 4.9, we find that the syntax of the UNASSEMBLE command is

U [STARTING ADDRESS] [ENDING ADDRESS]

We can use this command to verify that the machine code entered for an instruction is correct. To do this for our earlier example, the command that follows is issued

U CS:100 101 (↵)

This results in display of the starting memory location followed by both the machine-code and assembler forms of the instruction. This gives

08F1:0100 88C3 MOV BL,AL

The entry sequence and displayed information for loading, verification, and unassembly of the instruction is shown in Fig. 4.30.

```
-E CS:100 88 C3
-D CS:100 101
08F1:0100   88 C3                                        .C
-U CS:100 101
08F1:0100 88C3          MOV      BL,AL
-
```

Figure 4.30 Loading, verifying, and unassembly of an instruction.

Example 4.20

Use a series of commands to load, verify loading, and unassemble the machine code for the ADD instruction encoded in Example 4.2. Load the instruction at address CS:0200.

Solution:

In Example 4.2 we found that the machine code for the instruction was 0304_{16}. It is loaded into the code segment of the microcomputer's memory with the command

E CS:200 03 04 (↵)

Next, we can verify that it was loaded correctly with the command

D CS:200 201 (↵)

and finally unassemble the instruction with

U CS:200 201 (↵)

The results produced by this sequence of commands are shown in Fig. 4.31. Here we see that the instruction entered is

ADD AX,[SI]

```
-E CS:200 03 04
-D CS:200 201
08F1:0200   03 04                                    . .
-U CS:200 201
08F1:0200 0304        ' ADD      AX,[SI]
-
```

Figure 4.31 Displayed information for Example 4.20.

Before going further we will cover two more commands that are useful for loading programs. They are the *WRITE* (W) *command* and *LOAD* (L) *command*. These commands give the ability to save data stored in memory on a diskette and to reload memory from a diskette, respectively. We can load the machine code of a program with the E command the first time we use it and then save it on a diskette. In this way, we can simply reload the program from the diskette the next time we need to work with it.

Figure 4.9 shows that their general forms are

W [STARTING ADDRESS] [DRIVE] [STARTING SECTOR] [NUMBER OF SECTORS]

L [STARTING ADDRESS] [DRIVE] [STARTING SECTOR] [NUMBER OF SECTORS]

For instance, to save the ADD instruction we just loaded at address CS:200 in Example 4.20 we can issue the WRITE command

W CS:200 1 10 1 (↵)

Notice that we have selected for the specification on the disk drive 1 (drive B), 10 as an arbitrary starting sector on the diskette, and an arbitrary length of 1 sector. Before the command is issued, a formatted data diskette must be inserted into drive B. Then issuing the command causes one sector of data starting at address CS:200 to be read from memory and written into sector 10 on the diskette in drive B. Unlike the earlier commands we have studied, the W command automatically references the CS register instead of the DS register. For this reason, the command

$$\text{W} \quad 200 \quad 1 \quad 10 \quad 1 \quad (\hookleftarrow)$$

will perform the same operation.

Let us digress for a moment to examine the file specification of the W command in more detail. The diskettes for an IBM PC that has double-sided, double-density drives are organized into 10,001 sectors that are assigned sector numbers over the range 0_{16} through $27F_{16}$. Moreover, each sector is capable of storing 512 bytes of data. With the file specification in a W command, we can select any one of these sector numbers as the starting sector. The value of the number of sectors should be specified based on the number of bytes of data that are to be saved. The specification we made earlier for our example of a write command selected one sector (sector number 10_{16}) and for this reason could only save up to 512 bytes of data. The maximum value of sectors that can be specified with a write command is 80_{16}.

The LOAD command can be used to reload a file of data stored on a diskette anywhere in memory. As an example, let us load the instruction that we just saved on disk with a W command at a new address (CS:300). This is done with the L command

$$\text{L} \quad 300 \quad 1 \quad 10 \quad 1 \quad (\hookleftarrow)$$

The reloading of the instruction can be verified by issuing the UNASSEMBLE command

$$\text{U} \quad \text{CS:300} \quad 301 \quad (\hookleftarrow)$$

This causes the display

$$\text{08F1:300} \quad 0301 \quad \text{ADD AX,[SI]}$$

Example 4.21

Show the sequence of keyboard entries needed to enter the machine-code program of Fig. 4.7(c) into memory of the PC. The program is to be loaded into memory starting at address CS:100. Verify that the hexadecimal machine code was entered correctly and then unassemble the machine code to assure that it represents the source program of Fig. 4.7(c). Save the program in sector 100 of a data diskette.

Solution:

We will use the ENTER command to load the program.

```
E CS:100:0 B8 20 0 8E D8 BE 0 01 BF 20 01 B9 10 0 8A 24 88 25 46
47 49 75 F7 90 (↵)
```

First we verify that the machine code has loaded correctly with the command

D CS:100 117 (⏎)

Comparing the displayed data in Fig. 4.32 to the machine code in Fig. 4.7(c), we see that it has been loaded correctly. Now the machine code can be unassembled by the command

U CS:100 117 (⏎)

Comparing the displayed program of Fig. 4.32 to that in Fig. 4.7(c), it again verifies correct entry. Finally the program is saved on the data diskette with the command

W CS:100 1 100 1 (⏎)

```
-E CS:100 B8 20 0 8E D8 BE 0 01 BF 20 01 B9 10 0 8A 24 88 25 46 47 49 75 F7 90
-D CS:100 117
08F1:0100   B8 20 00 8E D8 BE 00 01-BF 20 01 B9 10 00 8A 24   8 ..X>..? .9...$
08F1:0110   88 25 46 47 49 75 F7 90                           .%FGIuw.
-U CS:100 117
08F1:0100 B82000        MOV     AX,0020
08F1:0103 8ED8          MOV     DS,AX
08F1:0105 BE0001        MOV     SI,0100
08F1:0108 BF2001        MOV     DI,0120
08F1:010B B91000        MOV     CX,0010
08F1:010E 8A24          MOV     AH,[SI]
08F1:0110 8825          MOV     [DI],AH
08F1:0112 46            INC     SI
08F1:0113 47            INC     DI
08F1:0114 49            DEC     CX
08F1:0115 75F7          JNZ     010E
08F1:0117 90            NOP
-W CS:100 1 100 1
-
```

Figure 4.32 Displayed information for Example 4.21.

4.7 ASSEMBLING INSTRUCTIONS WITH THE ASSEMBLE COMMAND

All the instructions we have worked with up to this point in the chapter have been hand assembled into machine code. The DEBUG program of the IBM PC has a command that lets us automatically assemble the instructions of a program, one after the other, and store them in memory. It is called the *ASSEMBLE* (A) *command.* Unlike the other commands we have introduced, ASSEMBLE is only available in revision levels 2.0 and 2.1 of DOS.

The general syntax of ASSEMBLE is given in Fig. 4.9 as

A [STARTING ADDRESS]

Here, "starting address" is the address at which the machine code of the first instruction of the program is to be stored. For example, to assemble the instruction ADD [BX + SI + 1234], AX and store its machine code in memory starting at address CS:100, the command entry is

A CS:100 (↲)

The response to this command input is the display of the starting address in the form

08F1:0100_

The instruction to be assembled is typed in following this address, and when the (↲) key is depressed, the instruction is assembled into machine code, then it is stored in memory, and the starting address of the next instruction is displayed. As shown in Fig. 4.33, for our example, we get

08F1:0100 ADD [BX+SI+1234],AX (↲)
08F1:0104 _

Now either the next instruction is entered or the (↲) key is depressed to complete the ASSEMBLE command.

Assuming that the assemble operation we just performed was completed by entering (↲), we can view the machine code that was produced for the instruction by issuing a DUMP command. Notice that the address displayed as the starting point of the next instruction is 08F1:0104. Therefore, the machine code for the ADD instruction took up four bytes of memory: CS:100, CS:101, CS:102, and CS:103. The command needed to display this machine code is

D CS:100 103 (↲)

In Fig. 4.33, we find that the machine code stored for the instruction is 01803412H.

```
-A CS:100
08F1:0100 ADD [BX+SI+1234],AX
08F1:0104
-D CS:100 103
08F1:0100  01 80 34 12                                    ..4.
-W CS:100 1 75 1
-
```

Figure 4.33 Assembling the instruction ADD [BX + SI + 1234], AX.

At this point, the instruction can be executed or saved on a data diskette. For instance, to save the machine code at file specification 1 75 1 on a data diskette, we can issue the command

W CS:100 1 75 1 (↵)

Now that we have showed how to assemble an instruction, view its machine code, and save the machine code on a data diskette, let us look into how a complete program can be assembled with the A command. For this purpose, we will use the program shown in Fig. 4.34(a). This is the same program that was hand assembled to machine code in Example 4.7.

We will begin by assuming that the program is to be stored in memory starting at address CS:200. For this reason, the *line-by-line assembler* is invoked with the command

A CS:200 (↵)

This gives the response

08F1:0200_

Now we type in each instruction of the program as follows:

```
08F1:0200  MOV  AX,020  (↵)
08F1:0203  MOV  DS,AX  (↵)
08F1:0205  MOV  SI,0100  (↵)
             •       •    •
             •       •    •
08F1:0217  NOP  (↵)
08F1:0218  (↵)
```

The details of the instruction entry sequence are shown in Fig. 4.34(b).

Now that the complete program has been entered, let us verify that it has been assembled correctly. This can be done with an UNASSEMBLE command. Notice in Fig. 4.34(b) that the program resides in memory over the address range CS:200 through CS:217. To unassemble the machine code in this part of memory, we issue the command

U CS:200 217 (↵)

The results produced with this command are shown in Fig. 4.34(c). Comparing the source statements to those in Fig. 4.34(a) confirms that the program has assembled correctly.

```
MOV   AX,020
MOV   DS,AX
MOV   SI,0100                    -A CS:200
                                 08F1:0200 MOV AX,020
MOV   DI,0120                    08F1:0203 MOV DS,AX
MOV   CX,010                     08F1:0205 MOV SI,0100
                                 08F1:0208 MOV DI,0120
MOV   AH,[SI]                    08F1:020B MOV CX,010
MOV   [DI],AH                    08F1:020E MOV AH,[SI]
                                 08F1:0210 MOV [DI],AH
INC   SI                         08F1:0212 INC SI
INC   DI                         08F1:0213 INC DI
                                 08F1:0214 DEC CX
DEC   CX                         08F1:0215 JNZ 20E
JNZ   20E                        08F1:0217 NOP
                                 08F1:0218
NOP                              -
        (a)                                (b)
```

```
-U CS:200 217
08F1:0200 B82000       MOV       AX,0020
08F1:0203 8ED8         MOV       DS,AX
08F1:0205 BE0001       MOV       SI,0100
08F1:0208 BF2001       MOV       DI,0120
08F1:020B B91000       MOV       CX,0010
08F1:020E 8A24         MOV       AH,[SI]
08F1:0210 8825         MOV       [DI],AH
08F1:0212 46           INC       SI
08F1:0213 47           INC       DI
08F1:0214 49           DEC       CX
08F1:0215 75F7         JNZ       020E
08F1:0217 90           NOP
-
                        (c)
```

Figure 4.34 (a) Block move program; (b) assembling the program; (c) verifying the assembled program with the U command.

4.8 EXECUTING INSTRUCTIONS AND PROGRAMS WITH THE TRACE AND GO COMMANDS

Once the program has been entered into the memory of the PC, it is ready to be executed. The DEBUG program allows us to execute the entire program with one *GO* (G) *command* or to execute the program in several segments of instructions by using *breakpoints* in the GO command. Moreover, by using the *TRACE* (T) *command,* the program can be stepped through by executing one or more instructions at a time.

Let us begin by examining the TRACE command in more detail. This command provides the programmer with the ability to execute one instruction at a time. This mode of operation is also known as *single-stepping the program;* it is very useful during early phases of program debugging. This is because the contents of registers or memory can be viewed both before and after the execution of each instruction to determine whether or not the correct operation was performed.

The general form of the command is shown in Fig. 4.9 as

$$T = [ADDRESS] \ [NUMBER]$$

Notice that a *starting address* may be specified as part of the command. This is the address of the instruction at which execution is to begin. It is followed by a *number* that tells how many instructions are to be executed. If an instruction count is not specified in the command, just one instruction is executed. For instance, the command

$$T = CS:100 \ (↵)$$

causes the instruction starting at address CS:100 to be executed. At completion of the instruction's execution, the complete state of the 8088's internal registers is automatically displayed. At this point other debug commands can be issued—for instance, to display the contents of memory—or the next instruction can be executed.

This TRACE command can also be issued as

$$T \ (↵)$$

In this case the instruction pointed to by the current values of CS and IP (CS:IP) is executed. This is the form of the TRACE command that is used just to execute the next instruction.

If we want to single-step through several instructions, the TRACE command must include the number of instructions to be executed. This number is included after the address. For example, to trace through three instructions, the command is issued as

$$T = CS:100 \ 3 \ (↵)$$

Again, the internal state of the 8088 is displayed after each instruction is executed.

Example 4.22

Load the instruction stored at file specification 1 10 1 at offset 100 of the current code segment. Unassemble the instruction. Then initialize $AX = 1111_{16}$, $SI = 1234_{16}$, and the contents of memory address 1234_{16} to 2222_{16}. Next, display the internal state of the 8088 and the contents of address 1234_{16} to verify their initialization. Finally, execute the instruction with the TRACE command. What operation is performed by the instruction?

Solution:

First the instruction is loaded from diskette at CS:100 with the command

L CS:100 1 10 1 (↵)

Now the machine code is unassembled to verify that the instruction has loaded correctly.

U 100 101 (↵)

Looking at the displayed information in Fig. 4.35, we see that it is an add instruction. Next we initialize the internal registers and memory with the command sequence

R AX (↵)
AX 0000
:1111 (↵)
R SI (↵)
SI 0000
:1234 (↵)
E DS:1234 22 22 (↵)

Now the initialization is verified with the commands

R (↵)
D DS:1234 1235 (↵)

In Fig. 4.35 we see that AX, SI, and the contents of address 1234_{16} were correctly initialized. Therefore, we are ready to execute the instruction. This is done with the command

T =CS:100 (↵)

From the displayed trace information in Fig. 4.35, we find that the value 2222_{16} at address 1234_{16} was added to the value 1111_{16} that is held in AX. Therefore, the new contents of AX are 3333_{16}.

The GO command is typically used to execute programs that are already debugged or to aid in the process of debugging programs in the latter stages of debugging. For example, if the beginning part of a program is already operating correctly, a GO command can be issued to execute this group of instructions and then stop execution at a point in the program where additional debugging is to begin.

```
-L CS:100 1 10 1
-U 100 101
08F1:0100 0304          ADD      AX,[SI]
-R AX
AX 0000
:1111
-R SI
SI 0000
:1234
-E DS:1234 22 22
-T =CS:100

AX=3333  BX=0000  CX=0000  DX=0000  SP=70EE  BP=0000  SI=1234  DI=0000
DS=08F1  ES=08F1  SS=08F1  CS=08F1  IP=0102   NV UP DI PL NZ NA PE NC
08F1:0102 0000          ADD      [BX+SI],AL                    DS:1234=22
-
```

Figure 4.35 Displayed information for Example 4.22.

The table in Fig. 4.9 shows that the general form of the GO command is

G =[STARTING ADDRESS] [BREAKPOINT ADDRESS]

The first address is the starting address of the program segment that is to be executed—that is, the address of the instruction at which execution is to begin. The second address, the *breakpoint address,* is the address of the end of the program segment—that is, the address of the instruction at which execution is to stop. The breakpoint address that is specified must correspond to the first byte of an instruction. A list of up to 10 breakpoint addresses can be supplied with the command.

An example of the GO command is

G =CS:200 217 (↵)

This command loads the IP register with 200_{16}, sets a breakpoint at address CS:217, and then begins program execution at address CS:200. Instruction execution proceeds until address CS:217 is accessed. When the breakpoint address is reached, program execution is terminated, the complete internal status of the 8088 is displayed, and control is returned to DEBUG.

Sometimes we just want to execute a program without using a breakpoint. This can also be done with the GO command. For instance, to execute a program that starts at offset 100_{16} in the current CS, we can issue the GO command without a breakpoint address as follows

G =CS:100 (↵)

This command will cause the program to run to completion. In the case of a program where CS and IP are already initialized with the correct values, we can just enter

G (↵)

Example 4.23

In Example 4.21 we saved the block move program at file specification 1 100 1 of a data diskette. Load this program into memory starting at address CS:200. Then initialize the microcomputer by loading the DS register with 0020_{16}; fill the block of memory from DS:100 through DS:10F with FF_{16}, and the block of memory from DS:120 through DS:12F with 00_{16}. Verify that the blocks of memory were initialized correctly, restore DS to $08F1_{16}$, and display the state of the 8088's registers. Display the assembly language version of the program from CS:200 through CS:217. Now execute down through address CS:215. What changes are found in the blocks of data? Next execute the program down to address CS:217. What new changes are found in the blocks of data?

Solution:

The command needed to load the program is

                    L CS:200 1 100 1 (↵)

Next we initialize the DS register and memory.

                    R DS (↵)
                    DS 08F1
                    :0020 (↵)
                    F DS:100 10F FF (↵)
                    F DS:120 12F 00 (↵)

Now the blocks of data in memory are displayed.

                    D DS:100 10F (↵)
                    D DS:120 12F (↵)

This displayed information is shown in Fig. 4.36. DS is restored with the commands

                    R DS (↵)
                    DS 0020
                    :08F1 (↵)

and the state of the 8088's registers is displayed with the command

                    R (↵)

Before beginning to execute the program, we will display the source code with the command

                    U CS:200 217 (↵)

The program that is displayed is shown in Fig. 4.36.

```
-L CS:200 1 100 1
-R DS
DS 08F1
:0020
-F DS:100 10F FF
-F DS:120 12F 00
-D DS:100 10F
0020:0100  FF FF FF FF FF FF FF FF-FF FF FF FF FF FF FF FF    ................
-D DS:120 12F
0020:0120  00 00 00 00 00 00 00 00-00 00 00 00 00 00 00 00    ................
-R DS
DS 0020
:08F1
-R
AX=3333  BX=0000  CX=0000  DX=0000  SP=70EE  BP=0000  SI=1234  DI=0000
DS=08F1  ES=08F1  SS=08F1  CS=08F1  IP=0102    NV UP DI PL NZ NA PE NC
08F1:0102 0000          ADD     [BX+SI],AL                     DS:1234=22
-U CS:200 217
08F1:0200 B82000        MOV     AX,0020
08F1:0203 8ED8          MOV     DS,AX
08F1:0205 BE0001        MOV     SI,0100
08F1:0208 BF2001        MOV     DI,0120
08F1:020B B91000        MOV     CX,0010
08F1:020E 8A24          MOV     AH,[SI]
08F1:0210 8825          MOV     [DI],AH
08F1:0212 46            INC     SI
08F1:0213 47            INC     DI
08F1:0214 49            DEC     CX
08F1:0215 75F7          JNZ     020E
08F1:0217 90            NOP
-G =CS:200 20E

AX=0020  BX=0000  CX=0010  DX=0000  SP=70EE  BP=0000  SI=0100  DI=0120
DS=0020  ES=08F1  SS=08F1  CS=08F1  IP=020E    NV UP DI PL NZ NA PE NC
08F1:020E 8A24          MOV     AH,[SI]                        DS:0100=FF
-G =CS:20E 215

AX=FF20  BX=0000  CX=000F  DX=0000  SP=70EE  BP=0000  SI=0101  DI=0121
DS=0020  ES=08F1  SS=08F1  CS=08F1  IP=0215    NV UP DI PL NZ AC PE NC
08F1:0215 75F7          JNZ     020E
-D DS:100 10F
0020:0100  FF FF FF FF FF FF FF FF-FF FF FF FF FF FF FF FF    ................
-D DS:120 12F
0020:0120  FF 00 00 00 00 00 00 00-00 00 00 00 00 00 00 00    ................
-G =CS:215 217

AX=FF20  BX=0000  CX=0000  DX=0000  SP=70EE  BP=0000  SI=0110  DI=0130
DS=0020  ES=08F1  SS=08F1  CS=08F1  IP=0217    NV UP DI PL ZR NA PE NC
08F1:0217 90            NOP
-D DS:100 10F
0020:0100  FF FF FF FF FF FF FF FF-FF FF FF FF FF FF FF FF    ................
-D DS:120 12F
0020:0120  FF FF FF FF FF FF FF FF-FF FF FF FF FF FF FF FF    ................
-
```

Figure 4.36 Displayed information for Example 4.23.

Now the first segment of program is executed with the command

$$G =CS:200 \ 20E \ (\lrcorner)$$

Looking at the displayed state of the 8088 in Fig. 4.36, we see that DS was loaded with 0020_{16}, AX was loaded with 0020_{16}, SI was loaded with 0100_{16}, and CX was loaded with 0010_{16}.

Next another GO command is used to execute the program down through address CS:215.

$$G\ =CS:20E\ \ 215\ (\downarrow)$$

We can check the state of the blocks of memory with the commands

$$D\ \ DS:100\ \ 10F\ (\downarrow)$$
$$D\ \ DS:120\ \ 12F\ (\downarrow)$$

From the display information in Fig. 4.36 we see that FF_{16} was copied from the first element of the source block to the first element of the destination block. Now we can execute through CS:217 with the command

$$G\ =CS:215\ \ 217\ (\downarrow)$$

and examining the blocks of data with the commands

$$D\ \ DS:100\ \ 10F\ (\downarrow)$$
$$D\ \ DS:120\ \ 12F\ (\downarrow)$$

we find that the complete source block has been copied into the destination block.

4.9 DEBUGGING A PROGRAM

In sections 4.6, 4.7, and 4.8 we learned how to use DEBUG to load a machine-code program into the memory of the PC, assemble a program, and execute the program. However, we did not determine if the program when executed performed the operation for which it was written. It is common to have errors in programs, and even a single error can render the program useless. For instance, if the address to which a "jump" instruction passes control is wrong, the program may get hung up. Errors in a program are also referred to as *bugs;* the process of removing them is called *debugging.*

The two types of errors that can be made by a programmer are the *syntax error* and the *execution error.* A syntax error is an error caused by not following the rules for coding or entering an instruction. These types of errors are typically identified by the microcomputer and signaled to the user with an error message. For this reason, they are usually easy to find and correct. For example, if an ENTER command was keyed in as

$$E\ DS:100120\ (\downarrow)$$

an error condition exists. This is because the space between the starting and ending address is left out. This incorrect entry is signaled by the warning "Error" in the display and the spot where the error begins, the 1 in 120, is marked with the symbol "^".

An execution error is an error in the logic behind the development of the program. That is, the program is correctly coded and entered, but still it does not perform the operation for which it was planned. This type of error can be identified by entering the program into the microcomputer and observing its operation. Even when an execution error problem has been identified, it is usually not easy to find the exact cause of the problem.

Our ability to debug execution errors in a program is aided by the commands of the DEBUG program. For instance, the TRACE command allows us to step through the program by executing just one instruction at a time. We can use the display of the internal-register state produced by TRACE and the memory dump command to determine the state of the 8088 and memory prior to execution of an instruction and again after its execution. This information will tell us whether the instruction has performed the operation planned for it. If an error is found, its cause can be identified and corrected.

To demonstrate the process of debugging a program, let us once again use the program that we stored at file specification 1 100 1 of the data diskette. We load it into the code segment at address CS:200 with the command

```
L CS:200 1 100 1 (⏎)
```

Now the program resides in memory at addresses CS:200 through CS:217. The program is displayed with the command

```
U CS:200 217 (⏎)
```

The program that is displayed is shown in Fig. 4.37. This program implements a block data transfer operation. The block of data to be moved starts at memory address DS:100 and is 16 bytes in length. It is to be moved to another block location starting at address DS:120.

Before executing the program, let us issue commands to initialize the source block of memory locations from address 100_{16} through $10F_{16}$ to FF_{16}, and the bytes in the destination block starting at 120_{16} can be initialized to 00_{16}. To do this, we issue the command sequence

```
R DS (⏎)
DS 08F1
:0020 (⏎)
F DS:100 10F FF (⏎)
F DS:120 12F 00 (⏎)
```

Now we will reset DS to its original value

```
R DS (⏎)
DS 0020
:08F1 (⏎)
```

```
-L CS:200 1 100 1
-U CS:200 217
08F1:0200 B82000      MOV     AX,0020
08F1:0203 8ED8        MOV     DS,AX
08F1:0205 BE0001      MOV     SI,0100
08F1:0208 BF2001      MOV     DI,0120
08F1:020B B91000      MOV     CX,0010
08F1:020E 8A24        MOV     AH,[SI]
08F1:0210 8825        MOV     [DI],AH
08F1:0212 46          INC     SI
08F1:0213 47          INC     DI
08F1:0214 49          DEC     CX
08F1:0215 75F7        JNZ     020E
08F1:0217 90          NOP
-R DS
DS 08F1
:0020
-F DS:100 10F FF
-F DS:120 12F 00
-R DS
DS 0020
:08F1
-T =CS:200 4

AX=0020  BX=0000  CX=0000  DX=0000  SP=70EE  BP=0000  SI=0000  DI=0000
DS=08F1  ES=08F1  SS=08F1  CS=08F1  IP=0203    NV UP DI PL NZ NA PO NC
08F1:0203 8ED8.          MOV     DS,AX

AX=0020  BX=0000  CX=0000  DX=0000  SP=70EE  BP=0000  SI=0100  DI=0000
DS=0020  ES=08F1  SS=08F1  CS=08F1  IP=0208    NV UP DI PL NZ NA PO NC
08F1:0208 BF2001         MOV     DI,0120

AX=0020  BX=0000  CX=0000  DX=0000  SP=70EE  BP=0000  SI=0100  DI=0120
DS=0020  ES=08F1  SS=08F1  CS=08F1  IP=020B    NV UP DI PL NZ NA PO NC
08F1:020B B91000         MOV     CX,0010

AX=0020  BX=0000  CX=0010  DX=0000  SP=70EE  BP=0000  SI=0100  DI=0120
DS=0020  ES=08F1  SS=08F1  CS=08F1  IP=020E    NV UP DI PL NZ NA PO NC
08F1:020E 8A24           MOV     AH,[SI]                      DS:0100=FF
-D DS:120 12F
0020:0120  00 00 00 00 00 00 00 00-00 00 00 00 00 00 00 00   ................
-T 2

AX=FF20  BX=0000  CX=0010  DX=0000  SP=70EE  BP=0000  SI=0100  DI=0120
DS=0020  ES=08F1  SS=08F1  CS=08F1  IP=0210    NV UP DI PL NZ NA PO NC
08F1:0210 8825           MOV     [DI],AH                      DS:0120=00

AX=FF20  BX=0000  CX=0010  DX=0000  SP=70EE  BP=0000  SI=0100  DI=0120
DS=0020  ES=08F1  SS=08F1  CS=08F1  IP=0212    NV UP DI PL NZ NA PO NC
08F1:0212 46             INC     SI
-D DS:120 12F
0020:0120  FF 00 00 00 00 00 00 00-00 00 00 00 00 00 00 00   ................
-T 3

AX=FF20  BX=0000  CX=0010  DX=0000  SP=70EE  BP=0000  SI=0101  DI=0120
DS=0020  ES=08F1  SS=08F1  CS=08F1  IP=0213    NV UP DI PL NZ NA PO NC
08F1:0213 47             INC     DI

AX=FF20  BX=0000  CX=0010  DX=0000  SP=70EE  BP=0000  SI=0101  DI=0121
DS=0020  ES=08F1  SS=08F1  CS=08F1  IP=0214    NV UP DI PL NZ NA PE NC
08F1:0214 49             DEC     CX

AX=FF20  BX=0000  CX=000F  DX=0000  SP=70EE  BP=0000  SI=0101  DI=0121
```

Figure 4.37 Program debugging demonstration.

```
DS=0020  ES=08F1  SS=08F1  CS=08F1  IP=0215    NV UP DI PL NZ AC PE NC
08F1:0215 75F7          JNZ     020E
-T

AX=FF20  BX=0000  CX=000F  DX=0000  SP=70EE  BP=0000  SI=0101  DI=0121
DS=0020  ES=08F1  SS=08F1  CS=08F1  IP=020E    NV UP DI PL NZ AC PE NC
08F1:020E 8A24          MOV     AH,[SI]                         DS:0101=FF
-G =CS:20E 215

AX=FF20  BX=0000  CX=000E  DX=0000  SP=70EE  BP=0000  SI=0102  DI=0122
DS=0020  ES=08F1  SS=08F1  CS=08F1  IP=0215    NV UP DI PL NZ NA PO NC
08F1:0215 75F7          JNZ     020E
-D DS:120 12F
0020:0120  FF FF 00 00 00 00 00 00-00 00 00 00 00 00 00 00   ................
-T

AX=FF20  BX=0000  CX=000E  DX=0000  SP=70EE  BP=0000  SI=0102  DI=0122
DS=0020  ES=08F1  SS=08F1  CS=08F1  IP=020E    NV UP DI PL NZ NA PO NC
08F1:020E 8A24          MOV     AH,[SI]                         DS:0102=FF
-G =CS:20E 215

AX=FF20  BX=0000  CX=000D  DX=0000  SP=70EE  BP=0000  SI=0103  DI=0123
DS=0020  ES=08F1  SS=08F1  CS=08F1  IP=0215    NV UP DI PL NZ NA PO NC
08F1:0215 75F7          JNZ     020E
-T

AX=FF20  BX=0000  CX=000D  DX=0000  SP=70EE  BP=0000  SI=0103  DI=0123
DS=0020  ES=08F1  SS=08F1  CS=08F1  IP=020E    NV UP DI PL NZ NA PO NC
08F1:020E 8A24          MOV     AH,[SI]                         DS:0103=FF
-G =CS:20E 215

AX=FF20  BX=0000  CX=000C  DX=0000  SP=70EE  BP=0000  SI=0104  DI=0124
DS=0020  ES=08F1  SS=08F1  CS=08F1  IP=0215    NV UP DI PL NZ NA PE NC
08F1:0215 75F7          JNZ     020E
-T

AX=FF20  BX=0000  CX=000C  DX=0000  SP=70EE  BP=0000  SI=0104  DI=0124
DS=0020  ES=08F1  SS=08F1  CS=08F1  IP=020E    NV UP DI PL NZ NA PE NC
08F1:020E 8A24          MOV     AH,[SI]                         DS:0104=FF
-G =CS:20E 215

AX=FF20  BX=0000  CX=000B  DX=0000  SP=70EE  BP=0000  SI=0105  DI=0125
DS=0020  ES=08F1  SS=08F1  CS=08F1  IP=0215    NV UP DI PL NZ NA PO NC
08F1:0215 75F7          JNZ     020E
-T

AX=FF20  BX=0000  CX=000B  DX=0000  SP=70EE  BP=0000  SI=0105  DI=0125
DS=0020  ES=08F1  SS=08F1  CS=08F1  IP=020E    NV UP DI PL NZ NA PO NC
08F1:020E 8A24          MOV     AH,[SI]                         DS:0105=FF
-G =CS:20E 215

AX=FF20  BX=0000  CX=000A  DX=0000  SP=70EE  BP=0000  SI=0106  DI=0126
DS=0020  ES=08F1  SS=08F1  CS=08F1  IP=0215    NV UP DI PL NZ NA PE NC
08F1:0215 75F7          JNZ     020E
-T

AX=FF20  BX=0000  CX=000A  DX=0000  SP=70EE  BP=0000  SI=0106  DI=0126
DS=0020  ES=08F1  SS=08F1  CS=08F1  IP=020E    NV UP DI PL NZ NA PE NC
08F1:020E 8A24          MOV     AH,[SI]                         DS:0106=FF
-G =CS:20E 215

AX=FF20  BX=0000  CX=0009  DX=0000  SP=70EE  BP=0000  SI=0107  DI=0127
DS=0020  ES=08F1  SS=08F1  CS=08F1  IP=0215    NV UP DI PL NZ NA PE NC
08F1:0215 75F7          JNZ     020E
-T
```

Figure 4.37 (continued)

```
AX=FF20  BX=0000  CX=0009  DX=0000  SP=70EE  BP=0000  SI=0107  DI=0127
DS=0020  ES=08F1  SS=08F1  CS=08F1  IP=020E   NV UP DI PL NZ NA PE NC
08F1:020E 8A24         MOV     AH,[SI]                             DS:0107=FF
-G =CS:20E 215

AX=FF20  BX=0000  CX=0008  DX=0000  SP=70EE  BP=0000  SI=0108  DI=0128
DS=0020  ES=08F1  SS=08F1  CS=08F1  IP=0215   NV UP DI PL NZ NA PO NC
08F1:0215 75F7         JNZ     020E
-T

AX=FF20  BX=0000  CX=0008  DX=0000  SP=70EE  BP=0000  SI=0108  DI=0128
DS=0020  ES=08F1  SS=08F1  CS=08F1  IP=020E   NV UP DI PL NZ NA PO NC
08F1:020E 8A24         MOV     AH,[SI]                             DS:0108=FF
-G =CS:20E 215

AX=FF20  BX=0000  CX=0007  DX=0000  SP=70EE  BP=0000  SI=0109  DI=0129
DS=0020  ES=08F1  SS=08F1  CS=08F1  IP=0215   NV UP DI PL NZ NA PO NC
08F1:0215 75F7         JNZ     020E
-T

AX=FF20  BX=0000  CX=0007  DX=0000  SP=70EE  BP=0000  SI=0109  DI=0129
DS=0020  ES=08F1  SS=08F1  CS=08F1  IP=020E   NV UP DI PL NZ NA PO NC
08F1:020E 8A24         MOV     AH,[SI]                             DS:0109=FF
-G =CS:20E 215

AX=FF20  BX=0000  CX=0006  DX=0000  SP=70EE  BP=0000  SI=010A  DI=012A
DS=0020  ES=08F1  SS=08F1  CS=08F1  IP=0215   NV UP DI PL NZ NA PE NC
08F1:0215 75F7         JNZ     020E
-T

AX=FF20  BX=0000  CX=0006  DX=0000  SP=70EE  BP=0000  SI=010A  DI=012A
DS=0020  ES=08F1  SS=08F1  CS=08F1  IP=020E   NV UP DI PL NZ NA PE NC
08F1:020E 8A24         MOV     AH,[SI]                             DS:010A=FF
-G =CS:20E 215

AX=FF20  BX=0000  CX=0005  DX=0000  SP=70EE  BP=0000  SI=010B  DI=012B
DS=0020  ES=08F1  SS=08F1  CS=08F1  IP=0215   NV UP DI PL NZ NA PE NC
08F1:0215 75F7         JNZ     020E
-T

AX=FF20  BX=0000  CX=0005  DX=0000  SP=70EE  BP=0000  SI=010B  DI=012B
DS=0020  ES=08F1  SS=08F1  CS=08F1  IP=020E   NV UP DI PL NZ NA PE NC
08F1:020E 8A24         MOV     AH,[SI]                             DS:010B=FF
-G =CS:20E 215

AX=FF20  BX=0000  CX=0004  DX=0000  SP=70EE  BP=0000  SI=010C  DI=012C
DS=0020  ES=08F1  SS=08F1  CS=08F1  IP=0215   NV UP DI PL NZ NA PO NC
08F1:0215 75F7         JNZ     020E
-T

AX=FF20  BX=0000  CX=0004  DX=0000  SP=70EE  BP=0000  SI=010C  DI=012C
DS=0020  ES=08F1  SS=08F1  CS=08F1  IP=020E   NV UP DI PL NZ NA PO NC
08F1:020E 8A24         MOV     AH,[SI]                             DS:010C=FF
-G =CS:20E 215

AX=FF20  BX=0000  CX=0003  DX=0000  SP=70EE  BP=0000  SI=010D  DI=012D
DS=0020  ES=08F1  SS=08F1  CS=08F1  IP=0215   NV UP DI PL NZ NA PE NC
08F1:0215 75F7         JNZ     020E
-T

AX=FF20  BX=0000  CX=0003  DX=0000  SP=70EE  BP=0000  SI=010D  DI=012D
DS=0020  ES=08F1  SS=08F1  CS=08F1  IP=020E   NV UP DI PL NZ NA PE NC
08F1:020E 8A24         MOV     AH,[SI]                             DS:010D=FF
-G =CS:20E 215

AX=FF20  BX=0000  CX=0002  DX=0000  SP=70EE  BP=0000  SI=010E  DI=012E
```

Figure 4.37 (continued)

135

```
DS=0020  ES=08F1  SS=08F1  CS=08F1  IP=0215   NV UP DI PL NZ NA PO NC
08F1:0215 75F7           JNZ     020E
-T

AX=FF20  BX=0000  CX=0002  DX=0000  SP=70EE  BP=0000  SI=010E  DI=012E
DS=0020  ES=08F1  SS=08F1  CS=08F1  IP=020E   NV UP DI PL NZ NA PO NC
08F1:020E 8A24           MOV     AH,[SI]                      DS:010E=FF
-G =CS:20E 215

AX=FF20  BX=0000  CX=0001  DX=0000  SP=70EE  BP=0000  SI=010F  DI=012F
DS=0020  ES=08F1  SS=08F1  CS=08F1  IP=0215   NV UP DI PL NZ NA PO NC
08F1:0215 75F7           JNZ     020E
-T

AX=FF20  BX=0000  CX=0001  DX=0000  SP=70EE  BP=0000  SI=010F  DI=012F
DS=0020  ES=08F1  SS=08F1  CS=08F1  IP=020E   NV UP DI PL NZ NA PO NC
08F1:020E 8A24           MOV     AH,[SI]                      DS:010F=FF
-G =CS:20E 215

AX=FF20  BX=0000  CX=0000  DX=0000  SP=70EE  BP=0000  SI=0110  DI=0130
DS=0020  ES=08F1  SS=08F1  CS=08F1  IP=0215   NV UP DI PL ZR NA PE NC
08F1:0215 75F7           JNZ     020E
-T

AX=FF20  BX=0000  CX=0000  DX=0000  SP=70EE  BP=0000  SI=0110  DI=0130
DS=0020  ES=08F1  SS=08F1  CS=08F1  IP=0217   NV UP DI PL ZR NA PE NC
08F1:0217 90            NOP
-D DS:120 12F
0020:0120  FF FF FF FF FF FF FF FF-FF FF FF FF FF FF FF FF    ................
-
-
```

Figure 4.37 (continued)

The first two instructions of the program in Fig. 4.37 are

MOV AX,0020

and

MOV DS,AX

These two instructions, when executed, load the data-segment register with the value 0020_{16}. In this way, they define a data segment starting at address 200_{16}. The next three instructions are used to load the SI, DI, and CX registers with 100_{16}, 120_{16}, and 10_{16}, respectively. Let us now show how to execute these instructions and then determine if they perform the correct function. They are executed by issuing the command

T =CS:200 4 (↵)

To determine if the five instructions that were executed performed the correct operation, we just need to look at the trace display that they produce. This display trace is shown in Fig. 4.37. Here we see that the first instruction loads AX with 0020_{16} and the second moves this value into the DS register. Also notice in the last trace displayed that SI contains 0100_{16}, DI contains 0120_{16}, and CX contains 0010_{16}.

The next two instructions copy the contents of memory location 100_{16} into the storage location at address 120_{16}. Let us first check the contents of the destination block with the D command

D DS:120 12F (⏎)

Looking at the dump display, we see that the original contents of these locations are 00_{16}. Now the two instructions are executed with the command

T 2 (⏎)

and the contents of address DS:120 are checked once again with the command

D DS:120 12F (⏎)

The display dump in Fig. 4.37 shows that the first element of the source block was copied to the location of the first element of the destination block. Therefore, both address 100_{16} and address 120_{16} now contain the same data.

The next three instructions are used to increment pointers SI and DI and decrement block counter CX. To execute them, we issue the command

T 3 (⏎)

Referring to the trace display in Fig. 4.37 to verify their operation, we find that the new values in SI and DI are 0101_{16} and 0121_{16}, respectively, and CX is now $000F_{16}$.

The jump instruction transfers control to the instruction eight bytes back. It is executed with the command

T (⏎)

Notice that the result of executing this instruction is that the value in IP is changed to $020E_{16}$. This corresponds to the location of the instruction

MOV AH,[SI]

In this way we see that control has been returned to the part of the program that performs the block-move operation.

The move operation performed by this part of the program was already checked; however, we must still determine if it runs to completion when the count in CX decrements to zero. Therefore, we will execute the complete loop with a GO command. This command is

G =CS:20E 215 (⏎)

Correct operation is verified because the trace shows that CX has been decremented by one more and equals E. The fact that the second element has been moved can be verified by dumping the destination block with the command

D DS:120 12F (⏎)

Now we are again at address CS:215. To execute the jump instruction at this location, we can again use the T command

T (⏎)

This returns control to the instruction at CS:20E. The previous two commands can be repeated until the complete block is moved and CX equals 0_{16}.

At completion, the overall operation of the program can be verified by examining the contents of the destination block with the command sequence

D DS:120 12F (⏎)

FF_{16} should be displayed as the data held in each storage location.

ASSIGNMENT

Section 4.2

1. Encode the following instruction using the information in Figs. 4.1 through 4.4.

ADD AX,DX

Assume that the opcode for the add operation is 000000_{16}.

2. Encode the following instructions using the information in the tables of Figs. 4.2 through 4.6.

    (a) MOV [DI],DX
    (b) MOV [BX+SI],BX
    (c) MOV DL,[BX+10]

3. Encode the instructions that follow using the tables in Figs. 4.2 through 4.6.

    (a) PUSH DS
    (b) ROL BL,CL
    (c) ADD AX,[1234]

Section 4.3

4. How many bytes are required to encode the instruction MOV SI,0100?
5. How many bytes of memory are required to store the machine code for the program in Fig. 4.7(a)?

Section 4.4

6. On which DOS diskette does the DEBUG program reside?
7. Bring up DEBUG on your PC; type it in using lowercase letters.
8. Enter the command R AXBX on your PC. What happens?
9. Use the REGISTER command to change the value in CX to 10_{16}.
10. Change the state of the parity flag to PE with a REGISTER command.
11. Dump the state of the 8088's internal registers and verify that the change of CX in problem 9 and the change of the parity flag in problem 10 were correctly made.

Section 4.5

12. Use the DUMP command to display the contents of the first 16 bytes of the current code segment.
13. Use the ENTER command to examine the contents of the same 16 bytes of memory that were displayed in problem 12.
14. Use the ENTER command to load five consecutive bytes of memory starting at address CS:100 of the current code segment with FF_{16}. Before terminating the command, verify that the memory contents have been changed by stepping back through the memory locations by depressing the " $-$ " key.
15. Use the FILL command to initialize the first 32 bytes at the top of the stack to 00_{16}. Verify the new contents of memory with the DUMP command.
16. Fill the first six storage locations starting at address CS:100 with 11_{16}, the second six with 22_{16}, the third six with 33_{16}, the fourth six with 44_{16}, and the fifth six with 55_{16}. Next change the contents of storage locations CS:105 and CS:113 to FF_{16}. Issue a DUMP command to display the first 30 bytes of the data segment. Then issue a SEARCH command that searches the block of memory for those storage locations that contain FF_{16}.

Section 4.6

17. Load the machine code found for the instruction in Example 4.3 starting at address CS:100, unassemble it to verify that the correct instruction was loaded, and save it on a data diskette at file specification 1 50 1.
18. Do Example 4.20 on your PC and save the machine code, using file specification 1 10 1.
19. Reload the instruction saved on the data diskette in problem 18 into memory at offset 400 in the current code segment and unassemble it to verify correct loading.
20. Do Example 4.21 on your PC.

Section 4.7

21. Repeat problem 2, but this time use the ASSEMBLE and UNASSEMBLE commands to obtain the machine code.
22. Use the ASSEMBLE and UNASSEMBLE commands to find the machine code for each of the instructions given in problem 3.

Section 4.8

23. Load the instruction saved on the data diskette in problem 17 at address CS:300. Unassemble it to verify correct loading and then initialize the contents of register CX to $000F_{16}$ and the contents of the word memory location starting at DS:1234 to $00FF_{16}$. Execute the instruction with the TRACE command and verify its operation by examining the contents of CX and the word of data stored starting at DS:1234 in memory.
24. Repeat Example 4.23; however, this time execute the complete program with one GO command. Verify the operation of the program by examining the blocks of data in memory.

Section 4.9

25. What is the difference between a syntax error and an execution error?
26. Repeat the debug demonstration presented in section 4.9, but this time use only GO commands to execute the program.

5

ASSEMBLY LANGUAGE PROGRAM DEVELOPMENT AND THE IBM PC MACROASSEMBLER

5.1 INTRODUCTION

In the last chapter we learned how assembly language instructions are encoded using 8088 machine language and how to use the program development tools available in the PC's DOS 2.1 operating system. We did find that there is a line-by-line assembler included in the DEBUG program; however, this assembler is not practical to use when writing programs for useful applications. In this chapter we will study in detail the steps involved in developing larger assembly language application programs for the PC and how to use IBM's 8088 macroassembler and the LINK programs. The topics covered in the chapter are as follows:

1. Assembly language program development on the IBM PC
2. Statement syntax for the source program
3. Pseudo operations
4. Generating an assembler source file with EDLIN
5. Assembling source programs with MASM
6. The LINK program—creating a run module
7. Loading and executing run modules with DEBUG

5.2 ASSEMBLY LANGUAGE PROGRAM DEVELOPMENT ON THE IBM PC

An assembly language program is written to solve a specific problem. For instance, the example program we used in Chapter 4 was a *block-move program.* Its function was to move a fixed-length block of data, called the *source block,* from one location in memory to another location in memory, called the *destination block.* When we ran this program on the PC with the debugger, we were able to trace its operation and observe each element of data as it was moved from the source to the destination block. In this way, we verified its operation. The development of an assembler language program, such as the block-move program, involves many steps. A flowchart that outlines the steps in this development process is shown in Fig. 5.1. Let us now look at each of these steps in detail.

Looking at Fig. 5.1, we see that the first step in the *program development process* is to plan a solution for the problem. This assumes that we are provided with a complete and clear description of the problem to be solved. Once we have this information, it can be analyzed and the problem broken down into a series of basic operations which, when performed, will produce an efficient solution to the problem. These basic operations must be ones that can be implemented in 8088 assembler language. The solution is normally presented in a pictorial form called a *flowchart.* A flowchart uses a set of symbols to identify both the operations required in the solution and the sequence in which they are performed.

The second step of the program development process, as shown in Fig. 5.1, is the translation of the flowchart solution into its equivalent assembly language program. This requires the programmer to describe the operation for each symbol in the flowchart with a series of 8088 assembler instructions. These instruction sequences are combined together to form a handwritten assembly language program called the *source program.* The source program uses Englishlike statements that are either instructions to be performed by the microprocessor or instructions to the program that is used to convert the assembly language program into machine code.

To do this step, the programmer must know the instruction set of the 8088 microprocessor, the assembler instruction syntax, and the assembler's pseudo-operations. We will discuss assembler instruction syntax and pseudo-operations in this chapter. The instruction set of the 8088 will be covered in the next two chapters.

After having handwritten the assembly language program, we are ready to enter it into the computer. This is done with a program called an *editor,* which is available as part of the PC's DOS operating system. Using the editor program, we type in each of the statements of the assembler program. If errors are made as they are keyed in, the corrections can be made either at the time of entry or edited at a later time. The source program is saved by storing it in a file

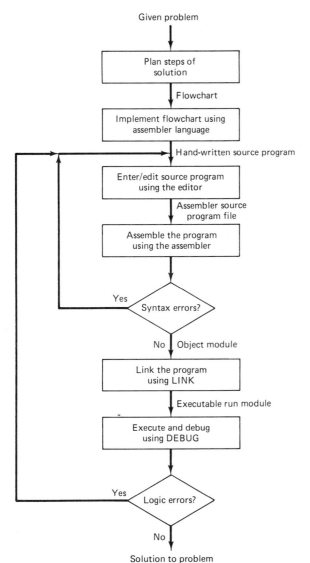

Figure 5.1 General program development cycle.

on a data diskette. The use of the DOS editor to create a source file is covered later in this chapter.

The fourth step in the flowchart of Fig. 5.1 is the point at which the assembly language source program is converted to its corresponding 8088 machine-language program. To do this, we use a program called an *assembler*. The assembler program reads as its input the contents of the *assembler source file;* it converts this program statement by statement to machine code, and produces a machine-code program as its output. This machine-code output is stored in another file called the *object module.*

If during the conversion operation syntax errors are found—that is, violations in the rules of writing 8088 assembly language instructions for the IBM PC—they are automatically flagged by the assembler. As shown in the flowchart, before going on, the cause of each error in the source program must be identified and then corrected. The corrections are made using the editor program. After the corrections are made, the source program must be reassembled. This edit-assemble sequence must be repeated until the program assembles with no errors. We will discuss the use of IBM's macroassembler (MASM) later in this chapter.

The object module produced by the assembler cannot be run directly on the 8088 microprocessor. As shown in Fig. 5.1, this module must be processed by the *LINK program* to produce an executable object module, which is known as a *run module.* The linker program converts the object module to a run module by making it address compatible with the microcomputer on which it is to be run. For instance, if our system is implemented with memory at addresses $A000_{16}$ through $FFFF_{16}$, the executable machine-code output by the linker will also have addresses in this range.

There is another purpose for the use of a linker. This is that it is used to link together different object modules to generate one executable object module.

Now the executable object module is ready to be run on the microcomputer. Once again, the PC's DOS operating system provides us with a program, which is called DEBUG, to perform this function. DEBUG provides an environment in which we can run the program instruction by instruction or run a group of instructions at a time, look at intermediate results, display the contents of the registers within the microprocessor, and so on. If the program when run correctly performs the function for which it was written, the program development process is complete.

On the other hand, Fig. 5.1 shows that if errors are discovered in the logic of the solution, they must be corrected by going back and editing the source program. Then the edited source file must be reassembled, relinked, and retested by running it with DEBUG. This edit-assemble-link-debug loop must be repeated until the program correctly performs the operation for which it was written.

The edit, assemble, link, and debug parts of the general program development cycle in Fig. 5.1 are performed directly on the IBM PC. Figure 5.2 shows the names of the programs and typical file names with extensions used as inputs and outputs during this process. For example, the *EDLIN program* is the editor that is used to create and correct assembly language source files. The program that results is shown to have the name PROG1.SRC. This stands for *program 1 source code.*

There are two programs that can be used to assemble source files into ob-

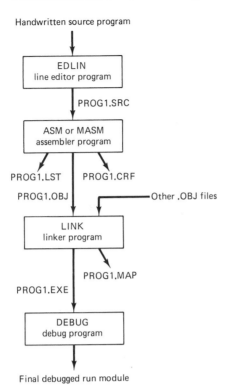

Figure 5.2 The DOS program development programs and user files.

ject modules. They are called ASM and MASM, which stand for *small assembler* and *macroassembler,* respectively. The assembler converts the contents of the source input file PROG1.SRC into three output files called PROG1.OBJ, PROG1.LST, and PROG1.CRF. The file PROG1.OBJ contains the object code module. The other two files are provided for debugging support.

Object module PROG1.OBJ can be linked to other object modules with the LINK program. This program produces a *run module* in file PROG1.EXE and a *map file* called PROG1.MAP as outputs. The executable object module, PROG1.EXE, can be run with the debugger program, which is called DEBUG. PROG1.MAP is provided as support for the debugging operation.

5.3 STATEMENT SYNTAX FOR THE SOURCE PROGRAM

A source program is a series of assembly language and pseudo-operation statements that solve a specific problem. The *assembly language statements* of the program tell the 8088 microprocessor the operations to be performed. On the other hand, the *pseudo-operation statements* are directions that tell the assembler program how the assembly is to be done. In this section we will look into the syntax that must be used when writing assembly language and pseudo-operation statements for IBM's 8088 macroassembler.

Syntax of an Assembly Language Statement

For a source program to be read correctly from a file, it must be written using the syntax understood by the assembler program. By *statement syntax,* we mean the form in which statements must be written—that is, the different elements that are part of the statement, sequence of elements, and any restrictions or exceptions that must be obeyed. The general format of an assembly language statement is

LABEL OPCODE OPERAND COMMENT

Note that it contains four separate fields: the *label field, opcode field, operand field,* and *comment field.* An example is the instruction

START MOV CX,10 ;Load a count of 10 into register CX

Here we find that START is in the label field, MOV (for "move operation") is the opcode field, the operands are CX and decimal number 10, and the comment field tells us that execution of the instruction loads a count of 10 into register CX.

Not all the fields need to be included in an instruction. In fact, the only part of the format that is always required is the opcode. For instance, the instruction

MOV CX,10 ;Initialize the count in CX

has nothing in the label field. Other instructions may not need anything in the operand field. The instruction

CLC   ;Clear the carry flag

is an example.

The one rule that must be followed when writing assembly language statements is that the fields must be separated by at least one blank space and that if no label is used, the opcode field must be preceded by at least one blank.

Let us now look at each field of the assembly language source statement in more detail. We will begin with the label field. It is used to give a *symbolic name* to an assembly language statement. By doing this, other instructions in the program can reference the instruction by simply referring to this symbol instead of the actual memory address where the instruction is stored.

For example, it is common to use a jump instruction to pass control to an instruction elsewhere in the program. An example is the instruction sequence

```
JMP   START
      .
      .
      .
START   MOV   CX,10   ;Initialize the count in CX
```

Execution of the jump instruction causes program execution to pass to the point in the program corresponding to label START—that is, the MOV instruction that is located further down in the program.

The label is an arbitrarily selected string of alphanumeric characters optionally followed by ":". If no colon is used, as in our example START, the address represented by the label is in the current segment. On the other hand, putting a colon after the label, for instance START:, means that the address corresponding to the label is in a segment that is not currently active. Some examples of valid labels are: START, LOOPA, SUBROUTINE_A, and COUNT_ROUTINE. As in our earlier example, the names used for labels are typically selected to help document what is happening at that point of the program.

There are some limitations on the selection of labels. For one, only the first 31 characters of the label are recognized by the assembler. Moreover, the first character of the label must be either a letter or the symbol ".". A period cannot be used at any other point in the label except as the first character.

Another restriction is that *reserved symbols,* such as those used to refer to the internal registers of the 8088 (AH, AL, AX, etc.) cannot be used. A last restriction is that a label cannot include embedded blanks. This is the reason that the earlier example COUNT_ROUTINE has an underscore character (_) separating the two words. Use of the underscore makes the assembler view the character string as a single label.

As we found in Chapter 4, each of the basic operations that can be performed by the 8088 microprocessor is identified with a three- to six-letter mnemonic, which is called its *operation code* (opcode). For example, the *mnemonics* for the add, subtract, and move operations are ADD, SUB, and MOV, respectively. It is these mnemonics that are entered into the opcode field when writing assembly language statements.

The entries in the operand field tell where the data that is to be processed is located and how it is to be accessed. An instruction may have one, two, or even no operands. For example, the MOV instruction requires two operands. An example is the statement

```
MOV   AX,BX
```

Here the two operands are the accumulator (AX) register and the base (BX) register of the 8088. Note that the operands are separated by a comma. A question that we may now ask is How do we tell which is the source operand and which is the destination operand? The answer is quite simple: 8088 assembly language instructions are written with the destination operand first. Therefore, BX is the source operand (the "move from" location) and AX is the destination operand (the "move to" location). In this way, we see that the operation performed by the instruction is to move the value held in BX into AX. The notations used to identify the 8088's internal registers are shown in Fig. 5.3.

In section 3.13 we saw that a large number of addressing modes are provided for the 8088 to help us in specifying the location of operands. Examples using each of the addressing modes are provided in Fig. 5.4. For example, the instruction that specifies an immediate data operand simply includes the value of the piece of data in the operand location. On the other hand, if the operand is a direct address it is specified using a label for the memory address.

The *comment* field can be used to describe the operation performed by the instruction. It is always preceded by ";". For instance, in the instruction

MOV   AX,BX   ;Copy BX into AX

Symbol	Register
AX	Accumulator register
AH	Accumulator register high byte
AL	Accumulator register lower byte
BX	Base register
BH	Base register high byte
BL	Base register low byte
CX	Count register
CH	Count register high byte
CL	Count register low byte
DX	Data register
DH	Data register high byte
DL	Data register low byte
SI	Source index register
DI	Destination index register
SP	Stack pointer register
BP	Base pointer register
CS	Code segment register
DS	Data segment register
SS	Stack segment register
ES	Extra segment register

Figure 5.3 Symbols for specifying register operands.

Addressing mode	Operand	Example	Segment
Register	Destination	MOV AX,LABEL	—
Immediate	Source	MOV AL,15H	—
Direct	Destination	MOV LABEL,AX	Data
Register indirect	Source	MOV AX,[SI]	Data
		MOV AX,[BP]	Stack
		MOV AX,[DI]	Data
		MOV AX,[BX]	Data
Based	Destination	MOV [BX]+DISP,AL	Data
		MOV [BP]+DISP,AL	Stack
Indexed	Source	MOV AL,[SI]	Data
		MOV AL,[DI]	Data
Based indexed	Destination	MOV [BX][SI]+DISP,AH	Data
		MOV [BX][DI]+DISP,AH	Data
		MOV [BP][SI]+DISP,AH	Stack
		MOV [BP][DI]+DISP,AH	Stack

Figure 5.4 Examples using the various 8088 addressing modes.

the comment tells us that execution of the instruction causes the value in the source register BX to be copied into destination register AX.

The assembler program ignores comments when it assembles a program into an object module. Comments are only produced in the source listing. This does not mean that comments are not important. In fact, they are very important. This is because they document the operation of the source program. If a program is picked up a long time after it was written, for instance, for a software update, the comments permit the programmer to quickly understand its operation.

Syntax of a Pseudo-Operation Statement

The syntax used to write pseudo-operation statements is essentially the same as that for an assembly language statement. The general form is

```
LABEL  PSEUDO-OPCODE  OPERAND  COMMENT
```

Notice that the only difference is that the instruction opcode is replaced with a *pseudo-opcode.* It tells the assembler which type of operation is to be performed. For example, the pseudo-opcode DB stands for *define byte,* and if a statement is written as

```
DB  0FFH  ;Allocate byte locations initialized to FFH
```

it causes the next byte location in memory to be loaded with the value FF_{16}. This type of command can be used to initialize memory locations with data.

Another difference between the pseudo-operation statement and an assembly language statement is that pseudo-operations frequently have more than two operands. For instance, the statement

```
DB   0FFH,0FFH,0FFH,0FFH,0FFH
```

causes the assembler to load the next five consecutive bytes in memory with the value FF_{16}.

Constants in a Statement

Constants, such as an immediate value of data or an address, in an instruction or pseudo-operation can be expressed in any of five data types: *binary, decimal, hexadecimal, octal,* or *character*. The first four types of data are defined by including the letter B, D, H, or Q, respectively, after the number. For example, decimal number 9 is expressed in each of these four data forms as follows:

```
1001B
9D
9H
11Q
```

One exception is that decimal numbers do not have to be followed by a D. Therefore, 9D can also be written simply as 9.

Another variation is that the first digit of a hexadecimal number must always be one of the numbers in the range 0 through 9. For this reason, hexadecimal A must be written as 0AH instead of just as AH.

Typically, data and addresses are expressed in hexadecimal form. On the other hand, it is more common to express the count for shift, rotate, and string instructions in decimal form.

Example 5.1

The repeat count in CX for a string instruction is to be equal to decimal 255. Assume that the instruction that is to load the count has the form

```
MOV   CX,XX
```

where XX stands for the count, which is an immediate operand, that is to be loaded into CX. Show how the instruction would be written using first decimal notation for the immediate operand and then a second time using hexadecimal notation.

Solution:

Using decimal notation, we get

```
MOV   CX,255D
```

or just

MOV CX,255

In hexadecimal form, 255 is represented by FF_{16}. Therefore, the instruction becomes

MOV CX,0FFH

The numbers used as operands in assembly language and pseudo-op statements can also be *signed* (positive or negative) *numbers.* For decimal numbers, this is simply done by preceding it with a + or − sign. For example, an immediate count of − 10 that is to be loaded into the CX register with a MOV instruction can be written as

MOV CX, − 10

However, for negative numbers expressed in binary, hexadecimal, or octal form, the 2's complement of the number must be entered.

Example 5.2

The count in a MOV instruction that is to load CX is to be − 10. Write the instruction and express the immediate operand in binary form.

Solution:

The binary form of 10_{10} is 01010_2. Forming the 2's complement, we get

$$\begin{array}{r} 10101 \\ + 1 \\ \hline 10110 \end{array}$$

Therefore, the instruction is written as

MOV CX,10110B

Character data can also be used as an operand. For instance, a string-search operation may be used to search through a block of ASCII data in memory looking for a specific ASCII character, such as the letter A. When ASCII data are used as an operand, the character or string of characters must be enclosed by quotes. For example, if the number 1 is to be expressed as character data, instead of numeric data, it is written as "1". In a string-compare operation, the data in memory is always compared to the contents of the AL register. Therefore, the character being searched for must be loaded into this register. For instance, to load the ASCII value of 1 into AL, we use the instruction

MOV AL,"1"

A second kind of operand specifies a storage location in memory. Such operands are written using the memory-addressing modes of the 8088, which are shown in Fig. 5.4. For instance, to specify that an operand is held in a storage location that is the tenth byte from the beginning of a source block of data located in the current data segment, we can use indirect addressing through source-index register SI. In this way, the location of the operand is specified as

10[SI]   or   [SI] + 10

SI must be loaded with an offset that points to the beginning of the source-data block in memory.

Certain instructions require operands that are a memory address instead of data. Two examples are the *jump* (JMP) instruction and the *call* (CALL) instruction. Labels can be used to identify these addresses. For instance, in the instruction

JMP   LOOP

LOOP is a label that specifies the "jump to" address. *Attributes* may also be assigned to the label. An attribute specifies whether or not a given label is a *near, far, external,* or *internal label.* The different types of labels are covered in detail along with the JMP instruction in Chapter 7.

Operand Expressions using the Arithmetic, Relational, and Logical Operators

The operands we have used up to this point have all been either constants, variables, or labels. However, it is also possible to have an expression as an operand. For example, the instruction

MOV   AH,A+2

has an expression for its source operand. That is, the source operand is written as the sum of variable A and the number 2.

Figure 5.5 lists the *arithmetic, relational,* and *logical operators* that can be used to form operand expressions for use with IBM's 8088 macroassembler. Expressions that are used for operands are evaluated as part of the assembly process. As the source program is assembled into an object module, the numeric values for the terms in the operand expressions are combined together based on a *precedence* of the operators in the expression, and then the expression is replaced with the resulting operand value in the final object code.

In Fig. 5.5 the operators are listed in the order of their precedence. By precedence we mean the order in which the 8088 assembler performs their

Type	Operator	Example	Function
Arithmetic	*	A * B	Multiplies A with B and makes the operand equal to the product
	/	A / B	Divides A by B and makes the operand equal to the quotient
	MOD	A MOD B	Divides A by B and assigns the remainder to the operand
	SHL	A SHL n	Shifts the value in A left by n bit positions and assigns this shifted value to the operand
	SHR	A SHR n	Shifts the value in A right by n bit positions and assigns this shifted value to the operand
	+	A + B	Adds A to B and makes the operand equal to the sum
	−	A − B	Subtracts B from A and makes the operand equal to the difference
Relational	EQ	A EQ B	Compares value of A to that of B. If A equals B, the operand is set to FFFFH and if they are not equal it is set to 0H
	NE	A NE B	Compares value of A to that of B. If A is not equal to B, the operand is set to FFFFH and if they are equal it is set to 0H
	LT	A LT B	Compares value of A to that of B. If A is less than B, the operand is set to FFFFH and if it is equal or greater than it is set to 0H
	GT	A GT B	Compares value of A to that of B. If A is greater than B, the operand is set to FFFFH and if it is equal or less than it is set to 0H
	LE	A LE B	Compares value of A to that of B. If A is less than or equal to B, the operand is set to FFFFH and if it is greater than it is set to 0H
	GE	A GE B	Compares value of A to that of B. If A is greater than or equal to B, the operand is set to FFFFH and if it is less than it is set to 0H
Logical	NOT	NOT A	Takes the logical NOT of A and makes the value that results equal to the operand
	AND	A AND B	A is ANDed with B and makes the value that results equal to the operand
	OR	A OR B	A is ORed with B and makes the value that results equal to the operand
	XOR	A XOR B	A is XORed with B and makes the value that results equal to the operand

Figure 5.5 Arithmetic, relational, and logical operators.

operations as it evaluates an expression. For instance, if the expression for an operand is

$$A + B * 2 / D$$

when the assembler evaluates the expression, the multiplication is performed first, the division second, and the addition third.

The order of precedence can be overcome by using parentheses. When parentheses are in use, what is enclosed within them is evaluated first. For example, if we modify the example we just used as follows:

$$(A + B * 2) / D$$

the multiplication still takes place first, but now it is followed by the addition and then the division. Use of the set of parentheses has changed the order of precedence.

In Fig. 5.5 we have shown a simple expression using each of the operators and described the function performed by the assembler for these expressions. For example, we find that the operand expression

$$A \text{ SHL } n$$

causes the assembler to shift the value of A to the left by "n" bits.

Example 5.3

Find the value the assembler assigns to the source operand for the instruction

$$MOV \ BH,(A * 4 - 2) / (B - 3)$$

for A = 8 and B = 5.

Solution:

The expression is calculated as

$$(8 * 4 - 2) / (5 - 3)$$
$$(30) / (2)$$
$$15$$

and using hexadecimal notation, we get the instruction

$$MOV \ BH,0EH$$

All the examples we have considered so far have used arithmetic operators. Let us now take an example of a relational operator. In Fig. 5.5 we find that there are six relational operators: *equal* (EQ), *not equal* (NE), *less than* (LT), *greater than* (GT), *less than or equal* (LE), and *greater than or equal* (GE). The example expression given for equal is

$$A \text{ EQ } B$$

When the assembler evaluates this relational expression, it determines whether or not the value of A equals that of B. If they are equal to each other, the operand is made equal to $FFFF_{16}$; if they are unequal, the operand is made equal to 0_{16}.

This result is true for all relational operators. If by evaluating a relational expression, we find that the conditions it specifies are satisfied, the operand expression is replaced with $FFFF_{16}$; if the conditions are not satisfied, it is replaced by 0_{16}.

Example 5.4

What value is used for the source operand in the expression

```
MOV  AX,A LE (B − C)
```

if A = 234, B = 345, and C = 111?

Solution:

Substituting into the expression, we get

```
234 LE (345 − 111)
234 LE 234
```

Since the relational operator is satisfied, the instruction is equivalent to

```
MOV  AX,0FFFFH
```

The logical operators are similar to the arithmetic and relational operator; however, when they are used, the assembler performs the appropriate sequence of logic operations and then assigns the result that is produced to the operand.

The Value-Returning and Attribute Operators

Two other types of operators are available for use with operands: the *value-returning operators* and the *attribute operators*. The operators in each group along with an example expression and description of their function are given in Fig. 5.6.

The value-returning operators return the attribute (segment, offset, or type) value of a variable or label operand. For instance, assuming that the variable A is in a data segment, the instructions

```
MOV  AX,SEG A
MOV  SI,OFFSET A
MOV  CL,TYPE A
```

when assembled cause the 16-bit value in the DS register to replace SEG A, the 16-bit offset of the location of variable A from the current value in DS to replace OFFSET A, and the type number of the variable to replace TYPE A, re-

Type	Operator	Example	Function
Value-returning	SEG	SEG A	Assigns the contents held in the segment register corresponding to the segment in which A resides to the operand
	OFFSET	OFFSET A	Assigns the offset of the location A in its corresponding segment to the operand
	TYPE	TYPE A	Returns to the operand a number representing the type of A; 1 for a byte variable and 2 for a word variable; NEAR or FAR for the label
	SIZE	SIZE A	Returns the byte count of variable A to the operand
	LENGTH	LENGTH A	Returns the number of units (as specified by TYPE) allocated for the variable A to the operand
Attribute	PTR	NEAR PTR A	Overrides the current type of label operand A and assigns a new pointer type: BYTE, WORD, NEAR, or FAR to A
	DS:,ES:,SS:	ES:A	Overrides the normal segment for operand A and assigns a new segment to A
	SHORT	JMP SHORT A	Assigns to operand A an attribute that indicates that it is within +127 or −128 bytes of the next instruction. This lets the instruction be encoded with the minimum number of bytes
	THIS	THIS BYTE A	Assigns to operand A a distance or type attribute: BYTE, WORD, NEAR, or FAR, and the corresponding segment attribute
	HIGH	HIGH A	Returns to the operand A the high byte of the word of A
	LOW	LOW A	Returns to the operand A the low byte of the word of A

Figure 5.6 Value-returning and attribute operators.

spectively. Assuming that A is a data byte, the value 1 will be assigned to TYPE A.

The attribute operators give the programmer the ability to change the attributes of an operand or label. For example, operands that use the BX, SI, or DI registers to hold the offsets to their storage locations in memory are automatically referenced with respect to the contents of the DS register. An example is the instruction

```
MOV   AX,[SI]
```

We can use the *segment override* attribute operator to select another segment register. For instance, to select the extra segment register the instruction is written as

```
MOV   AX,ES:[SI]
```

5.4 PSEUDO-OPERATIONS

The primary function of an assembler program is to convert the assembly language instructions of the assembly language source program to their corresponding machine instructions. However, practical assembly language source programs do not consist of just assembly language statements, they also contain what are called *pseudo-operation statements* (*pseudo-op* statements for short). In this section, we will look more closely at what pseudo-ops are, which ones are available in the 8088 macroassembler for the IBM PC, and how they are used as part of the assembly language source program.

The Pseudo-Op

In section 5.3 we introduced the syntax of pseudo-op statements and found that they differ from assembly language instruction statements in that they are directions to tell the assembler how to assemble the source program instead of instructions to be processed by the microprocessor. That is, pseudo-ops are statements written in the source program but meant only for use by the assembler program. The assembler program follows these *directives* (directions) during the assembling of the program, but does not produce machine code for them.

A list of the pseudo-ops provided in IBM's 8088 macroassembler for the PC is shown in Fig. 5.7. Notice that the pseudo-ops are grouped into categories

Type	Pseudo-ops		
Data	ASSUME	ENDS	NAME
	COMMENT	EQU	ORG
	DB	= (Equal	PROC
	DD	Sign)	PUBLIC
	DQ	EVEN	.RADIX
	DT	EXTRN	RECORD
	DW	GROUP	SEGMENT
	END	INCLUDE	STRUC
	ENDP	LABEL	
Conditional	ELSE	IFDEF	IFNB
	ENDIF	IFDIF	IFNDEF
	IF	IFE	IF1
	IFB	IFIDN	IF2
Macro	ENDM	IRPC	PURGE
	EXITM	LOCAL	REPT
	IRP	MACRO	
Listing	.CREF	PAGE	TITLE
	.LALL	.SALL	.XALL
	.LFCOND	.SFCOND	.XCREF
	.LIST	SUBTTL	.XLIST
	%OUT	.TFCOND	

Figure 5.7 Pseudo-ops of IBM's 8088 macroassembler. (*Courtesy International Business Machine Corporation*)

based on the type of operation they specify to the assembler. These categories are the *data pseudo-ops, conditional pseudo-ops, macro pseudo-ops,* and *listing pseudo-ops.* Notice that each category contains a number of different pseudo-ops. Here we will consider only a subset of the pseudo-ops in these categories, a subset that represents those used most frequently. For information on those pseudo-ops not covered here, the reader should consult the manual provided with IBM's 8088 macroassembler.

Data Pseudo-Ops

The function of the pseudo-ops in the data pseudo-op group is to define values for constants, variables, and labels. Other functions that can be performed by these pseudo-ops are to assign a size to variables and to reserve storage locations for them in memory. The most commonly used pseudo-ops to handle these types of data operations are those listed in Fig. 5.8.

The first two data pseudo-ops in Fig. 5.8 are *equate* and *equal to.* Their pseudo-opcodes are EQU and =, respectively. Both these pseudo-ops can be used to assign a constant value to a symbol. For example, the symbol AA can be set equal to 0100_{16} with the equate statement

AA EQU 0100H

The value of the operand can also be assigned using expressions such as those discussed in section 5.3. Another example of the EQU pseudo-op, which uses an arithmetic expression to define the operand, is

BB EQU AA+5H

In this statement, the symbol BB is assigned the value of symbol AA plus 5.

Pseudo-op	Meaning	Function
EQU	Equate	Assign a permanent value to a symbol
=	Equal to	Set or redefine the value of a symbol
DB	Define byte	Define or initialize byte size variables or locations
DW	Define word	Define or initialize word size (2 byte) variables or locations
DD	Define double word	Define or initialize double word size (4 byte) variables or locations

Figure 5.8 Data pseudo-ops.

Thus its value will turn out to be 0105_{16}. These two operations can also be done using the = pseudo-op. This gives the statements

```
AA  =  0100H
BB  =  AA+5H
```

Once these values are assigned to AA and BB, they can be referenced elsewhere in the program by just using the symbol.

The difference between the EQU and = pseudo-ops lies in the fact that the values assigned to the symbol using EQU cannot be changed, whereas when = is used to define the symbol its value can be changed later in the program. For instance, in the first case AA and BB are defined as follows

```
AA  EQU  0100 H
BB  EQU  AA+5H
        •
        •
        •
BB  EQU  AA+10H   ;This is illegal
```

Here AA is set equal to 0100_{16} and BB to 0105_{16}; the value of BB cannot be changed with the third EQU statement. On the other hand, if we use the = pseudo-ops as follows

```
AA = 0100H
BB = AA+ 5H
    •
    •
    •
BB = AA+ 10H   ;This is legal
```

BB is assigned the new value of AA+10H as the third = pseudo-op is processed by the assembler.

The other three pseudo-ops given in Fig. 5.8 are *define byte* (DB), *define word* (DW), and *define double word* (DD). The function of these pseudo-ops is to define the size of variables as being byte, word, or double word in length and to assign them initial values. If the initial values of a variable is not known, the DB, DW, or DD statement allocates a byte, word, or double word of memory to the variable name.

An example of the DB pseudo-op is

```
CC  DB  7
```

Here variable CC is defined as byte size and assigned the value 7. It is important to note that the value assigned with a DB, DW, or DD statement must not be larger than the maximum number that can be stored in the specified-size storage location. For instance, for a byte-size variable, the maximum decimal values are 255 for an unsigned number and $+127$ or -128 for a signed number.

Here is another example

```
EE  DB  ?
```

In this case, a byte of memory is allocated to the variable EE, but no value is assigned to it. Notice that use of a ? as the operand means that an initial value is not to be assigned.

Look at another example

```
MESSAGE  DB  'JASBIR'
```

Here each character in the string JASBIR is allocated a byte in memory, and these bytes are initialized with the ASCII values for the characters. This is the way ASCII data are assigned to a name.

If we need to initialize a large block of storage locations with the same value, the macroassembler provides a way of using the define byte, word, or double-word pseudo-ops to repeat a value. An example is the statement

```
TABLE_A  DB  10  DUP(?),5  DUP(7)
```

This statement causes the assembler to allocate 15 bytes of memory for TABLE_A. The first ten bytes of this block of memory are left uninitialized and the next five bytes are all initialized with the value 7. Notice that use of *duplicate* (DUP) tells the assembler to duplicate the value enclosed in parentheses a number of times equal to the number that precedes DUP.

If each element of the table was to be initialized to a different value, the DB command is written in a different way. For example, the command

```
TABLE_B  DB  0,1,2,3,4,5,6,7,8,9
```

sets up a table called TABLE_B and assigns to its ten storage locations the decimal values 0 through 9.

Segment Control Pseudo-Ops

In Chapter 3 we found that memory for the 8088 microprocessor is partitioned into four kinds of segments: the code segment, data segment, extra segment, and stack segment. The code segment is where 8088 machine-code instructions are stored, the data and extra segments are for storage of data, and the stack segment is for a temporary storage location called the stack. Using the *segment-control pseudo-ops* in Fig. 5.9, the statements of a source program

Pseudo-op	Function
SEGMENT	Defines the beginning of a segment and specifies its kind, at what type of address boundary it is to be stored in memory, and how it is to be positioned with respect to other similar segments in memory
ENDS	Specifies the end of a segment
ASSUME	Specifies the segment address register for a given segment

Figure 5.9 Segment pseudo-ops.

written for the 8088 can be partitioned and assigned to a specific memory segment. These pseudo-ops can be used to specify the beginning and end of a segment in a source program and assign to them attributes such as a starting address boundary, the kind of segment, and how the segment is to be combined with other segments of the same name.

The beginning of a segment is identified by the *segment* (SEGMENT) pseudo-op and its end is marked by the *end of segment* (ENDS) pseudo-op. Here is an example of a segment definition

```
SEGA  SEGMENT    PARA  PUBLIC  'CODE'
      MOV        AX,BX
        .
        .
SEGA  ENDS
```

As shown, the information between the two pseudo-op statements would be the instructions of the assembly language program.

In this example, SEGA is the name given to the segment. The pseudo-op SEGMENT is followed by the operand PARA PUBLIC 'CODE'. Here *paragraph* (PARA) defines that this segment is to be aligned in memory on a 16-byte address boundary. This part of the operand is called the *align-type* attribute. There are other align-type entries that can be used instead of PARA. They are given in Fig. 5.10 with a brief description of their function.

Attribute	Function
PARA	Segment begins on a 16 byte address boundary in memory (4 LSBs of the address are equal to 0)
BYTE	Segment begins anywhere in memory
WORD	Segment begins on a word (2 byte) address boundary in memory (LSB of the address is 0)
PAGE	Segment begins on a 256 byte address boundary in memory (8 LSBs of the address are equal to 0)

Figure 5.10 Align-type attributes.

No specific of align type, you will get Para type

Attribute	Function
PUBLIC	Concatenates segments with the same name
COMMON	Overlaps from the beginning segments with the same name
AT [expression]	Locates the segment at the 16-bit paragraph number evaluated from the expression
STACK	The segment is part of the run-time stack segment
MEMORY	Locates the segment at an address above all other segments

Figure 5.11 Combine-type attributes.

PUBLIC, which follows PARA in the operand of the example SEGMENT pseudo-op, defines what is called a *combine-type* attribute. It specifies that this segment is to be concatenated with all other segments that are assigned the name SEGA to generate one physical segment called SEGA. Other combine-type attributes are shown in Fig. 5.11.

The last part of the operand in the SEGMENT statement is 'CODE'; it specifies that the segment is a code segment. This entry is called a *class* attribute. All of the allowed segment classes are shown in Fig. 5.12.

At the end of the group of statements that are to be assigned to the code segment, there must be an ENDS pseudo-op. In Fig. 5.9 we find that this statement is used to mark the end of the segment. ENDS must also be preceded by the segment name, which is SEGA in our example.

The third pseudo-op in Fig. 5.9 is *assume* (ASSUME). It is used to assign the segment registers which hold the base addresses to the program segments. For instance, with the statement

ASSUME   CS:SEGA,DS:SEGB,SS:SEGC

we specify that register CS holds the base address for segment SEGA, register DS holds the base address for segment SEGB, and register SS holds the base address for segment SEGC. The ASSUME pseudo-op is written at the beginning of a code segment just after the SEGMENT pseudo-op.

Figure 5.13 shows the general structure of a segment assignment using the segment control pseudo-ops.

Attribute	Function
CODE	Specifies the code segment
DATA	Specifies the data segment
STACK	Specifies the stack segment
EXTRA	Specifies the extra segment

Figure 5.12 Class attributes.

```
SEGA      SEGMENT     PARA PUBLIC 'CODE'
          ASSUME      CS:SEGA
          MOV         AX,BX
            .
            .
            .
SEGA      ENDS
```

Figure 5.13 Example using segment control pseudo-ops.

Modular Programming Pseudo-Ops

For the purpose of development, larger programs are broken down into smaller segments called *modules*. Typically, each module implements a specific function and has its own code segment and data segment. However, it is common that during the execution of a module a part of some other module may need to be called for execution or that data that resides in another module may need to be accessed for processing. To support capabilities such that a section of code in one module can be executed from another module or for data to be passed between modules, IBM's macroassembler provides *modular programming pseudo-ops*. The most frequently used modular programming pseudo-ops are listed in Fig. 5.14.

A section of program that can be called for execution from other modules is called a *procedure*. Just like for the definition of a segment of a program, the beginning and end of a procedure must be marked with pseudo-op statements. The beginning of the procedure is marked by the *procedure* (PROC) pseudo-op and its end by the *end of procedure* (ENDP) pseudo-op.

There are two kinds of procedures: a *near procedure* and a *far procedure*. When a near procedure is called into operation, only the code offset address (IP) is saved on the stack. Therefore, a near procedure can only be called from the same code segment. On the other hand, when a far procedure is called, both the contents of the code segment (CS) register and the code offset (IP) are saved on

Pseudo-op	Function
proc-name PROC [NEAR]	Defines the beginning of a near-proc procedure
proc-name PROC FAR	Defines the beginning of a far-proc procedure
proc-name ENDP	Defines the end of a procedure
PUBLIC Symbol[.......]	The defined symbols can be referenced from other modules
EXTRN name:type[....]	The specified symbols are defined in other modules and are to be used in this module

Figure 5.14 Modular programming pseudo-ops.

the stack. For this reason, a far procedure can be called from any code segment. Depending upon the kind of procedure, the *return* (RET) instruction at the end of the procedure restores either IP or both IP and CS from the stack.

If a procedure can be called from other modules, its name must be made *public* by using the PUBLIC pseudo-op. Typically this is done just before entering the procedure. Thus the complete structure for defining a procedure with name SUB_NEAR will be

```
                    PUBLIC   SUB_NEAR
      SUB_NEAR  PROC
                    MOV      AX,BX
                      •
                      •
                    RET
      SUB_NEAR  ENDP
```

In this example the PROC does not have either the NEAR or FAR attribute in its operand field. When no attribute is specified as an operand, NEAR is assumed as the default attribute by the assembler. In this way, we see that this procedure can only be called from other modules in the same code segment.

The structure of a far procedure that can be called from modules in other segments would be

```
                    PUBLIC   SUB_FAR
      SUB_FAR   PROC     FAR
                    MOV      AX,BX
                      •
                      •
                    RET
      SUB_FAR   ENDP
```

If a procedure in another module is to be called from the current module, its name must be declared external in the current procedure by using the *external reference* (EXTRN) pseudo-op. It is also important to know whether this call is to a module in the same code segment or in a different code segment. Depending upon the code segments, the name of the procedure must be assigned either a NEAR or FAR attribute as part of the EXTRN statement.

The example in Fig. 5.15 illustrates the use of the EXTRN pseudo-op. Here we find that an external call is made from module 2 to the procedure SUB that resides in module 1. Therefore, the procedure SUB is defined as PUBLIC in module 1. Notice that the two modules have different code segments, which are called CSEG1 and CSEG2. Thus the external call in module 2 is to a far procedure. Therefore the PROC pseudo-op for SUB in module 1 and the external label definition of SUB in module 2 have the FAR attribute attached to them.

	PUBLIC	SUB			EXTRN	SUB:FAR
CSEG1	SEGMENT			CSEG2	SEGMENT	
	.				.	
	.				.	
SUB	PROC	FAR			CALL	SUB
	MOV	AX,BX			.	
	.				.	
	.				.	
	RET				.	
SUB	ENDP				.	
	.			CSEG2	ENDS	
	.					
	.					
CSEG1	ENDS					

| Module 1 | Module 2 |

Figure 5.15 An example showing use of the EXTRN pseudo-op.

ORG Pseudo-Op for Memory Usage Control

If the machine code generated by the assembler must reside in a specific part of the memory address space, an *origin* (ORG) pseudo-op can be used to specify the starting point of that memory area. In Fig. 5.16 we see that the operand in the ORG statement can be an expression. The value that results from this expression is the address at which the machine code is to begin loading. For example, the statement

ORG   100H

simply tells the assembler that the machine code for subsequent instructions is to be placed in memory starting at address 100_{16} of the current code segment. This pseudo-op statement is normally located near the beginning of the program.

Pseudo-op	Function
ORG [expression]	Specifies the memory address starting from which the machine code must be placed
END [expression]	Specifies the end of the source program

Figure 5.16 ORG and END pseudo-ops.

current value

If specific memory locations must be skipped—for example, because they are in a read-only area of memory—one can use ORG pseudo-ops as follows

ORG   100H
ORG $+201H

in which case memory locations 100_{16} to 300_{16} are skipped and the machine code of the program can start at address 301_{16}.

The End of Program Pseudo-Op—END

The *end* (END) pseudo-op, which is also described in Fig. 5.16, tells the assembler when to stop assembling. It must always be included at the end of the source program. Optionally we can specify the starting point of the program with an expression in the operand field of the END statement. For instance, an END statement can be written as

END   PROG_BLOCK

where PROG_BLOCK identifies the beginning address of the program.

Listing Control Pseudo-Ops

The last group of pseudo-ops we will consider are called the *listing control pseudo-ops*. The most widely used pseudo-ops in this group are shown in Fig. 5.17. The purpose of the listing control pseudo-ops is to give the programmer some options related to the way in which source program listings are produced by the assembler. For instance, we may want to set the print output such that a certain number of lines are printed per page. Moreover, we may want to title the pages of the listing with certain information, such as the name of the program.

The *page* (PAGE) pseudo-op lets us set the page width and length of the

lines per page & characters

Pseudo-op	Function
PAGE operand_1 operand_2	Selects the number of lines printed per page and the maximum number of characters printed per line in the listing
TITLE text	Prints 'text' on the second line of each page of the listing
SUBTTL text	Prints 'text' on the third line of each page of the listing

Figure 5.17 Listing control pseudo-ops.

source listing produced as part of the assembly process. For example, if the PAGE pseudo-op

PAGE 50 100

is encountered at the beginning of a source program, then each printed page will have 50 lines and up to 100 characters in a line. The first operand, which specifies the number of lines per page, can be any number from 10 through 255. The second operand, which specifies the maximum number of characters per line, can range from 60 through 132. The default values for these parameters are 66 lines per page and 80 characters per line. The default parameters are selected if the pseudo-op is specified as just

PAGE

Chapter and page numbers are always printed at the top of each page in a source listing. They are in the form

[chapter number] – [page number]

As the source listing is produced by the assembler, the page number automatically increments each time a full page of listing information is generated. On the other hand, the chapter number does not change as the listing is generated. The only way to change the chapter number is by using the pseudo-op

PAGE +

When this form of the PAGE pseudo-op is processed by the assembler, it increments the chapter count and at the same time resets the page number to 1.

The second pseudo-op in Fig. 5.17 is *title* (TITLE). When this pseudo-op is included in a program, it causes the text in the operand field to be printed on the second line of each page of the source listing. Similarly, the third pseudo-op, *subtitle* (SUBTTL), prints the text included in the pseudo-op statement on the third line of each page.

Example Source Program Using Pseudo-Ops

In order to have our first experience in using pseudo-ops in a source program, let us look at the program in Fig. 5.18. This program is written to copy a given block of data from a location in memory known as the source block to another block location known as the destination block. This program is similar to the one we used as an example in Chapter 4; however, here we have included pseudo-ops to prepare the program for assembly by IBM's 8088 macroassem-

```
TITLE    BLOCK-MOVE PROGRAM

COMMENT *This program moves a block of specified number of bytes
        from one place to another place*

;Define constants used in program

        N          =          16
        BLK1ADDR=             100H              ;Source block offset address
        BLK2ADDR=             120H              ;Destination block offset addr
        DATASEGADDR=          0020H             ;Data segment start address


STACK_SEG          SEGMENT          STACK 'STACK'
                   DB               128 DUP(?)
STACK_SEG          ENDS


CODE_SEG           SEGMENT          'CODE'
BLOCK    PROC      FAR
         ASSUME    CS:CODE_SEG,SS:STACK_SEG

;To return to DEBUG program put return address on the stack

         PUSH      DS
         MOV       AX, 0
         PUSH      AX

;Set up the data segment address

         MOV       AX,DATASEGADDR
         MOV       DS, AX

;Set up the source and destination offset adresses

         MOV       SI, BLK1ADDR
         MOV       DI, BLK2ADDR

;Set up the count of bytes to be moved

         MOV       CX, N

;Copy source block to destination block

NXTPT:   MOV       AH, [SI]
         MOV       [DI], AH
         INC       SI
         INC       DI
         DEC       CX
         JNZ       NXTPT
         RET                                    ;Return to DEBUG program
BLOCK    ENDP
CODE_SEG     ENDS
         END       BLOCK                        ;End of program
```

Figure 5.18 Example program that employs pseudo-op statements.

bler. In the sections of this chapter that follow, we will use this program to learn the various aspects of program development, such as creating a source file, assembling, linking, and debugging. For now we will just look at the pseudo-ops used in the program.

The program starts with a TITLE pseudo-op statement. The text "BLOCK_MOVE PROGRAM" that is included in this statement will be printed on the second line of each page of the source listing. This text should be limited to 60 characters. The second and third statements in the program are also a pseudo-op. This is a *comment* pseudo-op and is used to introduce descriptive comments into the program. Note that it begins with the pseudo-opcode COMMENT and is followed by the comment enclosed within the delimiter "*". This comment gives a brief description of the function of the program.

There is another way of including comments in a program. This is by using ";" followed by the text of the comment. The next line in the program is an example of this type of comment. It indicates that the next part of the program is used to define variables that are used in the program. Four "equal to" (=) pseudo-op statements follow the comment. Notice that they equate N to the value 16_{10}, BLK1ADDR to the value 100_{16}, BLK2ADDR to the value 120_{16}, and DATASEGADDR to the value 020_{16}.

There are two segments in the program: the stack segment and the code segment. The next three pseudo-op statements define the stack segment. They are

```
STACK_SEG  SEGMENT  STACK 'STACK'
           DB            128  DUP ?
STACK_SEG  ENDS
```

In the first statement, the stack segment is assigned the name STACK_SEG; the second statement allocates a block of 128 bytes of memory for use as stack and leaves this area uninitialized.

The code segment is defined between the statements

```
CODE_SEG  SEGMENT      'CODE'
```

and

```
CODE_SEG  ENDS
```

Here CODE_SEG is the name we have used for the code segment. At the beginning of the code segment an ASSUME pseudo-op is used to specify the base registers for the code and stack segments. Notice that CS is given as the base register for the code segment and SS as the base register for the stack segment.

We also find at the end of the program an END pseudo-op. It identifies the end of the program and BLOCK in this statement defines the starting address of the source program. Processing of this statement tells the assembler that the assembly is complete.

A PROC pseudo-op is included at the beginning of the source program and the ENDP pseudo-op at the end of the program. This makes the program segment into a procedure that can be referenced as a module in a larger program.

5.5 CREATING AN ASSEMBLER SOURCE FILE

Now that we have introduced assembly language syntax, the pseudo-ops, and an example of an assembly language program, let us continue by looking at how the source-program file is created on the IBM PC. Source-program files are generated using a program called an *editor*. Basically two types of editors are available on computers: the *screen editor* and the *line editor*. They differ in that a screen editor works on a full screen of text at a time, while a line editor works on one text line at a time. The editor program provided in the IBM PC's DOS 2.1 operating system is called *EDLIN;* it is a line editor. In this book we have assumed that the reader is already familiar with the commands of the DOS operating system and the use of the EDLIN program. For this reason, we will just briefly describe the use of EDLIN in creating a source-program file. If additional details are required, the "Disk Operating System" manual that is provided with version 2.1 of the operating system should be consulted.

The diagram in Fig. 5.19 outlines the sequence of events that take place during a typical editing session. We are interested in creating, with the editor, a source program in a file called BLOCK.SRC; this file will be stored on a data diskette in drive B. To bring up the editor, the DOS diskette is placed in drive A and a data diskette in drive B. Once DOS is booted up, it displays the prompt

A>_

At this point we enter the command that follows to bring up the line-editor program

A>EDLIN B:BLOCK.SRC   (↵)

In response to this input, the EDLIN program is first loaded from the operating system diskette and then executed. Once EDLIN is running, it checks to determine whether or not the file BLOCK.SRC already exists on the data diskette. If it does exist, the file is loaded into memory and the response "End of input file" is displayed; on the next line the prompt *_ is displayed. On the other hand, if the file does not exist, "New file" is displayed and it is followed by the prompt *_.

Let us assume that BLOCK.SRC is a new file. Then the system will respond with the prompt

New file

*_

As shown in Fig. 5.19, the next input should be I followed by (↵). This is the *insert line* command; its entry causes line number 1:* to be displayed. We are now in the *line input mode* of editor operation. This is the mode used when creating

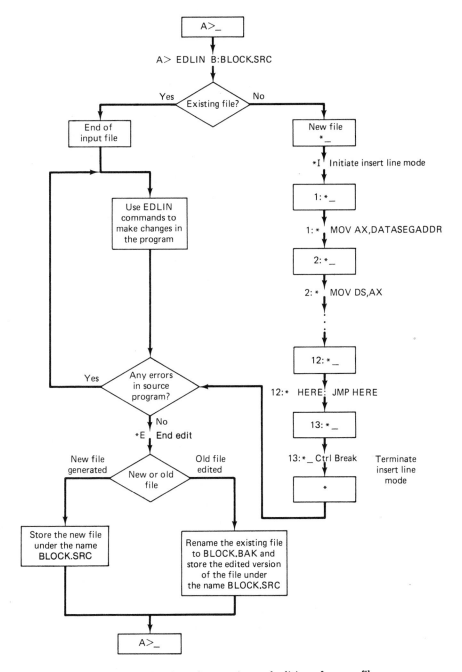

Figure 5.19 Flowchart for creating and editing of source files.

new source-program files. Next the text for the first line of the program is keyed in following the line number; then the (↵) key is depressed. For instance, in Fig. 5.19 we entered the statement

1:＊   MOV AX,DATASEGADDR   (↵)

When (↵) is depressed, the entry of line 1 is completed and line number 2:＊ is displayed. Its text is now entered and (↵) depressed once more. For example, in Fig. 5.19 we find

2:＊   MOV DS,AX   (↵)

Repeating this sequence, the complete program is entered line by line. Here are some additional line entries for the program

3:＊   MOV SI,BLK1ADDR   (↵)
4:＊   MOV DI,BLK2ADDR   (↵)
•   •   •   •
•   •   •   •
11:＊   JNZ NXTPT   (↵)

After the last line of the program is entered, we must come out of the line input mode. This is done by depressing the "Ctrl" (control) and "Break" (break) keys together. Notice on the keyboard of the PC that the break key is marked "Scroll Lock" on the top and "Break" on the front. Depression of these two keys together takes EDLIN out of the line input mode and puts it into the *edit mode*. Figure 5.20 shows the information displayed during the entry of this segment of program.

Once we are in the edit mode, the program should be looked over closely for errors. If errors are found, they can be corrected using other editor com-

```
A>EDLIN B:BLOCK.SRC
New file
*I
     1:*       MOV      AX,DATASEGADDR
     2:*       MOV      DS,AX
     3:*       MOV      SI,BLK1ADDR
     4:*       MOV      DI,BLK1ADDR
     5:*       MOV      CX,N
     6:*NXTPT: MOV      AH,[SI]
     7:*       MOV      [DI],AH
     8:*       INC      SI
     9:*       INC      DI
    10:*       DEC      CX
    11:*       JNZ      NXTPT
    12:*^C

*E

A>
```

Figure 5.20 Entry of example program with the EDLIN editor.

Command	Format
Append Lines	[n] A
Copy Lines	[line] ,[line] ,line,[count] C
Delete Lines	[line] [,line] D
Edit Line	[line]
End Edit	E
Insert Lines	[line] I
List Lines	[line] [,line] L
Quit Edit	Q
Move Lines	[line] ,[line] ,lineM
Page	[line] [,line] P
Replace Text	[line] [,line] [?] R [string] [<F6>string]
Search Text	[line] [,line] [?] S [string]
Transfer Lines	[line] T filename [.ext]
Write Lines	[n] W

Figure 5.21 EDLIN commands. (*Courtesy International Business Machine Corporation*)

mands. The commands provided in EDLIN and the syntax in which they must be entered are shown in Fig. 5.21. Notice that commands are provided that let us delete a line or lines, insert a new line or lines, list lines, delete or insert characters in a line, and replace or search for a string of characters. For instance, after loading a program that already exists in a file on the data diskette, the "List Lines" command can be used to display the lines of the program. The file created in our earlier example can be reloaded and displayed with the command sequence

```
A>EDLIN  B:BLOCK.SRC   (↵)
1,11 L                 (↵)
```

A printout of the displayed information is shown in Fig. 5.22.

```
A>EDLIN  B:BLOCK.SRC
End of input file
*1,11L
      1:*      MOV     AX,DATASEGADDR
      2:       MOV     DS,AX
      3:       MOV     SI,BLK1ADDR
      4:       MOV     DI,BLK1ADDR
      5:       MOV     CX,N
      6: NXTPT: MOV    AH,[SI]
      7:       MOV     [DI],AH
      8:       INC     SI
      9:       INC     DI
     10:       DEC     CX
     11:       JNZ     NXTPT
*Q
Abort edit (Y/N)? Y
A>
```

Figure 5.22 Listing of the example source program produced with the List Lines command.

After all corrections have been made, the editing session is complete and it must be ended. The "End Edit" command is used for this purpose. Looking at Fig. 5.19, we see that it is entered as

⋆E (↵)

The response of EDLIN to this entry depends on whether the current editing was done on an existing file or a new file that was just being created. In Fig. 5.19 we find that if it is a new file, such as in our earlier example, the edit mode is terminated and the lines of text that were entered are stored in a file called BLOCK.SRC and then the DOS prompt A > is displayed.

On the other hand, if we were editing an existing file called BLOCK.SRC, the original file (before editing) is renamed using the original file name with the extension BAK. This file, BLOCK.BAK, is called the *backup file*. Next, the edited version of the program is saved in the file BLOCK.SRC. Then the DOS prompt A > is displayed. The creation of this backup file provides us with a way to get back to the original version of the program if necessary. It should be noted that a file with the extension BAK cannot be edited. However, this backup file can either be copied to another file or have its extension changed with a RENAME command, and then it can be edited.

5.6 ASSEMBLING SOURCE PROGRAMS WITH MASM

Up to this point in the chapter, we have studied the steps involved in writing a program, the assembly language syntax and pseudo-op statements provided in IBM's 8088 macroassembler, the structure of an assembly language program, and how to create a source program using the EDLIN editor. Here we continue by learning how to bring up the 8088 assembler, use it to assemble a source-program file into an object-code module, and examine the outputs that are produced by the assembler.

Earlier we found that an *assembler* is a program used to convert a file that contains an assembly language source program to its equivalent object file of 8088 machine code. Figure 5.23 shows that the input to the assembler program is the assembly language source program. This is the program that is to be assembled. The source file is read by the assembler program from its file on the diskette and translated into three outputs. As shown in Fig. 5.23, these outputs are the *object module,* the *source listing,* and a *cross-reference table.*

Initiating the Assembly Process

To use the macroassembler we first insert the diskette that contains it into drive A and a data diskette that contains the source file to be assembled into

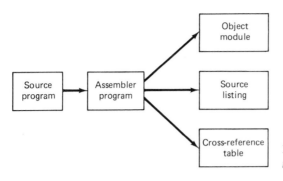

Figure 5.23 Assembling a source program.

drive B. The data diskette must not be write protected. Now the assembler program is loaded by keying in

A > MASM   (↵)

In response to this entry, the following prompt is displayed.

Source filename[.ASM]:

Now we must enter the name of the source file with its extension and then depress (↵). Let us assume that we are assembling the source program that was shown in Fig. 5.18 and that its file was assigned the name BLOCK.SRC. Therefore, the input is

Source filename[.ASM]:B:BLOCK.SRC   (↵)

Next the assembler program displays a second prompt, which asks for entry of the file name (with extension) that is to be used to save the object-code module that it creates during the assembly process. This prompt is

Object filename[BLOCK.OBJ]:

Notice that the assembler automatically fills in the file name entered for the source file and appends this file name with the default extension OBJ. In our example, the file is to be created on the data diskette in drive B. For this reason, we will reenter the name for the object file with drive B specified.

Object filename[BLOCK.OBJ]:B:BLOCK.OBJ   (↵)

Actually, the response can simply be

Object filename[BLOCK.OBJ]:B: (↵)

After this entry is made, a third prompt is displayed. This prompt is

Source listing[NUL.LST]:

Note that a file name of NUL.LST is automatically assigned for the source list-ing if the (↵) key is depressed without entry of an alternate file name. This de-fault file name causes suppression of a source listing, and none will be pro-duced. If we want the assembler to create a source listing during the assembly process, we can enter a name for a listing file. Let us use a file BLOCK.LST to save our source listing. This is done by entering

Source listing[NUL.LST]:B:BLOCK.LST   (↵)

Another way of issuing the source listing response lets us just print the listing instead of saving it in a file. This is done by simply entering LPT1 in place of a file name.

The last prompt displayed is for the name of a cross-reference table file. This prompt is

Cross reference[NUL.CRF]:

Again, depressing (↵) without entering a file name causes creation of a cross-reference file to be suppressed. However, for our example, let us create one by assigning the name BLOCK.CRF to the file. This is done by making the entry

Cross reference[NUL.CRF]:B:BLOCK.CRF   (↵)

This completes the input needed to initiate the assembler.

As soon as the cross-reference file name entry is made, the assembly pro-cess begins and runs through to completion without any additional entries. First the contents of the source file are read from the file BLOCK.SRC on the diskette in drive B; it is translated and information for the listing and cross-reference table is produced; finally the object code, source listing, and cross-reference table are saved on the diskette in drive B in files BLOCK.OBJ, BLOCK.LST, and BLOCK.CRF, respectively. The displayed information for the start-up and execution of the assembler for our example program is shown in Fig. 5.24(a), the contents of the source-code file is shown in Fig. 5.24(b), the source listing file in Fig. 5.24(c), and the cross-reference file in Fig. 5.24(d). We printed the contents of these files with the TYPE command in DOS 2.1.

```
A>MASM
The IBM Personal Computer MACRO Assembler
Version 1.00 (C)Copyright IBM Corp 1981

Source filename [.ASM]: B:BLOCK.SRC
Object filename [BLOCK.OBJ]: B:
Source listing  [NUL.LST]: B:BLOCK
Cross reference [NUL.CRF]: B:BLOCK

Warning Severe
Errors  Errors
0       0

A>
```

```
A>TYPE B:BLOCK.SRC

TITLE   BLOCK-MOVE PROGRAM

        PAGE    ,132

COMMENT *This program moves a block of specified number of bytes
        from one place to another place*


;Define constants used in this program

        N          =        16           ;Bytes to be moved
        BLK1ADDR=            100H         ;Source block offset address
        BLK2ADDR=            120H         ;Destination block offset addr
        DATASEGADDR=        0020H         ;Data segment start address


STACK_SEG       SEGMENT         STACK 'STACK'
                DB              64 DUP(?)
STACK_SEG       ENDS


CODE_SEG        SEGMENT         'CODE'
BLOCK           PROC            FAR
        ASSUME  CS:CODE_SEG,SS:STACK_SEG

;To return to DEBUG program put return address on the stack

        PUSH    DS
        MOV     AX, 0
        PUSH    AX

;Set up the data segment address

        MOV     AX, DATASEGADDR
        MOV     DS, AX

;Set up the source and destination offset adresses

        MOV     SI, BLK1ADDR
        MOV     DI, BLK2ADDR

;Set up the count of bytes to be moved

        MOV     CX, N

;Copy source block to destination block

NXTPT:  MOV     AH, [SI]                 ;Move a byte
        MOV     [DI], AH
        INC     SI                       ;Update pointers
        INC     DI
        DEC     CX                       ;Update byte counter
        JNZ     NXTPT                    ;Repeat for next byte
        RET                              ;Return to DEBUG program
BLOCK           ENDP
CODE_SEG        ENDS
        END     BLOCK                    ;End of program

A>
```

(b)

Figure 5.24 (a) Display sequence for assembly of a program; (b) source program file; (c) source listing file; (d) cross-reference table file.

A>TYPE B:BLOCK.LST

```
  The IBM Personal Computer Assembler 01-15-84              PAGE    1-1
  BLOCK-MOVE PROGRAM


  1
  2
  3                                     TITLE    BLOCK-MOVE PROGRAM
  4
  5                                              PAGE    ,132
  6
  7                                     COMMENT *This program moves a block of specified number of bytes
  8                                              from one place to another place*
  9
 10
 11                                     ;Define constants used in this program
 12
 13      = 0010                         N          =        16                 ;Bytes to be moved
 14      = 0100                         BLK1ADDR=            100H               ;Source block offset address
 15      = 0120                         BLK2ADDR=            120H               ;Destination block offset addr
 16      = 0020                         DATASEGADDR=         0020H              ;Data segment start address
 17
 18
 19      0000                           STACK_SEG           SEGMENT            STACK 'STACK'
 20      0000       40 [                                    DB                 64 DUP(?)
 21                        ??
 22                              ]
 23
 24      0040                           STACK_SEG           ENDS
 25
 26
 27      0000                           CODE_SEG            SEGMENT            'CODE'
 28      0000                           BLOCK               PROC               FAR
 29                                                ASSUME  CS:CODE_SEG,SS:STACK_SEG
 30
 31                                     ;To return to DEBUG program put return address on the stack
 32
 33      0000  1E                                           PUSH     DS
 34      0001  BB 0000                                      MOV      AX, 0
 35      0004  50                                           PUSH     AX
 36
 37                                     ;Set up the data segment address
 38
 39      0005  BB 0020                                      MOV      AX, DATASEGADDR
 40      0008  8E D8                                        MOV      DS, AX
 41
 42                                     ;Set up the source and destination offset adresses
 43
 44      000A  BE 0100                                      MOV      SI, BLK1ADDR
 45      000D  BF 0120                                      MOV      DI, BLK2ADDR
 46
 47                                     ;Set up the count of bytes to be moved
 48
 49      0010  B9 0010                                      MOV      CX, N
 50
 51                                     ;Copy source block to destination block
 52
 53      0013  8A 24                    NXTPT:  MOV          AH, [SI]           ;Move a byte
```

(c)

Figure 5.24 (continued)

```
The IBM Personal Computer Assembler 01-15-84              PAGE    1-2
BLOCK-MOVE PROGRAM

54        0015  88 25                    MOV    [DI], AH
55        0017  46                       INC    SI             ;Update pointers
56        0018  47                       INC    DI
57        0019  49                       DEC    CX             ;Update byte counter
58        001A  75 F7                    JNZ    NXTPT          ;Repeat for next byte
59        001C  CB                       RET                   ;Return to DEBUG program
60        001D           BLOCK           ENDP
61        001D           CODE_SEG        ENDS
62                       END             BLOCK                 ;End of program
```

```
The IBM Personal Computer Assembler 01-15-84              PAGE    Symbols-1
BLOCK-MOVE PROGRAM


Segments and groups:

               N a m e                 Size    align   combine class

CODE_SEG . . . . . . . . . . . .       001D    PARA    NONE    'CODE'
STACK_SEG. . . . . . . . . . . .       0040    PARA    STACK   'STACK'

Symbols:

               N a m e                 Type    Value   Attr

BLK1ADDR . . . . . . . . . . . .       Number  0100
BLK2ADDR . . . . . . . . . . . .       Number  0120
BLOCK. . . . . . . . . . . . . .       F PROC  0000    CODE_SEG       Length =001D
DATASEGADDR. . . . . . . . . . .       Number  0020
N. . . . . . . . . . . . . . . .       Number  0010
NXTPT. . . . . . . . . . . . . .       L NEAR  0013    CODE_SEG

Warning Severe
Errors  Errors
0       0

A>
```

(c)

Figure 5.24 (continued)

```
Symbol Cross Reference              (# is definition)        Cref-1

BLK1ADDR . . . . . . . . . . . .     14#    44
BLK2ADDR . . . . . . . . . . . .     15#    45
BLOCK. . . . . . . . . . . . . .     28#    60      62

CODE . . . . . . . . . . . . . .     27
CODE_SEG . . . . . . . . . . . .     27#    29      61

DATASEGADDR. . . . . . . . . . .     16#    39

N. . . . . . . . . . . . . . . .     13#    49
NXTPT. . . . . . . . . . . . . .     53#    58

STACK. . . . . . . . . . . . . .     19
STACK_SEG. . . . . . . . . . . .     19#    24      29

A>
```

(d)

Figure 5.24 (continued)

The default file extensions specified in the prompts can also be used. Assuming that the source file has the extension ASM, the responses to the prompts would be

```
Source filename[.ASM]:B:BLOCK      (↵)
Object filename[BLOCK.OBJ]:B:      (↵)
Source listing[NUL.LST]:           (↵)
Cross reference[NUL.CRF]:          (↵)
```

Initiating the assembler with this sequence results in no source listing or cross-reference file.

If the files reside on the diskette in drive A instead of drive B, the responses to the prompts could be

```
Source filename[.ASM]:BLOCK        (↵)
Object filename[BLOCK.OBJ]:        (↵)
Source listing[NUL.LST]:LPT1       (↵)
Cross reference[NUL.CRF]:          (↵)
```

In this example, we have elected to print the source listing instead of saving it in a file.

Alternate Approach for Calling up the Assembler

Once familiar with the use of the assembler, a shorter entry sequence can be used to call it up. This is done by specifying the file names in the entry sequence that calls MASM from DOS 2.1. For our original example, the command would be issued as

A > MASM   B:BLOCK.SRC,B:BLOCK.OBJ,B:BLOCK.LST,B:BLOCK.CRF   (↵)

If any of the default names are to be used, simply enter a comma.

Syntax Errors in an Assembled File

If the assembler program identifies syntax errors in the source file while it is being assembled, the locations of the errors are marked in the source listing file with an error number and error message. Moreover, the total number of errors is displayed on the screen at the end of the assembly process. Looking at the displayed information for our assembly example in Fig. 5.24(a), we find that no errors occurred.

Figure 5.25(a) shows the response on the display when four syntax errors are found during the assembly process. The listing for the program, which is shown in Fig. 5.25(b), contains four syntax errors. Notice how the errors are marked in the source listing. For instance, in Fig. 5.25(b) we find error number 10 following the instruction DCR CX. Looking in Fig. 5.25(a), we find that this error message stands for a syntax error. The error that was made is that the mnemonic was spelled wrong. It should be DEC CX. The source program must first be edited to correct this error and the other three errors, and then it must be reassembled.

```
A>MASM
The IBM Personal Computer MACRO Assembler
Version 1.00 (C)Copyright IBM Corp 1981

Source filename [.ASM]: EBLOCK.SRC
Object filename [EBLOCK.OBJ]:
Source listing  [NUL.LST]: EBLOCK
Cross reference [NUL.CRF]: EBLOCK
                                      N                16              ;Bytes t
o be moved
  E r r o r    ---          10:Syntax error
                                 Set up the data segment address
  E r r o r    ---          10:Syntax error
  0010  8B 0E 0000 U                   MOV      CX, N
  E r r o r    ---           9:Symbol not defined
                                      DCR      CX                     ;Update
byte counter
  E r r o r    ---          10:Syntax error

Warning Severe
Errors  Errors
0        4

A>
```

(a)

Figure 5.25 (a) Displayed information for a source file with assembly syntax errors; (b) source listing for a file with syntax errors.

A>TYPE B:EBLOCK.LST

The IBM Personal Computer Assembler 06-24-84   PAGE   1-1
BLOCK-MOVE PROGRAM


```
                              TITLE   BLOCK-MOVE PROGRAM

                              PAGE    ,132

                              COMMENT *This program moves a block of specified number of bytes
                                       from one place to another place*


                              ;Define constants used in this program

                              N               16              ;Bytes to be moved
Error    ---        10
= 0100                        BLK1ADDR=       100H            ;Source block offset address
= 0120                        BLK2ADDR=       120H            ;Destination block offset addr
= 0020                        DATASEGADDR=    0020H           ;Data segment start address


0000                          STACK_SEG       SEGMENT         STACK 'STACK'
0000    40 [                                  DB              64 DUP(?)
            ??
                 ]

0040                          STACK_SEG       ENDS


0000                          CODE_SEG        SEGMENT         'CODE'
0000                          BLOCK           PROC            FAR
                                      ASSUME  CS:CODE_SEG,SS:STACK_SEG

                              ;To return to DEBUG program put return address on the stack

0000    1E                                    PUSH    DS
0001    B8 0000                               MOV     AX, O
0004    50                                    PUSH    AX

                              Set up the data segment address
Error    ---        10
0005    B8 0020                               MOV     AX, DATASEGADDR
0008    8E D8                                 MOV     DS, AX

                              ;Set up the source and destination offset adresses

000A    BE 0100                               MOV     SI, BLK1ADDR
000D    BF 0120                               MOV     DI, BLK2ADDR

                              ;Set up the count of bytes to be moved

0010    8B 0E 0000 U                          MOV     CX, N
Error    ---         9
```

(b)

Figure 5.25 (continued)

```
The IBM Personal Computer Assembler 06-24-84              PAGE    1-2
BLOCK-MOVE PROGRAM


                          ;Copy source block to destination block

0014  8A 24    NXTPT:  MOV     AH, [SI]              ;Move a byte
0016  88 25            MOV     [DI], AH
0018  46               INC     SI                    ;Update pointers
0019  47               INC     DI
                       DCR     CX                    ;Update byte counter
E r r o r  ---      10
001A  75 F8            JNZ     NXTPT                 ;Repeat for next byte
001C  CB               RET                           ;Return to DEBUG program
001D            BLOCK          ENDP
001D            CODE_SEG       ENDS
                       END     BLOCK                 ;End of program




The IBM Personal Computer Assembler 06-24-84              PAGE    Symbols-1
BLOCK-MOVE PROGRAM


Segments and groups:

              N a m e                    Size    align   combine class

CODE_SEG . . . . . . . . . . . .         001D    PARA    NONE    'CODE'
STACK_SEG. . . . . . . . . . .           0040    PARA    STACK   'STACK'

Symbols:

              N a m e                    Type    Value   Attr

BLK1ADDR . . . . . . . . . . . .         Number  0100
BLK2ADDR . . . . . . . . . . . .         Number  0120
BLOCK. . . . . . . . . . . . . .         F PROC  0000    CODE_SEG      Length =001D
DATASEGADDR. . . . . . . . . .           Number  0020
NXTPT. . . . . . . . . . . . .           L NEAR  0014    CODE_SEG

Warning Severe
Errors  Errors
0       4

A>
```

(b)

Figure 5.25 (continued)

Example 5.5

What is the meaning of the error code at line 0010 of the program source listing in Fig. 5.25(b)?

Solution:

Looking at Fig. 5.25(b) we get the error number as 9 and in Fig. 5.25(a) we see that it means that a symbol was not defined. The undefined symbol is N.

Object Module

The most important output produced by the assembler is in the object-code file. The contents of this file are called the object module; it is a machine-language version of the program. Even though the object module is the machine code for the source program, it cannot be directly run on the 8088. It must first be processed by the linker to create an executable run module.

Source Listing

Let us now look more closely at the source listing in Fig. 5.24(c). Notice that the first column gives the line numbers that were assigned to the statements when the source file was created on the EDLIN editor. The second column is the starting offset address of the machine-language instruction from the beginning of the current code segment. In the next column we find the bytes of machine code for the instructions. They are expressed in hexadecimal form. If an "R" is listed after a number, it means that an *external reference* exists and that the link operation may modify this value. The machine-code instructions are followed by the original source-code instructions in the next column, and the comments in the last column.

For instance, at line number 38 the machine code for the assembly language instruction MOV AX,DATASEGADDR is found. This instruction is encoded with 3 bytes and is

MOV   AX,DATASEGADDR = B80020H

A symbol table is also produced as part of the source listing. It is a list of all of the symbols defined in the program. The symbol table for our example program is shown at the bottom of the source listing in Fig. 5.24(c). Notice that the name of each symbol is listed along with its type (and length for data), value, and attribute. The types of symbols identified are *label, variable, number,* and *procedure.* For example, in Fig. 5.24(c) we find that the symbol BLK1ADDR is a number and its value is 0100_{16}. For this symbol, no attribute is indicated. On the other hand, for the symbol NXTPT, which is a near-label with value 0013_{16}, the attribute is CODE_SEG.

The source listing is a valuable aid in correcting errors in the program. For instance, earlier we found that syntax errors are marked into the source listing. Therefore, they can be easily found and corrected. Since both the source and corresponding machine code are provided in the source listing, it also serves as a valuable tool for identifying and correcting logical errors in the writing of the program.

Cross-Reference Table

The cross-reference table is also useful when debugging programs that contain logical errors. The cross-reference table is a table that tells the number of the line in the source program at which each symbol is defined and the number of each line in which it is referenced. The line number followed by the symbol # is the location at which the symbol is defined. For instance, in the table of Fig. 5.24(d), we find that the label NXTPT is defined in line 52 and is referenced in line 57.

Another use of the cross-reference table is when a program is to be modified in such a way that the name of a symbol must be changed. The cross-reference table can be used to find all of the locations where the symbol is used. In this way, they can be easily found and changed with the editor.

The cross-reference-table file produced by the assembler of the IBM PC is not in the correct form to be printed. This is because it is not yet an ASCII file. To convert it to ASCII form, we must use the CREF program in DOS 2.1. For instance, to convert the cross-reference file for our example to an ASCII file, we issue the command

A > CREF   B:BLOCK.REF B:BLOCK.CRF   (⏎)

This command reads the file BLOCK.CRF on the diskette in drive B as its input, converts it to an ASCII file, and outputs it to a new file called BLOCK.REF, also on the diskette in drive B. Now the file BLOCK.REF can be displayed or printed with the TYPE command. The command needed to do this is

A > TYPE B:BLOCK.REF   (⏎)

5.7 THE LINK PROGRAM—CREATING A RUN MODULE

In section 5.6 we indicated that the object module produced by the assembler is not yet an executable file. That is, in its current state it cannot be loaded with the DEBUG program and run on the 8088 microprocessor in the PC. To convert an object module to an executable machine-code file (*run module*), we must process it with a linker. The link operation for 8088 object code is performed by the *LINK program*, which is part of DOS 2.1.

Modular Programming

At this point we may ask the question, Why doesn't the macroassembler directly produce an executable run module? To answer this question, let us look into the real idea behind the use of the LINK program, *modular programming*. The program we have been using as an example in this chapter is quite simple. For this reason, it can be easily contained in a single source file. However, most practical application programs are very large. For example, a source program may contain 2,000 assembly language statements. When assembled, this can result in as many as 4,000 to 8,000 bytes of machine code. For development purposes, programs of this size are frequently broken down into a number of parts called *modules* and the individual modules worked on by different programmers. Each module is written, assembled, and debugged separately. When they are all complete, the object codes for all modules are combined together to form a single executable run module. This idea is illustrated in Fig. 5.26. Notice that the LINK program is the software tool that is used to combine the modules together. Its inputs are the object code for modules 1, 2, and 3. Execution of the linker combines these programs into a single run module.

The technique of writing larger programs as a series of modules has several benefits. First, since several programmers are working on the project in parallel, the program can be completed in a much shorter period of time. Another benefit is that the smaller size of the modules requires less time to edit and assemble. For instance, if we were not using modular programming, to make a change in just one statement the complete program would have to be edited, reassembled, and relinked. On the other hand, when using modular programming, just the module containing the statement that needs to be changed can be edited and reassembled. Then the new object module is relinked with the rest of the old object modules to give a new run module.

A third benefit derived from modular programming is that it makes it easier to reuse old software. For instance, the next software design may need some functions for which modules have already been written. If these modules were integrated into a single large program, we would need to edit them out carefully and transfer them to the new source file. However, if these segments of program exist as separate modules, we may need to do no additional work to integrate them into the new application.

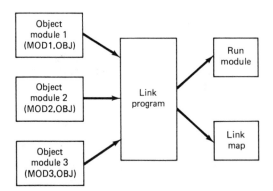

Figure 5.26 Linking object modules.

Initiating the LINK Program

Even though our example program has just one object module, we must still perform the link operation on it to obtain a run module. Let us now look at how this is done using the LINK program available on the IBM PC. First the DOS 2.1 diskette is inserted into drive A and the data diskette that contains object file BLOCK.OBJ is inserted into drive B. Now we invoke the linker with the command

                          A > LINK   (↵)

The linker program is loaded from the DOS diskette and starts to run. It begins by prompting for input of the object file name. This prompt is

                   Object Modules[.OBJ]:

In response to this prompt, we enter the names of all object modules that are to be linked together. The file names are listed, separated by the + sign. For example, to link three object modules named MOD1.OBJ, MOD2.OBJ, and MOD3.OBJ, the input would be

           Object Modules[.OBJ]:B:MOD1+B:MOD2+B:MOD3   (↵)

The file names are to be listed in the order they are to be linked.

    For our earlier example, we just have one object file, which is called BLOCK.OBJ. Therefore, the input is

           Object Modules[.OBJ]: B:BLOCK.OBJ   (↵)

Here, entry of the extension OBJ is optional. That is, we could have entered just B:BLOCK followed by (↵).

    Next, the linker program asks for input of the name of the file into which it is to save the run module. It does this with the prompt

                   Run File[BLOCK.EXE]:

Notice that it automatically creates a default file name by appending the EXE extension to the first file name entered as part of the object module prompt. For this prompt, the file name can be changed, but the EXE extension cannot. This is because all run modules loaded by the DEBUG program must have the extension EXE. Let us use the default file name but assign it to drive B instead of A. To do this, the input entry is

               Run File[BLOCK.EXE]:B: (↵)

At completion of this entry, a third prompt is displayed by the program. It is

List File[NUL.MAP]:

Selection of the default name NUL.MAP causes the linker to suppress formation of a link map file. For our example, we will request one to be generated and assign it the file name BLOCK.MAP. This is done by issuing the command.

List File[NUL.MAP]:B:BLOCK.MAP   (↵)

The last prompt is

Libraries[.LIB]:

It asks us whether or not we want to include subroutines from a *library* in the link process. If so, just enter the name of the file that contains the libraries and depress (↵). Libraries are more widely used with high-level languages. For our example, we will not require use of a library; therefore, (↵) is simply depressed.

Libraries[.LIB]:   (↵)

This completes the start-up of the linker.

After the response to the library prompt, the linker program reads the object files, combines them, and resolves all external references. Moreover, it produces the information for the link map. Finally, it saves the run module on the diskette in drive B in file BLOCK.EXE and the link map information in BLOCK.MAP. The sequence of entries made to invoke the linker for our example is shown in Fig. 5.27(a) and the map file BLOCK.MAP is shown in Fig. 5.27(b).

The link map shows the start address, stop address, and length for each memory segment employed by the program that was linked. Looking at the link map for our program, which is shown in Fig. 5.27(b), we find that the code segment starts at address 00000_{16} and ends at address $0001C_{16}$. The program is $1D_{16}$ equals 30 bytes long.

Example 5.6

From the link map in Fig. 5.27(b), find the range of addresses used for the stack segment. How many bytes are in use?

Solution:

The link map indicates that addresses from 00020_{16} to $0009F_{16}$ are used for storage of stack data. From the length we find that this represents 80_{16} bytes.

```
A>LINK

IBM Personal Computer Linker
Version 2.10 (C)Copyright IBM Corp 1981, 1982, 1983

Object Modules [.OBJ]: B:BLOCK
Run File [A:BLOCK.EXE]: B:
List File [NUL.MAP]: B:BLOCK
Libraries [.LIB]:

A>
```

(a)

```
A>TYPE B:BLOCK.MAP

 Start   Stop   Length   Name              Class
 00000H  0001CH  001DH   CODE_SEG          CODE
 00020H  0005FH  0040H   STACK_SEG         STACK

 Origin   Group

Program entry point at 0000:0000

A>
```

(b)

Figure 5.27 (a) Display sequence for initiating linking of object files; (b) link map file.

5.8 LOADING AND EXECUTING A RUN MODULE WITH DEBUG

In Chapter 4 we learned how to bring up the DEBUG program; the operation of each of its commands; and how to load, execute, and debug the operation of a program. At that time we loaded the machine code for the program and data with memory-modify commands. Up to this point in this chapter, we have learned how to form a source program using assembly language and pseudo-op statements, how to assemble the program into an object module, and how to use the linker to produce a run module. Here we will load and execute the run module BLOCK.EXE that was produced in section 5.7 for the source program BLOCK.SRC.

When the DEBUG program was loaded in Chapter 4, we did not have a run module available. For this reason, we just brought up the debugger by typing in DEBUG and depressing (↵). Now that we do have a run module, the debugger will be brought up in a different way and the run module will be loaded at the same time. This is done by issuing the command

A>DEBUG B:BLOCK.EXE (↵)

In response to this command, both the DEBUG program and the run module BLOCK.EXE are loaded into the PC's memory. As shown in Fig. 5.28, after loading, the debug prompt "_" is displayed. Next the register status is dumped with an R command. Notice that DS is initialized with the value 0905_{16}.

```
A>DEBUG B:BLOCK.EXE
-R
AX=0000  BX=0000  CX=001D  DX=0000  SP=0040  BP=0000  SI=0000  DI=0000
DS=0905  ES=0905  SS=0917  CS=0915  IP=0000   NV UP DI PL NZ NA PO NC
0915:0000 1E         PUSH    DS
-U CS:000 01C
0915:0000 1E         PUSH    DS
0915:0001 B80000     MOV     AX,0000
0915:0004 50         PUSH    AX
0915:0005 B82000     MOV     AX,0020
0915:0008 8ED8       MOV     DS,AX
0915:000A BE0001     MOV     SI,0100
0915:000D BF2001     MOV     DI,0120
0915:0010 B91000     MOV     CX,0010
0915:0013 8A24       MOV     AH,[SI]
0915:0015 8825       MOV     [DI],AH
0915:0017 46         INC     SI
0915:0018 47         INC     DI
0915:0019 49         DEC     CX
0915:001A 75F7       JNZ     0013
0915:001C CB         RETF
-R DS
DS 0905
:0020
-F DS:100 10F FF
-F DS:120 12F 00
-R DS
DS 0020
:0905
-G =CS:00 01C

AX=0020  BX=0000  CX=0010  DX=0000  SP=003C  BP=0000  SI=0100  DI=0120
DS=0020  ES=0905  SS=0917  CS=0915  IP=0013   NV UP DI PL NZ NA PO NC
0915:0013 8A24         MOV     AH,[SI]                        DS:0100=FF
-G =CS:013 01A

AX=FF20  BX=0000  CX=000F  DX=0000  SP=003C  BP=0000  SI=0101  DI=0121
DS=0020  ES=0905  SS=0917  CS=0915  IP=001A   NV UP DI PL NZ AC PE NC
0915:001A 75F7         JNZ     0013
-D DS:100 10F
0020:0100  FF FF FF FF FF FF FF FF-FF FF FF FF FF FF FF FF   ................
-D DS:120 12F
0020:0120  FF 00 00 00 00 00 00 00-00 00 00 00 00 00 00 00   ................
-G =CS:01A 01C

AX=FF20  BX=0000  CX=0000  DX=0000  SP=003C  BP=0000  SI=0110  DI=0130
DS=0020  ES=0905  SS=0917  CS=0915  IP=001C   NV UP DI PL ZR NA PE NC
0915:001C CB           RETF
-D DS:100 10F
0020:0100  FF FF FF FF FF FF FF FF-FF FF FF FF FF FF FF FF   ................
-D DS:120 12F
0020:0120  FF FF FF FF FF FF FF FF-FF FF FF FF FF FF FF FF   ................
-Q

Insert COMMAND.COM disk in drive A
and strike any key when ready

A>
```

Figure 5.28 Loading and executing the run module BLOCK.EXE.

Let us now verify that the program has loaded correctly. This is done with
the commands

$$U \quad CS:000 \quad 01C \quad (\lrcorner)$$

Comparing the program displayed in Fig. 5.28 as a result of the command to the
source program in Fig. 5.24(b), we see that they are essentially the same. Therefore, the program has loaded correctly.

190

Next the value in DS is changed to 0020_{16} with an R command and then the FILL command is used to initialize the bytes of data in the source and destination blocks. The storage locations in the source block are loaded with FF_{16} with the command

```
F  DS:100  10F  FF  (↵)
```

and the storage locations in the destination block are loaded with 00_{16} with the command

```
F  DS:120  12F  00  (↵)
```

Finally, the value in DS is changed back to 0905_{16} with another R command.

Now we will execute the first eight instructions of the program and verify the operation they perform. To do this, we issue the command

```
G  =CS:000  013  (↵)
```

The information displayed at the completion of this command is also shown in Fig. 5.28. Here we find that the registers have been initialized as follows: DS contains 0020_{16}, AX contains 0020_{16}, SI contains 0100_{16}, DI contains 0120_{16}, and CX contains 0010_{16}.

Next we will execute down through the program to the JNZ instruction, address $01A_{16}$,

```
G  =CS:013  01A  (↵)
```

To check the state of the data blocks, we use the commands

```
D  DS:100  10F  (↵)
D  DS:120  12F  (↵)
```

Looking at the displayed blocks of data in Fig. 5.28, we see that the source block is unchanged and that FF_{16} has been copied into the first element of the destination block.

Finally, the program is run to completion with the command

```
G  =CS:01A  01C  (↵)
```

By once more looking at the two blocks of data with the commands

```
D  DS:100  10F  (↵)
D  DS:120  12F  (↵)
```

we find that the contents of the source block have been copied into the destination block.

ASSIGNMENT

Section 5.2

1. What is a flowchart?
2. List the six basic steps in the general development cycle for an assembly language program.
3. In which part of the development cycle is the EDLIN program used? The MASM program? The LINK program? The DEBUG program?
4. Assuming that the file name is PROG_A, give typical names for the files that result from use of the EDLIN program? The MASM program? The LINK program?

Section 5.3

5. What are the two types of statements in a source program?
6. What is the function of an assembly language instruction?
7. What is the function of a pseudo-operation?
8. What are the four elements of an assembly language statement?
9. What part of the instruction format is always required?
10. What are the two limitations on format when writing source statements for the 8088 macroassembler of the IBM PC?
11. What is the function of a label?
12. What is the maximum number of characters of a label that will be recognized by the 8088 macroassembler of the IBM PC?
13. What is the function of the opcode?
14. What is the function of operands?
15. In the instruction statement

SUB_A MOV CL,0FFH

what are the source and destination operands?
16. What is the purpose of the comment field? How are comments processed by an assembler?
17. Give two differences between the syntax of an assembly language statement and a pseudo-operation statement.
18. Write the instruction MOV AX,[32728D] with the source operand expressed both in binary and hexadecimal forms.
19. Rewrite the jump instruction JMP +25D with the operand expressed both in binary and hexadecimal forms.
20. Repeat Example 5.4 with the values A = 345, B = 234, and C = 111.

Section 5.4

21. What is the function of the data pseudo-ops?
22. What happens when the statements

```
SRC_BLOCK = 0100H
DEST_BLOCK = SRC_BLOCK + 20H
```

are processed by the 8088 macroassembler?

23. What does the statement

```
SEG_ADDR  DW  1234H
```

do when processed by the macroassembler?

24. What happens when the statement

```
BLOCK_1  DB  128  DUP(?)
```

is processed by the macroassembler?

25. Show how the segment-control pseudo-ops are used to define a segment called DATA_SEG that is aligned on a word address boundary, overlaps other segments with the same name, and is a data segment.
26. Show the general structure of a far procedure called BLOCK that is to be accessible from other modules.
27. Write an origin statement that causes machine code to be loaded at offset 1000H of the current code segment.
28. Write a page statement that will set up the printout for 55 lines per page and 80 characters per line and a title statement that will title pages of the source listing with "BLOCK—MOVE PROGRAM".

Section 5.5

29. What type of editor is EDLIN?
30. Use EDLIN to repeat the entry of the source statements in Fig. 5.20. Make the file name EXAMPLE.SRC.
31. Create a source file for the program shown in Fig. 5.18 under the file name BLOCK.ASM.

Section 5.6

32. What is the input to the assembler program?
33. What are the output files of the assembler? Give a brief description of each.
34. Assemble the file created in problem 31.

Section 5.7

35. Can the output of the assembler be directly executed by the 8088 microprocessor?
36. Give three benefits of modular programming.
37. What is the input to the LINK program?
38. What are the outputs of the LINK program? Give a brief description of each.
39. Link the program assembled in problem 34.

Section 5.8

40. Use DEBUG to load and execute the run module created in problem 39. Before executing the program, initialize all storage locations in the source block with the value FF_{16} and all locations in the destination block with the value 00_{16}. Execute the program with a single GO command.

6

8088 MICROPROCESSOR PROGRAMMING 1

6.1 INTRODUCTION

Up to this point in the book, we have studied the software architecture of the 8088 microprocessor, the software development tools provided by the DEBUG program on the IBM PC, how to write source programs, and how to use the macroassembler and linker programs to develop an assembly language run module. In this chapter we begin a detailed study of the instruction set of the 8088 microprocessor. A large part of the instruction set is covered in this chapter. These instructions provide the ability to write straight-line programs. The rest of the instruction set and some more sophisticated programming concepts are covered in Chapter 7. The following topics are presented in this chapter.

1. The 8088's instruction set
2. Data transfer instructions
3. Arithmetic instructions
4. Logic instructions
5. Shift instructions
6. Rotate instructions

6.2 THE 8088'S INSTRUCTION SET

The instruction set of a microprocessor defines the basic operations that a programmer can make the device perform. The 8088 microprocessor provides a powerful instruction set containing 117 basic instructions. The wide range of operands and addressing modes permitted for use with these instructions further expand the instruction set into many more instructions executable at the machine-code level. For instance, the basic MOV instruction expands into 28 different machine-level instructions.

For the purpose of discussion, the instruction set will be divided into a number of groups of functionally related instructions. In this chapter we consider the data-transfer instructions, arithmetic instructions, the logic instructions, shift instructions, and rotate instructions. Advanced instructions such as those for program and processor control are described in Chapter 7.

6.3 DATA TRANSFER INSTRUCTIONS

The 8088 microprocessor has a group of *data-transfer instructions* that are provided to move data either between its internal registers or between an internal register and a storage location in memory. This group includes the *move byte or word* (MOV) instruction, *exchange byte or word* (XCHG) instruction, *translate byte* (XLAT) instruction, *load effective address* (LEA) instruction, *load data segment* (LDS) instruction, and *load extra segment* (LES) instruction. These instructions are discussed in this section.

The MOV Instruction

The MOV instruction of Fig. 6.1(a) is used to transfer a byte or a word of data from a source operand to a destination operand. These operands can be internal

Mnemonic	Meaning	Format	Operation	Flags affected
MOV	Move	MOV D,S	(S) → (D)	None

(a)

Destination	Source
Memory	Accumulator
Accumulator	Memory
Register	Register
Register	Memory
Memory	Register
Register	Immediate
Memory	Immediate
Seg–reg	Reg16
Seg–reg	Mem16
Reg16	Seg–reg
Memory	Seg–reg

(b)

Figure 6.1 (a) MOV data transfer instruction; (b) allowed operands; (c) MOV DX,CS instruction before execution; (d) after execution.

registers of the 8088 and storage locations in memory. Figure 6.1(b) shows the valid source and destination operand variations. This large choice of operands results in many different MOV instructions. Looking at this list of operands, we see that data can be moved between general-purpose registers, between a general-purpose register and a segment register, between a general-purpose register or segment register and memory, or between a memory location and the accumulator.

Notice that the MOV instruction cannot transfer data directly between a source and a destination that both reside in external memory. Instead, the data must first be moved from memory into an internal register, such as to the accumulator (AX), with one move instruction and then moved to the new location in memory with a second move instruction.

All transfers between general-purpose registers and memory can involve either a byte or word of data. The fact that the instruction corresponds to byte

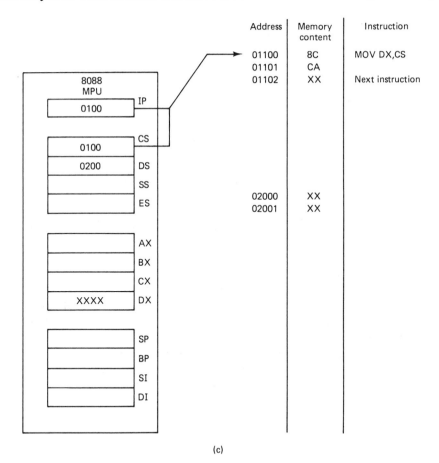

(c)

Figure 6.1 (continued)

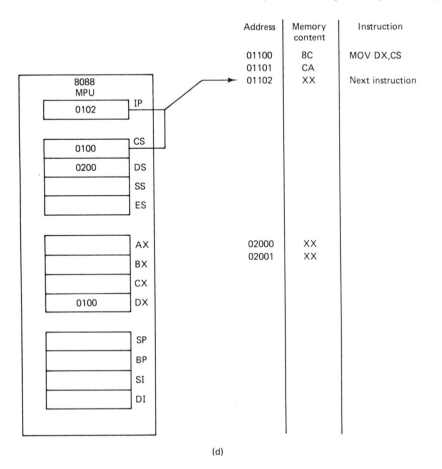

(d)

Figure 6.1 (continued)

or word data is designated by the way in which its operands are specified. For instance, AL or AH would be used to specify a byte operand, and AX—a word operand. On the other hand, data moved between one of the general-purpose registers and a segment register or between a segment register and a memory location must always be word-wide.

In Fig. 6.1(a) we also find additional important information. For instance, flag bits within the 8088 are not modified by execution of a MOV instruction.

An example of a segment register to general-purpose register MOV instruction shown in Fig. 6.1(c) is

MOV   DX,CS

In this instruction, the code-segment register is the source operand and the data register is the destination. It stands for "move the contents of CS into DX." That is,

$$(CS) \rightarrow (DX)$$

For example, if the contents of CS are 0100_{16}, execution of the instruction MOV DX,CS as shown in Fig. 6.1(d) makes

$$(DX) = (CS) = 0100_{16}$$

In all memory reference MOV instructions, the machine code for the instruction includes an offset address relative to the contents of the data-segment register. An example of this type of instruction is

MOV   SUM,AX

In this instruction, the memory location identified by the variable SUM is specified using direct addressing. That is, the value of the offset is included in the two byte locations that follow its opcode in program memory.

Let us assume that the contents of DS equals 0200_{16} and that SUM corresponds to a displacement of 1212_{16}. Then this instruction means "move the contents of accumulator AX to the memory location offset by 1212_{16} from the starting location of the current data segment." The physical address of this location is obtained as

$$PA = 02000_{16} + 1212_{16} = 03212_{16}$$

Thus the effect of the instruction is

$$(AL) \rightarrow (\text{Memory Location } 03212_{16})$$

and

$$(AH) \rightarrow (\text{Memory Location } 03213_{16})$$

Example 6.1

What is the effect of executing the instruction

MOV   CX,SOURCE_MEM

where SOURCE_MEM is the memory location offset by 20_{16} relative to the data segment starting at address $A000_{16}$?

Solution:

Execution of this instruction results in the following:

$$((DS)0 + 20_{16}) \rightarrow (CL)$$

$$((DS)0 + 20_{16} + 1_{16}) \rightarrow (CH)$$

In other words, CL is loaded with the contents held at memory address

$$0A000_{16} + 20_{16} = 0A020_{16}$$

and CH is loaded with the contents of memory address

$$0A000_{16} + 20_{16} + 1_{16} = 0A021_{16}$$

Example 6.2

Use the DEBUG program on the IBM PC to verify the operation of the instruction in Example 6.1. Initialize the word-storage location pointed to by SOURCE_MEM to the value $AA55_{16}$ before executing the instruction.

Solution:

First the DEBUG program is invoked by entering the command

A>DEBUG (↵)

As shown in Fig. 6.2, this results in the display of the debugger's prompt

—

To determine the memory locations the debugger assigns for use in entering instructions and data, we can examine the state of the internal registers with the command

—R (↵)

Looking at the displayed information for this command in Fig. 6.2, we find that the contents of CS and IP indicate that the starting address in the current code

```
A>DEBUG
-R
AX=0000  BX=0000  CX=0000  DX=0000  SP=70EE  BP=0000  SI=0000  DI=0000
DS=08F1  ES=08F1  SS=08F1  CS=08F1  IP=0100   NV UP DI PL NZ NA PO NC
08F1:0100 0000         ADD     [BX+SI],AL                        DS:0000=CD
-A
08F1:0100 MOV  CX,[20]
08F1:0104
-R DS
DS 08F1
:A00
-E 20 55 AA
-T

AX=0000  BX=0000  CX=AA55  DX=0000  SP=70EE  BP=0000  SI=0000  DI=0000
DS=0A00  ES=08F1  SS=08F1  CS=08F1  IP=0104   NV UP DI PL NZ NA PO NC
08F1:0104 0000         ADD     [BX+SI],AL                        DS:0000=00
-Q

A>
```

Figure 6.2 Display sequence for Example 6.2.

segment is 08F1:0100 and the current data segment starts at address 08F1:0000. Also note that the initial value in CX is 0000H.

To enter the instruction from Example 6.1 at location 08F1:0100 we use the ASSEMBLE command

```
        —A                          (↵)
        08F1:0100  MOV  CX,[20]  (↵)
        08F1:0104                   (↵)
        —
```

Note that we must enter the value of the offset address instead of the symbol SOURCE_MEM and that it must be enclosed in brackets to indicate that it is a direct address.

Let us now redefine the data segment so that it starts at $A000_{16}$. This is done by loading the DS register with $A00_{16}$ with the REGISTER command. As shown in Fig. 6.2, we do this with the entries

```
        —R  DS   (↵)
        DS  08F1
        :A00     (↵)
        —
```

Now we initialize the memory locations at addresses 0A00:20 and 0A00:21 to 55_{16} and AA_{16}, respectively, with the ENTER command

```
        —E  20  55  AA  (↵)
```

Notice that the bytes of the word of data must be entered in the reverse order. Finally, to execute the instruction we issue the trace command

```
        —T  (↵)
```

The results of executing the instruction are shown in Fig. 6.2. Note that CX has been loaded with $AA55_{16}$.

The XCHG Instruction

In our study of the move instruction, we found that it could be used to copy the contents of a register or memory location into a register or contents of a register into a storage location in memory. In all cases, the original contents of the source location are preserved and the original contents of the destination are destroyed. In some applications it is required to interchange the contents of two registers. For instance, we might want to exchange the data in the AX and BX registers.

This could be done using multiple move instructions and storage of the data in a temporary register such as DX. However, to perform the exchange function more efficiently, a special instruction has been provided in the instruction set of the 8088. This is the exchange (XCHG) instruction. The forms of the XCHG instruction and its allowed operands are shown in Fig. 6.3(a) and (b). Here we see that it can be used to swap data between two general-purpose registers or between a general-purpose register and a storage location in memory. In particular, it allows for the exchange of words of data between one of the general-purpose registers, including the pointers and index registers, and the accumulator (AX), exchange of a byte or word of data between one of the general-purpose registers and a location in memory, or between two of the general-purpose registers.

Let us consider an example of an exchange between two internal registers. Here is a typical instruction.

$$XCHG \ \ AX,DX$$

Its execution by the 8088 swaps the contents of AX with that of DX. That is,

$$(AX \ original) \rightarrow (DX)$$

$$(DX \ original) \rightarrow (AX)$$

or

$$(AX) \leftrightarrow (DX)$$

Example 6.3

For the data shown in Fig. 6.3(c), what is the result of executing the instruction

$$XCHG \ \ SUM,BX$$

Mnemonic	Meaning	Format	Operation	Flags affected
XCHG	Exchange	XCHG D,S	(D) ↔ (S)	None

(a)

Destination	Source
Accumulator	Reg16
Memory	Register
Register	Register

(b)

Figure 6.3 (a) Exchange data transfer instruction; (b) allowed operands; (c) XCHG SUM,BX instruction before execution; (d) after execution.

Solution:

Execution of this instruction performs the function

$$((DS)0 + SUM) \leftrightarrow (BX)$$

In Fig. 6.3(c) we see that $(DS) = 0200_{16}$ and the direct address $SUM = 1234_{16}$. Therefore, the physical address is

$$PA = 02000_{16} + 1234_{16} = 03234_{16}$$

Notice that this location contains FF_{16} and the address that follows contains 00_{16}. Moreover, note that BL contains AA_{16} and BH contains 11_{16}.

Execution of the instruction performs the following 16-bit swap.

$$(03234_{16}) \leftrightarrow (BL)$$

$$(03235_{16}) \leftrightarrow (BH)$$

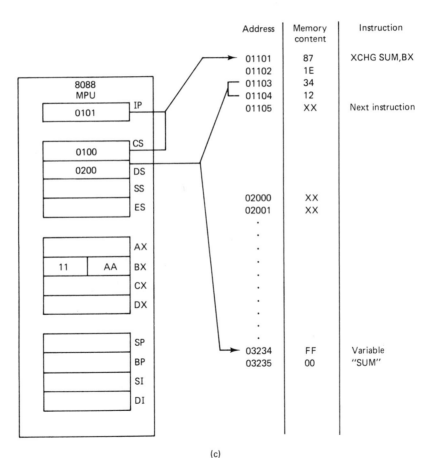

(c)

Figure 6.3 (continued)

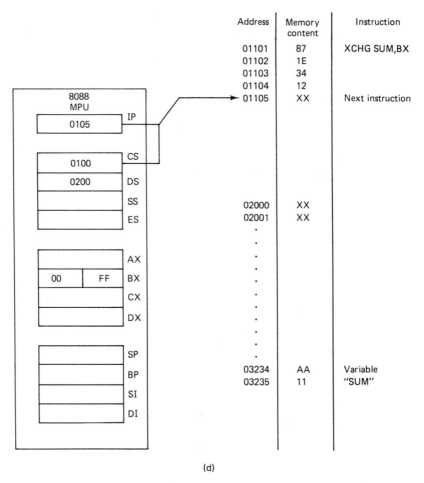

(d)

Figure 6.3 (continued)

As shown in Fig. 6.3(d), we get

$$(BX) = 00FF_{16}$$

$$(SUM) = 11AA_{16}$$

Example 6.4

Use the IBM PC's DEBUG program to verify the operation of the instruction in Example 6.3.

Solution:

The DEBUG operations needed to enter the instruction, enter the data, execute the instruction, and verify the result of its operation are shown in Fig. 6.4. Here we

```
A>DEBUG
-R
AX=0000  BX=0000  CX=0000  DX=0000  SP=70EE  BP=0000  SI=0000  DI=0000
DS=08F1  ES=08F1  SS=08F1  CS=08F1  IP=0100   NV UP DI PL NZ NA PO NC
08F1:0100 8B0E2000      MOV     CX,[0020]                          DS:0020=FFFF
-A 0100:101
0100:0101 XCHG  [1234],BX
0100:0105
-R BX
BX 0000
:11AA
-R DS
DS 08F1
:0200
-R CS
CS 08F1
:0100
-R IP
IP 0100
:0101
-R
AX=0000  BX=11AA  CX=0000  DX=0000  SP=70EE  BP=0000  SI=0000  DI=0000
DS=0200  ES=08F1  SS=08F1  CS=0100  IP=0101   NV UP DI PL NZ NA PO NC
0100:0101 871E3412      XCHG    [1234],BX                          DS:1234=11AA
-E 1234 FF 00
-U 0101 0104
0100:0101 871E3412      XCHG    [1234],BX
-T

AX=0000  BX=00FF  CX=0000  DX=0000  SP=70EE  BP=0000  SI=0000  DI=0000
DS=0200  ES=08F1  SS=08F1  CS=0100  IP=0105   NV UP DI PL NZ NA PO NC
0100:0105 B20A          MOV     DL,0A
-D 1234 1235
0200:1234  AA 11                                           *.
-Q

A>
```

Figure 6.4 Display sequence for Example 6.4.

see that after invoking DEBUG and displaying the initial state of the 8088's
registers, the instruction is loaded into memory with the command

```
—A  0100:101                (⏎)
0100:0101  XCHG  [1234],BX  (⏎)
0100:0105                   (⏎)
—
```

Next, as shown in Fig. 6.4, R commands are used to initialize the contents of
registers BX, DS, CS, and IP to $11AA_{16}$, 0200_{16}, 0100_{16}, and 0101_{16}, respectively,
and then the updated register states are verified with another R command. Now
memory locations DS:1234 and DS:1235 are loaded with the values FF_{16} and 00_{16},
respectively, with the E command

```
—E  1234  FF  00   (⏎)
—
```

Before executing the instruction, its loading is verified with an unassemble command. Looking at Fig. 6.4, we see that it has been correctly loaded. Therefore, the instruction is executed by issuing the TRACE command

$$-\text{T} \qquad (\lrcorner)$$

The displayed trace information in Fig. 6.4 shows that BX now contains 00FF_{16}. To verify that the memory location was loaded with data from BX, we must display the data held at addresses DS:1234 and DS:1235. This is done with the DUMP command

$$-\text{D } 1234\ 1235\ (\lrcorner)$$
$$0200{:}1234\ \ \text{AA}\ \ 11$$

In this way, we see that the word contents of memory location DS:1234 have been exchanged with the contents of the BX register.

The XLAT Instruction

The translate (XLAT) instruction has been provided in the instruction set of the 8088 to simplify implementation of the lookup-table operation. This instruction is described in Fig. 6.5. When using XLAT, the contents of register BX represent the offset of the starting address of the lookup table from the beginning of the current data segment. Also, the contents of AL represent the offset of the element to be accessed from the beginning of the lookup table. This eight-bit element address permits a table with up to 256 elements. The values in both of these registers must be initialized prior to execution of the XLAT instruction.

Execution of XLAT replaces the contents of AL by the contents of the accessed lookup-table location. The physical address of this element in the table is derived as

$$\text{PA} = (\text{DS})0 + (\text{BX}) + (\text{AL})$$

An example of the use of this instruction would be for software code conversions: for instance, an ASCII-to-EBCDIC conversion. This requires an EBCDIC table in memory. The individual EBCDIC codes are located in the

Mnemonic	Meaning	Format	Operation	Flags affected
XLAT	Translate	XLAT Source-table	$((\text{AL})+(\text{BX})+(\text{DS})0) \rightarrow (\text{AL})$	None

Figure 6.5 Translate data transfer instruction.

table at element displacements (AL) equal to their equivalent ASCII character values. That is, the EBCDIC code $B1_{16}$ for letter A would be positioned at displacement 41_{16}, which equals ASCII A, from the start of the table. The start of this ASCII-to-EBCDIC table in the current data segment is identified by the contents of BX.

As an illustration of XLAT, let us assume that the $(DS)=0300_{16}$, $(BX) = 0100_{16}$, and $(AL)=0D_{16}$. $0D_{16}$ represents the ASCII character CR (carriage return). Execution of XLAT replaces the contents of AL by the contents of the memory location given by

$$PA = (DS)0 + (BX) + (AL)$$
$$= 03000_{16} + 0100_{16} + 0D_{16} = 0310D_{16}$$

Thus the execution can be described by

$$(0310D_{16}) \rightarrow (AL)$$

Assuming that this memory location contains 52_{16}, this value is placed in AL.

$$(AL) = 52_{16}$$

The LEA, LDS, and LES Instructions

Another type of data-transfer operation that is important is to load a segment or general-purpose register with an address directly from memory. Special instructions are provided in the instruction set of the 8088 to give a programmer this capability. These instructions are described in Fig. 6.6. They are load register with effective address (LEA), load register and data segment register (LDS), and load register and extra segment register (LES).

Looking at Fig. 6.6(a), we see that these instructions provide the ability to manipulate memory addresses by loading a specific register with a 16-bit offset address or a 16-bit offset address together with a 16-bit segment address into either DS or ES.

Mnemonic	Meaning	Format	Operation	Flags affected
LEA	Load effective address	LEA Reg16,Mem16	(Mem16) → (Reg16)	None
LDS	Load register and DS	LDS Reg16,Mem32	(Mem32) → (Reg16) (Mem32+2) → (DS)	None
LES	Load register and ES	LES Reg16,Mem32	(Mem32) → (Reg16) (Mem32+2) → (ES)	None

(a)

Figure 6.6 (a) LEA, LDS, and LES data transfer instructions; (b) LEA SI,[200] instruction before execution; (c) after execution.

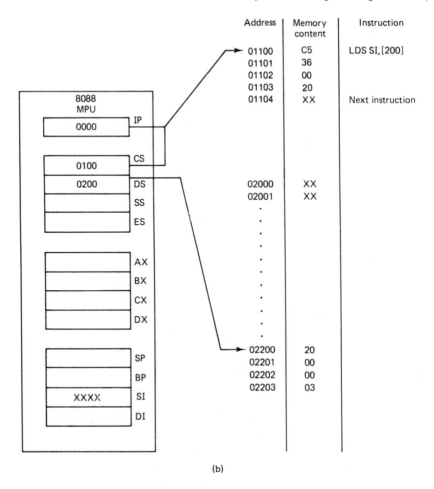

(b)

Figure 6.6 (continued)

The LEA instruction is used to load a specified register with a 16-bit offset address. An example of this instruction is

                                          LEA   SI,INPUT

When executed, it loads the SI register with an offset address value. The value of this offset is represented by the value of INPUT. INPUT is encoded following the instruction opcode in the code segment of memory.

The other two instructions, LDS and LES, are similar to LEA except that they load the specified register as well as the DS or ES segment register.

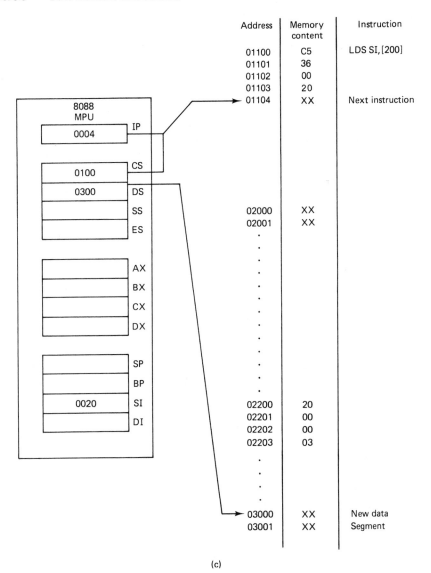

Address	Memory content	Instruction
01100	C5	LDS SI, [200]
01101	36	
01102	00	
01103	20	
01104	XX	Next instruction
02000	XX	
02001	XX	
02200	20	
02201	00	
02202	00	
02203	03	
03000	XX	New data
03001	XX	Segment

8088 MPU

IP 0004
CS 0100
DS 0300
SS
ES
AX
BX
CX
DX
SP
BP
SI 0020
DI

(c)

Figure 6.6 (continued)

Example 6.5

Assuming that the 8088 is set up as shown in Fig. 6.6(b), what is the result of executing the instruction:

LDS   SI, [200]

Solution:

Execution of the instruction loads the SI register from the word location in memory whose offset address with respect to the current data segment is 200_{16}. Figure 6.6(b) shows that the contents of DS are 0200_{16}. This gives a physical address of

$$PA = 02000_{16} + 0200_{16} = 02200_{16}$$

It is the contents of this location and the one that follows that are loaded into SI. Therefore, in Fig. 6.6 (c) we find that SI contains 0020_{16}. The next two bytes—that is, the contents of addresses 2202_{16} and 2203_{16}—are loaded into the DS register. As shown, this defines a new data-segment address of 03000_{16}.

Example 6.6

Verify the execution of the instruction in Example 6.5 using the debugger of the IBM PC. The memory and register contents are to be those shown in Fig. 6.6(b).

Solution:

As shown in Fig. 6.7, DEBUG is first brought up and then REGISTER commands are used to initialize registers IP, CS, DS, and SI with values 0100_{16}, 0100_{16}, 0200_{16}, and 0000_{16}. Next the instruction is assembled at address CS:100 with the command

```
—A CS:100              (↵)
0100:0100  LDS  SI,[200]  (↵)
0100:0104              (↵)
—
```

```
A>DEBUG
-R IP
IP 0100
:
-R CS
CS 08F1
:0100
-R DS
DS 08F1
:0200
-R SI
SI 0000
:
-A CS:100
0100:0100 LDS   SI,[200]
0100:0104
-E 200 20 00 00 03
-T

AX=0000  BX=0000  CX=0000  DX=0000  SP=70EE  BP=0000  SI=0020  DI=0000
DS=0300  ES=08F1  SS=08F1  CS=0100  IP=0104    NV UP DI PL NZ NA PO NC
0100:0104 06           PUSH     ES
-Q

A>
```

Figure 6.7 Display sequence for Example 6.6.

Before executing the instruction, we still need to initialize two words of data starting at location DS:200 in memory. As shown in Fig. 6.7, this is done with an E command. Then the instruction is executed with the TRACE command

$$-\text{T} \quad (\downarrow)$$

Looking at the displayed-register status in Fig. 6.7, we see that SI has been loaded with the value 0020_{16} and DS with the value 0300_{16}.

6.4 ARITHMETIC INSTRUCTIONS

The instruction set of the 8088 microprocessor contains an extensive complement of *arithmetic instructions.* They include instructions for the *addition, subtraction, multiplication,* and *division* operations. Moreover, these operations can be performed on numbers expressed in a variety of numeric data formats. They include: *unsigned or signed binary bytes or words, unpacked or packed decimal bytes,* or *ASCII numbers.* By *packed decimal* we mean that two BCD digits are packed into a byte register or memory location. Unpacked decimal numbers are stored one BCD digit per byte. These decimal numbers are always unsigned. Moreover, ASCII numbers are expressed in ASCII code and stored one number per byte.

The status that results from the execution of an arithmetic instruction is recorded in the flags of the 8088. The flags that are affected by the arithmetic instructions are: carry flag (CF), auxiliary flag (AF), sign flag (SF), zero flag (ZF), parity flag (PF), and overflow flag (OF). Each of these flags was discussed in Chapter 3.

For the purpose of discussion, we will divide the arithmetic instructions into the subgroups shown in Fig. 6.8.

Addition Instructions—ADD, ADC, INC, AAA, and DAA

The form of each of the instructions in the *addition group* is shown in Fig. 6.9 (a); the allowed operand variations, for all but the INC instruction, are shown in Fig. 6.9(b). Let us begin by looking more closely at the *add* (ADD) instruction. Notice in Fig. 6.9(b) that it can be used to add to the contents of the accumulator an immediate operand, the contents of another register, or the contents of a storage location in memory. It also allows us to add the contents of two registers or the contents of a register and a memory location.

In general, the result of executing the instruction is expressed as

$$(S) + (D) \rightarrow (D)$$

That is, the contents of the source operand are added to those of the destination operand and the sum that results is put into the location of the destination operand.

Addition	
ADD	Add byte or word
ADC	Add byte or word with carry
INC	Increment byte or word by 1
AAA	ASCII adjust for addition
DAA	Decimal adjust for addition
Subtraction	
SUB	Subtract byte or word
SBB	Subtract byte or word with borrow
DEC	Decrement byte or word by 1
NEG	Negate byte or word
AAS	ASCII adjust for subtraction
DAS	Decimal adjust for subtraction
Multiplication	
MUL	Multiply byte or word unsigned
IMUL	Integer multiply byte or word
AAM	ASCII adjust for multiply
Division	
DIV	Divide byte or word unsigned
IDIV	Integer divide byte or word
AAD	ASCII adjust for division
CBW	Convert byte to word
CWD	Convert word to doubleword

Figure 6.8 Arithmetic instructions.

Mnemonic	Meaning	Format	Operation	Flags affected
ADD	Addition	ADD D,S	(S) + (D) → (D) carry → (CF)	OF,SF,ZF,AF,PF,CF
ADC	Add with carry	ADC D,S	(S)+(D)+(CF) → (D) carry → (CF)	OF,SF,ZF,AF,PF,CF
INC	Increment by 1	INC D	(D)+1 → (D)	OF,SF,ZF,AF,PF,CF
DAA	Decimal adjust for addition	DAA		OF,SF,ZF,AF,PF,CF
AAA	ASCII adjust for addition	AAA		OF,SF,ZF,AF,PF,CF

(a)

Destination	Source
Register	Register
Register	Memory
Memory	Register
Register	Immediate
Memory	Immediate
Accumulator	Immediate

Destination
Reg16
Reg8
Memory

(b)

(c)

Figure 6.9 (a) Addition arithmetic instructions; (b) allowed operands for ADD and ADC instructions; (c) allowed operands for INC instruction.

212

Example 6.7

Assume that the AX and BX registers contain 1100_{16} and $0ABC_{16}$, respectively. What are the results of executing the instruction ADD AX,BX?

Solution:

Execution of the ADD instruction causes the contents of source operand BX to be added to the contents of destination register AX. This gives

$$(BX) + (AX) = 0ABC_{16} + 1100_{16} = 1BBC_{16}$$

This sum ends up in destination register AX.

$$(AX) = 1BBC_{16}$$

Execution of this instruction is illustrated in Fig. 6.10(a) and (b).

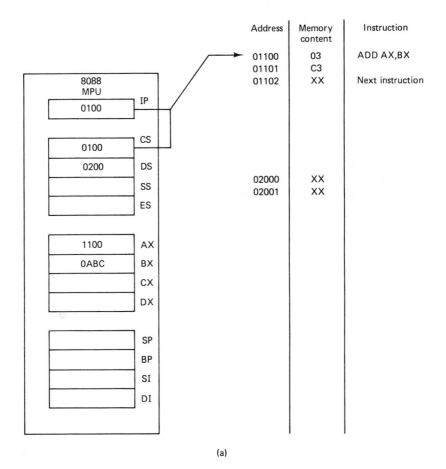

(a)

Figure 6.10 (a) ADD instruction before execution; (b) after execution.

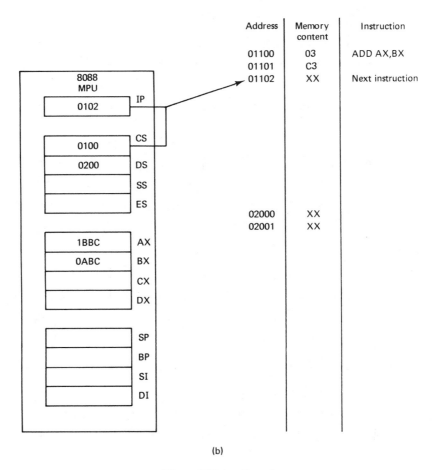

(b)

Figure 6.10 (continued)

Example 6.8

Use the debugger on the IBM PC to verify the execution of the instruction in Example 6.7. Assume that the registers are to be initialized with the values shown in Fig. 6.10(a).

Solution:

The debug sequence for this problem is shown in Fig. 6.11. After DEBUG is brought up, the instruction is assembled into memory with the command

```
        —A  0100:0100              (↵)
        0100:0100  ADD  AX,BX  (↵)
        0100:0102                  (↵)
        —
```

```
A>DEBUG
-A 0100:0100
0100:0100 ADD    AX,BX
0100:0102
-R AX
AX 0000
:1100
-R BX
BX 0000
:0ABC
-U 0100:0100 0100
0100:0100 01D8          ADD      AX,BX
-T =0100:0100

AX=1BBC  BX=0ABC  CX=0000  DX=0000  SP=70EE  BP=0000  SI=0000  DI=0000
DS=08F1  ES=08F1  SS=08F1  CS=0100  IP=0102    NV UP DI PL NZ NA PO NC
0100:0102 2F          DAS
-Q

A>
```

Figure 6.11 Display sequence for Example 6.8.

Next, as shown in Fig. 6.11, the AX and BX registers are loaded with the values 1100_{16} and $0ABC_{16}$, respectively, using R commands. Next, the loading of the instruction is verified with the unassemble command

$$-U \ 0100{:}0100 \ 0100 \ (\lrcorner)$$

and is shown in Fig. 6.11 to be correct.

We are now ready to execute the instruction with the TRACE command

$$-T \ =0100{:}0100 \ (\lrcorner)$$

From the trace dump in Fig. 6.11, we see that the sum of AX and BX, which equals $1BBC_{16}$, is now held in destination register AX.

The instruction *add with carry* (ADC) works similarly to ADD. But in this case, the content of the carry flag is also added; that is,

$$(S) + (D) + (CF) \rightarrow (D)$$

The valid operand combinations are the same as those for the ADD instruction.

Another instruction that can be considered as part of the addition subgroup of arithmetic instructions is the *increment* (INC) instruction. As shown in Fig. 6.9(c), its operands can be the contents of a 16-bit internal register, an 8-bit internal register, or a storage location in memory. Execution of the INC instruction adds one to the specified operand. An example of an instruction that increments the high byte of AX is

INC AH

Looking at Fig. 6.9(a), we see that execution of any one of these three instructions affects all six of the flags earlier mentioned.

Example 6.9

The original contents of AX, BL, memory location SUM, and carry flag (CF) are 1234_{16}, AB_{16}, $00CD_{16}$, and 0_{16}, respectively. Describe the results of executing the following sequence of instructions.

```
ADD   AX,SUM
ADC   BL,05H
INC   SUM
```

Solution:

By executing the first instruction, we add the word in the accumulator to the contents of the memory location identified as SUM. The result is placed in the accumulator. That is,

$$(AX) \leftarrow (AX) + (SUM) = 1234_{16} + 00CD_{16} = 1301_{16}$$

The carry flag remains reset.

The second instruction adds the lower byte of the base register (BL), immediate operand 5_{16}, and the carry flag, which is 0_{16}. This gives

$$(BL) \leftarrow (BL) + IOP + (CF) = AB_{16} + 5_{16} + 0_{16} = B0_{16}$$

Again CF stays reset.

The last instruction increments the contents of memory location SUM by one. That is,

$$(SUM) \leftarrow (SUM) + 1_{16} = 00CD_{16} + 1_{16} = 00CE_{16}$$

These results are summarized in Fig. 6.12.

Instruction	(AX)	(BL)	(SUM)	(CF)
Initial state	1234	AB	00CD	0
ADD AX,SUM	1301	AB	00CD	0
ADC BL,05H	1301	B0	00CD	0
INC SUM	1301	B0	00CE	0

Figure 6.12 Results due to execution of arithmetic program.

Example 6.10

Verify the operation of the instruction sequence in Example 6.9 by executing it with DEBUG on the IBM PC. A source program that includes this sequence of instructions is shown in Fig. 6.13(a) and the source listing produced when the program is assembled is shown in Fig. 6.13(b). A run module that was produced by linking this program is stored in file EX610.EXE.

Solution:

The DEBUG program is called up and at the same time the run module from file
EX610.EXE is loaded with the command

>DEBUG   B:EX610.EXE   (↵)

Next, we will verify the loading of the program by unassembling it with the command

—U 0 12   (↵)

Looking at the displayed instruction sequence in Fig. 6.13(c) and comparing it to
the source listing in Fig. 6.13(b), we find that the program has loaded correctly.

```
A>TYPE B:EX610.ASM


TITLE    EXAMPLE 6.10

         PAGE       ,132

STACK_SEG          SEGMENT            STACK 'STACK'
                   DB                 64 DUP(?)
STACK_SEG          ENDS


DATA_SEG           SEGMENT
SUM                DW                 OCDH
DATA_SEG           ENDS

CODE_SEG           SEGMENT            'CODE'
EX610    PROC      FAR
         ASSUME    CS:CODE_SEG, SS:STACK_SEG, DS:DATA_SEG

;To return to DEBUG program put return address on the stack

         PUSH      DS
         MOV       AX, 0
         PUSH      AX

;Following code implements the Example 6.10

         MOV       AX, DATA_SEG      ;Establish data segment
         MOV       DS, AX

         ADD       AX, SUM
         ADC       BL, 5H
         INC       SUM

         RET                         ;Return to DEBUG program
EX610    ENDP

CODE_SEG           ENDS

         END       EX610

A>
```

(a)

Figure 6.13 (a) Source program for Example 6.10; (b) source listing produced
by assembler; (c) debug session for execution of program EX610.EXE.

A>TYPE B:EX610.LST

```
                              TITLE    EXAMPLE 6.10

                                  PAGE      ,132

0000                          STACK_SEG        SEGMENT       STACK 'STACK'
0000     40 [                                  DB            64 DUP(?)
                ??
            ]

0040                          STACK_SEG        ENDS


0000                          DATA_SEG         SEGMENT
0000    00CD                  SUM              DW            OCDH
0002                          DATA_SEG         ENDS

0000                          CODE_SEG         SEGMENT       'CODE'
0000                          EX610   PROC     FAR
                                      ASSUME   CS:CODE_SEG, SS:STACK_SEG, DS:DATA_SEG

                              ;To return to DEBUG program put return address on the stack

0000    1E                            PUSH     DS
0001    B8 0000                       MOV      AX, 0
0004    50                            PUSH     AX

                              ;Following code implements the Example 6.10

0005    B8 ---- R                     MOV      AX, DATA_SEG   ;Establish data segment
0008    8E D8                         MOV      DS, AX

000A    03 06 0000 R                  ADD      AX, SUM
000E    80 D3 05                      ADC      BL, 5H
0011    FF 06 0000 R                  INC      SUM

0015    CB                            RET                     ;Return to DEBUG program
0016                          EX610   ENDP

0016                          CODE_SEG         ENDS

                                      END      EX610
```

Segments and groups:

N a m e	Size	align	combine	class
CODE_SEG	0016	PARA	NONE	'CODE'
DATA_SEG	0002	PARA	NONE	
STACK_SEG.	0040	PARA	STACK	'STACK'

Symbols:

N a m e	Type	Value	Attr	
EX610.	F PROC	0000	CODE_SEG	Length =0016
SUM.	L WORD	0000	DATA_SEG	

Warning Severe
Errors Errors
0   0

A>   (b)

Figure 6.13 (continued)

```
A>DEBUG B:EX610.EXE
-U 0 12
0915:0000 1E            PUSH    DS
0915:0001 B80000        MOV     AX,0000
0915:0004 50            PUSH    AX
0915:0005 B81709        MOV     AX,0917
0915:0008 8ED8          MOV     DS,AX
0915:000A 03060000      ADD     AX,[0000]
0915:000E 80D305        ADC     BL,05
0915:0011 FF060000      INC     WORD PTR [0000]
-G A

AX=0917  BX=0000  CX=0022  DX=0000  SP=003C  BP=0000  SI=0000  DI=0000
DS=0917  ES=0905  SS=0918  CS=0915  IP=000A   NV UP DI PL NZ NA PO NC
0915:000A 03060000      ADD     AX,[0000]                           DS:0000=00CD
-R AX
AX 0917
:1234
-R BX
BX 0000
:AB
-R F
NV UP DI PL NZ NA PO NC -
-E 0 CD 00
-D 0 1
0917:0000  CD 00                                                    M.
-T

AX=1301  BX=00AB  CX=0022  DX=0000  SP=003C  BP=0000  SI=0000  DI=0000
DS=0917  ES=0905  SS=0918  CS=0915  IP=000E   NV UP DI PL NZ AC PO NC
0915:000E 80D305        ADC     BL,05
-T

AX=1301  BX=00B0  CX=0022  DX=0000  SP=003C  BP=0000  SI=0000  DI=0000
DS=0917  ES=0905  SS=0918  CS=0915  IP=0011   NV UP DI NG NZ AC PO NC
0915:0011 FF060000      INC     WORD PTR [0000]                     DS:0000=00CD
-T

AX=1301  BX=00B0  CX=0022  DX=0000  SP=003C  BP=0000  SI=0000  DI=0000
DS=0917  ES=0905  SS=0918  CS=0915  IP=0015   NV UP DI PL NZ NA PO NC
0915:0015 CB            RETF
-D 0 1
0917:0000  CE 00                                                    N.
-G

Program terminated normally
-Q
```

(c)

Figure 6.13 (continued)

Notice in Fig. 6.13(c) that the instructions for which we are interested in veri-fying operation start at address 0915:000A. For this reason, a GO command will be used to execute down to this point in the program. This command is

$$-G \quad A \qquad (\leftarrow)$$

Notice in the trace information displayed for this command that now CS contains 0915_{16} and IP contains $000A_{16}$; therefore, the next instruction to be executed is at address 0915:000A. This is the ADD instruction.

Now we need to initialize registers AX, BX, and the memory location pointed to by SUM (WORD PTR [0000]). We must also verify that the CF status flag is set to NC (no carry). In Fig. 6.13(c), we find that these operations are done with the following sequence of commands.

$$
\begin{array}{ll}
-R \ AX & (\leftarrow) \\
AX \ 0917 & \\
:1234 & (\leftarrow) \\
-R \ BX & (\leftarrow) \\
\end{array}
$$

```
BX  0000
:AB                                    (↵)
—R  F                                  (↵)
NV  UP  DI  PL  NZ  NA  PO  NC  —  (↵)
—E  0  CD  00                          (↵)
—D  0  1                               (↵)
0917:0000  CD  00
```

Now we are ready to execute the ADD instruction. This is done by issuing the TRACE command

$$—T \quad (↵)$$

From the state information displayed for this command in Fig. 6.13(c), notice that the value CD_{16} has been added to the original value in AX, which was 1234_{16}, and the sum that results in AX is 1301_{16}.

Next the ADC instruction is executed with another T command.

$$—T \quad (↵)$$

It causes the immediate operand value 05_{16} to be added to the original contents of BL, which is AB_{16}, and the sum that is produced in BL is $B0_{16}$.

The last instruction is executed with one more T command, and it causes the SUM (WORD PTR [0000]) to be incremented by one. This can be verified by issuing the DUMP command

$$—D \quad 0 \quad 1 \quad (↵)$$

The addition instructions we just covered can also be used to directly add numbers expressed in ASCII code. This eliminates the need for doing a code conversion on ASCII data prior to processing it with addition operations. Whenever the 8088 does an addition on ASCII format data, an adjustment must be performed on the result to convert it to a decimal number. It is specifically for this purpose that the *ASCII adjust for addition* (AAA) instruction is provided in the instruction set of the 8088. The AAA instruction should be executed immediately after the instruction that adds ASCII data.

Assuming that AL contains the result produced by adding two ASCII-coded numbers, execution of the AAA instruction causes the contents of AL to be replaced by its equivalent decimal value. If the sum is greater than nine, AL contains the LSDs and AH is incremented by one. Otherwise, AL contains the sum and AH is cleared. Both the AF and CF flags can get affected. Since AAA can only adjust data that are in AL, the destination register for ADD instructions that process ASCII numbers should be AL.

Example 6.11

What is the result of executing the following instruction sequence?

$$\text{ADD AL,BL}$$
$$\text{AAA}$$

Assume that AL contains 32_{16}, which is the ASCII code for number 2, BL contains 34_{16}, which is the ASCII code for number 4, and AH has been cleared.

Solution:

Executing the ADD instruction gives

$$(AL) \leftarrow (AL) + (BL) = 32_{16} + 34_{16} = 66_{16}$$

Next, the result is adjusted to give its equivalent decimal number. This is done by execution of the AAA instruction. The equivalent of adding 2 and 4 is decimal 6 with no carry. Therefore, the result after the AAA instruction is

$$(AL) = 06_{16}$$
$$(AH) = 00_{16}$$

and both AF and CF remain cleared.

The instruction set of the 8088 includes another instruction, called *decimal adjust for addition* (DAA). This instruction is used to perform an adjust operation similar to that performed by AAA but for the addition of packed BCD numbers instead of ASCII numbers. Information about this instruction is also provided in Fig. 6.9. Similar to AAA, DAA performs an adjustment on the value in AL. A typical instruction sequence is

$$\text{ADD AL,BL}$$
$$\text{DAA}$$

Remember that the contents of AL and BL must be packed BCD numbers, that is, two BCD digits packed into a byte. The adjusted result in AL is again a packed BCD byte.

Subtraction Instructions—SUB, SBB, DEC, AAS, DAS, and NEG

The instruction set of the 8088 includes an extensive set of instructions provided for implementing subtraction. As shown in Fig. 6.14, the subtraction subgroup is similar to the addition subgroup. It includes instructions for subtracting a source and destination operand, decrementing an operand, and for adjusting subtractions of ASCII and BCD data. An additional instruction in this subgroup is negate.

Mnemonic	Meaning	Format	Operation	Flags affected
SUB	Subtraction	SUB D,S	(D)−(S) → (D) Borrow → (CF)	OF,SF,ZF,AF,PF,CF
SBB	Subtract with borrow	SBB D,S	(D)−(S)−(CF) → (D)	OF,SF,ZF,AF,PF,CF
DEC	Decrement by 1	DEC D	(D)−1 → (D)	OF,SF,ZF,AF,PF,CF
NEG	Negate	NEG D	0−(D) → (D) 1 → (CF)	OF,SF,ZF,AF,PF,CF
DAS	Decimal adjust for subtraction	DAS		OF,SF,ZF,AF,PF,CF
AAS	ASCII adjust for subtraction	ASAS		OF,SF,ZF,AF,PF,CF

(a)

Destination	Source
Register	Register
Register	Memory
Memory	Register
Accumulator	Immediate
Register	Immediate
Memory	Immediate

(b)

Destination
Reg16
Reg8
Memory

(c)

Destination
Register
Memory

(d)

Figure 6.14 (a) Subtraction arithmetic instructions; (b) allowed operands for SUB and SBB instructions; (c) allowed operands for DEC instruction; (d) allowed operands for NEG instruction.

The *subtract* (SUB) instruction is used to subtract the value of a source operand from a destination operand. The result of this operation in general is given as

$$(D) \leftarrow (D) - (S)$$

As shown in Fig. 6.14(b), it can employ the identical operand combinations as the ADD instruction.

The *subtract with borrow* (SBB) instruction is similar to SUB; however, it also subtracts the content of the carry flag from the destination. That is,

$$(D) \leftarrow (D) - (S) - (CF)$$

Example 6.12

Assuming that the contents of registers BX and CX are 1234_{16} and 0123_{16}, respectively, and the carry flag is 0, what will be the result of executing the instruction

SBB   BX,CX?

Solution:

Since the instruction implements the operation,

$$(BX) - (CX) - (CF) \rightarrow (BX)$$

we get

$$(BX) = 1234_{16} - 0123_{16} - 0_{16}$$
$$= 1111_{16}$$

Example 6.13

Verify the operation of the subtract instruction in Example 6.12 by repeating the example using the debugger on the IBM PC.

Solution:

As shown in Fig. 6.15, we first bring up the debugger and then dump the initial state of the 8088 with a REGISTER command. Next we load registers BX, CX, and flag CF with the values 1234_{16}, 0123_{16}, and NC, respectively. Notice in Fig. 6.15 that this is done with three more R commands.

```
A>DEBUG
-R
AX=0000  BX=0000  CX=0000  DX=0000  SP=70EE  BP=0000  SI=0000  DI=0000
DS=08F1  ES=08F1  SS=08F1  CS=08F1  IP=0100   NV UP DI PL NZ NA PO NC
08F1:0100 8B0E2000      MOV     CX,[0020]                      DS:0020=FFFF
-R BX
BX 0000
:1234
-R CX
CX 0000
:0123
-R F
NV UP DI PL NZ NA PO NC -
-A
08F1:0100 SBB   BX,CX
08F1:0102
-R
AX=0000  BX=1234  CX=0123  DX=0000  SP=70EE  BP=0000  SI=0000  DI=0000
DS=08F1  ES=08F1  SS=08F1  CS=08F1  IP=0100   NV UP DI PL NZ NA PO NC
08F1:0100 19CB          SBB     BX,CX
-U 100 101
08F1:0100 19CB          SBB     BX,CX
-T

AX=0000  BX=1111  CX=0123  DX=0000  SP=70EE  BP=0000  SI=0000  DI=0000
DS=08F1  ES=08F1  SS=08F1  CS=08F1  IP=0102   NV UP DI PL NZ NA PE NC
08F1:0102 2000          AND     [BX+SI],AL                     DS:1111=AA
-Q

A>
```

Figure 6.15 Display sequence for Example 6.13.

Now the instruction is assembled at address CS:100 with the command

```
—A                              (↵)
08F1:0100  SBB  BX,CX  (↵)
08F1:0102                      (↵)
—
```

Before executing the instruction, we can verify the initialization of the register and the entry of the instruction by issuing the commands

```
—R                 (↵)
```

and

```
—U  100  101  (↵)
```

Looking at Fig. 6.15, we find that the registers have been correctly initialized and that the instruction SBB BX,CX has been correctly loaded.

Finally, the instruction is executed with a TRACE command. As shown in Fig. 6.15, the result of executing the instruction is that the contents of CX were subtracted from the contents of BX. The difference, which is 1111_{16}, resides in destination register BX.

Just as the INC instruction could be used to add one to an operand, the *decrement* (DEC) instruction can be used to subtract one from its operand. The allowed operands are shown in Fig. 6.14(c).

In Fig. 6.14(d) we see that the *negate* (NEG) instruction can operate on operands in a general-purpose register or a storage location in memory. Execution of this instruction causes the value of its operand to be replaced by its negative. The way this is actually done is through subtraction. That is, the contents of the specified operand are subtracted from zero using 2's-complement arithmetic, and the result is returned to the operand location.

Example 6.14

Assuming that register BX contains $003A_{16}$, what is the result of executing the instruction

```
NEG  BX ?
```

Solution:

Executing the NEG instruction causes the 2's-complement subtraction that follows:

$$0000_{16} - (BX) = 0000_{16} + 2\text{'s complement of } 003A_{16}$$
$$= 0000_{16} + FFC6_{16}$$
$$= FFC6_{16}$$

This value is returned to BX.

$$(BX) = FFC6_{16}$$

Example 6.15

Verify the operation of the NEG instruction in Example 6.14 by executing it with the debugger on the IBM PC.

Solution:

After loading the DEBUG program, we must initialize the contents of the BX register. This is done with the command

```
           —R            (↵)
           BX  0000
           :3A          . (↵)
           —
```

Next the instruction is assembled with the command

```
           —A                    (↵)
           08F1:0100  NEG  BX  (↵)
           08F1:0102            (↵)
           —
```

At this point, we can verify the initialization of BX by issuing the command

```
           —R  BX   (↵)
           BX  003A (↵)
           :        (↵)
           —
```

To check the assembly of the instruction, we can unassemble it with the command

```
           —U  100 101              (↵)
           08F1:0100 F7DB  NEG  BX
           —
```

Now the instruction is executed with the command

```
           —T      (↵)
```

The trace information that is dumped by issuing this command is shown in Fig. 6.16. Here the new contents in register BX are verified as $FFC6_{16}$, which is the negative of $003A_{16}$.

In our study of the addition instruction subgroup, we found that the 8088 was capable of directly adding ASCII and BCD numbers. The SUB and SBB instructions can also subtract numbers represented in these formats. Just as for

```
A>DEBUG
-R BX
BX 0000
:3A
-A
08F1:0100 NEG  BX
08F1:0102
-R BX
BX 003A
:
-U 100 101
08F1:0100 F7DB           NEG       BX
-T

AX=0000  BX=FFC6  CX=0000  DX=0000  SP=70EE  BP=0000  SI=0000  DI=0000
DS=08F1  ES=08F1  SS=08F1  CS=08F1  IP=0102    NV UP DI NG NZ AC PE CY
08F1:0102 2000           AND       [BX+SI],AL                    DS:FFC6=FF
-Q

A>
```

Figure 6.16 Display sequence for Example 6.15.

addition, the results that are obtained must be adjusted to produce their corresponding decimal numbers. In the case of ASCII subtraction, we use the
ASCII adjust for subtraction (AAS) instruction, and for packed BCD subtraction we use the *decimal adjust for subtract* (DAS) instruction.

An example of an instruction sequence for direct ASCII subtraction is

```
SUB  AL,BL
AAS
```

ASCII numbers must be loaded into AL and BL before execution of the subtract instruction. Notice that the destination of the subtraction should be AL.
After execution of AAS, AL contains the difference of the two numbers, and
AH is cleared if no borrow takes place or is decremented by one if a borrow occurs.

Multiplication and Division Instructions—MUL, DIV, IMUL, IDIV, AAM, AAD, CBW, and CWD

The 8088 has instructions to support multiplication and division of binary and
BCD numbers. Two basic types of multiplication and division instructions,
those for the processing of unsigned numbers and signed numbers, are available. To do these operations on unsigned numbers, the instructions are MUL
and DIV. On the other hand, to multiply or divide signed numbers, the instructions are IMUL and IDIV.

Figure 6.17(a) describes these instructions. Notice in Fig. 6.17(b) that a
single byte-wide or word-wide operand is specified in a multiplication instruction. It is the source operand. As shown in Fig. 6.17(a), the other operand, which
is the destination, is assumed already to be in AL for eight-bit multiplications
or in AX for 16-bit multiplications.

Mnemonic	Meaning	Format	Operation	Flags affected
MUL	Multiply (unsigned)	MUL S	$(AL)*(S8) \rightarrow (AX)$ $(AX)*(S16) \rightarrow (DX),(AX)$	OF,SF,ZF,AF,PF,CF
DIV	Division (unsigned)	DIV S	1) $Q((AX)/(S8)) \rightarrow (AL)$ $R((AX)/(S8)) \rightarrow (AH)$ 2) $Q((DX,AX)/(S16)) \rightarrow (AX)$ $R((DX,AX)/(S16)) \rightarrow (DX)$ If Q is FF_{16} in case 1 or $FFFF_{16}$ in case 2 then type 0 interrupt occurs	OF,SF,ZF,AF,PF,CF
IMUL	Integer multiply (signed)	IMUL S	$(AL)*(S8) \rightarrow (AX)$ $(AX)*(S16) \rightarrow (DX),(AX)$	OF,SF,ZF,AF,PF,CF
IDIV	Integer divide (signed)	IDIV S	1) $Q((AX)/(S8)) \rightarrow (AX)$ $R((AX)/(S8)) \rightarrow (AH)$ 2) $Q((DX,AX)/(S16)) \rightarrow (AX)$ $R((DX,AX)/(S16)) \rightarrow (DX)$ If Q is $7F_{16}$ in case 1 or $7FFF_{16}$ in case 2 then type 0 interrupt occurs	OF,SF,ZF,AF,PF,CF
AAM	Adjust AL for multiplication	AAM	$Q((AL)/10) \rightarrow AH$ $R((AL)/10) \rightarrow AL$	OF,SF,ZF,AF,PF,CF
AAD	Adjust AX for division	AAD	$(AH)*10 + AL \rightarrow AL$ $00 \rightarrow AH$	OF,SF,ZF,AF,PF,CF
CBW	Convert byte to word	CBW	$(MSB \ of \ AL) \rightarrow (All \ bits \ of \ AH)$	None
CWD	Convert word to double word	CWD	$(MSB \ of \ AX) \rightarrow (All \ bits \ of \ DX)$	None

(a)

Source
Reg8
Reg16
Mem8
Mem16

(b)

Figure 6.17 (a) Multiplication and division instructions; (b) allowed operands.

The result of executing a MUL or IMUL instruction on byte data can be represented as

$$(AX) \leftarrow (AL) \times (\text{8-Bit operand})$$

That is, the resulting 16-bit product is produced in the AX register. On the other hand, for multiplications of data words, the 32-bit result is given by

$$(DX,AX) \leftarrow (AX) \times (\text{16-Bit operand})$$

where AX contains the 16 LSBs and DX the 16 MSBs.

For the division operation, again just the source operand is specified. The other operand is either the contents of AX for 16-bit dividends or the contents of both DX and AX for 32-bit dividends. The result of a DIV or IDIV instruction for an eight-bit divisor is represented by

$$(AH),(AL) \leftarrow (AX)/(8\text{-Bit operand})$$

where (AH) is the remainder and (AL) the quotient. For 16-bit divisions, we get

$$(DX),(AX) \leftarrow (DX,AX)/(16\text{-Bit operand})$$

Here AX contains the quotient and DX contains the remainder.

Example 6.16

If the contents of AL equals -1_{10} and the contents of CL are -2_{10}, what will be the result produced in AX by executing the instructions

                    MUL CL

and

                    IMUL CL

Solution:

The first instruction multiplies the contents of AL and CL as unsigned numbers.

$$-1_{10} = 11111111_2 = FF_{16}$$

$$-2_{10} = 11111110_2 = FE_{16}$$

Thus executing the MUL instruction, we get

$$(AX) = 11111111_2 \times 11111110_2 = 1111110100000010_2$$
$$= FD02_{16}$$

The second instruction multiplies the same two numbers as signed numbers and gives

$$(AX) = -1_{16} \times -2_{16}$$
$$= 2_{16}$$

Example 6.17

Verify the operation of the MUL instruction obtained in Example 6.16 by performing the same operation on the IBM PC with the debugger.

Solution:

First the DEBUG program is loaded and then registers AX and CX are initialized with the values FF_{16} and FE_{16}, respectively. These registers are loaded as follows:

```
                              —R  AX   (↵)
                              AX  0000
                              :FF       (↵)
                              —R  CX   (↵)
                              CX  0000
                              :FE        (↵)
                              —
```

Next the instruction is loaded with the command

```
                    —A                    (↵)
                    08F1:0100  MUL  CL
                    08F1:0102              (↵)
                    —
```

Before executing the instruction, let us verify the loading of AX, CX, and the instruction. To do this, we use the commands

```
                    —R  AX                (↵)
                    AX  00FF
                    :                      (↵)
                    —R  CX                (↵)
                    CX  00FE
                    :                      (↵)
                    —U  100  101          (↵)
                    08F1:0100  MUL  CL
                    —
```

To execute the instruction, we issue the T command.

```
                              —T         (↵)
```

The displayed result in Fig. 6.18 shows that AX now contains FD02$_{16}$, which is the product that was expected.

As shown in Fig. 6.17(a), adjust instructions for BCD multiplication and division are also provided. They are *adjust AX for multiply* (AAM) and *Adjust AX for divide* (AAD). The multiplication performed just before execution of the AAM instruction is assumed to have been performed on two unpacked BCD numbers with the product produced in AL. The AAD instruction assumes that AH and AL contain unpacked BCD numbers.

The division instructions can also be used to divide an eight-bit dividend in AL by an eight-bit divisor. However, to do this, the sign of the dividend must first be extended to fill the AX register. That is, AH is filled with zeros if the number in AL is positive or with ones if it is negative. This conversion is automatically done by executing the *convert byte to word* (CBW) instruction.

```
A>DEBUG
-R AX
AX 0000
:FF
-R CX
CX 0000
:FE
-A
08F1:0100 MUL  CL
08F1:0102
-R AX
AX 00FF
:
-R CX
CX 00FE
:
-U 100 101
08F1:0100 F6E1          MUL     CL
-T

AX=FD02  BX=0000  CX=00FE  DX=0000  SP=70EE  BP=0000  SI=0000  DI=0000
DS=08F1  ES=08F1  SS=08F1  CS=08F1  IP=0102    OV UP DI NG NZ NA PO CY
08F1:0102 2000          AND     [BX+SI],AL                    DS:0000=CD
-Q

A>
```

Figure 6.18 Display sequence for Example 6.17.

In a similar way, the 32-bit by 16-bit division instructions can be used to divide a 16-bit dividend in AX by a 16-bit divisor. In this case, the sign bit of AX must be extended by 16 bits into the DX register. This can be done by another instruction, which is known as *convert word to double word* (CWD). These two sign-extension instructions are also shown in Fig. 6.17(a).

Notice that the CBW and CWD instructions are provided to handle operations where the result or intermediate results of an operation cannot be held in the correct word length for use in other arithmetic operations. Using these instructions, we can extend a byte or word of data to its equivalent word or double word.

Example 6.18

What is the result of executing the following sequence of instructions?

$$\text{MOV AL,0A1H}$$
$$\text{CBW}$$
$$\text{CWD}$$

Solution:

The first instruction loads AL with $A1_{16}$. This gives

$$(AL) = A1_{16} = 10100001_2$$

Executing the second instruction extends the most significant bit of AL, which is one, into all bits of AH. The result is

$$(AH) = 11111111_2 = FF_{16}$$

$$(AX) = 1111111110100001_2 = FFA1_{16}$$

This completes conversion of the byte in AL to a word in AX.

The last instruction loads each bit of DX with the most significant bit of AX. This bit is also one. Therefore, we get

$$(DX) = 1111111111111111_2 = FFFF_{16}$$

Now the word in AX has been extended to the double word

$$(AX) = FFA1_{16}$$

$$(DX) = FFFF_{16}$$

Example 6.19

Use an assembled version of the program in Example 6.18 to verify the results obtained when it is executed.

Solution:

The source program that is created using the EDLIN editor is shown in Fig. 6.19(a). Notice that this program differs from that described in Example 6.18 in

```
A>TYPE B:EX619.ASM


TITLE    EXAMPLE 6.19

        PAGE    ,132

STACK_SEG       SEGMENT         STACK 'STACK'
                DB              64 DUP(?)
STACK_SEG       ENDS


CODE_SEG        SEGMENT         'CODE'
EX619   PROC    FAR
        ASSUME  CS:CODE_SEG, SS:STACK_SEG

;To return to DEBUG program put return address on the stack

        PUSH    DS
        MOV     AX, 0
        PUSH    AX

;Following code implements Example 6.19

        MOV     AL, 0A1H
        CBW
        CWD

        RET                     ;Return to DEBUG program
EX619   ENDP

CODE_SEG        ENDS

        END     EX619

A>
```

(a)

Figure 6.19 (a) Source program for Example 6.19; (b) source listing produced by assembler; (c) debug session for execution of program EX619.EXE.

```
                              TITLE    EXAMPLE 6.19

                                  PAGE     ,132

0000                    STACK_SEG       SEGMENT         STACK 'STACK'
0000      40 [                          DB              64 DUP(?)
               ??
                    ]

0040                    STACK_SEG       ENDS


0000                    CODE_SEG        SEGMENT         'CODE'
0000                    EX619   PROC    FAR
                                ASSUME  CS:CODE_SEG, SS:STACK_SEG

                        ;To return to DEBUG program put return address on the stack

0000  1E                        PUSH    DS
0001  B8 0000                   MOV     AX, 0
0004  50                        PUSH    AX

                        ;Following code implements Example 6.19

0005  B0 A1                     MOV     AL, 0A1H
0007  98                        CBW
0008  99                        CWD

0009  CB                        RET                     ;Return to DEBUG program
000A                    EX619   ENDP

000A                    CODE_SEG        ENDS

                                END     EX619
```

Segments and groups:

	Size	align	combine	class
N a m e				
CODE_SEG	000A	PARA	NONE	'CODE'
STACK_SEG.	0040	PARA	STACK	'STACK'

Symbols:

	Type	Value	Attr
N a m e			
EX619.	F PROC	0000	CODE_SEG Length =000A

Warning Severe
Errors Errors
0   0

A>

(b)

Figure 6.19 (continued)

that it includes the pseudo-op statements that are needed to assemble it and some
additional instructions so that it can be executed through the debugger.

This source file is assembled with the macroassembler and then linked with
the LINK program to give a run module stored in the file EX619.EXE. The source
listing (EX619.LST) produced by the assembly of this source file, which is called
EX619.ASM, is shown in Fig. 6.19(b).

232

```
A>DEBUG B:EX619.EXE
-U 0 9
0915:0000 1E          PUSH    DS
0915:0001 B80000       MOV     AX,0000
0915:0004 50          PUSH    AX
0915:0005 B0A1         MOV     AL,A1
0915:0007 98          CBW
0915:0008 99          CWD
0915:0009 CB          RETF
-G 5

AX=0000  BX=0000  CX=000A  DX=0000  SP=003C  BP=0000  SI=0000  DI=0000
DS=0905  ES=0905  SS=0916  CS=0915  IP=0005    NV UP DI PL NZ NA PO NC
0915:0005 B0A1         MOV     AL,A1
-T

AX=00A1  BX=0000  CX=000A  DX=0000  SP=003C  BP=0000  SI=0000  DI=0000
DS=0905  ES=0905  SS=0916  CS=0915  IP=0007    NV UP DI PL NZ NA PO NC
0915:0007 98          CBW
-T

AX=FFA1  BX=0000  CX=000A  DX=0000  SP=003C  BP=0000  SI=0000  DI=0000
DS=0905  ES=0905  SS=0916  CS=0915  IP=0008    NV UP DI PL NZ NA PO NC
0915:0008 99          CWD
-T

AX=FFA1  BX=0000  CX=000A  DX=FFFF  SP=003C  BP=0000  SI=0000  DI=0000
DS=0905  ES=0905  SS=0916  CS=0915  IP=0009    NV UP DI PL NZ NA PO NC
0915:0009 CB          RETF
-G

Program terminated normally
-Q
```

(c)

Figure 6.19 (continued)

As shown in Fig. 6.19(c), the run module is loaded for execution as part of calling up the DEBUG program. This is done with the command

A > DEBUG B:EX619.EXE   ($\hookleftarrow$)

The program load can now be verified with the UNASSEMBLE command

—U 0 9   ($\hookleftarrow$)

Looking at the instructions displayed in Fig. 6.19(c), we see that the program is correct.

From the unassembled version of the program in Fig. 6.19(c), we find that the instructions we are interested in start at address 0915:0005. Thus we will execute the instructions prior to the MOV   AL,A1 instruction by issuing the command

—G 5   ($\hookleftarrow$)

The state information that is displayed in Fig. 6.19(b) shows that $(AX) = 0000_{16}$ and $(DX) = 0000_{16}$. Moreover, $(IP) = 0005_{16}$ and points to the first instruction that we are interested in. This instruction is executed with the command

—T   ($\hookleftarrow$)

In the trace dump information of Fig. 6.19(c), we see that AL has been loaded with $A1_{16}$ and DX contains 0000_{16}.

Now the second instruction is executed with the command

$$-\text{T} \quad (\leftarrow\!\lrcorner)$$

Again looking at the trace information, we see that AX now contains the value FFA1_{16} and DX still contains 0000_{16}.

To execute the third instruction, the command is

$$-\text{T} \quad (\leftarrow\!\lrcorner)$$

Then looking at the trace information produced, we find that AX still contains FFA1_{16} and the value in DX has changed to FFFF_{16}. This shows us that the word in AX has been extended to a double word in DX and AX.

To run the program to completion enter the command

$$-\text{G} \quad (\leftarrow\!\lrcorner)$$

This executes the remaining instructions, which cause control to be returned to the DEBUG program.

6.5 LOGIC INSTRUCTIONS

The 8088 has instructions for performing the logic operations *AND, OR, exclusive-OR,* and *NOT.* As shown in Fig. 6.20(a), the AND, OR, and XOR instructions perform their respective logic operations bit by bit on the specified source and destination operands, the result being represented by the final contents of the destination operand. Figure 6.20(b) shows the allowed operand combinations for the AND, OR, and XOR instructions.

For example, the instruction

$$\text{AND} \quad \text{AX,BX}$$

causes the contents of BX to be ANDed with the contents of AX. The result is reflected by the new contents of AX. If AX contains 1234_{16} and BX contains 000F_{16}, the result produced by the instruction is

$$1234_{16} \bullet 000\text{F}_{16} = 0001001000110100_2 \bullet 0000000000001111_2$$
$$= 0000000000000100_{16}$$
$$= 0004_{16}$$

This result is stored in the destination operand.

$$(\text{AX}) = 0004_{16}$$

In this way we see that the AND instruction was used to mask off the 12 most significant bits of the destination operand.

Mnemonic	Meaning	Format	Operation	Flags affected
AND	Logical AND	AND D,S	$(S) \cdot (D) \rightarrow (D)$	OF,SF,ZF,AF,PF,CF
OR	Logical inclusive OR	OR D,S	$(S) + (D) \rightarrow (D)$	OF,SF,ZF,AF,PF,CF
XOR	Logical exclusive OR	XOR D,S	$(S) \oplus (D) \rightarrow (D)$	OF,SF,ZF,AF,PF,CF
NOT	Logical NOT	NOT D	$(\overline{D}) \rightarrow (D)$	None

(a)

Destination	Source
Register	Register
Register	Memory
Memory	Register
Register	Immediate
Memory	Immediate
Accumulator	Immediate

(b)

Destination
Register
Memory

(c)

Figure 6.20 (a) Logic instructions; (b) allowed operands for the AND, OR, and XOR instructions; (c) allowed operands for the NOT instruction.

The NOT logic instruction differs from those for AND, OR, and exclusive-OR in that it operates on a single operand. Looking at Fig. 6.20(c), which shows the allowed operands of the NOT instruction, we see that this operand can be the contents of an internal register or a location in memory.

Example 6.20

Describe the result of executing the following sequence of instructions.

```
MOV  AL,01010101B
AND  AL,00011111B
OR   AL,11000000B
XOR  AL,00001111B
NOT  AL
```

Solution:

The first instruction moves the immediate operand 01010101_2 into the AL register. This loads the data that are to be manipulated with the logic instructions. The next instruction performs a bit-by-bit AND operation of the contents of AL with immediate operand 00011111_2. This gives

$$01010101_2 \bullet 00011111_2 = 00010101_2$$

This result is produced in destination register AL. Note that this operation has masked off the three most significant bits of AL. The next instruction performs a bit-by-bit logical OR of the present contents of AL with immediate operand $C0_{16}$.

This gives

$$00010101_2 + 11000000_2 = 11010101_2$$
$$(AL) = 11010101$$

This operation is equivalent to setting the two most significant bits of AL.

The fourth instruction is an exclusive-OR operation of the contents of AL with immediate operand 00001111_2. We get

$$11010101_2 \oplus 00001111_2 = 11011010_2$$
$$(AL) = 11011010$$

Note that this operation complements the logic state of those bits in AL that are ones in the immediate operand.

The last instruction, NOT AL, inverts each bit of AL. Therefore, the final contents of AL become

$$(AL) = \overline{11011010_2} = 00100101_2$$

These results are summarized in Fig. 6.21.

Instruction	(AL)
MOV AL,01010101B	01010101
AND AL,00011111B	00010101
OR AL,11000000B	11010101
XOR AL,00001111B	11011010
NOT AL	00100101

Figure 6.21 Results of example program using logic instructions.

Example 6.21

Use the IBM PC's debugger to verify the operation of the program in Example 6.20.

Solution:

After the debugger is brought up, the line-by-line assembler is used to enter the program as shown in Fig. 6.22.

Now the first instruction is executed by issuing the T command

$$-T \quad (\lrcorner)$$

The trace dump given in Fig. 6.22 shows that the value 55_{16} has been loaded into the AL register.

The second instruction is executed by issuing another T command.

$$-T \quad (\lrcorner)$$

Execution of this instruction causes $1F_{16}$ to be ANDed with the value 55_{16} in AL. Looking at the trace information displayed in Fig. 6.22, we see that the three most significant bits of AL have been masked off to produce the result 15_{16}.

```
A>DEBUG
-A
08F1:0100 MOV   AL,55
08F1:0102 AND   AL,1F
08F1:0104 OR    AL,C0
08F1:0106 XOR   AL,OF
08F1:0108 NOT   AL
08F1:010A
-T

AX=0055  BX=0000  CX=0000  DX=0000  SP=70EE  BP=0000  SI=0000  DI=0000
DS=08F1  ES=08F1  SS=08F1  CS=08F1  IP=0102    NV UP DI PL NZ NA PO NC
08F1:0102 241F         AND       AL,1F
-T

AX=0015  BX=0000  CX=0000  DX=0000  SP=70EE  BP=0000  SI=0000  DI=0000
DS=08F1  ES=08F1  SS=08F1  CS=08F1  IP=0104    NV UP DI PL NZ NA PO NC
08F1:0104 0CC0          OR        AL,C0
-T

AX=00D5  BX=0000  CX=0000  DX=0000  SP=70EE  BP=0000  SI=0000  DI=0000
DS=08F1  ES=08F1  SS=08F1  CS=08F1  IP=0106    NV UP DI NG NZ NA PO NC
08F1:0106 340F         XOR       AL,OF
-T

AX=00DA  BX=0000  CX=0000  DX=0000  SP=70EE  BP=0000  SI=0000  DI=0000
DS=08F1  ES=08F1  SS=08F1  CS=08F1  IP=0108    NV UP DI NG NZ NA PO NC
08F1:0108 F6D0         NOT       AL
-T

AX=0025  BX=0000  CX=0000  DX=0000  SP=70EE  BP=0000  SI=0000  DI=0000
DS=08F1  ES=08F1  SS=08F1  CS=08F1  IP=010A    NV UP DI NG NZ NA PO NC
08F1:010A 0000         ADD       [BX+SI],AL     ·                    DS:0000=CD
-Q


A>
```

Figure 6.22 Display sequence for Example 6.21.

The third instruction is executed in the same way.

$$-\text{T} \quad (\dashv)$$

It causes the value $C0_{16}$ to be ORed with the value $1F_{16}$ in AL. This gives the result $D5_{16}$ in AL.

A fourth T command is used to execute the XOR instruction

$$-\text{T} \quad (\dashv)$$

and the trace dump that results shows that the new value in AL is DA_{16}.

The last instruction is a NOT instruction and its execution with the command

$$-\text{T} \quad (\dashv)$$

causes the bits of DA_{16} to be inverted. This gives 25_{16} as the final result in AL.

6.6 SHIFT INSTRUCTIONS

The four *shift instructions* of the 8088 can perform two basic types of shift operations. They are the *logical shift* and the *arithmetic shift.* Moreover, each of these operations can be performed to the right or to the left. The shift instructions are *shift logical left* (SHL), *shift arithmetic left* (SAL), *shift logical right* (SHR), and *shift arithmetic right* (SAR).

The logical shift instructions, SHL and SHR, are described in Fig. 6.23(a). Notice in Fig. 6.23(b) that the destination operand, the data whose bits are to be shifted, can be either the contents of an internal register or a storage location in memory. Moreover, the source operand can be specified in two ways. If it is assigned the value of one, a one-bit shift will take place. For instance, as illustrated in Fig. 6.24(a), executing

SHL AX,1

causes the 16-bit contents of the AX register to be shifted one bit position to the

Mnemonic	Meaning	Format	Operation	Flags affected
SAL/SHL	Shift arithmetic left/shift logical left	SAL/SHL D,Count	Shift the (D) left by the number of bit positions equal to count and fill the vacated bit positions on the right with zeros.	OF,CF
SHR	Shift logical right	SHR D,Count	Shift the (D) right by the number of bit positions equal to count and fill the vacated bit positions on the left with zeros.	OF,CF
SAR	Shift arithmetic right	SAR D,Count	Shift the (D) right by the number of bit positions equal to count and fill the vacated bit positions on the left with the original most significant bit.	OF,SF,ZF,AF,PF,CF

(a)

Destination	Count
Register	1
Register	CL
Memory	1
Memory	CL

(b)

Figure 6.23 (a) Shift instructions; (b) allowed operands.

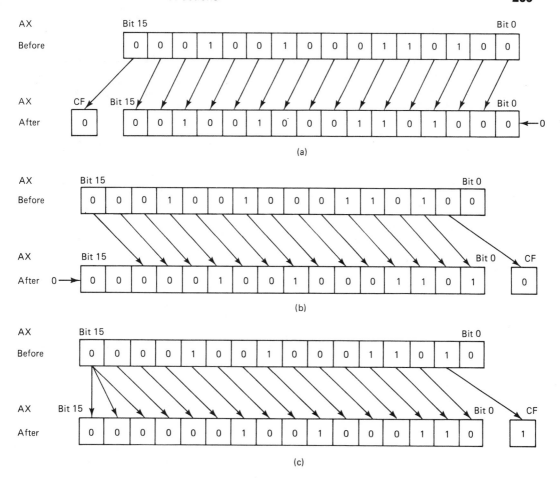

Figure 6.24 (a) Results of executing SHL AX,1; (b) result of executing SHR AX,CL; (c) results of executing SAR AX,CL.

left. Here we see that the vacated LSB location is filled with zero and the bit shifted out of the MSB is saved in CF.

On the other hand, if the source operand is specified as CL instead of one, the count in this register represents the number of bit positions the operand is to be shifted. This permits the count to be defined under software control and allows a range of shifts from 1 to 256 bits.

An example of an instruction specified in this way is

SHR   AX,CL

Assuming that CL contains the value 02_{16}, the logical shift right that occurs is as shown in Fig. 6.24(b). Notice that the two MSBs have been filled with zeros and the last bit shifted out at the LSB, which is zero, is maintained in the carry flag.

In an arithmetic shift to the left, SAL operation, the vacated bits at the right of the operand are filled with zeros, whereas in an arithmetic shift to the right, SAR operation, the vacated bits at the left are filled with the value of the original MSB of the operand. Thus in an arithmetic shift to the right, the original sign of the number is extended. This operation is equivalent to division by powers of two as long as the bits shifted out of the LSB are zeros.

Example 6.22

Assume that CL contains 02_{16} and AX contains $091A_{16}$. Determine the new contents of AX and the carry flag after the instruction

```
SAR   AX,CL
```

is executed.

Solution:

Figure 6.24(c) shows the effect of executing the instruction. Here we see that since CL contains 02_{16}, a shift right by two bit locations takes place and the original sign bit, which is logic 0, is extended to the two vacated bit positions. Moreover, the last bit shifted out from the LSB location is placed in CF. This makes CF equal to 1. Therefore, the results produced by execution of the instruction are

$$(AX) = 0246_{16}$$

and

$$(CF) = 1_2$$

Example 6.23

Verify the operation of the SAR instruction in Example 6.22 by executing the DEBUG program on the IBM PC.

Solution:

After invoking the debugger, we enter the instruction by assembling it with the command

```
—A                          (↵)
08F1:0100  SAR  AX,CL  (↵)
08F1:0102                   (↵)

—
```

Next, registers AX and CL are loaded with data and the carry flag is reset. This is done with the command sequence

```
—R AX                            (↵)
AX 0000
```

```
:091A                              (↵)
—R CX                              (↵)
CX  0000
:2                                 (↵)
—R F
NV UP DI PL NZ NA PO NC —  (↵)
—
```

Notice that the carry flag was already clear so no status entry was made.
Now the instruction is executed with the T command

$$-T \qquad (↵)$$

Note in Fig. 6.25 that the value in AX has become 0246_{16} and a carry (CY) has occurred. These results are identical to those obtained in Example 6.22.

```
A>DEBUG
-A
08F1:0100 SAR   AX,CL
08F1:0102
-R AX
AX 0000
:091A
-R CX
CX 0000
:2
-R F
NV UP DI PL NZ NA PO NC -
-T

AX=0246  BX=0000  CX=0002  DX=0000  SP=70EE  BP=0000  SI=0000  DI=0000
DS=08F1  ES=08F1  SS=08F1  CS=08F1  IP=0102   NV UP DI PL NZ NA PO CY
08F1:0102 241F           AND     AL,1F
-Q

A>
```

Figure 6.25 Display sequence for Example 6.23.

6.7 ROTATE INSTRUCTIONS

Another group of instructions, known as the *rotate instructions,* are similar to
the shift instructions we just introduced. This group, as shown in Fig. 6.26(a),
includes the *rotate left* (ROL), *rotate right* (ROR), *rotate left through carry*
(RCL), and *rotate right through carry* (RCR) instructions.

As shown in Fig. 6.26(b), the rotate instructions are similar to the shift instructions in several ways. They have the ability to shift the contents of either
an internal register or storage location in memory. Also, the shift that takes
place can be from 1 to 256 bit positions to the left or to the right. Moreover, in
the case of a multibit shift, the number of bit positions to be shifted is again

Mnemonic	Meaning	Format	Operation	Flags affected
ROL	Rotate left	ROL D,Count	Rotate the (D) left by the number of bit positions equal to count. Each bit shifted out from the left-most bit goes back into the rightmost bit position.	OF,CF
ROR	Rotate right	ROR D,Count	Rotate the (D) right by the number of bit positions equal to count. Each bit shifted out from the rightmost bit goes into the leftmost bit position.	OF,CF
RCL	Rotate left through carry	RCL D,Count	Same as ROL except carry is attached to (D) for rotation.	OF,CF
RCR	Rotate right through carry	RCR D,Count	Same as ROR except carry is attached to (D) for rotation.	OF,CF

(a)

Destination	Count
Register	1
Register	CL
Memory	1
Memory	CL

(b)

Figure 6.26 (a) Rotate instructions; (b) allowed operands.

specified by the contents of CL. Their difference from the shift instructions lies in the fact that the bits moved out at either the MSB or LSB end are not lost; instead, they are reloaded at the other end.

As an example, let us look at the operation of the ROL instruction. Execution of ROL causes the contents of the selected operand to be rotated left the specified number of bit positions. Each bit shifted out at the MSB end is reloaded at the LSB end. Moreover, the content of CF reflects the state of the last bit that was shifted out. For instance, the instruction

ROL AX,1

causes a one-bit rotate to the left. Figure 6.27(a) shows the result produced by executing this instruction. Notice that the original value of bit 15 is zero. This value has been rotated into CF and bit 0 of AX. All other bits have been rotated one bit position to the left.

The ROR instruction operates the same way as ROL except that it causes data to be rotated to the right instead of to the left. For example, execution of

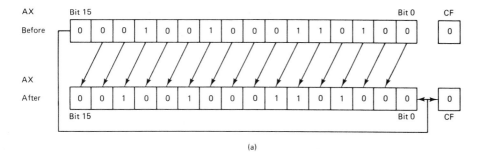

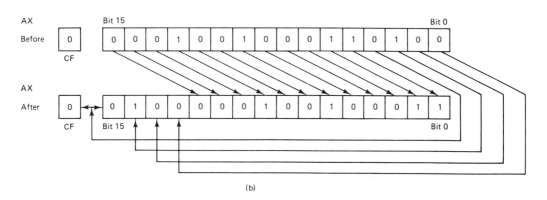

Figure 6.27 (a) Results of executing ROL AX,1; (b) results of executing ROR AX,CL.

ROR AX,CL

causes the contents of AX to be rotated right by the number of bit positions specified in CL. The result for CL equal to four is illustrated in Fig. 6.27(b).

The other two rotate instructions, RCL and RCR, differ from ROL and ROR in that the bits are rotated through the carry flag. Figure 6.28 illustrates the rotation that takes place due to execution of the RCL instruction. Notice that the bit returned to bit 0 is the prior contents of CF and not bit 15. The bit shifted out of bit 15 goes into the carry flag. Thus the bits rotate through carry.

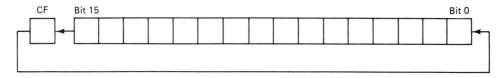

Figure 6.28 Rotation caused by execution of the RCL instruction.

Example 6.24

What is the result in BX and CF after execution of the following instruction:

RCR BX,CL ?

Assume that prior to execution of the instruction (CL) = 04_{16}, (BX) = 1234_{16}, and (CF) = 0.

Solution:

The original contents of BX are

$$(BX) = 0001001000110100_2 = 1234_{16}$$

Execution of the ROR instruction causes a four-bit rotate right through carry to take place on the data in BX. Therefore, the original content of bit 3, which is zero, resides in carry; CF=0 and 1000_2 has been reloaded from bit 15. The resulting contents of BX are

$$(BX) = 1000000100100011_2 = 8123_{16}$$

Example 6.25

Use the debugger to verify the operation found for the RCR instruction in Example 6.24 on the PC.

Solution:

After loading DEBUG, the instruction is assembled into memory with the command

```
        —A                    (↵)
        08F1:0100  RCR  BX,CL
        08F1:0102             (↵)
```

Next BX and CX are loaded with data and CF is cleared by issuing the commands

```
      —R  BX                   (↵)
      BX 0000
      :1234                    (↵)
      —R  CX                   (↵)
      CX 0000
      :4                       (↵)
      R  F                     (↵)
      NV UP DI PL NZ NA PO NC — (↵)
      —
```

Notice that CF is already cleared (NC); therefore, no entry is made for the flag register command.

```
A>DEBUG
-A
08F1:0100 RCR   BX,CL
08F1:0102
-R BX
BX 0000
:1234
-R CX
CX 0000
:4
-R F
NV UP DI PL NZ NA PO NC -
-T

AX=0000  BX=8123  CX=0004  DX=0000  SP=70EE  BP=0000  SI=0000  DI=0000
DS=08F1  ES=08F1  SS=08F1  CS=08F1  IP=0102     OV UP DI PL NZ NA PO NC
08F1:0102 241F          AND     AL,1F
-Q

A>
```

Figure 6.29 Display sequence for Example 6.25.

Now we can execute the instruction with the command

$$-T \qquad (\dashv)$$

Looking at the trace information displayed in Fig. 6.29, we see that the new contents of BX are 8123_{16}. This is the same result obtained in Example 6.24.

ASSIGNMENT

Section 6.3

1. Describe the operation performed by each of the following instructions.

    (a) MOV SI,[0ABC]

    (b) MOV WORD PTR [SI],ABCD

2. Use DEBUG to assemble and execute the instruction in problem 1 (a). Initialize the contents of memory location $0ABC_{16}$ to $FFFF_{16}$.

3. Use DEBUG to assemble and execute the instruction in problem 1 (b). Initialize the contents of SI to $0ABC_{16}$ before executing the instruction.

4. Write an instruction sequence using MOV instructions that is equivalent to

    XCHG AX,BX

Load the instruction sequence with the line-by-line assembler in DEBUG starting at address 100_{16} of the current code segment, initialize AX to 1111_{16} and BX to 2222_{16}, and then verify their operation by executing them with the GO command and examining the contents of AX and BX.

5. Assuming that $(AL) = 0010_{16}$, $(BX) = 0100_{16}$, and $DS = 1000_{16}$, what happens if the XLAT instruction is executed?

6. Two code-conversion tables starting with offsets TABL1 and TABL2 in the current data segment are to be accessed. Write a routine that initializes the needed registers and then replaces the contents of memory locations MEM1 and MEM2 (offsets in the data segment) by the equivalent converted codes from the code-conversion tables. Assemble the program with MASM and execute it using DEBUG.

7. Write a single instruction to load AX from address 0200_{16} and DS from address 0202_{16}. Use DEBUG to load 0200_{16} with 0030_{16} and 0202_{16} with 0040_{16}, assemble the instruction and execute it with a trace command to verify loading of the registers.

Section 6.4

8. Two word-wide unsigned integers are stored at the memory addresses $0A00_{16}$ and $0A02_{16}$, respectively. Write an instruction sequence that computes and stores their sum, difference, product, and quotient. Store these results at consecutive memory locations starting at address $0A10_{16}$ in memory. To obtain the difference, subtract the integer at $0A02_{16}$ from the integer at $0A00_{16}$. For the division, divide the integer at $0A00_{16}$ by the integer at $0A02_{16}$. Use register indirect relative addressing mode to store the various results.

9. Assuming that $(AX) = 0123_{16}$ and $(BL) = 10_{16}$, what will be the new contents of AX after executing the instruction DIV BL? Find the results by executing the instruction on the PC.

10. Two byte-size BCD integers are stored at the symbolic addresses NUM1 and NUM2, respectively. Write an instruction sequence to generate their difference and store it at NUM3. The difference is to be formed by subtracting the value at NUM1 from that at NUM2. Assemble the program with MASM and execute it with DEBUG for $(NUM1) = 45_{16}$ and $(NUM2) = 72_{16}$.

Section 6.5

11. Specify the relation between the old and new contents of AX after executing the following instructions.

$$\text{NOT} \quad \text{AX}$$
$$\text{ADD} \quad \text{AX,1}$$

Use DEBUG to initialize AX to $FFFF_{16}$, assemble the instructions starting at 100_{16} of the current code segment, and trace the operation of the instructions.

12. Write an instruction sequence that generates a byte-size integer in the memory location identified by label RESULT. The value of the byte integer is to be calculated as follows:

$$\text{RESULT} = \text{AL} \cdot \text{NUM1} + (\overline{\text{NUM2} \cdot \text{AL} + \text{BL}})$$

Assume that all parameters are byte-size.

Section 6.6

13. Identify the condition under which the contents of AX would remain unchanged after executing any of the instructions that follow.

```
MOV  CL,4
SHL  AX,CL
SHR  AX,CL
```

Verify your answers by executing the instruction sequence for this condition on the PC.

Section 6.7

14. Write a program that saves the content of bit 5 in AL in BX as a word. Assemble the program with MASM and execute with DEBUG to verify its operation.

7

8088 MICROPROCESSOR PROGRAMMING 2

7.1 INTRODUCTION

In Chapter 6 we discussed many of the instructions that can be executed by the 8088 microprocessor. Furthermore, we used these instructions in simple programs. In this chapter we introduce the rest of the instruction set and at the same time cover some more complicated programming techniques. The following topics are discussed in this chapter:

1. Flag-control instructions
2. Compare instruction
3. Jump instructions
4. Subroutines and subroutine handling instructions
5. Loop instruction
6. String instruction

7.2 FLAG-CONTROL INSTRUCTIONS

The 8088 microprocessor has a set of flags that either monitor the status of executing instructions or control options available in its operation. These flags were described in detail in Chapter 3. The instruction set includes a group of instructions which when executed directly affect the setting of the flags. These

Mnemonic	Meaning	Operation	Flags affected
LAHF	Load AH from flags	(AH) ← (Flags)	None
SAHF	Store AH into flags	(Flags) ← (AH)	SF,ZF,AF,PF,CF
CLC	Clear carry flag	(CF) ← 0	CF
STC	Set carry flag	(CF) ← 1	CF
CMC	Complement carry flag	(CF) ← ($\overline{CF}$)	CF
CLI	Clear interrupt flag	(IF) ← 0	IF
STI	Set interrupt flag	(IF) ← 1	IF

Figure 7.1 Flag control instructions of the 8088.

instructions, shown in Fig. 7.1, are: *load AH from flags* (LAHF), *store AH into flags* (SAHF), *clear carry* (CLC), *set carry* (STC), *complement carry* (CMC), *clear interrupt* (CLI), and *set interrupt* (STI). A few more instructions exist that can directly affect the flags; however, we will not cover them until later in the chapter when we introduce the subroutine and string instructions.

Looking at Fig. 7.1, we see that the first two instructions, LAHF and SAHF, can be used either to read the flags or to change them, respectively. Notice that the data transfer that takes place is always between the AH register and the flag register. For instance, we may want to start an operation with certain flags set or reset. Assume that we want to preset all flags to logic 1. To do this, we can first load AH with FF_{16} and then execute the SAHF instruction.

Example 7.1

Write an instruction sequence to save the current contents of the 8088's flags in memory location MEM1 and then reload the flags with the contents of memory location MEM2.

Solution:

To save the current flags, we must first load them into the AH register and then move them to the location MEM1. The instructions that do this are

```
LAHF
MOV  MEM1,AH
```

Similarly, to load the flags with the contents of MEM2, we must first copy the contents of MEM2 into AH and then store the contents of AH into the flags. The instructions for this are

```
MOV  AH,MEM2
SAHF
```

The entire instruction sequence is shown in Fig. 7.2.

```
LAHF
MOV     MEM1,AH
MOV     AH,MEM2
SAHF
```

Figure 7.2 Instruction sequence for saving the contents of the flag register and reloading from memory.

Example 7.2

Use the DEBUG program on the IBM PC to enter the instruction sequence in Example 7.1 starting at memory address 00110_{16}. Assign memory addresses 00150_{16} and 00151_{16} to symbols MEM1 and MEM2, respectively. Then initialize the values of MEM1 and MEM2 to FF_{16} and 01_{16}, respectively. Verify the operation of the instructions by executing them one after the other with the TRACE command.

Solution:

As shown in Fig. 7.3, the DEBUG program is called up with the DOS command

```
A>DEBUG              (↵)
```

Now we are ready to assemble the program into memory. This is done by making the ASSEMBLE command entries

```
—A 0:0110                        (↵)
0000:0110  LAHF                  (↵)
0000:0111  MOV [0150],AH  (↵)
0000:0115  MOV AH,[0151]  (↵)
0000:0119  SAHF                  (↵)
```

Now the values of MEM1 and MEM2 are initialized with the ENTER command

```
—E 0:0150 FF 01          (↵)
```

Moreover, the registers CS, IP, and DS must be initialized with the values 0000_{16}, 0110_{16}, and 0000_{16}, respectively. This is done with the commands

```
—R CS            (↵)
CS 08F1
:0                (↵)
—R IP            (↵)
IP 0100
:0110            (↵)
—R DS            (↵)
DS 08F1
:0                (↵)
```

```
A>DEBUG
-A 0:0110
0000:0110 LAHF
0000:0111 MOV   [0150],AH
0000:0115 MOV   AH,[0151]
0000:0119 SAHF
0000:011A
-E 0:0150 FF 01
-R CS
CS 08F1
:0
-R IP
IP 0100
:0110
-R DS
DS 08F1
:0
-R
AX=0000  BX=0000  CX=0000  DX=0000  SP=70EE  BP=0000  SI=0000  DI=0000
DS=0000  ES=08F1  SS=08F1  CS=0000  IP=0110   NV UP DI PL NZ NA PO NC
0000:0110 9F            LAHF
-T

AX=0200  BX=0000  CX=0000  DX=0000  SP=70EE  BP=0000  SI=0000  DI=0000
DS=0000  ES=08F1  SS=08F1  CS=0000  IP=0111   NV UP DI PL NZ NA PO NC
0000:0111 88265001       MOV    [0150],AH                     DS:0150=FF
-T

AX=0200  BX=0000  CX=0000  DX=0000  SP=70EE  BP=0000  SI=0000  DI=0000
DS=0000  ES=08F1  SS=08F1  CS=0000  IP=0115   NV UP DI PL NZ NA PO NC
0000:0115 8A265101       MOV    AH,[0151]                     DS:0151=01
-D 150 151
0000:0150  02 01                                   ..
-T

AX=0100  BX=0000  CX=0000  DX=0000  SP=70EE  BP=0000  SI=0000  DI=0000
DS=0000  ES=08F1  SS=08F1  CS=0000  IP=0119   NV UP DI PL NZ NA PO NC
0000:0119 9E            SAHF
-T

AX=0100  BX=0000  CX=0000  DX=0000  SP=70EE  BP=0000  SI=0000  DI=0000
DS=0000  ES=08F1  SS=08F1  CS=0000  IP=011A   NV UP DI PL NZ NA PO CY
0000:011A 0000           ADD    [BX+SI],AL                    DS:0000=72
-Q

A>
```

Figure 7.3 Display sequence for Example 7.2.

Before going further, let us verify the initialization of the internal registers. This is done by displaying their state with the R command

$$-R \qquad (\lrcorner)$$

Looking at the information displayed in Fig. 7.3, we see that all three registers have been correctly initialized.

Now we are ready to step through the execution of the program. The first instruction is executed with the command

$$-T \qquad (\lrcorner)$$

Notice from the displayed trace information in Fig. 7.3 that the contents of the status register, which are 02_{16}, have been copied into the AH register.

The second instruction is executed by issuing another T command

$$-T \qquad (\lrcorner)$$

This instruction causes the status, which is now in AH, to be saved in memory at address 0000:0150. The fact that this operation has occurred is verified with the D command

$$-D\ 150\ 151 \qquad (\lrcorner)$$

In Fig. 7.3 we see that the data held at address 0000:0150 is displayed by this command as 02_{16}. This verifies that status was saved at MEM1.

The third instruction is now executed with the command

$$-T \qquad (\lrcorner)$$

Its function is to copy the new status from MEM2 (0000:0151) into the AH register. From the data displayed in the earlier D command, we see that this value is 01_{16}. Looking at the displayed information for the third instruction, we find that 01_{16} has been copied into AH.

The last instruction is executed with another T command and as shown by its trace information in Fig. 7.3, it has caused the carry flag to set. That is, CF is displayed with the value CY.

The next three instructions, CLC, STC, and CMC, are used to manipulate the carry flag. They permit CF to be cleared, set, or complemented to its inverse logic level, respectively. For example, if CF is 1 and the CMC instruction is executed, it becomes 0.

The last two instructions are used to manipulate the interrupt flag. Executing the clear interrupt (CLI) instruction sets IF to logic 0 and disables the interrupt interface. On the other hand, executing the STI instruction sets IF to 1, and the microprocessor starts accepting interrupts from that point on.

Example 7.3

Of the three carry-flag instructions CLC, STC, and CMC, only one is really an independent instruction. That is, the operation that it provides cannot be performed by a series of the other two instructions. Determine which one of the carry instructions is the independent instruction.

Solution:

Let us begin with the CLC instruction. The clear carry operation can be performed by an STC instruction followed by a CMC instruction. Therefore, CLC is not an independent instruction. Moreover, the operation of the set carry (STC) instruction is equivalent to the operation performed by a CLC instruction followed by a CMC instruction. Thus, STC is also not an independent instruction. On the other hand, the operation performed by the last instruction, complement carry (CMC), cannot be expressed in terms of the CLC and STC instructions. Therefore, it is the independent instruction.

Example 7.4

Verify the operation of the following instructions which affect the carry flag:

CLC

STC

CMC

by executing them with the debugger on the IBM PC. Start with CF equal to one (CY).

Solution:

After bringing up the debugger, we enter the instructions with the A command as

—A   (⏎)

08F1:0100 CLC (⏎)

08F1:0101 STC (⏎)

08F1:0102 CMC (⏎)

08F1:0103   (⏎)

—

These inputs are shown in Fig. 7.4.

```
A>DEBUG
-A
08F1:0100 CLC
08F1:0101 STC
08F1:0102 CMC
08F1:0103
-R F
NV UP DI PL NZ NA PO NC -CY
-R F
NV UP DI PL NZ NA PO CY -
-T

AX=0000  BX=0000  CX=0000  DX=0000  SP=70EE  BP=0000  SI=0000  DI=0000
DS=08F1  ES=08F1  SS=08F1  CS=08F1  IP=0101  NV UP DI PL NZ NA PO NC
08F1:0101 F9              STC
-T

AX=0000  BX=0000  CX=0000  DX=0000  SP=70EE  BP=0000  SI=0000  DI=0000
DS=08F1  ES=08F1  SS=08F1  CS=08F1  IP=0102  NV UP DI PL NZ NA PO CY
08F1:0102 F5              CMC
-T

AX=0000  BX=0000  CX=0000  DX=0000  SP=70EE  BP=0000  SI=0000  DI=0000
DS=08F1  ES=08F1  SS=08F1  CS=08F1  IP=0103  NV UP DI PL NZ NA PO NC
08F1:0103 0000            ADD    [BX+SI],AL                        DS:0000=CD
-Q

A>
```

Figure 7.4 Display sequence for Example 7.4.

Next, the carry flag is initialized to CY with the R command

—R F   (↵)
NV UP DI PL NZ NA PO NC —CY   (↵)

and in Fig. 7.4 the updated status is displayed with another R command to verify that CF was set to the CY state.

Now the first instruction is executed with the TRACE command

—T   (↵)

Looking at the displayed state information in Fig. 7.4, we see that CF has been cleared and its new state is NC.

The other two instructions are also executed with T commands and, as shown in Fig. 7.4, the STC instruction sets CF (CY in the state dump) and CMC inverts CF (NC in the state dump).

7.3 COMPARE INSTRUCTION

There is an instruction included in the instruction set of the 8088 which can be used to compare two 8-bit or 16-bit numbers. It is the *compare* (CMP) instruction of Fig. 7.5(a). Figure 7.5(b) shows that the operands can reside in a storage location in memory, a register within the MPU, or as part of the instruction. For instance, a byte-wide wide number in a register such as BL can be compared to a second byte-number that is supplied as immediate data.

The result of the comparison is reflected by changes in six of the status

Mnemonic	Meaning	Format	Operation	Flags affected
CMP	Compare	CMP D,S	(D) − (S) is used in setting or resetting the flags	CF,AF,OF,PF,SF,ZF

(a)

Destination	Source
Register	Register
Register	Memory
Memory	Register
Register	Immediate
Memory	Immediate
Accumulator	Immediate

(b)

Figure 7.5 (a) Compare instruction; (b) operand combinations.

flags of the 8088. Notice in Fig. 7.5(a) that it affects the overflow flag, sign flag, zero flag, auxiliary carry flag, parity flag, and carry flag. The logic state of these flags can be referenced by instructions in order to make a decision whether or not to alter the sequence in which the program executes.

The process of comparison performed by the CMP instruction is basically a subtraction operation. The source operand is subtracted from the destination operand. However, the result of this subtraction is not saved. Instead, based on the result, the appropriate flags are set or reset.

The subtraction is done using 2's-complement arithmetic. For example, let us assume that the destination operand equals $10011001_2 = -103_{10}$ and that the source operand equals $00011011_2 = +27_{10}$. Subtracting the source from the destination, we get

$$10011001_2 = \quad -103_{10}$$
$$-00011011_2 = -(\ +27_{10})$$

Replacing the destination operand with its 2's complement and adding yields

$$10011001_2 = -103_{10}$$
$$+11100101_2 = -\ 27_{10}$$
$$101111110_2 = +126_{10}$$

In the process of obtaining this result, we get the status that follows:

1. No carry is generated from bit 3 to bit 4; therefore, the auxiliary carry flag AF is at logic 0.
2. There is a carry-out from bit 7. Thus, carry flag CF is set.
3. Even though a carry-out of bit 7 is generated, there is no carry from bit 6 to bit 7. This is an overflow condition and the OF flag is set.
4. There are an even number of ones; therefore, this makes parity flag PF equal to one.
5. Bit 7 is zero and therefore sign flag SF is at logic 0.
6. The result that is produced is nonzero, which makes zero flag ZF logic 0.

Notice that the result produced by the subtraction of the two 8-bit numbers is not correct. This condition was indicated by setting the overflow flag.

Example 7.5

Describe what happens to the status flags as the sequence of instructions that follows is executed.

```
MOV AX,1234H
MOV BX,0ABCDH
CMP AX,BX
```

Assume that flags ZF, SF, CF, AF, OF, and PF are all initially reset.

Solution:

The first instruction loads AX with 1234_{16}. No status flags are affected by the execution of a MOV instruction.

The second instruction puts $ABCD_{16}$ into the BX register. Again, status is not affected. Thus, after execution of these two move instructions, the contents of AX and BX are

$$(AX) = 1234_{16} = 0001001000110100_2$$

and

$$(BX) = ABCD_{16} = 1010101111001101_2$$

The third instruction is a 16-bit comparison with AX representing the destination and BX the source. Therefore, the contents of BX are subtracted from that of AX.

$$(AX) - (BX) = 0001001000110100_2 - 1010101111001101_2$$

Replacing (BX) with its 2's complement and adding, we get

$$(AX) + 2\text{'s complement }(BX) = 0001001000110100_2 + 0101010000110010_2 + 1_2$$
$$= 0110011001100111_2$$

The flags are either set or reset based on the result of this subtraction. Notice that the result is nonzero and positive. This makes ZF and SF equal to zero. Moreover, the overflow condition has not occurred. Therefore, OF is also at logic 0. The carry and auxiliary carry conditions have occurred; therefore, CF and AF are 1. Finally, the result has odd parity; therefore, PF is 0. These results are summarized in Fig. 7.6.

Example 7.6

Verify the execution of the instruction sequence in Example 7.5 on the PC. Use DEBUG and a run module formed with the macroassembler and linker programs.

Solution:

A source program written to implement a procedure that contains the instruction sequence executed in Example 7.5 is shown in Fig. 7.7(a). This program was assembled with MASM and linked with LINK to form a run module in file EX76.EXE. The source listing produced by the assembler is shown in Fig. 7.7(b).

Instruction	ZF	SF	CF	AF	OF	PF
Initial state	0	0	0	0	0	0
MOV AX,1234H	0	0	0	0	0	0
MOV BX,0ABCDH	0	0	0	0	0	0
CMP AX,BX	0	0	1	1	0	0

Figure 7.6 Effect on flags of executing instructions.

To execute this program with DEBUG, we bring up the debugger and load the file from a data diskette in drive B with the DOS command

A > DEBUG B:EX76.EXE (⏎)

To verify its loading, the UNASSEMBLE command that follows can be used

—U 0 D   (⏎)

As shown in Fig. 7.7(c), the instructions of the source program are correctly displayed.

First we will execute the instructions up to the CMP instruction. This is done with the GO command

—G B   (⏎)

Note in Fig. 7.7(c) that AX has been loaded with 1234_{16} and BX with the value $ABCD_{16}$.

```
A>TYPE B:EX76.ASM


TITLE    EXAMPLE 7.6

         PAGE       ,132

STACK_SEG          SEGMENT          STACK  'STACK'
                   DB               64 DUP(?)
STACK_SEG          ENDS


CODE_SEG           SEGMENT          'CODE'
EX76     PROC      FAR
         ASSUME    CS:CODE_SEG, SS:STACK_SEG

;To return to DEBUG program put return address on the stack

         PUSH      DS
         MOV       AX, 0
         PUSH      AX

;Following code implements Example 7.6

         MOV       AX, 1234H
         MOV       BX, 0ABCDH
         CMP       AX, BX

         RET                        ;Return to DEBUG program
EX76     ENDP

CODE_SEG           ENDS

         END       EX76

A>
```

(a)

Figure 7.7 (a) Source program for Example 7.6; (b) source listing produced by assembler; (c) execution of the program with DEBUG.

```
A>TYPE B:EX76.LST


The IBM Personal Computer Assembler 02-01-84              PAGE    1-1
EXAMPLE 7.6


                              TITLE   EXAMPLE 7.6

                              PAGE      ,132

0000                          STACK_SEG       SEGMENT        STACK 'STACK'
0000    40 [                                  DB             64 DUP(?)
              ??
            ]

0040                          STACK_SEG       ENDS


0000                          CODE_SEG        SEGMENT        'CODE'
0000                          EX76   PROC     FAR
                                     ASSUME   CS:CODE_SEG, SS:STACK_SEG

                              ;To return to DEBUG program put return address on the stack

0000  1E                              PUSH     DS
0001  B8 0000                         MOV      AX, 0
0004  50                              PUSH     AX

                              ;Following code implements Example 7.6

0005  B8 1234                         MOV      AX, 1234H
0008  BB ABCD                         MOV      BX, 0ABCDH
000B  3B C3                           CMP      AX, BX

000D  CB                              RET                      ;Return to DEBUG program
000E                          EX76    ENDP

000E                          CODE_SEG        ENDS

                                      END      EX76



The IBM Personal Computer Assembler 02-01-84              PAGE    Symbols-1
EXAMPLE 7.6

Segments and groups:

                N a m e             Size    align   combine class

CODE_SEG . . . . . . . . . . . .    000E    PARA    NONE    'CODE'
STACK_SEG. . . . . . . . . . . .    0040    PARA    STACK   'STACK'

Symbols:

                N a m e             Type    Value   Attr

EX76 . . . . . . . . . . . . . .    F PROC  0000    CODE_SEG        Length =000E

Warning Severe
Errors  Errors
0       0

A>
```

(b)

Figure 7.7 (continued)

```
A>DEBUG B:EX76.EXE
-U 0 D
0915:0000 1E              PUSH    DS
0915:0001 B80000          MOV     AX,0000
0915:0004 50              PUSH    AX
0915:0005 B83412          MOV     AX,1234
0915:0008 BBCDAB          MOV     BX,ABCD
0915:000B 3BC3            CMP     AX,BX
0915:000D CB              RETF
-G B

AX=1234  BX=ABCD  CX=000E  DX=0000  SP=003C  BP=0000  SI=0000  DI=0000
DS=0905  ES=0905  SS=0916  CS=0915  IP=000B   NV UP DI PL NZ NA PO NC
0915:000B 3BC3            CMP     AX,BX
-T

AX=1234  BX=ABCD  CX=000E  DX=0000  SP=003C  BP=0000  SI=0000  DI=0000
DS=0905  ES=0905  SS=0916  CS=0915  IP=000D   NV UP DI PL NZ AC PO CY
0915:000D CB              RETF
-G

Program terminated normally
-Q
```

(c)

Figure 7.7 (continued)

Next the compare instruction is executed with the command

$$-T \qquad (\leftarrow)$$

By comparing the state information before and after execution of the CMP instruction, we find that auxiliary carry flag and carry flag are the only flags that have changed states and they have both been set. Their new states are identified as AC and CY, respectively. These results are identical to those found in Example 7.5.

7.4 JUMP INSTRUCTIONS

The purpose of a *jump* instruction is to alter the execution path of instructions in the program. In the 8088 microprocessor, the code-segment register and instruction pointer keep track of the next instruction to be executed. Thus a jump instruction involves altering the contents of these registers. In this way, execution continues at an address other than that of the next sequential instruction. That is, a jump occurs to another part of the program. Typically, program execution is not intended to return to the next sequential instruction after the jump instruction. Therefore, no return linkage is saved when the jump takes place.

The Unconditional and Conditional Jump

The 8088 microprocessor allows two different types of jump instructions. They are the *unconditional jump* and the *conditional jump*. In an unconditional jump, no status requirements are imposed for the jump to occur. That is, as the instruction is executed, the jump always takes place to change the execution sequence.

This concept is illustrated in Fig. 7.8(a). Notice that when the instruction JMP AA in part I is executed, program control is passed to a point in part III identified by the label AA. Execution resumes with the instruction corresponding to AA. In this way, the instructions in part II of the program have been bypassed; that is, they have been jumped over.

On the other hand, for a conditional jump instruction, status conditions that exist at the moment the jump instruction is executed decide whether or not the jump will occur. If this condition or conditions are met, the jump takes place; otherwise, execution continues with the next sequential instruction of the program. The conditions that can be referenced by a conditional jump instruction are status flags such as carry (CF), parity (PF), and overflow (OF).

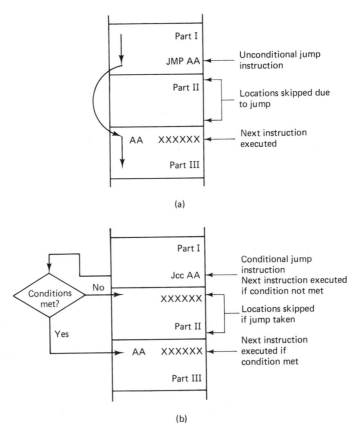

Figure 7.8 (a) Unconditional jump program sequence; (b) conditional jump program sequence.

Looking at Fig. 7.8(b), we see that execution of the conditional jump instruction in part I causes a test to be initiated. If the conditions of the test are not met, the NO path is taken and execution continues with the next sequential instruction. This corresponds to the first instruction in part II. However, if the result of the conditional test is YES, a jump is initiated to the segment of program identified as part III and the instructions in part II are bypassed.

Unconditional Jump Instruction

The unconditional jump instruction of the 8088 is shown in Fig. 7.9(a) together with its valid operand combinations in Fig. 7.9(b). There are two basic kinds of unconditional jumps. The first, called an *intrasegment jump,* is limited to addresses within the current code segment. This type of jump is achieved by just modifying the value in IP. The other kind of jump, the *intersegment jump,* permits jumps from one code segment to another. Implementation of this type of jump requires modification of the contents of both CS and IP.

Jump instructions specified with a *Short-label, Near-label, Memptr16,* or *Regptr16 operand* represent intrasegment jumps. The Short-label and Near-label operands specify the jump relative to the address of the jump instruction itself. For example, in a Short-label jump instruction an eight-bit number is coded as an immediate operand to specify the *signed displacement* of the next instruction to be executed from the location of the jump instruction. When the jump instruction is executed, IP is reloaded with a new value equal to the updated value in IP, which is (IP) + 2, plus the signed displacement. The new value of IP and current value in CS give the address of the next instruction to

Mnemonic	Meaning	Format	Operation	Affected flags
JMP	Unconditional jump	JMP Operand	Jump is initiated to the address specified by operand	None

(a)

Operands
Short-label
Near-label
Far-label
Memptr16
Regptr16
Memptr32

(b)

Figure 7.9 (a) Unconditional jump instruction; (b) allowed operands.

be fetched and executed. With an eight-bit displacement, the Short-label operand can only be used to initiate a jump in the range -126 to $+129$ bytes from the location of the jump instruction.

On the other hand, Near-label operands specify the displacement with a 16-bit immediate operand. This corresponds to a range equal to 32K bytes forward or backward from the jump instruction. The displacement is automatically calculated by the 8088's assembler. Thus a programmer can use symbolic labels as operands.

An example is the instruction

JMP LABEL

This means to jump to the point in the program corresponding to the tag LABEL. In this way, the programmer does not have to worry about counting the number of bytes from the jump instruction to the location to which control is to be passed. Moreover, the fact that it is coded as a Short- or Near-label displacement is also determined by the assembler.

The jump to address can also be specified indirectly by the contents of a memory location or the contents of a register. These two types correspond to the Memptr16 and Regptr16 operands, respectively. Just as for the Near-label operand, they both permit a jump of $+$ or $-$ 32K bytes from the address of the jump instruction.

For example,

JMP BX

uses the contents of register BX for the displacement. That is, the value in BX is copied into IP. Then the physical address of the next instruction is obtained by using the current contents of CS and the new value in IP.

Example 7.7

Verify the operation of the instruction JMP BX using the DEBUG program on the IBM PC. Let the contents of BX by 0010_{16}.

Solution:

As shown in Fig. 7.10, DEBUG is invoked and then the line-by-line assembler is used to load the instruction with the command

```
            —A                 (↵)
            08F1:0100  JMP  BX (↵)
            08F1:0102          (↵)
```

Next BX is initialized with the command

```
            —R  BX             (↵)
            BX 0000
            :10                (↵)
```

```
A>DEBUG
-A
08F1:0100 JMP BX
08F1:0102
-R BX
BX 0000
:10
-R
AX=0000  BX=0010  CX=0000  DX=0000  SP=70EE  BP=0000  SI=0000  DI=0000
DS=08F1  ES=08F1  SS=08F1  CS=08F1  IP=0100  NV UP DI PL NZ NA PO NC
08F1:0100 FFE3          JMP     BX
-T

AX=0000  BX=0010  CX=0000  DX=0000  SP=70EE  BP=0000  SI=0000  DI=0000
DS=08F1  ES=08F1  SS=08F1  CS=08F1  IP=0010  NV UP DI PL NZ NA PO NC
08F1:0010 0006E204      ADD     [04E2],AL                    .DS:04E2=52
-Q

A>
```

Figure 7.10 Display sequence for Example 7.7.

Let us check the value in IP before executing the JMP instruction. This is done with another R command as

$$-R \qquad (\hookleftarrow)$$

Looking at the state information displayed in Fig. 7.10, we see that IP contains 0100_{16} and BX contains 0010_{16}.

Now, executing the instruction with the command

$$-T \qquad (\hookleftarrow)$$

and then looking at Fig. 7.10, we see that the value in IP has become 10_{16}. Therefore, the address at which execution picks up is 08F1:0010.

To specify an operand to be used as a pointer, the various addressing modes available with the 8088 can be used. For instance,

JMP [BX]

uses the contents of BX as the address of the memory location that contains the offset address. This offset is loaded into IP, where it is used together with the current contents of CS to compute the "jump to" address.

Example 7.8

Use the DEBUG program to observe the operation of the instruction

JMP [BX]

Assume that the pointer held in BX is 1000_{16} and the value held at memory location DS:1000 is 200_{16}. What is the address of the next instruction to be executed?

Solution:

Figure 7.11 shows that first the debugger is brought up and then an ASSEMBLE command issued to load the instruction. This assemble command is

```
—A                          (↵)
08F1:0100  JMP  [BX]  (↵)
08F1:0102                   (↵)
```

Next BX is loaded with the pointer address using the R command

```
—R BX                       (↵)
BX 0000
:1000                       (↵)
```

and the memory location is initialized with the command

```
—E  1000  00  02      (↵)
```

As shown in Fig. 7.11, the loading of memory location DS:1000 and the BX register are next verified with D and R commands, respectively.

Now the instruction is executed with the command

```
                —T         (↵)
```

Notice from the state information displayed in Fig. 7.11 that the new value in IP is 0200_{16}. This value was loaded from memory location 08F1:1000. Therefore, program execution continues with the instruction at address 08F1:0200.

```
A>DEBUG
-A
08F1:0100 JMP   [BX]
08F1:0102
-R BX
BX 0000
:1000
-E 1000 00 02
-D 1000 1001
08F1:1000   00 02                                         ..
-R
AX=0000  BX=1000  CX=0000  DX=0000  SP=70EE  BP=0000  SI=0000  DI=0000
DS=08F1  ES=08F1  SS=08F1  CS=08F1  IP=0100   NV UP DI PL NZ NA PO NC
08F1:0100 FF27           JMP     [BX]                          DS:1000=0200
-T

AX=0000  BX=1000  CX=0000  DX=0000  SP=70EE  BP=0000  SI=0000  DI=0000
DS=08F1  ES=08F1  SS=08F1  CS=08F1  IP=0200   NV UP DI PL NZ NA PO NC
08F1:0200 0000           ADD     [BX+SI],AL                    DS:1000=00
-Q

A>
```

Figure 7.11 Display sequence for Example 7.8.

The intersegment unconditional jump instructions correspond to the *Far-label* and *Memptr32 operands* that are shown in Fig. 7.9(b). Far-label uses a 32-bit immediate operand to specify the jump to address. The first 16 bits of this 32-bit pointer are loaded into IP and are an offset address relative to the contents of the code-segment register. The next 16 bits are loaded into the CS register and define the new 64K-byte code segment.

An indirect way to specify the offset and code segment address for an intersegment jump is by using the Memptr32 operand. This time four consecutive memory bytes starting at the specified address contain the offset address and the new code-segment address, respectively. Just like the Memptr16 operand, the Memptr32 operand may be specified using any one of the various addressing modes of the 8088.

An example is the instruction

```
JMP  DWORD  PTR  [DI]
```

It uses the contents of DS and DI to calculate the address of the memory location that contains the first word of the pointer that identifies the location to which the jump will take place. The two-word pointer starting at this address is read into IP and CS to pass control to the new point in the program.

Conditional Jump Instruction

The second type of jump instruction is that which performs conditional jump operations. Figure 7.12(a) shows a general form of this instruction; Fig. 7.12(b) is a list of each of the conditional jump instructions in the 8088's instruction set. Notice that each of these instructions tests for the presence or absence of certain status conditions.

For instance, the *jump on carry* (JC) instruction makes a test to determine if carry flag (CF) is set. Depending on the result of the test, the jump to the location specified by its operand either takes place or does not. If CF equals zero, the test fails and execution continues with the instruction at the address following the JC instruction. On the other hand, if CF is set to one, the test condition is satisfied and the jump is performed.

Notice that for some of the instructions in Fig. 7.12(b) two different mnemonics can be used. This feature can be used to improve program readability. That is, for each occurrence of the instruction in the program, it can be identified with the mnemonic that best describes its function.

For instance, the instruction *jump on parity* (JP)/*jump on parity even* (JPE) can be used to test parity flag PF for logic 1. Since PF is set to one if the result from a computation has even parity, this instruction can initiate a jump based on the occurrence of even parity. The reverse instruction JNP/JPO is also provided. It can be used to initiate a jump based on the occurrence of a result with odd parity instead of even parity.

Mnemonic	Meaning	Format	Operation	Flags affected
Jcc	Conditional jump	Jcc Operand	If the specified condition cc is true the jump to the address specified by the operand is initiated; otherwise the next instruction is executed.	None

(a)

Mnemonic	Meaning
JA/JNBE	Jump if above/jump if not below or equal
JAE/JNB	Jump if above or equal/jump if not below
JB/JNAE	Jump if below/jump if not above or equal
JBE/JNA	Jump if below or equal/jump if not above
JC	Jump if carry
JCXZ	Jump if CX is zero
JE/JZ	Jump if equal/jump if zero
JG/JNLE	Jump if greater/jump if not less or equal
JGE/JNL	Jump if greater or equal/jump if not less
JLE/JNG	Jump if less or equal/jump if not greater
JNC	Jump if not carry
JNE/JNZ	Jump if not equal/jump if not zero
JNO	Jump if not overflow
JNP/JPO	Jump if not parity/jump if parity odd
JNS	Jump if not sign
JO	Jump if overflow
JP/JPE	Jump if parity/jump if parity even
JS	Jump if sign

(b)

Figure 7.12 (a) Conditional jump instruction; (b) types of conditional jump instructions.

In a similar manner, the instructions *jump if equal* (JE) and *jump if zero* (JZ) have the same function. Either notation can be used in a program to determine if the result of a computation was zero.

All other conditional jump instructions work in a similar way except that they test different conditions to decide whether or not the jump is to take place. Examples of these conditions are that the contents of CX are zero, an overflow has occurred, or the result is negative.

To distinguish between comparisons of signed and unsigned numbers by jump instructions, two different names, which seem to be the same, have been devised. They are *above* and *below* for comparison of unsigned numbers and *less* and *greater* for comparison of signed numbers. For instance, the number $ABCD_{16}$ is above the number 1234_{16} if considered as an unsigned number. On the other hand, if they are considered as signed numbers, $ABCD_{16}$ is negative and 1234_{16} is positive. Therefore, $ABCD_{16}$ is less than 1234_{16}.

Example 7.9

The source program in Fig. 7.13(a) is used to implement the instruction sequence

```
        CMP  AX,BX
        JB   DIFF2
DIFF1:  MOV  DX,AX
        SUB  DX,BX  ;DX = AX − BX
        JMP  DONE
DIFF2:  MOV  DX,BX
        SUB  DX,AX  ;DX = BX − AX
DONE:   NOP
```

as a procedure. This sequence of instructions calculates the absolute difference between the contents of AX and BX and places it in DX. Use the run module pro-

```
A>TYPE B:EX79.ASM


TITLE    EXAMPLE 7.9

         PAGE     ,132

STACK_SEG       SEGMENT         STACK 'STACK'
                DB              64 DUP(?)
STACK_SEG       ENDS


CODE_SEG        SEGMENT         'CODE'
EX79     PROC   FAR
         ASSUME  CS:CODE_SEG, SS:STACK_SEG

;To return to DEBUG program put return address on the stack

         PUSH   DS
         MOV    AX, 0
         PUSH   AX

;Following code implements Example 7.9

         CMP    AX, BX
         JC     DIFF2
DIFF1:   MOV    DX, AX
         SUB    DX, BX          ; DX = AX − BX
         JMP    DONE
DIFF2:   MOV    DX, BX
         SUB    DX, AX          ; DX = BX − AX
DONE:    NOP

         RET                    ;Return to DEBUG program
EX79     ENDP

CODE_SEG        ENDS

         END    EX79

A>
```

(a)

Figure 7.13 (a) Source program for Example 7.9; (b) source listing produced by the assembler; (c) executing the program with DEBUG.

A>TYPE B:EX79.LST

```
                              TITLE    EXAMPLE 7.9

                              PAGE      ,132
0000                  STACK_SEG    SEGMENT        STACK 'STACK'
0000      40 [                     DB             64 DUP(?)
               ??
                  ]

0040                  STACK_SEG    ENDS

0000                  CODE_SEG     SEGMENT        'CODE'
0000                  EX79    PROC FAR
                              ASSUME  CS:CODE_SEG, SS:STACK_SEG

                      ;To return to DEBUG program put return address on the stack

0000  1E                      PUSH    DS
0001  B8 0000                 MOV     AX, 0
0004  50                      PUSH    AX

                      ;Following code implements Example 7.9

0005  3B C3                   CMP     AX, BX
0007  72 07                   JC      DIFF2
0009  8B D0         DIFF1:    MOV     DX, AX
000B  2B D3                   SUB     DX, BX         ; DX = AX - BX
000D  EB 05 90                JMP     DONE
0010  8B D3         DIFF2:    MOV     DX, BX
0012  2B D0                   SUB     DX, AX         ; DX = BX - AX
0014  90            DONE:     NOP

0015  CB                      RET                    ;Return to DEBUG program
0016                  EX79    ENDP

0016                  CODE_SEG     ENDS

                              END     EX79
```

Segments and groups:

Name	Size	align	combine	class
CODE_SEG	0016	PARA	NONE	'CODE'
STACK_SEG.	0040	PARA	STACK	'STACK'

Symbols:

Name	Type	Value	Attr	
DIFF1.	L NEAR	0009	CODE_SEG	
DIFF2.	L NEAR	0010	CODE_SEG	
DONE	L NEAR	0014	CODE_SEG	
EX79	F PROC	0000	CODE_SEG	Length =0016

Warning Severe
Errors Errors
0   0

A>

(b)

Figure 7.13 (continued)

268

```
A>DEBUG B:EX79.EXE
-U 0 15
0915:0000 1E            PUSH    DS
0915:0001 B80000        MOV     AX,0000
0915:0004 50            PUSH    AX
0915:0005 3BC3          CMP     AX,BX
0915:0007 7207          JB      0010
0915:0009 8BD0          MOV     DX,AX
0915:000B 2BD3          SUB     DX,BX
0915:000D EB05          JMP     0014
0915:000F 90            NOP
0915:0010 8BD3          MOV     DX,BX
0915:0012 2BD0          SUB     DX,AX
0915:0014 90            NOP
0915:0015 CB            RETF
-G 5

AX=0000  BX=0000  CX=0016  DX=0000  SP=003C  BP=0000  SI=0000  DI=0000
DS=0905  ES=0905  SS=0917  CS=0915  IP=0005   NV UP DI PL NZ NA PO NC
0915:0005 3BC3          CMP       AX,BX
-R AX
AX 0000
:6
-R BX
BX 0000
:2
-T

AX=0006  BX=0002  CX=0016  DX=0000  SP=003C  BP=0000  SI=0000  DI=0000
DS=0905  ES=0905  SS=0917  CS=0915  IP=0007   NV UP DI PL NZ NA PO NC
0915:0007 7207          JB        0010
-G 14

AX=0006  BX=0002  CX=0016  DX=0004  SP=003C  BP=0000  SI=0000  DI=0000
DS=0905  ES=0905  SS=0917  CS=0915  IP=0014   NV UP DI PL NZ NA PO NC
0915:0014 90            NOP
-G

Program terminated normally
-R
AX=0006  BX=0002  CX=0016  DX=0004  SP=003C  BP=0000  SI=0000  DI=0000
DS=0905  ES=0905  SS=0917  CS=0915  IP=0014   NV UP DI PL NZ NA PO NC
0915:0014 90            NOP
-R IP
IP 0014
:0
-G 5

AX=0000  BX=0002  CX=0016  DX=0004  SP=0038  BP=0000  SI=0000  DI=0000
DS=0905  ES=0905  SS=0917  CS=0915  IP=0005   NV UP DI PL NZ NA PO NC
0915:0005 3BC3          CMP       AX,BX
-R AX
AX 0000
:2
-R BX
BX 0002
:6
-T

AX=0002  BX=0006  CX=0016  DX=0004  SP=0038  BP=0000  SI=0000  DI=0000
DS=0905  ES=0905  SS=0917  CS=0915  IP=0007   NV UP DI NG NZ AC PE CY
0915:0007 7207          JB        0010
-G 14

AX=0002  BX=0006  CX=0016  DX=0004  SP=0038  BP=0000  SI=0000  DI=0000
DS=0905  ES=0905  SS=0917  CS=0915  IP=0014   NV UP DI PL NZ NA PO NC
0915:0014 90            NOP
-G

Program terminated normally
-Q
```

(c)

Figure 7.13 (continued)

duced by assembling and linking the source program in Fig. 7.13(a) to verify the operation of the program for the two cases that follow:

(a) (AX) = 6, (BX) = 2
(b) (AX) = 2, (BX) = 6

Solution:

The source program in Fig. 7.13(a) can be assembled with MASM and linked with LINK to produce a run module called EX79.EXE. The source listing produced as part of the assembly process is shown in Fig. 7.13(b).

As shown in Fig. 7.13(c), the run module can be loaded as part of calling up the debugger by issuing the DOS command

A>DEBUG B:EX79.EXE   (↵)

Next, the loading of the program is verified with the UNASSEMBLE command

—U 0 15

Notice in Fig. 7.13(c) that the CMP instruction, which is the first instruction of the sequence that generates the absolute difference, is located at address 0915:0005. Let us execute down to this statement with the GO command

—G 5   (↵)

Now we will load AX and BX with the case (a) data. This is done with the R commands

—R AX   (↵)
AX 0000
:6   (↵)
— R B X   (↵)
BX 0000
: 2   (↵)

Next we execute the compare instruction with the command

—T   (↵)

Note in the trace information display in Fig. 7.13(c) that the carry flag is reset (NC). Therefore, no jump will take place when the JB instruction is executed.

The rest of the program can be executed by inputting the command

—G 14   (↵)

From Fig. 7.13(c), we find that DX contains 4. This result was produced by executing the SUB instruction at 0915:000B. Before executing the program for the (b) set of data, the command

$$-G \qquad (\leftarrow)$$

must be issued. This command causes the program to terminate normally.

The R command shows that the value in IP must be reset and then we can execute down to the CMP instruction. This is done with the commands

$$
\begin{array}{ll}
-R\ IP & (\leftarrow) \\
IP\ 0014 & \\
:0 & (\leftarrow)
\end{array}
$$

and

$$-G\ 5 \qquad (\leftarrow)$$

Notice in Fig. 7.13(c) that IP again contains 0005_{16} and points to the CMP instruction. Next the data for case (b) are loaded with R commands. This gives

$$
\begin{array}{ll}
-R\ AX & (\leftarrow) \\
AX\ 0000 & \\
:2 & (\leftarrow) \\
-R\ BX & (\leftarrow) \\
BX\ 0002 & \\
:6 & (\leftarrow)
\end{array}
$$

Now a T command is used to execute the CMP instruction. Notice that CY is set this time. Therefore, control is passed to the instruction at 0915:0010.

A GO command is now used to execute down to the NOP instruction at 0915:0014. This command is

$$-G\ 14 \qquad (\leftarrow)$$

Notice that DX again contains 4; however, this time it was calculated with the SUB instruction at 0915:0012.

7.5 SUBROUTINES AND THE SUBROUTINE HANDLING INSTRUCTIONS

Subroutines are procedures written separate from the main program. Whenever the main program must perform a function that is defined by a subroutine, it calls the subroutine into operation. In order to do this, control must be passed from the main program to the starting point of the subroutine. Execution continues with the subroutine and upon completion, control is returned back to the main program at the instruction that follows the one that called the subroutine. Notice that the difference between the operation of a subroutine call and a jump is that a call to a subroutine not only produces a jump to an appropriate address in the code segment of memory, but it also has a mechanism for saving information such as IP and CS, which is needed to return back to the main program.

CALL and RET Instructions

There are two basic instructions in the instruction set of the 8088 for subroutine handling. They are the *call* (CALL) and *return* (RET) instructions. Together they provide the mechanism for calling a subroutine into operation and returning control back to the main program at its completion. We will first discuss these two instructions and later introduce other instructions which can be used in conjunction with subroutines.

Just like the JMP instruction, CALL allows implementation of two types of operations, the *intrasegment call* and the *intersegment call*. The CALL instruction is shown in Fig. 7.14(a); its allowed operand variations are shown in Fig. 7.14(b).

It is the operand that initiates either an intersegment or intrasegment call. The operands Near-proc, Memptr16, and Regptr16 all specify intrasegment calls to a subroutine. In all three cases, execution of the instruction causes the contents of IP to be saved on the stack. Then the stack pointer (SP) is decremented by two. The saved value of IP is the address of the instruction that follows the CALL instruction. After saving the return address, a new

Mnemonic	Meaning	Format	Operation	Affected flags
CALL	Subroutine call	CALL Operand	Execution continues from the address of the subroutine specified by the operand. Information required to return back to the main program such as IP and CS is saved on the stack.	None

(a)

Operands
Near-proc
Far-proc
Memptr16
Regptr16
Memptr32

(b)

Figure 7.14 (a) Subroutine call instruction; (b) allowed operands.

16-bit value, which points to the storage location of the first instruction in the subroutine, is loaded into IP.

The three types of intrasegment operands represent different ways of specifying this new value of IP. In a Near-proc operand, the displacement of the first instruction of the subroutine from the current value of IP is supplied directly by the instruction. An example is

CALL WORD PTR NEAR

Here the label NEAR determines the 16-bit displacement and is coded as an immediate operand following the opcode for the call instruction. This form of call is actually a relative addressing-mode instruction; that is, the offset address is calculated relative to the address of the call instruction itself. With 16 bits, the displacement is limited to + or − 32K bytes.

The Memptr16 and Regptr16 operands provide indirect subroutine addressing by specifying a memory location or an internal register, respectively, as the source of a new value for IP. The value specified in this way is not a displacement. It is the actual offset that is to be loaded into IP. An example of the Regptr16 operand is

CALL BX

When this instruction is executed, the contents of BX are loaded into IP and execution continues, with the subroutine starting at a physical address derived from CS and IP.

By using one of the various addressing modes of the 8088, an internal register can be used as a pointer to an operand that resides in memory. This represents a Memptr16 type of operand. In this case, the value of the physical address of the offset is obtained from the current contents of the data-segment register DS and the address or addresses held in the specified registers. For instance, the instruction

CALL WORD PTR [BX]

has its subroutine offset address at the memory location whose physical address is derived from the contents of DS and BX. The value stored at this memory location is loaded into IP. Again, the current contents of CS and the new value in IP point to the first instruction of the subroutine.

Notice that in both intrasegment call examples the subroutine was located within the same code segment as the call instruction. The other type of CALL instruction, the intersegment call, permits the subroutine to reside in another code segment. It corresponds to the Far-proc and Memptr32 operands. These operands specify both a new offset address for IP and a new segment address for CS. In both cases, execution of the call instruction causes the contents of the CS and IP registers to be saved on the stack, and then new values are loaded into IP and CS. The saved values of CS and IP permit return to the main program from a different code segment.

Far-proc represents a 32-bit immediate operand that is stored in the four bytes that follow the opcode of the call instruction in program memory. These two words are loaded directly from code-segment memory into IP and CS with execution of the CALL instruction. An example is the instruction

CALL FAR

On the other hand, when the operand is Memptr32 the pointer for the subroutine is stored as four bytes in data memory. The location of the first byte of the pointer can be specified indirectly by one of the 8088's registers. An example is

CALL DWORD PTR [DI]

Here the physical address of the first byte of the four-byte pointer in memory is derived from the contents of DS and DI.

Every subroutine must end by executing an instruction that returns control to the main program. This is the return (RET) instruction. It is described in Fig. 7.15(a) and (b). Notice that its execution causes the value of IP or both the values of IP and CS that were saved on the stack to be returned back to their corresponding registers. In general, an intrasegment return results from an intrasegment call and an intersegment return results from an intersegment call.

There is an additional option with the return instruction: A two-byte code can be included following the return instruction. This code is added to the stack pointer after restoring the return address into IP or IP and CS for Far-proc

Mnemonic	Meaning	Format	Operation	Affected flags
RET	Return	RET or RET Operand	Return to the main program by restoring IP (and CS for far-procedure). If operand is present it is added to the content of SP.	None

(a)

Operands
None
Disp16

(b)

Figure 7.15 (a) Return instruction; (b) allowed operands.

calls. The purpose of this stack pointer displacement is to provide a simple means by which the *parameters* that were saved on the stack before the call to the subroutine was initiated can be discarded.

Example 7.10

The source program in Fig. 7.16(a) can be used to demonstrate the use of the call and return instructions to implement a subroutine. This program was assembled and linked on the IBM PC to produce a run module in file EX710.EXE. Its source listing is provided for reference in Fig. 7.16(b). Trace the operation of the program by executing it with DEBUG for data (AX) = 2 and (BX) = 4.

Solution:

We begin by calling up DEBUG and loading the program with the DOS command

A > DEBUG B:EX710.EXE   (⤶)

```
A>TYPE B:EX710.ASM

TITLE    EXAMPLE 7.10

         PAGE       ,132

STACK_SEG        SEGMENT        STACK 'STACK'
                 DB             64 DUP(?)
STACK_SEG        ENDS


CODE_SEG         SEGMENT        'CODE'
EX710   PROC     FAR
        ASSUME   CS:CODE_SEG, SS:STACK_SEG

;To return to DEBUG program put return address on the stack

        PUSH     DS
        MOV      AX, 0
        PUSH     AX

;Following code implements Example 7.10

        CALL     SUM
        RET

SUM     PROC     NEAR
        MOV      DX, AX
        ADD      DX, BX         ; DX = AX + BX
        RET
SUM     ENDP

EX710   ENDP
CODE_SEG         ENDS

        END      EX710

A>
```

(a)

Figure 7.16 (a) Source program for Example 7.10; (b) source listing produced by assembler; (c) executing the program with DEBUG.

The IBM Personal Computer Assembler 02-01-84   PAGE   1-1
EXAMPLE 7.10

```
                              TITLE   EXAMPLE 7.10

                                 PAGE    ,132

0000                          STACK_SEG     SEGMENT       STACK 'STACK'
0000      40 [                              DB            64 DUP(?)
              ??
                  ]

0040                          STACK_SEG     ENDS


0000                          CODE_SEG      SEGMENT         'CODE'
0000                          EX710   PROC  FAR
                                      ASSUME  CS:CODE_SEG, SS:STACK_SEG

                              ;To return to DEBUG program put return address on the stack

0000  1E                              PUSH    DS
0001  B8 0000                         MOV     AX, O
0004  50                              PUSH    AX

                              ;Following code implements Example 7.10

0005  E8 0009 R                       CALL    SUM
0008  CB                              RET

0009                          SUM     PROC    NEAR
0009  8B D0                           MOV     DX, AX
000B  03 D3                           ADD     DX, BX          ; DX = AX + BX
000D  C3                              RET
000E                          SUM     ENDP

000E                          EX710   ENDP
000E                          CODE_SEG      ENDS

                                      END     EX710
```

The IBM Personal Computer Assembler 02-01-84   PAGE   Symbols-1
EXAMPLE 7.10

Segments and groups:

N a m e	Size	align	combine	class
CODE_SEG	000E	PARA	NONE	'CODE'
STACK_SEG.	0040	PARA	STACK	'STACK'

Symbols:

N a m e	Type	Value	Attr	
EX710.	F PROC	0000	CODE_SEG	Length =000E
SUM.	N PROC	0009	CODE_SEG	Length =0005

Warning Severe
Errors Errors
O   O

A>

(b)

Figure 7.16 (continued)

```
A>DEBUG B:EX710.EXE
-U O D
0915:0000 1E               PUSH    DS
0915:0001 B80000           MOV     AX,0000
0915:0004 50               PUSH    AX
0915:0005 E80100           CALL    0009
0915:0008 CB               RETF
0915:0009 8BD0             MOV     DX,AX
0915:000B 03D3             ADD     DX,BX
0915:000D C3               RET
-G 5

AX=0000  BX=0000  CX=000E  DX=0000  SP=003C  BP=0000  SI=0000  DI=0000
DS=0905  ES=0905  SS=0916  CS=0915  IP=0005  NV UP DI PL NZ NA PO NC
0915:0005 E80100           CALL    0009
-R AX
AX 0000
:2
-R BX
BX 0000
:4
-T

AX=0002  BX=0004  CX=000E  DX=0000  SP=003A  BP=0000  SI=0000  DI=0000
DS=0905  ES=0905  SS=0916  CS=0915  IP=0009  NV UP DI PL NZ NA PO NC
0915:0009 8BD0             MOV     DX,AX
-D SS:3A 3B
0916:003A  08 00                                                  ..
-T

AX=0002  BX=0004  CX=000E  DX=0002  SP=003A  BP=0000  SI=0000  DI=0000
DS=0905  ES=0905  SS=0916  CS=0915  IP=000B  NV UP DI PL NZ NA PO NC
0915:000B 03D3             ADD     DX,BX
-T

AX=0002  BX=0004  CX=000E  DX=0006  SP=003A  BP=0000  SI=0000  DI=0000
DS=0905  ES=0905  SS=0916  CS=0915  IP=000D  NV UP DI PL NZ NA PE NC
0915:000D C3               RET
-T

AX=0002  BX=0004  CX=000E  DX=0006  SP=003C  BP=0000  SI=0000  DI=0000
DS=0905  ES=0905  SS=0916  CS=0915  IP=0008  NV UP DI PL NZ NA PE NC
0915:0008 CB               RETF
-G

Program terminated normally
-Q
```

(c)

Figure 7.16 (continued)

The loading of the program is now verified with the UNASSEMBLE command

$$-U\ 0\ D \qquad (\downarrow)$$

Looking at Fig. 7.16(c), we see that the program has correctly loaded. Moreover, we find that the CALL instruction is located at offset 0005_{16} of the current code segment. The command

$$-G\ 5 \qquad (\downarrow)$$

executes the program down to the CALL instruction. The state information displayed in Fig. 7.16(c) shows that $(CS) = 0915_{16}$, $(IP) = 0005_{16}$, and $(SP) =$

$003C_{16}$. Now let us load the AX and BX registers with R commands. This gives

```
—R AX              (⏎)
AX 0000
:2                 (⏎)
— R  B X           (⏎)
BX 0000
:4                 (⏎)
```

Now the CALL instruction is executed with the T command

$$—T \qquad (⏎)$$

and, looking at the displayed-state information in Fig. 7.16(c), we find that CS still contains 0915_{16}, IP has been loaded with 0009_{16}, and SP has been decremented to $003A_{16}$. This information tells us that the next instruction to be executed is the move instruction at address 0915:0009 and a word of data has been pushed to the stack.

Before executing another instruction, let us look at what got pushed onto the stack. This is done by issuing the memory dump command

$$—D \ SS:3A \ 3B \qquad (⏎)$$

Note from Fig. 7.16(c) that the value 0008_{16} has been pushed onto the stack. This is the address offset of the RETF instruction that follows the CALL instruction and is the address of the instruction to which control is to be returned at completion of the subroutine.

Two more TRACE commands are used to execute the move and add instructions of the subroutine. From the state information displayed in Fig. 7.16(c), we see that their execution causes the value 2_{16} in AX to be copied into DX and then the value 4_{16} in BX to be added to the value in DX. This results in the value 6_{16} in DX.

Now the RET instruction is executed by issuing another T command. In Fig. 7.16(c) we see that execution of this instruction causes the value 0008_{16} to be popped off the stack and put back into the IP register. Therefore, the next instruction to be executed is that located at address 0915:0008; this is the RETF instruction. Moreover, notice that as the word is popped from the stack back into IP, the value in SP is incremented by two. After this, the program is run to completion by issuing a GO command.

PUSH and POP Instructions

After the context switch to a subroutine, we find that it is usually necessary to save the contents of certain registers or some other main program parameters. These values are saved by pushing them onto the stack. Typically, these data

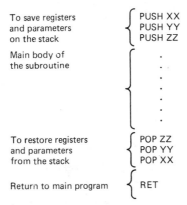

To save registers and parameters on the stack	PUSH XX PUSH YY PUSH ZZ
Main body of the subroutine	.
To restore registers and parameters from the stack	POP ZZ POP YY POP XX
Return to main program	RET

Figure 7.17 Structure of a subroutine.

correspond to registers and memory locations that are used by the subroutine. In this way, their original contents are kept intact in the stack segment of memory during the execution of the subroutine. Before a return to the main program takes place, the saved registers and main program parameters are restored. This is done by popping the saved values from the stack back into their original locations. Thus, a typical structure of a subroutine is that shown in Fig. 7.17.

The instruction that is used to save parameters on the stack is the *push* (PUSH) instruction, and that used to retrieve them back is the *pop* (POP) instruction. These instructions are shown in Fig. 7.18(a). Notice in Fig. 7.18(b) that the standard PUSH and POP instructions can be written with a general-purpose register, a segment register (excluding CS), or a storage location in memory as their operand.

Execution of a PUSH instruction causes the data corresponding to the

Mnemonic	Meaning	Format	Operation	Flags affected
PUSH	Push word onto stack	PUSH S	$((SP)) \leftarrow (S)$	None
POP	Pop word off stack	POP D	$(D) \leftarrow ((SP))$	None

(a)

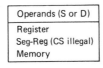

Operands (S or D)
Register Seg-Reg (CS illegal) Memory

(b)

Figure 7.18 (a) Push and pop instructions; (b) allowed operands.

operand to be pushed onto the top of the stack. For instance, if the instruction is

PUSH AX

the result is as follows:

$$((SP) - 1) \leftarrow (AH)$$
$$((SP) - 2) \leftarrow (AL)$$
$$(SP) \leftarrow (SP) - 2$$

This shows that the two bytes of AX are saved in the stack part of memory and the stack pointer is decremented by two such that it points to the new top of the stack.

On the other hand, if the instruction is

POP AX

its execution results in

$$(AL) \leftarrow ((SP))$$
$$(AH) \leftarrow ((SP) + 1)$$
$$(SP) \leftarrow (SP) + 2$$

In this manner, the saved contents of AX are restored back into the register.

Example 7.11

Write a procedure named SUM that adds two numbers, 5_{10} and 31_{16}, together and places their sum in DX. Assume that this procedure is to be called from another procedure in the same code segment and that at the time it is to be called, DX contains the value $ABCD_{16}$ and this value must be saved at entry of the procedure and restored at its completion.

Solution:

The beginning of the procedure is defined with the pseudo-op statement

SUM PROC NEAR

At entry of the procedure, we must save the value currently held in DX. This is done by pushing its contents to the stack with the instruction

PUSH DX

Now we load DX with the value 5_{10} using the instruction

MOV DX,5

and add 31_{16} to it with the instruction

ADD DX,31H

This completes the addition operation, but before we return to the main part of the program, the original contents of DX that were saved on the stack are restored with the pop instruction

POP DX

Then a return instruction is used to pass control back to the main program.

RET

The procedure must be terminated with the end procedure pseudo-op statement that follows

SUM ENDP

The complete instruction sequence is shown in Fig. 7.19.

SUM PROC NEAR
     PUSH DX
     MOV   DX,5
     ADD   DX,31H
     POP   DX
     RET
SUM ENDP

Figure 7.19 Program for Example 7.11.

Example 7.12

A source program that can be used to demonstrate execution of the procedure written in Example 7.11 is shown in Fig. 7.20(a). The source listing produced when this program was assembled is given in Fig. 7.20(b), and the run module produced when it was linked is stored in file EX712.EXE. Use the DEBUG program to load this run module and verify its operation by executing it on the IBM PC.

Solution:

The DEBUG program and run module can be loaded with the DEBUG DOS command. Looking at Fig. 7.20(c), we see that this command is

> DEBUG B:EX712.EXE   (↵)

After loading is completed, the instructions of the program are unassembled with the command

—U 0 14   (↵)

The displayed information in Fig. 7.20(c) shows that the program did load correctly. Next the contents of the 8088's internal registers are displayed with an R command. The displayed information produced for this command shows that CS contains 0915_{16} and IP contains 0000_{16}. Therefore, the first instruction to be executed is the PUSH DS instruction at 0915:0000.

From the instruction sequence in Fig. 7.20(c), we find that the part of the program whose operation we are interested in observing starts with the CALL instruction at address 0915:0008. Now we execute down to this point in the program with the GO command

$$-G\ 8\qquad(\lrcorner)$$

Looking at the trace information displayed, we see that DX has been initialized with the value $ABCD_{16}$.

```
A>TYPE B:EX712.ASM


TITLE    EXAMPLE 7.12

        PAGE      ,132

STACK_SEG         SEGMENT        STACK 'STACK'
                  DB             64 DUP(?)
STACK_SEG         ENDS


CODE_SEG          SEGMENT        'CODE'
EX712   PROC      FAR
        ASSUME  CS:CODE_SEG, SS:STACK_SEG

;To return to DEBUG program put return address on the stack

        PUSH      DS
        MOV       AX, 0
        PUSH      AX

;Following code implements Example 7.12

        MOV       DX, 0ABCDH
        CALL      SUM
        RET                      ;Return to DEBUG program
EX712   ENDP

SUM     PROC      NEAR
        PUSH      DX
        MOV       DX, 5
        ADD       DX, 31H        ;DX = 5 + 31H
        POP       DX
        RET
SUM     ENDP

CODE_SEG          ENDS

        END       EX712

A>
```

(a)

Figure 7.20 (a) Source program for Example 7.12; (b) source listing produced by the assembler; (c) DEBUG sequence for execution of run module EX712.EXE.

```
A>TYPE B:EX712.LST
```

```
                              TITLE   EXAMPLE 7.12

                              PAGE      ,132
0000                     STACK_SEG      SEGMENT         STACK 'STACK'
0000      40 [                         DB              64 DUP(?)
             ??
          ]

0040                     STACK_SEG      ENDS


0000                     CODE_SEG       SEGMENT         'CODE'
0000                     EX712   PROC   FAR
                              ASSUME  CS:CODE_SEG, SS:STACK_SEG

                         ;To return to DEBUG program put return address on the stack

0000  1E                         PUSH    DS
0001  B8 0000                    MOV     AX, 0
0004  50                         PUSH    AX

                         ;Following code implements Example 7.12

0005  BA ABCD                    MOV     DX, 0ABCDH
0008  E8 000C R                  CALL    SUM
000B  CB                         RET                   ;Return to DEBUG program
000C                     EX712   ENDP


000C                     SUM     PROC    NEAR
000C  52                         PUSH    DX
000D  BA 0005                    MOV     DX, 5
0010  83 C2 31                   ADD     DX, 31H        ;DX = 5 + 31H
0013  5A                         POP     DX
0014  C3                         RET
0015                     SUM     ENDP

0015                     CODE_SEG       ENDS

                              END     EX712
```

```
Segments and groups:

              N a m e                  Size   align   combine class

CODE_SEG . . . . . . . . . . . .       0015   PARA    NONE   'CODE'
STACK_SEG. . . . . . . . . . . .       0040   PARA    STACK  'STACK'

Symbols:

              N a m e                  Type   Value   Attr

EX712. . . . . . . . . . . . . .       F PROC 0000    CODE_SEG    Length =000C
SUM. . . . . . . . . . . . . . .       N PROC 000C    CODE_SEG    Length =0009

Warning Severe
Errors  Errors
0       0

A>
```

(b)

Figure 7.20 (continued)

```
A>DEBUG B:EX712.EXE
-U 0 14
0915:0000 1E              PUSH    DS
0915:0001 B80000          MOV     AX,0000
0915:0004 50              PUSH    AX
0915:0005 BACDAB          MOV     DX,ABCD
0915:0008 E80100          CALL    000C
0915:000B CB              RETF
0915:000C 52              PUSH    DX
0915:000D BA0500          MOV     DX,0005
0915:0010 83C231          ADD     DX,+31
0915:0013 5A              POP     DX
0915:0014 C3              RET
-R
AX=0000  BX=0000  CX=0015  DX=0000  SP=0040  BP=0000  SI=0000  DI=0000
DS=0905  ES=0905  SS=0917  CS=0915  IP=0000   NV UP DI PL NZ NA PO NC
0915:0000 1E              PUSH    DS
-G 8

AX=0000  BX=0000  CX=0015  DX=ABCD  SP=003C  BP=0000  SI=0000  DI=0000
DS=0905  ES=0905  SS=0917  CS=0915  IP=0008   NV UP DI PL NZ NA PO NC
0915:0008 E80100          CALL    000C
-T

AX=0000  BX=0000  CX=0015  DX=ABCD  SP=003A  BP=0000  SI=0000  DI=0000
DS=0905  ES=0905  SS=0917  CS=0915  IP=000C   NV UP DI PL NZ NA PO NC
0915:000C 52              PUSH    DX
-D SS:3A 3B
0917:003A  0B 00                                                          ..
-T

AX=0000  BX=0000  CX=0015  DX=ABCD  SP=0038  BP=0000  SI=0000  DI=0000
DS=0905  ES=0905  SS=0917  CS=0915  IP=000D   NV UP DI PL NZ NA PO NC
0915:000D BA0500          MOV     DX,0005
-D SS:38 39
0917:0038  CD AB                                                          M+
-G 13

AX=0000  BX=0000  CX=0015  DX=0036  SP=0038  BP=0000  SI=0000  DI=0000
DS=0905  ES=0905  SS=0917  CS=0915  IP=0013   NV UP DI PL NZ NA PE NC
0915:0013 5A              POP     DX
-T

AX=0000  BX=0000  CX=0015  DX=ABCD  SP=003A  BP=0000  SI=0000  DI=0000
DS=0905  ES=0905  SS=0917  CS=0915  IP=0014   NV UP DI PL NZ NA PE NC
0915:0014 C3              RET
-T

AX=0000  BX=0000  CX=0015  DX=ABCD  SP=003C  BP=0000  SI=0000  DI=0000
DS=0905  ES=0905  SS=0917  CS=0915  IP=000B   NV UP DI PL NZ NA PE NC
0915:000B CB              RETF
-G

Program terminated normally
-Q
```

(c)

Figure 7.20 (continued)

Now the call instruction is executed with the command

$$-T \qquad (↵)$$

Notice from the displayed information for this command in Fig. 7.20(c) that the value held in IP has been changed to $000C_{16}$. Therefore, control has been passed to address 0915:000C, which is the first instruction of procedure SUM. Moreover, note that stack pointer (SP) has been decremented to the value $003A_{16}$. The new top of the stack is at address SS:SP equal 0917:003A. The word held at the top of the stack can be examined with the command

—D SS:3A 3B   (↵)

Notice in Fig. 7.20(c) that its value is $000B_{16}$. From the instruction sequence in Fig. 7.20(c), we see that this is the address of the RETF instruction. This is the instruction to which control is to be returned at the completion of the procedure.
    Next, the PUSH DX instruction is executed with the command

—T   (↵)

and again looking at the displayed-state information, we find that SP has been decremented to the value 0038_{16}. Displaying the word at the top of the stack with the command

—D SS:38 39   (↵)

we find that it is the word $ABCD_{16}$. This confirms that the original contents of DX are saved on the stack.
    Now we execute down to the POP DX instruction with the command

—G 13   (↵)

Looking at the displayed-state information in Fig. 7.20(c), we find that the sum $5_{10} + 31_{16} = 36_{16}$ has been formed in DX.
    Next the pop instruction is executed with the command

—T   (↵)

and the displayed information shows that the value $ABCD_{16}$ has been popped off the stack and put back into DX. Moreover, the value in SP has been incremented to $003A_{16}$ so that once again the return address is at the top of the stack.
    Finally, the RET instruction is executed with the command

—-T   (↵)

As shown in Fig. 7.20(c), this causes the value $000B_{16}$ to be popped from the top of the stack back into IP. Therefore, CS now equals 0915_{16} and IP equals $000B_{16}$. In this way, we see that control has been returned to the instruction at address 0915:000B of the main program.

    At times, we also want to save the contents of the flag register; if saved, we will later have to restore them. These operations can be accomplished with the *push flags* (PUSHF) and *pop flags* (POPF) instructions, respectively. These

Mnemonic	Meaning	Operation	Flags affected
PUSHF	Push flags onto stack	$((SP)) \leftarrow (Flags)$	None
POPF	Pop flags from stack	$(Flags) \leftarrow ((SP))$	OF,DF,IF,TF,SF,ZF,AF,PF,CF

Figure 7.21 Push flags and pop flags instructions.

instructions are shown in Fig. 7.21. Notice that PUSHF saves the contents of the flag register on the top of the stack. On the other hand, POPF returns the flags from the top of the stack to the flag register.

7.6 THE LOOP AND THE LOOP HANDLING INSTRUCTIONS

The 8088 microprocessor has three instructions specifically designed for implementing *loop operations*. These instructions can be used in place of certain conditional jump instructions and give the programmer a simpler way of writing loop sequences. The loop instructions are listed in Fig. 7.22.

The first instruction, *loop* (LOOP), works with respect to the contents of the CX register. CX must be preloaded with a count representing the number of times the loop is to be repeated. Whenever LOOP is executed, the contents of CX are first decremented by one and then checked to determine if they are equal to zero. If equal to zero, the loop is complete and the instruction following LOOP is executed; otherwise, control is returned to the instruction at the label specified in the loop instruction. In this way, we see that LOOP is a single instruction that functions the same as a decrement CX instruction followed by a JNZ instruction.

For example, the LOOP instruction sequence shown in Fig. 7.23 will cause

Mnemonic	Meaning	Format	Operation
LOOP	Loop	LOOP Short-label	$(CX) \leftarrow (CX) - 1$ Jump is initiated to location defined by Short-label if $(CX) \neq 0$; otherwise, execute next sequential instruction.
LOOPE/LOOPZ	Loop while equal/ loop while zero	LOOPE/LOOPZ Short-label	$(CX) \leftarrow (CX) - 1$ Jump to location defined by Short-label if $(CX) \neq 0$ and $(ZF) \neq 0$; otherwise, execute next sequential instruction.
LOOPNE/LOOPNZ	Loop while not equal/ loop while not zero	LOOPNE/LOOPNZ Short-label	$(CX) \leftarrow (CX) - 1$ Jump to location defined by Short-label if $(CX) \neq 0$ and $(ZF) = 0$; otherwise, execute next sequential instruction.

Figure 7.22 Loop instructions.

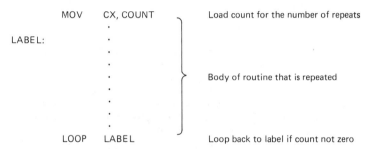

Figure 7.23 Typical loop routine structure.

the part of the program from the symbol LABEL through the instruction LOOP to be repeated a number of times equal to the value of COUNT stored in CX. For example, if CX contains $000A_{16}$, the sequence of instructions included in the loop is executed ten times.

Example 7.13

The source program in Fig. 7.24(a) demonstrates the use of the LOOP instruction to implement a software loop operation. This program was assembled by the macroassembler on the IBM PC and linked to produce a run module called EX713.EXE. The source listing is shown in Fig. 7.24(b). Observe the operation of the loop by executing the program through DEBUG.

Solution:

Looking at Fig. 7.24(c), we see that the run module is loaded with the DOS command

A > DEBUG B:EX713.EXE   (↵)

Now the loading of the program is verified by unassembling it with the command

—U 0 F   (↵)

By comparing the instruction sequence displayed in Fig. 7.24(c) with the listing in Fig. 7.24(b), we find that the program has loaded correctly.

Also we find from the instruction sequence in Fig. 7.24(c) that the loop whose operation we want to observe is located from address 0915:000B through 0915:000D. Therefore, we will begin by executing the instructions down to address 0915:000B with the GO command

—G B   (↵)

Again looking at Fig. 7.24(c), we see that these instructions initialize the count in CX to 0005_{16} and the contents of DX to 0000_{16}.

Now we execute the loop down to address 0915:000D with another GO command

$$-G \quad D \qquad (\lrcorner)$$

and looking at the displayed information, we find that the pass count in DX has been incremented by one to indicate that the first pass through the loop is about to be completed.

Next the LOOP instruction is executed with the TRACE command

$$-T \qquad (\lrcorner)$$

From Fig. 7.24(c), we find that the loop count CX has decremented by one, meaning that the first pass through the loop is complete, and the value in IP has been changed to $000B_{16}$. Therefore, control has been returned to the NOP instruction that represents the beginning of the loop.

```
A>TYPE B:EX713.ASM


TITLE    EXAMPLE 7.13

         PAGE     ,132

STACK_SEG        SEGMENT        STACK 'STACK'
                 DB             64 DUP(?)
STACK_SEG        ENDS


CODE_SEG         SEGMENT        'CODE'
EX713   PROC     FAR
        ASSUME   CS:CODE_SEG, SS:STACK_SEG

;To return to DEBUG program put return address on the stack

        PUSH     DS
        MOV      AX, 0
        PUSH     AX

;Following code implements Example 7.13

        MOV      CX, 5H
        MOV      DX, 0H
AGAIN:  NOP
        INC      DX
        LOOP     AGAIN

        RET                     ;Return to DEBUG program
EX713   ENDP
CODE_SEG         ENDS

        END      EX713

A>
```

(a)

Figure 7.24 (a) Source program for Example 7.13; (b) source listing produced by assembler; (c) executing the program with DEBUG.

```
                                    TITLE   EXAMPLE 7.13

                                    PAGE    ,132

0000                     STACK_SEG      SEGMENT     STACK 'STACK'
0000      40 [                         DB          64 DUP(?)
                ??
                   ]

0040                     STACK_SEG      ENDS


0000                     CODE_SEG       SEGMENT     'CODE'
0000                     EX713   PROC   FAR
                                 ASSUME  CS:CODE_SEG, SS:STACK_SEG

                         ;To return to DEBUG program put return address on the stack

0000  1E                         PUSH    DS
0001  B8 0000                    MOV     AX, 0
0004  50                         PUSH    AX

                         ;Following code implements Example 7.13

0005  B9 0005                    MOV     CX, 5H
0008  BA 0000                    MOV     DX, 0H
000B  90               AGAIN:    NOP
000C  42                         INC     DX
000D  E2 FC                      LOOP    AGAIN

000F  CB                         RET                    ;Return to DEBUG program
0010                     EX713   ENDP
0010                     CODE_SEG       ENDS

                                 END     EX713
```

Segments and groups:

Name	Size	align	combine	class
CODE_SEG	0010	PARA	NONE	'CODE'
STACK_SEG.	0040	PARA	STACK	'STACK'

Symbols:

Name	Type	Value	Attr	
AGAIN.	L NEAR	000B	CODE_SEG	
EX713.	F PROC	0000	CODE_SEG	Length =0010

```
Warning Severe
Errors  Errors
0       0
```

A>

(b)

Figure 7.24 (continued)

```
A>DEBUG B:EX713.EXE
-U 0 F
0915:0000 1E            PUSH    DS
0915:0001 B80000        MOV     AX,0000
0915:0004 50            PUSH    AX
0915:0005 B90500        MOV     CX,0005
0915:0008 BA0000        MOV     DX,0000
0915:000B 90            NOP
0915:000C 42            INC     DX
0915:000D E2FC          LOOP    000B
0915:000F CB            RETF
-G B

AX=0000  BX=0000  CX=0005  DX=0000  SP=003C  BP=0000  SI=0000  DI=0000
DS=0905  ES=0905  SS=0916  CS=0915  IP=000B   NV UP DI PL NZ NA PO NC
0915:000B 90            NOP
-G D

AX=0000  BX=0000  CX=0005  DX=0001  SP=003C  BP=0000  SI=0000  DI=0000
DS=0905  ES=0905  SS=0916  CS=0915  IP=000D   NV UP DI PL NZ NA PO NC
0915:000D E2FC          LOOP     000B
-T

AX=0000  BX=0000  CX=0004  DX=0001  SP=003C  BP=0000  SI=0000  DI=0000
DS=0905  ES=0905  SS=0916  CS=0915  IP=000B   NV UP DI PL NZ NA PO NC
0915:000B 90            NOP
-G F

AX=0000  BX=0000  CX=0000  DX=0005  SP=003C  BP=0000  SI=0000  DI=0000
DS=0905  ES=0905  SS=0916  CS=0915  IP=000F   NV UP DI PL NZ NA PE NC
0915:000F CB            RETF
-G

Program terminated normally
-Q
```

(c)

Figure 7.24 (continued)

Now that we have observed the basic loop operation, let us just execute the loop to completion with the command

$$-G \quad F \qquad (\hookleftarrow)$$

The displayed information for this command in Fig. 7.24(c) shows us that at completion of the program the loop count in CX has been decremented to 0000_{16} and the pass count in DX has been incremented to 0005_{16}.

The other two instructions in Fig. 7.22 operate in a similar way except that they check for two conditions. For instance, the instruction *loop while equal* (LOOPE)/*loop while zero* (LOOPZ) checks the contents of both CX and the ZF flag. Each time the loop instruction is executed, CX decrements by one without affecting the flags, its contents are checked for zero, and the state of ZF that results from execution of the previous instruction is tested for one. If CX equals zero and ZF equals one, a jump is initiated to the location specified with the Short-label operand and the loop continues. If either CX is not zero or ZF is not one, the loop is complete and the instruction following the loop instruction is executed.

Instruction *loop while not equal* (LOOPNE)/*loop while not zero* (LOOPNZ) works in a similar way to the LOOPE/LOOPZ instruction. The difference is that it checks ZF and CX looking for ZF equal to zero together with CX not equal to zero. If these conditions are met, the jump back to the location specified with the Short-label operand is performed and the loop continues.

Example 7.14

Given the following sequence of instructions:

```
            MOV   DL,05H
            MOV   AX,0A00H
            MOV   DS,AX
            MOV   SI,0H
            MOV   CX,0FH
AGAIN:      INC   SI
            CMP   [SI],DL
            LOOPNE  AGAIN
```

explain what happens as they are executed.

Solution:

The first five instructions are for initializing internal registers. Data register DL is loaded with 05_{16}; data segment register DS is loaded via AX with the value $0A00_{16}$; source index register SI is loaded with 0000_{16}; and count register CX is loaded with $0F_{16}$ (15_{10}). After initialization, a data segment is set up at address $0A000_{16}$ and SI points to the memory location at address 0000_{16} in this data segment. Moreover, DL contains the data 5_{10} and the CX register contains the loop count 15_{10}.

The part of the program that starts at the label AGAIN and ends with the LOOPNE instruction is a software loop. The first instruction in the loop increments SI by one. Therefore, the first time through the loop SI points to the memory address $A001_{16}$. The next instruction compares the contents of this memory location with the contents of DL, which are 5_{10}. If the data held at $A001_{16}$ are 5_{10}, the zero flag is set; otherwise, it is left at logic 0. The LOOPNE instruction then decrements CX (making it E_{16}) and then checks for CX = 0 or ZF = 1. If neither of these two conditions is satisfied, program control is returned to the instruction with the label AGAIN. This causes the comparison to be repeated for the examination of the contents of the next byte in memory. On the other hand, if either condition is satisfied, the loop is complete. In this way, we see that the loop is repeated until either a number 5_{16} is found or all locations in the address range $A001_{16}$ through $A00F_{16}$ have been tested and all are found not to contain 5_{16}.

Example 7.15

Figure 7.25(a) shows the source version of a program that is written to implement the memory-compare routine in Example 7.14. This program was assembled by the macroassembler on the IBM PC and linked to produce run module EX715.EXE. The source listing that resulted from the assembly process is shown in Fig. 7.25(b). Verify the operation of the program by executing it with the GO DEBUG command.

Solution:

As shown in Fig. 7.25(a), the run module is loaded with the DEBUG DOS command

A > DEBUG B:EX715.EXE   (↵)

The program loaded is verified with the command

—U 0 17   (↵)

Comparing the sequence of instructions displayed in Fig. 7.25(c) to those in the source listing of Fig. 7.25(b), we find that the program has loaded correctly.

```
A>TYPE B:EX715.ASM


TITLE    EXAMPLE 7.15

        PAGE      ,132

STACK_SEG         SEGMENT           STACK 'STACK'
                  DB                64 DUP(?)
STACK_SEG         ENDS


CODE_SEG          SEGMENT           'CODE'
EX715    PROC     FAR
         ASSUME   CS:CODE_SEG, SS:STACK_SEG

;To return to DEBUG program put return address on the stack

         PUSH     DS
         MOV      AX, 0
         PUSH     AX

;Following code implements Example 7.15

         MOV      DL, 5H
         MOV      AX, 0A00H
         MOV      DS, AX
         MOV      SI, 0H
         MOV      CX, 0FH
AGAIN:   INC      SI
         CMP      [SI], DL
         LOOPNE   AGAIN

         RET                        ;Return to DEBUG program
EX715    ENDP
CODE_SEG          ENDS

        END      EX715

A>
```

(a)

Figure 7.25 (a) Source program for Example 7.15; (b) source listing produced by assembler; (c) executing the program with DEBUG.

```
 The IBM Personal Computer Assembler 02-01-84              PAGE    1-1
EXAMPLE 7.15


                                TITLE    EXAMPLE 7.15

                                PAGE      ,132

0000                            STACK_SEG    SEGMENT       STACK 'STACK'
0000      40 [                               DB            64 DUP(?)
                ??
             ]

0040                            STACK_SEG    ENDS


0000                            CODE_SEG     SEGMENT       'CODE'
0000                            EX715   PROC  FAR
                                ASSUME  CS:CODE_SEG, SS:STACK_SEG

                             ;To return to DEBUG program put return address on the stack

0000  1E                                PUSH     DS
0001  B8 0000                           MOV      AX, 0
0004  50                                PUSH     AX

                             ;Following code implements Example 7.15

0005  B2 05                             MOV      DL, 5H
0007  B8 0A00                           MOV      AX, 0A00H
000A  8E D8                             MOV      DS, AX
000C  BE 0000                           MOV      SI, 0H
000F  B9 000F                           MOV      CX, 0FH
0012  46                      AGAIN:    INC      SI
0013  3B 14                             CMP      [SI], DL
0015  E0 FB                             LOOPNE   AGAIN

0017  CB                                RET                      ;Return to DEBUG program
0018                            EX715   ENDP
0018                            CODE_SEG     ENDS

                                END      EX715



 The IBM Personal Computer Assembler 02-01-84              PAGE    Symbols-1
EXAMPLE 7.15


Segments and groups:

               N a m e                  Size   align   combine class

CODE_SEG . . . . . . . . . . . .        0018   PARA    NONE    'CODE'
STACK_SEG. . . . . . . . . . . .        0040   PARA    STACK   'STACK'

Symbols:

               N a m e                  Type   Value   Attr

AGAIN. . . . . . . . . . . . . .        L NEAR 0012    CODE_SEG
EX715. . . . . . . . . . . . . .        F PROC 0000    CODE_SEG      Length =0018

Warning Severe
Errors  Errors
0       0

A>
```

(b)

293

```
A>DEBUG B:EX715.EXE
-U 0 17
0915:0000 1E            PUSH    DS
0915:0001 B80000        MOV     AX,0000
0915:0004 50            PUSH    AX
0915:0005 B205          MOV     DL,05
0915:0007 B8000A        MOV     AX,0A00
0915:000A 8ED8          MOV     DS,AX
0915:000C BE0000        MOV     SI,0000
0915:000F B90F00        MOV     CX,000F
0915:0012 46            INC     SI
0915:0013 3814          CMP     [SI],DL
0915:0015 E0FB          LOOPNZ  0012
0915:0017 CB            RETF
-G 12

AX=0A00  BX=0000  CX=000F  DX=0005  SP=003C  BP=0000  SI=0000  DI=0000
DS=0A00  ES=0905  SS=0917  CS=0915  IP=0012   NV UP DI PL NZ NA PO NC
0915:0012 46            INC     SI
-E A00:0 4,6,3,9,5,6,D,F,9
-D A00:0 F
0A00:0000  04 06 03 09 05 06 0D 0F-09 D0 D8 73 39 8A 5E F2   .........PXs9.^r
-G 17

AX=0A00  BX=0000  CX=000B  DX=0005  SP=003C  BP=0000  SI=0004  DI=0000
DS=0A00  ES=0905  SS=0917  CS=0915  IP=0017   NV UP DI PL ZR NA PE NC
0915:0017 CB            RETF
-G

Program terminated normally
-Q
```

(c)

Figure 7.25 (continued)

Notice that the loop that performs the memory-compare operation starts at address 0915:0012. Let us begin by executing down to this point with the GO command

$$-G\ 12\qquad (\leftarrow)$$

From the state information displayed in Fig. 7.25(c), we see that DL has been loaded with 0005_{16}, AX with $0A00_{16}$, DS with $0A00_{16}$, SI with 0000_{16}, and CX with $000F_{16}$.

Next, the table of data is loaded with the E command

$$-E\ A00:0\ 4,6,3,9,5,6,D,F,9\qquad (\leftarrow)$$

The nine values in this list are loaded into consecutive bytes of memory over the range 0A00:0000 through 0A00:0008. The compare routine actually also checks the storage locations from 0A00:0009 through 0A00:000F. Let us dump the data held in this part of memory to verify that it has been initialized correctly. In Fig. 7.25(c) we see that this is done with the command

$$-D\ A00:0\ F\qquad (\leftarrow)$$

and looking at the displayed data we find that it has loaded correctly.

Now the loop is executed with the command

$$-G\ 17 \qquad (\hookleftarrow)$$

In the display dump for this command in Fig. 7.25(c), we find that SI has incremented to the value 0004_{16}; therefore, the loop was only run four times. The fourth time through the loop SI equals four and the memory location pointed to by [SI], which is the address 0A00:0005, contains the value five. This value is equal to the value in DL; therefore, the instruction CMP [SI],DL results in a difference of zero and the zero flag is set. Notice in Fig. 7.25(c) that this flag is identified as ZR in the display dump. For this reason, execution of the LOOPNZ instruction causes the loop to be terminated, and control is passed to the RETF instruction.

7.7 STRINGS AND THE STRING HANDLING INSTRUCTIONS

The 8088 microprocessor is equipped with special instructions to handle *string operations*. By "string" we mean a series of data words or bytes that reside in consecutive memory locations. The string instructions of the 8088 permit a programmer to implement operations such as to move data from one block of memory to a block elsewhere in memory. A second type of operation that is easily performed is to scan a string of data elements stored in memory looking for a specific value. Other examples are to compare the elements of two strings together in order to determine whether they are the same or different, and to initialize a group of consecutive memory locations. Complex operations such as these typically require several nonstring instructions to be implemented.

There are five basic string instructions in the instruction set of the 8088. These instructions, as listed in Fig. 7.26, are *move byte* or *word string* (MOVS, MOVSB/MOVSW), *compare strings* (CMPS), *scan string* (SCAS), *load string* (LODS), and *store string* (STOS). They are called the *basic string instructions* because each defines an operation for one element of a string. Thus these operations must be repeated to handle a string of more than one element. Let us first look at the basic operations performed by these instructions.

Move String—MOVS, MOVSB/MOVSW

The instructions MOVS, MOVSB, and MOVSW all perform the same basic operation. An element of the string specified by the source index (SI) register with respect to the current data segment (DS) register is moved to the location specified by the destination index (DI) register with respect to the current extra segment (ES) register. The move can be performed on a byte or a word of data. After the move is complete, the contents of both SI and DI are automatically incremented or decremented by one for a byte move and by two for a word move. Remember the fact that the address pointers in SI and DI increment or

Mnemonic	Meaning	Format	Operation	Flags affected
MOVS	Move string	MOVS Operand	((ES)0 + (DI)) ← ((DS)0 + (SI)) (SI) ← (SI) ± 1 or 2 (DI) ← (DI) ± 1 or 2	None
MOVSB	Move string byte	MOVSB Operand	((ES)0 + (DI)) ← ((DS)0 + (SI)) (SI) ← (SI) ± 1 (DI) ← (DI) ± 1	None
MOVSW	Move string word	MOVSW Operand	((ES)0 + (DI)) ← ((DS)0 + (SI)) ((ES)0 + (DI) + 1) ← ((DS)0 + (SI) + 1) (SI) ← (SI) ± 2 (DI) ← (DI) ± 2	None
CMPS	Compare string	CMPS Operand	Set flags as per ((DS)0 + (SI)) − ((ES)0 + (DI)) (SI) ← (SI) ± 1 or 2 (DI) ← (DI) ± 1 or 2	CF,PF,AF,ZF,SF,OF
SCAS	Scan string	SCAS Operand	Set flags as per (AL or AX) − ((ES)0 + (DI)) (DI) ← (DI) ± 1 or 2	CF,PF,AF,ZF,SF,OF
LODS	Load string	LODS Operand	(AL or AX) ← ((DS)0 + (SI)) (SI) ← (SI) ± 1 or 2	None
STOS	Store string	STOS Operand	((ES)0 + (DI)) ← (AL or AX) ± 1 or 2 (DI) ← (DI) ± 1 or 2	None

Figure 7.26 Basic string instructions.

decrement depending on how the direction flag (DF) is set. The instruction MOVS requires that operands be specified, whereas MOVSB and MOVSW have no operands. This operand is simply either a word or byte size label whose size has been defined with a pseudo-op.

For example, one way of writing a MOVS instruction is

MOVS DESTINATION, SOURCE

This instruction could also be written simply as

MOVSB

In this case, SI and DI are used as pointers to the byte operands.

Compare Strings and Scan String—CMPS and SCAS

The CMPS instruction can be used to compare two elements in the same or different strings. It subtracts the destination operand from the source operand and adjusts flags CF, PF, AF, ZF, SF, and OF accordingly. The result of subtraction is not saved; therefore, the operation does not affect the operands in any way.

An example of a compare-strings instruction for bytes of data is

CMPSB

Again, the source element is pointed to by the address in SI with respect to the current value in DS, and the destination element is specified by the contents of DI relative to the contents of ES. Moreover, both SI and DI are updated such that they point to the next elements in their respective strings.

The scan-string (SCAS) instruction is similar to CMPS; however, it compares the byte or word element of the destination string at the physical address derived from DI and ES to the contents of AL or AX, respectively. The flags are adjusted based on this result and DI incremented or decremented.

Load and Store String—LODS and STOS

The last two instructions in Fig. 7.26, load string (LODS) and store string (STOS), are specifically provided to move string elements between the accumulator and memory. LODS loads either a byte or a word from a string in memory into AL or AX, respectively. The address in SI is used relative to DS to determine the address of the memory location of the string element. For instance, the instruction

```
                              LODSW
```

indicates that the word-string element at the physical address derived from DS and SI is to be loaded into AX. Then the index in SI is automatically incremented by two.

On the other hand, STOS stores a byte from AL or a word from AX into a string location in memory. This time the contents of ES and DI are used to form the address of the storage location in memory.

Repeat String—REP

In most applications, the basic string operations must be repeated in order to process arrays of data. This is done by inserting a repeat prefix before the instruction that is to be repeated. The *repeat prefixes* of the 8088 are shown in Fig. 7.27.

Prefix	Used with	Meaning
REP	MOVS STOS	Repeat while not end of string $CX \neq 0$
REPE/REPZ	CMPS SCAS	Repeat while not end of string and strings are equal $CX \neq 0$ and $ZF = 1$
REPNE/REPNZ	CMPS SCAS	Repeat while not end of string and strings are not equal $CX \neq 0$ and $ZF = 0$

Figure 7.27 Prefixes for use with the basic string instructions.

The first prefix, REP, causes the basic string operation to be repeated until the contents of register CX become equal to zero. Each time the instruction is executed, it causes CX to be tested for zero. If CX is found to be nonzero, it is decremented by one and the basic string operation is repeated. On the other hand, if it is zero, the repeat string operation is not done and the next instruction in the program is executed. The repeat count must be loaded into CX prior to executing the repeat string instruction.

The prefixes REPE and REPZ stand for the same function. They are meant for use with the CMPS and SCAS instructions. With REPE/REPZ, the basic compare or scan operation can be repeated as long as both the contents of CX are not equal to zero and the zero flag is one. The first condition, CX not equal to zero, indicates that the end of the string has not yet been reached; the second condition, ZF = 1, indicates that the elements that were compared are equal.

The last prefix, REPNE/REPNZ, works similarly to REPE/REPZ except that now the operation is repeated as long as CX is not equal to zero and ZF is zero. That is, the comparison or scanning is to be performed as long as the string elements are unequal and the end of the string is not yet found.

Autoindexing for String Instructions

Earlier we pointed out that during the execution of a string instruction the address indices in SI and DI are either automatically incremented or decremented. Moreover, we indicated that the decision to increment or decrement is made based on the setting of the direction flag DF. The 8088 provides two instructions, clear direction flag (CLD) and set direction flag (STD), to permit selection between *autoincrement* and *autodecrement modes* of operation. These instructions are shown in Fig. 7.28. When CLD is executed, DF is set to zero. This selects autoincrement mode, and each time a string operation is performed SI and/or DI are incremented by one if byte data are processed and by two if word data are processed.

Example 7.16

Describe what happens as the following sequence of instructions is executed.

```
        CLD
        MOV  AX,DATA_SEGMENT
        MOV  DS,AX
        MOV  AX,EXTRA_SEGMENT
        MOV  ES,AX
        MOV  CX,20H
        MOV  SI,OFFSET  MASTER
        MOV  DI,OFFSET  COPY
   REP  MOVS COPY,MASTER
```

Mnemonic	Meaning	Format	Operation	Affected flags
CLD	Clear DF	CLD	$(DF) \leftarrow 0$	DF
STD	Set DF	STD	$(DF) \leftarrow 1$	DF

Figure 7.28 Instructions for selection of autoincrementing and autodecrementing in string instructions.

Solution:

The first instruction clears the direction flag and selects autoincrement mode of operation for string addressing. The next two instructions initialize DS with the value DATA_SEGMENT. It is followed by two instructions that load ES with the value EXTRA_SEGMENT. Then the number of repeats, 20_{16}, is loaded into CX. The next two instructions load SI and DI with beginning offset addresses MASTER and COPY for the source and destination strings. Now we are ready to perform the string operation. Execution of REP MOVSB moves a block of 32 consecutive bytes from the block of memory locations starting at offset address MASTER with respect to the current data segment (DS) to a block of locations starting at offset address COPY with respect to the current extra segment (ES).

Example 7.17

The source program in Fig. 7.29(a) implements the block-move operation of Example 7.16. This program was assembled by the macroassembler on the IBM PC and linked to produce a run module called EX717.EXE. The source listing that was produced during the assembly process is shown in Fig. 7.29(b). Execute the program through DEBUG and verify its operation.

Solution:

The program is loaded with the DEBUG command

$$A > DEBUG\ B{:}EX717.EXE \qquad (\leftarrow\!\!\!\lrcorner)$$

and verified by the UNASSEMBLE command

$$-U\ \ 0\ \ 11 \qquad (\leftarrow\!\!\!\lrcorner)$$

Comparing the displayed instruction sequence in Fig. 7.29(c) with the source listing in Fig. 7.29(b), we find that the program has loaded correctly.

Now the storage locations in the 32-byte source block that starts at address DS:0000 are loaded with the value FF_{16} using the FILL command

$$-F\ \ DS{:}0\ \ 1F\ \ FF\ (\leftarrow\!\!\!\lrcorner)$$

and the 32 bytes of the destination block, which start at DS:0020, are loaded with the value 00_{16} with the FILL command

$$-F\ \ DS{:}20\ \ 3F\ \ 00\ (\leftarrow\!\!\!\lrcorner)$$

Now a memory dump command is used to verify the initialization of memory

$$-\text{D DS:0 3F} \qquad (\leftarrow)$$

Looking at the displayed information in Fig. 7.29(c), we see that memory has been initialized correctly.

First we execute down to the REPZ instruction with the G command

$$-\text{G F} \qquad (\leftarrow)$$

and looking at the state information displayed in Fig. 7.29(c), we see that CX has been loaded with 0020_{16}, SI with 0000_{16}, and DI with 0020_{16}.

```
A>TYPE B:EX717.ASM


TITLE   EXAMPLE 7.17

        PAGE        ,132

STACK_SEG       SEGMENT         STACK 'STACK'
                DB              64 DUP(?)
STACK_SEG       ENDS


DATA_SEG        SEGMENT         'DATA'
MASTER          DB              32 DUP(?)
COPY            DB              32 DUP(?)
DATA_SEG        ENDS


CODE_SEG        SEGMENT         'CODE'
EX717   PROC    FAR
        ASSUME  CS:CODE_SEG, SS:STACK_SEG, DS:DATA_SEG, ES:DATA_SEG

;To return to DEBUG program put return address on the stack

        PUSH    DS
        MOV     AX, 0
        PUSH    AX

;Following code implements Example 7.17

        MOV     AX, DATA_SEG    ;Set up data segment
        MOV     DS, AX
        MOV     ES, AX          ;Set up extra segment

        CLD
        MOV     CX, 20H
        MOV     SI, OFFSET MASTER
        MOV     DI, OFFSET COPY
REP     MOVS    COPY, MASTER

        RET                     ;Return to DEBUG program
EX717   ENDP
CODE_SEG        ENDS

        END     EX717

A>
```

(a)

Figure 7.29 (a) Source program for Example 7.17; (b) source listing produced by the assembler; (c) executing the program with DEBUG.

A>TYPE B:EX717.LST

```
The IBM Personal Computer Assembler 07-01-84          PAGE    1-1
EXAMPLE 7.17


                    TITLE    EXAMPLE 7.17

                         PAGE      ,132

0000                STACK_SEG      SEGMENT       STACK 'STACK'
0000    40 [                       DB            64 DUP(?)
            ??
                ]

0040                STACK_SEG      ENDS


0000                DATA_SEG       SEGMENT       'DATA'
0000    20 [        MASTER         DB            32 DUP(?)
            ??
                ]

0020    20 [        COPY           DB            32 DUP(?)
            ??
                ]

0040                DATA_SEG       ENDS


0000                CODE_SEG       SEGMENT       'CODE'
0000                EX717   PROC   FAR
                         ASSUME  CS:CODE_SEG, SS:STACK_SEG, DS:DATA_SEG, ES:DATA_SEG

                    ;To return to DEBUG program put return address on the stack

0000    1E                    PUSH    DS
0001    B8 0000               MOV     AX, 0
0004    50                    PUSH    AX

                    ;Following code implements Example 7.17

0005    B8  ---- R            MOV     AX, DATA_SEG   ;Set up data segment
0008    8E D8                 MOV     DS, AX
000A    8E C0                 MOV     ES, AX         ;Set up extra segment

000C    FC                    CLD
000D    B9 0020               MOV     CX, 20H
0010    BE 0000 R             MOV     SI, OFFSET MASTER
0013    BF 0020 R             MOV     DI, OFFSET COPY
0016    F3/ A4        REP     MOVS    COPY, MASTER

0018    CB                    RET                     ;Return to DEBUG program
0019                EX717   ENDP
0019                CODE_SEG       ENDS

                         END     EX717
```

(b)

Figure 7.29 (continued)

```
   The IBM Personal Computer Assembler 07-01-84          PAGE      Symbols-1
   EXAMPLE 7.17


Segments and groups:

              N a m e                   Size    align    combine class

CODE_SEG . . . . . . . . . . . .        0019    PARA     NONE    'CODE'
DATA_SEG . . . . . . . . . . . .        0040    PARA     NONE    'DATA'
STACK_SEG. . . . . . . . . . . .        0040    PARA     STACK   'STACK'

Symbols:

              N a m e                   Type    Value    Attr

COPY . . . . . . . . . . . . . .        L BYTE  0020     DATA_SEG     Length =0020
EX717. . . . . . . . . . . . . .        F PROC  0000     CODE_SEG     Length =0019
MASTER . . . . . . . . . . . . .        L BYTE  0000     DATA_SEG     Length =0020

Warning Severe
Errors  Errors
0       0

A>
```

(b)

```
A>DEBUG B:EX717.EXE
-U 0 11
0915:0000 1E              PUSH    DS
0915:0001 B80000          MOV     AX,0000
0915:0004 50              PUSH    AX
0915:0005 FC              CLD
0915:0006 B92000          MOV     CX,0020
0915:0009 BE0000          MOV     SI,0000
0915:000C BF2000          MOV     DI,0020
0915:000F F3              REPZ
0915:0010 A4              MOVSB
0915:0011 CB              RETF
-F DS:0 1F FF
-F DS:20 3F 00
-D DS:0 3F
0905:0000  FF FF FF FF FF FF FF FF-FF FF FF FF FF FF FF FF   ................
0905:0010  FF FF FF FF FF FF FF FF-FF FF FF FF FF FF FF FF   ................
0905:0020  00 00 00 00 00 00 00 00-00 00 00 00 00 00 00 00   ................
0905:0030  00 00 00 00 00 00 00 00-00 00 00 00 00 00 00 00   ................
-G F

AX=0000  BX=0000  CX=0020  DX=0000  SP=003C  BP=0000  SI=0000  DI=0020
DS=0905  ES=0905  SS=091B  CS=0915  IP=000F   NV UP DI PL NZ NA PO NC
0915:000F F3              REPZ
0915:0010 A4              MOVSB
-G 11

AX=0000  BX=0000  CX=0000  DX=0000  SP=003C  BP=0000  SI=0020  DI=0040
DS=0905  ES=0905  SS=091B  CS=0915  IP=0011   NV UP DI PL NZ NA PO NC
0915:0011 CB              RETF
-D DS:0 3F
0905:0000  FF FF FF FF FF FF FF FF-FF FF FF FF FF FF FF FF   ................
0905:0010  FF FF FF FF FF FF FF FF-FF FF FF FF FF FF FF FF   ................
0905:0020  FF FF FF FF FF FF FF FF-FF FF FF FF FF FF CA 2A   ...............J*
0905:0030  00 06 FF FF FF FF FF FF-FF FF FF FF FF FF FF FF   ................
-G
```

(c)

Figure 7.29 (continued)

Now we execute the string-move operation with the command

—G 11   (↵)

Again looking at the display in Fig. 7.29(c), we see that the repeat count in CX has been decremented to zero and that the source and destination pointers have been incremented to $(SI) = 0020_{16}$ and $(DI) = 0040_{16}$. In this way, we see that the string-move instruction was executed 32 times and that the source and destination addresses were correctly incremented to complete the block transfer. The block-transfer operation is verified by repeating the DUMP command

—D DS:0 3F   (↵)

Notice that both the source and destination blocks now contain FF_{16} in all byte-storage locations.

ASSIGNMENT

Section 7.2

1. Write an instruction sequence to configure the 8088 as follows: interrupts not accepted; save the original contents of flags SF, ZF, AF, PF, and CF at the address $A000_{16}$; and then clear CF.

Section 7.3

2. Describe the difference in operation and effect on status flags due to execution of the subtract-words and compare-words instructions.
3. What happens to the ZF and CF status flags as the following sequence of instructions is executed? Assume that they both are initially cleared.

```
MOV  BX,1111H
MOV  AX,0BBBBH
CMP  AX,BX
```

Use the IBM PC debugger to verify the operation of the sequence of instructions.

Section 7.4

4. The program that follows implements what is known as a *delay loop*.

```
        MOV  CX,1000H
DLY:    DEC  CX
        JNZ  DLY
NXT:    NOP
```

(a) How many times does the JNZ DLY instruction get executed?

(b) Change the program so that JNZ DLY is executed 2^{32} times.

5. Given a number N in the range $0 < N \le 5$, write a program that computes its factorial and saves the result in memory location FACT in the current data segment. Let N be contained in DL. Assemble and execute the program to test it for $N = 5$.

Section 7.5

6. Change the subroutine SUM program in Example 7.10 so that it implements

$$(DX) = (AX) + (BX) + (CX)$$

Execute the program on the IBM PC with $(AX) = -32$, $(BX) = 27$, and $(CX) = 10$.

7. Use appropriate PUSH and POP instructions in the subroutine SUM in problem 6 so that no register gets changed due to the execution of the subroutine. Execute the program on the IBM PC with the data in problem 6.

8. Write a subroutine that converts a BCD number in DL to an equivalent binary number in DL. The execution of the subroutine must not change any other register.

Section 7.6

9. Change the program in Example 7.14 to search for a number AB_{16} in memory range $B010_{16}$ to $B0AF_{16}$. Verify the programs execution on the IBM PC.

10. Write the program in problem 4(a) using the LOOP instruction.

11. Write the program in problem 4(b) using the appropriate loop instruction.

Section 7.7

12. Write a program that compares the elements of two arrays A(I) and B(I). Each array contains 100 16-bit signed numbers. The comparison is to be done by comparing the corresponding elements of the two arrays until either two elements are found to be equal or all elements are compared and found to be unequal. The arrays start at offsets MASTER and COPY of the current data and extra segments, respectively. Assemble and execute the program to verify its operation.

8

APPLICATION
EXAMPLES

8.1 INTRODUCTION

In the last two chapters we made a detailed study of the instruction set of the 8088 microprocessor and worked with some simple instruction sequences. Here we finish our study of assembly language programming for the 8088 microprocessor and IBM PC with a series of practical applications. Each application is illustrated with examples which step us through the writing of the program and then through its execution on the PC. All of the programs that are written in this chapter are set up as procedures so that they can be easily used as modules for programs you may write in the future. The application examples covered in this chapter are as follows:

1. Multiplication and division using the shift instructions
2. Memory test routine
3. Calculating the average of a series of numbers
4. Sorting a table of data
5. Generating elements for a mathematical series
6. Code conversions in software
7. Speaker-control routine
8. Searching a data structure
9. Keyboard and display interaction routine
10. Floating-point arithmetic calculations

8.2 MULTIPLICATION AND DIVISION
USING THE SHIFT INSTRUCTIONS

During our study of the shift instructions in Chapter 6, we found that if the bits of a number are shifted to the left using either an arithmetic or logical shift instruction, its value gets multiplied by 2^n where n is the number of bit positions shifted. We also found that if we shift the bits of a number to the right by n bit positions, the value of the number was divided by 2^n. In this way, we see that shift instructions can be used to multiply or divide a number by a power of two. Let us now look at an example that demonstrates the use of the shift instructions for performing multiplications.

Example 8.1

Write a program to implement the following expression, using shift instructions to perform the arithmetic.

$$3(AX) + 7(BX) \rightarrow (DX)$$

Solution:

Shifting left by one bit position causes a multiplication by two. To perform multiplication by an odd number we can use a shift instruction to multiply to the nearest multiple of two and then add or subtract the appropriate value to get the desired result.

The algorithm for performing the arithmetic operations in the expression starts by shifting (AX) left by one bit. This gives two times (AX). Then adding the original (AX) gives multiplication by three. Next, the contents of BX are shifted left by three bits to give eight times its value and subtracting the original (BX) once gives multiplication by seven. Expressing this with instructions, we get

```
MOV  SI,AX     ; COPY (AX) INTO SI
SAL  SI,1      ; 2(AX)
ADD  SI,AX     ; 3(AX)
MOV  DX,BX     ; COPY (BX) INTO DX
MOV  CL,03H    ; LOAD SHIFT COUNT
SAL  DX,CL     ; 8(BX)
SUB  DX,BX     ; 7(BX)
ADD  DX,SI     ; RESULT
```

It is important to note that we have assumed that to obtain any of the intermediate results and the final result, overflows do not occur. For instance, if the value 8 (BX) could not be accommodated in the 16 bits of BX, an overflow condition would occur and the result produced by executing the program may be incorrect.

Example 8.2

A source program for a procedure that includes the arithmetic routine developed in Example 8.1 is shown in Fig. 8.1(a). This program was assembled and linked to produce a run module in file EX82.EXE. The source listing produced as part of the assembly process is shown in Fig. 8.1(b). Load this run module with DEBUG, initialize AX to $FFFF_{16}$ and BX to 0002_{16}, and then run the program.

Solution:

As shown in Fig. 8.1(c), the program is loaded with the DOS command

A > DEBUG B:EX82.EXE (↵)

Next, the instruction sequence is displayed using the UNASSEMBLE command

—U 0 15   (↵)

Notice that the arithmetic routine starts at address 0915:0005. Let us execute to this point in the program with the command

—G 5   (↵)

```
A>TYPE B:EX82.ASM


TITLE    EXAMPLE 8.2

         PAGE    ,132

STACK_SEG       SEGMENT         STACK 'STACK'
                DB              64 DUP(?)
STACK_SEG       ENDS


CODE_SEG        SEGMENT         'CODE'
EX82    PROC    FAR
        ASSUME  CS:CODE_SEG, SS:STACK_SEG

;To return to DEBUG program put return address on the stack

        PUSH    DS
        MOV     AX, 0
        PUSH    AX

;Following code implements Example 8.2

        MOV     SI, AX          ;Copy (AX) into SI
        SAL     SI, 1           ;2(AX)
        ADD     SI, AX          ;3(AX)
        MOV     DX, BX          ;Copy (BX) into DX
        MOV     CL, 3H          ;Load shift count
        SAL     DX, CL          ;8(BX)
        SUB     DX, BX          ;7(BX)
        ADD     DX, SI          ;Result

        RET                     ;Return to DEBUG program
EX82    ENDP
CODE_SEG        ENDS

        END     EX82

A>
```

(a)

Figure 8.1 (a) Source program for Example 8.2; (b) source listing produced by assembler; (c) DEBUG sequence.

```
                                    TITLE    EXAMPLE 8.2

                                        PAGE      ,132

0000                                STACK_SEG        SEGMENT        STACK 'STACK'
0000      40 [                                       DB             64 DUP(?)
                  ??
                        ]

0040                                STACK_SEG        ENDS


0000                                CODE_SEG         SEGMENT        'CODE'
0000                                EX82     PROC    FAR
                                             ASSUME  CS:CODE_SEG, SS:STACK_SEG

                                    ;To return to DEBUG program put return address on the stack

0000      1E                                 PUSH    DS
0001      B8 0000                            MOV     AX, 0
0004      50                                 PUSH    AX

                                    ;Following code implements Example 8.2

0005      8B F0                              MOV     SI, AX          ;Copy (AX) into SI
0007      D1 E6                              SAL     SI, 1           ;2(AX)
0009      03 F0                              ADD     SI, AX          ;3(AX)
000B      8B D3                              MOV     DX, BX          ;Copy (BX) into DX
000D      B1 03                              MOV     CL, 3H          ;Load shift count
000F      D3 E2                              SAL     DX, CL          ;8(BX)
0011      2B D3                              SUB     DX, BX          ;7(BX)
0013      03 D6                              ADD     DX, SI          ;Result

0015      CB                                 RET                     ;Return to DEBUG program
0016                                EX82     ENDP
0016                                CODE_SEG         ENDS

                                             END     EX82
```

Segments and groups:

Name	Size	align	combine	class
CODE_SEG	0016	PARA	NONE	'CODE'
STACK_SEG.	0040	PARA	STACK	'STACK'

Symbols:

Name	Type	Value	Attr
EX82	F PROC	0000	CODE_SEG Length =0016

Warning Severe
Errors Errors
0   0

A>

(b)

Figure 8.1 (continued)

```
DEBUG B:EX82.EXE
-U 0 15
0915:0000 1E            PUSH    DS
0915:0001 B80000        MOV     AX,0000
0915:0004 50            PUSH    AX
0915:0005 8BF0          MOV     SI,AX
0915:0007 D1E6          SHL     SI,1
0915:0009 03F0          ADD     SI,AX
0915:000B 8BD3          MOV     DX,BX
0915:000D B103          MOV     CL,03
0915:000F D3E2          SHL     DX,CL
0915:0011 2BD3          SUB     DX,BX
0915:0013 03D6          ADD     DX,SI
0915:0015 CB            RETF
-G 5

AX=0000  BX=0000  CX=0016  DX=0000  SP=003C  BP=0000  SI=0000  DI=0000
DS=0905  ES=0905  SS=0917  CS=0915  IP=0005    NV UP DI PL NZ NA PO NC
0915:0005 8BF0          MOV     SI,AX
-R AX
AX 0000
:FFFF
-R BX
BX 0000
:2
-R
AX=FFFF  BX=0002  CX=0016  DX=0000  SP=003C  BP=0000  SI=0000  DI=0000
DS=0905  ES=0905  SS=0917  CS=0915  IP=0005    NV UP DI PL NZ NA PO NC
0915:0005 8BF0          MOV     SI,AX
-G 15

AX=FFFF  BX=0002  CX=0003  DX=000B  SP=003C  BP=0000  SI=FFFD  DI=0000
DS=0905  ES=0905  SS=0917  CS=0915  IP=0015    NV UP DI PL NZ AC PO CY
0915:0015 CB            RETF
-G

Program terminated normally
-Q
```

(c)

Figure 8.1 (continued)

Now registers AX and BX are initialized with the commands

```
—R  AX    (↵)
AX  0000
:FFFF     (↵)
—R  BX    (↵)
BX  0000
:2        (↵)
```

and the initialization of the registers is verified with the command

```
—R    (↵)
```

Notice in the displayed information in Fig. 8.1(c) that the contents of AX are $FFFF_{16}$, those of BX are 0002_{16}, and IP is 0005_{16}.

Now we are ready to run the program. This is done with the command

$$-\text{G} \quad 15 \qquad (\text{↵})$$

The result produced in DX is $000B_{16}$.

8.3 MEMORY TEST ROUTINE

The IBM PC's operating system software provides a *diagnostic routine* that tests the operation of the memory subsystem of the microcomputer. As this routine is run, it signals that the memory has passed the test and is verified to work correctly by generating a beep at the speaker.

Many programs are available to perform a memory test diagnostic operation. The basic idea behind all these programs is to write a known data pattern to a location in memory, read back the contents of the same location, and then compare the value written into memory to that read back. If these two values match, the memory location operates correctly; if they are different, it is malfunctioning. This sequence of events must be repeated for every storage location in the memory subsystem.

The memory test sequence we just described is not really as simple as it sounds. This is because theoretically we must write and read every possible binary combination to every storage location to verify that the memory subsystem operates correctly. At this point, we realize that it is not practical to execute a program that makes such an exhaustive test of a memory subsystem. Therefore, in typical memory test programs, the storage locations are just tested for specific data patterns or for random data. If the test is passed, the memory subsystem is considered to work correctly and is put into service. If the test fails, an error message can be displayed.

Here we will write a small program that is designed to test a portion of the IBM PC's memory. This test program is limited in functionality, but does illustrate the concept behind memory test routines.

Example 8.3

Write a memory test program to test the storage locations in the range from address offset MEM_START to offset MEM_STOP in the data segment starting at segment address DSEG_ADDR. Each memory address is to be tested by writing a word-size test pattern to it, reading the pattern back, and comparing the write and read data patterns. If the memory test fails, place the value $0BAD_{16}$ in the DX register; otherwise, load it with 1234_{16}.

Solution:

First we will initialize DS, SI, and CX so that they contain the data-segment address, the offset address of the first memory location to be tested, and the number of memory locations to be tested, respectively. This is done with the instruction sequence

```
MOV   AX,DSEG_ADDR
MOV   DS,AX
MOV   SI,MEM_START
MOV   CX, (MEM_STOP—MEM_START+1)/2
```

Next we write the word-size test pattern into the memory location pointed to by DS and SI, read it back, and compare the value read back to the test pattern. If the result of the comparison is that they are not equal, a jump is initiated to the statement with label BADMEM; otherwise, the next memory location is tested. This is done with the sequence of instructions that follows:

```
AGAIN:  MOV   WORD PTR [SI],PATTERN
        MOV   AX,[SI]
        CMP   AX,PATTERN
        JNE   BADMEM
```

Assuming that the memory location was found to be working correctly, we need to increment SI by two such that it points to the next word storage location in memory and then loop back to the label AGAIN to repeat the memory test. To do this, we use the instructions

```
INC   SI
INC   SI
LOOP  AGAIN
```

If the loop runs to completion without any error occurring, we must load DX with 1234_{16} and then jump to the end of the program. Therefore, the next two instructions are

```
MOV   DX,1234H
JMP   DONE
```

On the other hand, if during the execution of the loop a bad storage location was found, a jump was made to the statement with the label BADMEM. This statement must load DX with the value $0BAD_{16}$ and then pass control to the end of the program. This is done with the last two statements in the program. They are

```
BADMEM:  MOV   DX,0BADH
DONE:    NOP
```

The complete program is shown in Fig. 8.2.

```
              MOV     AX,DSEG_ADDR
              MOV     DS,AX
              MOV     SI,MEM_START
              MOV     CX,(MEM_STOP−MEM_START+1)/2
AGAIN:        MOV     WORD PTR [SI],PATTERN
              MOV     AX,[SI]
              CMP     AX,PATTERN
              JNE     BADMEM
              INC     SI
              INC     SI
              LOOP    AGAIN
              MOV     DX,1234H
              JMP     DONE
BADMEM:       MOV     DX,0BADH
DONE:         NOP
```

Figure 8.2 Source program for the memory test routine.

Example 8.4

Figure 8.3(a) is a source file set up as a procedure that can be used to test the operation of a segment of memory. Notice that the body of the program implements the memory test routine we developed in Example 8.3. Moreover, the constants are defined as PATTERN equals 5555_{16}, MEM_START equals 1000_{16}, MEM_STOP equals $107F_{16}$, and DSEG_ADDR equals 0000_{16} with pseudo-op statements. This program was assembled and linked to produce a run module in file EX84.EXE. The source listing that resulted during the assembly process is given in Fig. 8.3(b). Load and execute the program on the PC with DEBUG.

Solution:

The DEBUG sequence in Fig. 8.3(c) shows that the program is loaded with the DOS command

A>DEBUG   B:EX84.EXE   (↵)

Then it is unassembled with U commands to show the instruction sequence.
    Now the program is executed with the GO command

−G   28   (↵)

Looking at the displayed-state information produced for this command in Fig. 8.3(c), we see that DX contains 1234_{16}. This tells us that the memory test was passed. Notice that the contents of all memory locations tested have also been displayed with a DUMP command.

8.4 CALCULATING THE AVERAGE OF A SERIES OF NUMBERS

A mathematical operation we must frequently perform is to calculate the average of a group of numbers. This may need to be done for a number of reasons—for instance, to find the average grade for a large number of tests. In general, the average of a group of data points is computed by adding the values

```
A>TYPE B:EX84.ASM


TITLE    EXAMPLE 8.4

        PAGE        ,132

STACK_SEG        SEGMENT         STACK 'STACK'
                 DB              64 DUP(?)
STACK_SEG        ENDS


PATTERN          =        5555H
MEM_START        =        1000H
MEM_STOP         =        107FH
DSEG_ADDR        =        OH


CODE_SEG         SEGMENT          'CODE'
EX84     PROC    FAR
         ASSUME  CS:CODE_SEG, SS:STACK_SEG

;To return to DEBUG program put return address on the stack

         PUSH    DS
         MOV     AX, 0
         PUSH    AX

;Following code implements Example 8.4

         MOV     AX, DSEG_ADDR           ;Establish data segment
         MOV     DS, AX
         MOV     SI, MEM_START           ;Next memory address
         MOV     CX, (MEM_STOP-MEM_START+1)/2   ;No of locations
AGAIN:   MOV     WORD PTR [SI], PATTERN  ;Write the pattern
         MOV     AX, [SI]                ;Read it back
         CMP     AX, PATTERN             ;Same ?
         JNE     BADMEM
         INC     SI                      ;Repeat for next location
         INC     SI
         LOOP    AGAIN
         MOV     DX, 1234H               ;Code for test passed
         JMP     DONE
BADMEM:  MOV     DX, OBADH               ;Code for test failed
DONE:    NOP

         RET                             ;Return to DEBUG program
EX84     ENDP
CODE_SEG         ENDS

         END     EX84

A>
```

(a)

Figure 8.3 (a) Source program for Example 8.4; (b) source listing produced by assembler; (c) DEBUG sequence.

```
TYPE B:EX84.LST



The IBM Personal Computer Assembler 03-15-84              PAGE    1-1
EXAMPLE 8.4




                        TITLE    EXAMPLE 8.4

                               PAGE      ,132

0000                    STACK_SEG        SEGMENT        STACK 'STACK'
0000      40 [                           DB             64 DUP(?)
              ??
                  ]

0040                    STACK_SEG        ENDS


= 5555                  PATTERN          =       5555H
= 1000                  MEM_START        =       1000H
= 107F                  MEM_STOP         =       107FH
= 0000                  DSEG_ADDR        =       OH


0000                    CODE_SEG         SEGMENT        'CODE'
0000                    EX84     PROC    FAR
                                 ASSUME  CS:CODE_SEG, SS:STACK_SEG

                        ;To return to DEBUG program put return address on the stack

0000   1E                        PUSH    DS
0001   B8 0000                   MOV     AX, 0
0004   50                        PUSH    AX

                        ;Following code implements Example 8.4

0005   B8 0000                   MOV     AX, DSEG_ADDR           ;Establish data segment
0008   8E D8                     MOV     DS, AX
000A   BE 1000                   MOV     SI, MEM_START          ;Next memory address
000D   B9 0040                   MOV     CX, (MEM_STOP-MEM_START+1)/2    ;No of locations
0010   C7 04 5555      AGAIN:    MOV     WORD PTR [SI], PATTERN ;Write the pattern
0014   8B 04                     MOV     AX, [SI]               ;Read it back
0016   3D 5555                   CMP     AX, PATTERN            ;Same ?
0019   75 0A                     JNE     BADMEM
001B   46                        INC     SI                     ;Repeat for next location
001C   46                        INC     SI
001D   E2 F1                     LOOP    AGAIN
001F   BA 1234                   MOV     DX, 1234H              ;Code for test passed
0022   EB 04 90                  JMP     DONE
0025   BA 0BAD        BADMEM:    MOV     DX, 0BADH              ;Code for test failed
0028   90             DONE:      NOP         .

0029   CB                        RET                            ;Return to DEBUG program
002A                    EX84     ENDP
002A                    CODE_SEG         ENDS

                                 END     EX84
```

(b)

Figure 8.3 (continued)

```
The IBM Personal Computer Assembler 03-15-84          PAGE    Symbols-1
EXAMPLE 8.4


Segments and groups:

                N a m e                   Size    align    combine class

CODE_SEG . . . . . . . . . . . .          002A    PARA     NONE    'CODE'
STACK_SEG. . . . . . . . . . . .          0040    PARA     STACK   'STACK'

Symbols:

                N a m e                   Type    Value    Attr

AGAIN. . . . . . . . . . . . . .          L NEAR  0010     CODE_SEG
BADMEM . . . . . . . . . . . . .          L NEAR  0025     CODE_SEG
DONE . . . . . . . . . . . . . .          L NEAR  0028     CODE_SEG
DSEG_ADDR. . . . . . . . . . . .          Number  0000
EX84 . . . . . . . . . . . . . .          F PROC  0000     CODE_SEG        Length =002A
MEM_START. . . . . . . . . . . .          Number  1000
MEM_STOP . . . . . . . . . . . .          Number  107F
PATTERN. . . . . . . . . . . . .          Number  5555

Warning Severe
Errors  Errors
0       0

A>
```

(b)

```
A>DEBUG B:EX84.EXE
-U
0915:0000 1E           PUSH    DS
0915:0001 B80000       MOV     AX,0000
0915:0004 50           PUSH    AX
0915:0005 B80000       MOV     AX,0000
0915:0008 8ED8         MOV     DS,AX
0915:000A BE0010       MOV     SI,1000
0915:000D B94000       MOV     CX,0040
0915:0010 C7045555     MOV     WORD PTR [SI],5555
0915:0014 8B04         MOV     AX,[SI]
0915:0016 3D5555       CMP     AX,5555
0915:0019 750A         JNZ     0025
0915:001B 46           INC     SI
0915:001C 46           INC     SI
0915:001D E2F1         LOOP    0010
0915:001F BA3412       MOV     DX,1234
-U 22 29
0915:0022 EB04         JMP     0028
0915:0024 90           NOP
0915:0025 BAAD0B       MOV     DX,0BAD
0915:0028 90           NOP
0915:0029 CB           RETF
-G 28

AX=5555  BX=0000  CX=0000  DX=1234  SP=003C  BP=0000  SI=1080  DI=0000
DS=0000  ES=0905  SS=0918  CS=0915  IP=0028    NV UP DI PL NZ AC PO NC
0915:0028 90              NOP
-D 1000 107F
0000:1000   55 55 55 55 55 55 55 55-55 55 55 55 55 55 55 55   UUUUUUUUUUUUUUUU
0000:1010   55 55 55 55 55 55 55 55-55 55 55 55 55 55 55 55   UUUUUUUUUUUUUUUU
0000:1020   55 55 55 55 55 55 55 55-55 55 55 55 55 55 55 55   UUUUUUUUUUUUUUUU
0000:1030   55 55 55 55 55 55 55 55-55 55 55 55 55 55 55 55   UUUUUUUUUUUUUUUU
0000:1040   55 55 55 55 55 55 55 55-55 55 55 55 55 55 55 55   UUUUUUUUUUUUUUUU
0000:1050   55 55 55 55 55 55 55 55-55 55 55 55 55 55 55 55   UUUUUUUUUUUUUUUU
0000:1060   55 55 55 55 55 55 55 55-55 55 55 55 55 55 55 55   UUUUUUUUUUUUUUUU
0000:1070   55 55 55 55 55 55 55 55-55 55 55 55 55 55 55 55   UUUUUUUUUUUUUUUU
-G

Program terminated normally
-Q
```

(c)

Figure 8.3 (continued)

of the data points and then dividing their sum by the number of points. In the examples that follow, we develop an average calculation program and demonstrate its operation on the PC.

Example 8.5

It is required to determine the average of a set of data points stored in a buffer. The number of points in the buffer, the offset address of the beginning of the buffer, and the data-segment address are stored in a table called a *parameter table*. Figure 8.4(a) shows an example of the parameters needed for the average program. Notice that the beginning address of this table is $ABC0_{16}$. This first address holds the number that indicates how many data points are in the buffer. Since a byte is used to specify the number of data points, the size of the buffer is limited to 256 bytes. The offset address of the beginning of the buffer is stored at table locations $ABC1_{16}$ and $ABC2_{16}$. This buffer table offset address is taken with respect to the data segment defined by the address in locations $ABC3_{16}$ and $ABC4_{16}$. Assuming that the data points are signed eight-bit binary numbers, write a program to find their average.

Solution:

The average can be found by adding all the signed numbers and then dividing their sum by the number of points that were added. Even though eight-bit data points are being added, the sum that results can be more than eight bits. Therefore, we will consider a 16-bit result for the sum, and it will be held in register DX. The average that is obtained turns out to be just eight bits long. It will be available in AL at the completion of the program.

Our plan for the program that will solve this problem is shown in Fig. 8.4(b). This flowchart can be divided into six basic operations, which are: initialization, preparing the next point for addition, performing the addition, updating the counter and pointer, testing for the end of the summation, and computing the average.

Initialization involves establishing the data segment and data buffer addresses and loading the data point counter. This is achieved by loading the appropriate registers within the 8088 with parameters from the parameter table. The instructions that perform this initialization are:

```
MOV   AX,0A00H
MOV   DS,AX
MOV   DI,0BC0H
MOV   CL,[DI]
MOV   BL,CL
LDS   SI,[DI+1]
```

The first two instructions define the data segment in which the parameter table resides. This is achieved by first loading AX with the immediate operand $A00_{16}$ of a MOV instruction and then copying it into DS. Then another MOV instruction establishes a pointer to the parameter table in register DI. This is done by loading DI with immediate operand $BC0_{16}$. The instruction that follows this

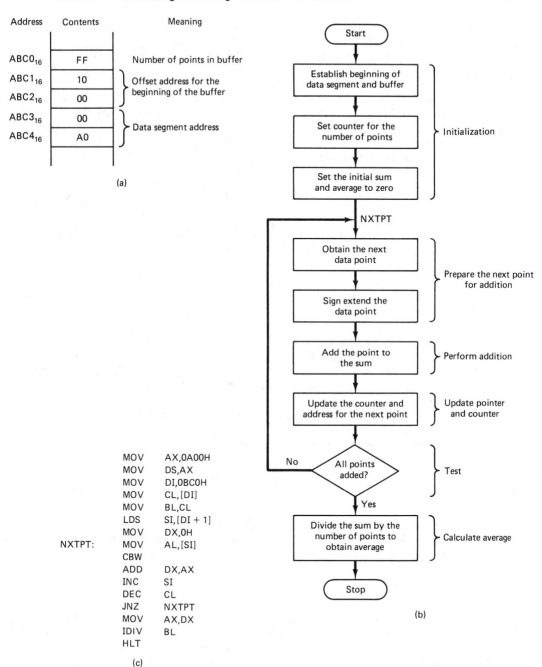

Address	Contents	Meaning
$ABC0_{16}$	FF	Number of points in buffer
$ABC1_{16}$	10	Offset address for the
$ABC2_{16}$	00	beginning of the buffer
$ABC3_{16}$	00	Data segment address
$ABC4_{16}$	A0	

(a)

Flowchart (b):

Start → Establish beginning of data segment and buffer → Set counter for the number of points → Set the initial sum and average to zero ⎤ Initialization

NXTPT → Obtain the next data point → Sign extend the data point ⎤ Prepare the next point for addition

Add the point to the sum ⎤ Perform addition

Update the counter and address for the next point ⎤ Update pointer and counter

All points added? ⎤ Test — No → NXTPT; Yes →

Divide the sum by the number of points to obtain average ⎤ Calculate average

Stop

(b)

```
            MOV     AX,0A00H
            MOV     DS,AX
            MOV     DI,0BC0H
            MOV     CL,[DI]
            MOV     BL,CL
            LDS     SI,[DI + 1]
            MOV     DX,0H
NXTPT:      MOV     AL,[SI]
            CBW
            ADD     DX,AX
            INC     SI
            DEC     CL
            JNZ     NXTPT
            MOV     AX,DX
            IDIV    BL
            HLT
```

(c)

Figure 8.4 (a) Parameter table for Example 8.5; (b) flowchart for average calculation; (c) program.

uses DI as a pointer to load CL from the first address in the parameter table. This address is $ABC0_{16}$ and contains the number of points to be used in forming the average. Looking at Fig. 8.4(a), we see that this value is FF_{16}. The next instruction copies the number in CL into BL for later use. The LDS instruction is used to define the buffer together with the data segment in which it resides. This instruction first loads SI with the offset address of the beginning of the buffer from table locations $ABC1_{16}$ and $ABC2_{16}$ and then DS with the address of the data segment in which the data table lies from table locations $ABC3_{16}$ and $ABC4_{16}$. The sum must start with zero; therefore, register DX, which is to hold the sum, is loaded with zeros by the instruction

```
MOV   DX,0H
```

The next operation involves obtaining a byte of data from the buffer, making it into a 16-bit number by sign extension, and adding it to the contents of the DX register. This is accomplished by the following sequence of instructions.

```
NXTPT:  MOV   AL,[SI]
        CBW
        ADD   DX,AX
```

The first instruction loads AL with the element in the buffer that is pointed to by the address in SI. The CBW instruction converts the signed byte in AL to a signed word in AX by extending its sign. Next the 16-bit signed number in AX is added to the sum in DX. Notice that the label NXTPT (next point) has been used on the first instruction.

To prepare for the next addition, we must increment the value in SI such that it points to the next element in the buffer and decrement the count in CL. To do this, we use the following instructions:

```
INC   SI
DEC   CL
```

If the contents of CL at this point are nonzero, we should go back to obtain and add the next element from the buffer; otherwise, we just proceed with the next instruction in the program. To do this, we execute the following instruction:

```
JNZ   NXTPT
```

Execution of this instruction tests the value in ZF that results from the DEC CL instruction. If this flag is not set to one, a jump is initiated to the instruction corresponding to the label NXTPT. Remember that NXTPT is placed at the instruction used to move a byte into AL for addition to the sum. In this way we see that this part of the program will be repeated until all data points have been added. After this is complete, the sum resides in DX.

The average is obtained by dividing the accumulated sum in DX by the number of data points. The count of data points was saved earlier in BL. However, the contents of DX cannot be divided directly. It must first be moved into AX. Once there, the signed divide instruction can be used to do the division. This gives the following instructions:

```
MOV  AX,DX
IDIV BL
```

The result of the division, which is the average, is now in AL. The entire average calculation program is shown in Fig. 8.4(c).

Example 8.6

The source program in Fig. 8.5(a) implements the average calculation routine we developed in Example 8.5 as a procedure. This program was assembled and linked to produce a run module in file EX86.EXE. The source listing produced by the assembler is shown in Fig. 8.5(b). Execute the program on the IBM PC with 16 arbitrarily selected data points.

Solution:

As shown in Fig. 8.5(c), we begin by loading the program with the DOS command

```
A>DEBUG  B:EX86.EXE  (↵)
```

and then it is unassembled with a U command to verify loading.

Next the program is executed down to the instruction at address 0915:000A with the command

```
—G  A    (↵)
```

Looking at the state information displayed for this command, we find that DS has been loaded with the value 0918_{16}. Next we can verify the data segment locations that are initialized with a D command. Notice that the location 0918:0000 contains the byte count and the next four locations contain the double word 10000000_{16}.

Next, the program is executed down to the instruction at 0915:0017 with the command

```
—G  17    (↵)
```

From the displayed information, we see that CL, BL, SI, and DX have been initialized.

Now CS:IP has the value 0915:0017 and points to the beginning of the loop that performs the summation part of the average calculation routine. Therefore, an E command is next used to initialize the buffer with random values of data; and a D command is used to verify that the data has been loaded.

Finally the program is run to completion with the command

$$-G \ 25 \qquad (\lrcorner)$$

In the state information displayed for this command, we find that the average, which is saved in BX, is 0010_{16}.

```
A>TYPE B:EX86.ASM


TITLE    EXAMPLE 8.6

         PAGE      ,132

STACK_SEG         SEGMENT        STACK 'STACK'
                  DB             64 DUP(?)
STACK_SEG         ENDS

DATA_SEG          SEGMENT        'DATA'
COUNT             DB      16
BUFFER            DD      10000000H
DATA_SEG          ENDS

CODE_SEG          SEGMENT        'CODE'
EX86     PROC     FAR
         ASSUME   CS:CODE_SEG, SS:STACK_SEG, DS:DATA_SEG

;To return to DEBUG program put return address on the stack

         PUSH     DS
         MOV      AX, 0
         PUSH     AX

;Following code implements Example 8.6

         MOV      AX, DATA_SEG        ;Establish data segment
         MOV      DS, AX
         MOV      CL, COUNT           ;Point count
         MOV      BL, CL
         LDS      SI, BUFFER          ;Pointer for data points
         MOV      DX, 0H              ;Sum = 0
NXTPT:   MOV      AL, [SI]            ;Get a byte size point
         CBW                          ;Convert to word size
         ADD      DX, AX              ;Add to last sum
         INC      SI                  ;Point to next point
         DEC      CL                  ;All points added ?
         JNZ      NXTPT               ;If not - repeat
         MOV      AX, DX              ;Compute average
         IDIV     BL

         RET                          ;Return to DEBUG program
EX86     ENDP
CODE_SEG          ENDS

         END      EX86

A>
```

(a)

Figure 8.5 (a) Source program for Example 8.6; (b) source listing produced by assembler; (c) DEBUG sequence.

A>TYPE B:EX86.LST

The IBM Personal Computer MACRO Assembler 04-15-84   PAGE   1-1
EXAMPLE 8.6

```
                      TITLE    EXAMPLE 8.6

                          PAGE     ,132
0000                  STACK_SEG       SEGMENT       STACK 'STACK'
0000      40 [                        DB            64 DUP(?)
            ??
                  ]

0040                  STACK_SEG       ENDS

0000                  DATA_SEG        SEGMENT       'DATA'
0000   10             COUNT           DB       16
0001   00 00 00 10    BUFFER          DD       10000000H
0005                  DATA_SEG        ENDS

0000                  CODE_SEG        SEGMENT       'CODE'
0000                  EX86      PROC  FAR
                          ASSUME  CS:CODE_SEG, SS:STACK_SEG, DS:DATA_SEG

                      ;To return to DEBUG program put return address on the stack

0000   1E                      PUSH    DS
0001   B8 0000                 MOV     AX, 0
0004   50                      PUSH    AX

                      ;Following code implements Example 8.6

0005   B8  ---- R              MOV     AX, DATA_SEG         ;Establish data segment
0008   8E D8                   MOV     DS, AX
000A   8A 0E 0000 R            MOV     CL, COUNT            ;Point count
000E   8A D9                   MOV     BL, CL
0010   C5 36 0001 R            LDS     SI, BUFFER           ;Pointer for data points
0014   BA 0000                 MOV     DX, 0H               ;Sum = 0
0017   8A 04         NXTPT:    MOV     AL, [SI]             ;Get a byte size point
0019   98                      CBW                          ;Convert to word size
001A   03 D0                   ADD     DX, AX               ;Add to last sum
001C   46                      INC     SI                   ;Point to next point
001D   FE C9                   DEC     CL                   ;All points added ?
001F   75 F6                   JNZ     NXTPT                ;If not - repeat
0021   8B C2                   MOV     AX, DX               ;Compute average
0023   F6 FB                   IDIV    BL

0025   CB                      RET                          ;Return to DEBUG program
0026                  EX86      ENDP
0026                  CODE_SEG        ENDS

                          END     EX86
```

(b)

Figure 8.5 (continued)

```
The IBM Personal Computer MACRO Assembler 04-15-84        PAGE    Symbols-1
EXAMPLE 8.6
```

Segments and groups:

N a m e	Size	align	combine	class
CODE_SEG	0026	PARA	NONE	'CODE'
DATA_SEG	0005	PARA	NONE	'DATA'
STACK_SEG.	0040	PARA	STACK	'STACK'

Symbols:

N a m e	Type	Value	Attr	
BUFFER	L DWORD	0001	DATA_SEG	
COUNT.	L BYTE	0000	DATA_SEG	
EX86	F PROC	0000	CODE_SEG	Length =0026
NXTPT.	L NEAR	0017	CODE_SEG	

```
Warning Severe
Errors  Errors
0       0

A>
```

(b)

```
A>DEBUG B:EX86.EXE
 -U
0915:0000 1E           PUSH    DS
0915:0001 B80000       MOV     AX,0000
0915:0004 50           PUSH    AX
0915:0005 B81809       MOV     AX,0918
0915:0008 8ED8         MOV     DS,AX
0915:000A 8A0E0000     MOV     CL,[0000]
0915:000E 8AD9         MOV     BL,CL
0915:0010 C5360100     LDS     SI,[0001]
0915:0014 BA0000       MOV     DX,0000
0915:0017 8A04         MOV     AL,[SI]
0915:0019 98           CBW
0915:001A 03D0         ADD     DX,AX
0915:001C 46           INC     SI
0915:001D FEC9         DEC     CL
0915:001F 75F6         JNZ     0017
 -G A

AX=0918  BX=0000  CX=0035  DX=0000  SP=003C  BP=0000  SI=0000  DI=0000
DS=0918  ES=0905  SS=0919  CS=0915  IP=000A   NV UP DI PL NZ NA PO NC
0915:000A 8A0E0000     MOV     CL,[0000]                          DS:0000=10
 -D 0 6
0918:0000   10 00 00 00 10 00 00                               .......
 -G 17

AX=0918  BX=0010  CX=0010  DX=0000  SP=003C  BP=0000  SI=0000  DI=0000
DS=1000  ES=0905  SS=0919  CS=0915  IP=0017   NV UP DI PL NZ NA PO NC
0915:0017 8A04         MOV     AL,[SI]                            DS:0000=00
 -E 1000:0 4 5 6 4 5 6 FF FE FF 1 2 0 1 5 5 5
 -D 0 F
```

(c)

Figure 8.5 (continued)

```
1000:0000  04 05 06 04 05 06 FF FE-FF 01 02 00 01 05 05 05    .......~.........
-U 17 25
0915:0017 8A04        MOV    AL,[SI]
0915:0019 98          CBW
0915:001A 03D0        ADD    DX,AX
0915:001C 46          INC    SI
0915:001D FEC9        DEC    CL
0915:001F 75F6        JNZ    0017
0915:0021 8BC2        MOV    AX,DX
0915:0023 F6FB        IDIV   BL
0915:0025 CB          RETF
-G 25

AX=0D02  BX=0010  CX=0000  DX=002D  SP=003C  BP=0000  SI=0010  DI=0000
DS=1000  ES=0905  SS=0919  CS=0915  IP=0025   NV UP DI NG NZ NA PO NC
0915:0025 CB          RETF
-G

Program terminated normally
-Q
```

(c)

Figure 8.5 (continued)

8.5 SORTING A TABLE OF DATA

Many applications require a large array of data to be rearranged in a specific way through software. For instance, a table of numbers, such as the grades of a group of tests, can be reorganized so that they are arranged in ascending order. That is, the program would examine all numbers in the table and then rearrange them with the lowest grade in the first location, the next to lowest in the second location, and so on up through the highest grade. Another example would be to rearrange the grades into descending order. In this case, they are arranged in order from the highest grade down through the lowest grade. This operation is called a *sort*.

This type of operation is so common that a number of excellent algorithms have been developed for implementing sort procedures. These algorithms have different properties that make them either efficient in terms of execution time or the amount of code needed to implement them. An example of a widely used sort algorithm is that known as the *bubble sort*.

Here we will develop a program for an algorithm that illustrates the sorting of a group of numbers into ascending order. The operation of this program is also demonstrated by executing it on the IBM PC.

Example 8.7

It is required to sort an array of 16-bit signed binary numbers such that they are arranged in ascending order. For instance, if the original array is

$$5, 1, 29, 15, 38, 3, -8, -32$$

after sorting, the array that results would be

$$-32, -8, 1, 3, 5, 15, 29, 38$$

Assume that the array of numbers is stored at consecutive memory locations from addresses $A400_{16}$ through $A41E_{16}$ in memory. Write a sort program.

Solution:

First we will develop an algorithm that can be used to sort an array of elements A(0), A(1), A(2), through A(N) into ascending order. One way of doing this is to take the first number in the array, which is A(0), and compare it to the second number, A(1). If A(0) is greater than A(1), the two numbers are swapped; otherwise, they are left alone. Next A(0) is compared to A(2) and, based on the result of this comparison, they are either swapped or left alone. This sequence is repeated until A(0) has been compared with all numbers up through A(N). When this is complete, the smallest number will be in the A(0) position.

Now A(1) must be compared to A(2) through A(N) in the same way. After this is done, the second smallest number is in the A(1) position. Up to this point, just two of the N numbers have been put in ascending order. Therefore, the procedure must be continued for A(2) through A(N-1) to complete the sort.

Figure 8.6(a) illustrates the use of this algorithm for an array with just four numbers. The numbers are A(0)=5, A(1)=1, A(2)=29, and A(3)=−8. During the sort sequence, A(0)=5 is first compared to A(1)=1. Since 5 is greater than 1, A(0) and A(1) are swapped. Now A(0)=1 is compared to A(2)=29. This time 1 is less than 29; therefore, the numbers are not swapped and A(0) remains equal to 1. Next A(0)=1 is compared with A(3)=−8. A(0) is greater than A(3). Thus A(0) and A(3) are swapped and A(0) becomes equal to −8. Notice in Fig. 8.6(a) that the lowest of the four numbers now resides in A(0).

The sort sequence in Fig. 8.6(a) continues with A(1)=5 being compared first to A(2)=29 and then to A(3)=1. In the first comparison, A(1) is less than A(2). For this reason, their values are not swapped. But in the second comparison, A(1) is greater than A(3); therefore, the two values are swapped. In this way, the second lowest number, which is 1, is sorted into A(1).

I	0	1	2	3	Status
A(I)	5	1	29	−8	Original array
A(I)	1	5	29	−8	Array after comparing A(0) and A(1)
A(I)	1	5	29	−8	Array after comparing A(0) and A(2)
A(I)	−8	5	29	1	Array after comparing A(0) and A(3)
A(I)	−8	5	29	1	Array after comparing A(1) and A(2)
A(I)	−8	1	29	5	Array after comparing A(1) and A(3)
A(I)	−8	1	5	29	Array after comparing A(2) and A(3)

(a)

Figure 8.6 (a) Sort algorithm demonstration; (b) flowchart for the sort program; (c) program.

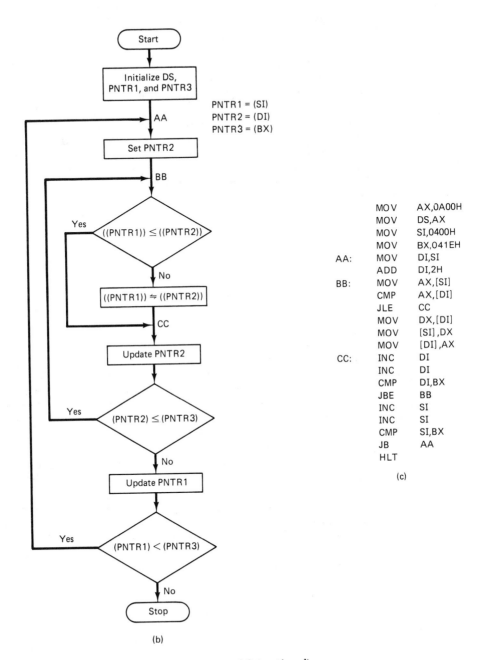

PNTR1 = (SI)
PNTR2 = (DI)
PNTR3 = (BX)

```
          MOV   AX,0A00H
          MOV   DS,AX
          MOV   SI,0400H
          MOV   BX,041EH
AA:       MOV   DI,SI
          ADD   DI,2H
BB:       MOV   AX,[SI]
          CMP   AX,[DI]
          JLE   CC
          MOV   DX,[DI]
          MOV   [SI],DX
          MOV   [DI],AX
CC:       INC   DI
          INC   DI
          CMP   DI,BX
          JBE   BB
          INC   SI
          INC   SI
          CMP   SI,BX
          JB    AA
          HLT
```

(c)

(b)

Figure 8.6 (continued)

It just remains to sort A(2) and A(3). Comparing these two values, we see that 29 is greater than 5. This causes the two values to be swapped such that A(2)=5 and A(3)=29. As shown in Fig. 8.6(a), the sorting of the array is now complete.

Now we will implement the algorithm on the 8088 microprocessor. The flowchart for its implementation is shown in Fig. 8.6(b).

The first block in the flowchart represents the initialization of data-segment register DS and pointers $PNTR_1$ and $PNTR_3$. The DS register is initialized with $0A00_{16}$ to define a data segment starting from memory address $0A000_{16}$. $PNTR_1$ points to the first element in the array. It will be register SI and will be initialized to 0400_{16}. Therefore, the first element of the array is at address $A400_{16}$. For pointer $PNTR_3$, we will use register BX and will initialize it to $041E_{16}$. It points to the last element in the array, which is at address $A41E_{16}$. Next, $PNTR_2$, the moving pointer, is initialized so that it points to the second element in the array. Register DI will be used for this pointer. This leads to the following instruction sequence for initialization.

```
        MOV   AX,0A00H
        MOV   DS,AX
        MOV   SI,0400H
        MOV   BX,041EH
AA:     MOV   DI,SI
        ADD   DI,02H
```

Notice that DS was loaded via AX with the immediate data $0A00_{16}$ to define a data segment starting at $0A000_{16}$. SI and BX, which are $PNTR_1$ and $PNTR_3$, respectively, are loaded with immediate operands 0400_{16} and $041E_{16}$. In this way they point to the first and last elements of the array, respectively. Finally, register DI, which is $PNTR_2$, is loaded with 0400_{16} from SI and then incremented by two with an ADD instruction such that it points to the second element in the array. This completes the initialization process.

Next, the array element pointed to by $PNTR_1$ is to be compared to the element pointed to by $PNTR_2$. If the element corresponding to $PNTR_1$ is arithmetically less than the element corresponding to pointer $PNTR_2$, the two elements are already in ascending order. But if this is not the case, the two elements must be interchanged. Both of these elements are in memory. However, the 8088 cannot directly compare two values in memory. For this reason, one of the two elements must be moved to a register within the 8088. We will use AX for this purpose. The resulting code is as follows:

```
BB:    MOV   AX,[SI]
       CMP   AX,[DI]
       JLE   CC
       MOV   DX,[DI]
       MOV   [SI],DX
       MOV   [DI],AX
CC:
```

The first instruction moves the element pointed to by $PNTR_1$ into AX. The second instruction compares the value in AX with the element pointed to by $PNTR_2$. The result of this comparison is reflected in the status flags. The jump on less-than or equal-to instruction that follows checks if the first element is arithmetically less than or equal to the second element. If the result of this check is yes, control is transferred to CC. CC is a label to be used in the segment of program that will follow. If the check fails, the two elements must be interchanged. In this case, the instructions executed next move the element pointed to by $PNTR_2$ into the location pointed to by $PNTR_1$. Then the copy of the original value pointed to by $PNTR_1$ which is saved in AX, is moved to the location pointed to by $PNTR_2$.

   To continue sorting through the rest of the elements in the array, we update $PNTR_2$ such that it points to the next element in the array. This comparison should be repeated until the first element has been compared to each of the other elements in the array. This condition is satisfied when $PNTR_2$ points to the last element in the array. That is, $PNTR_2$ equals $PNTR_3$. This part of the program can be done with the code that follows:

```
CC:   INC   DI
      INC   DI
      CMP   DI,BX
      JBE   BB
```

The first two instructions update $PNTR_2$ such that it points to the next element. The third instruction compares $PNTR_2$ to $PNTR_3$ to determine whether or not they are equal. If they are equal to each other, the first element has been compared to the last element and we are ready to continue with the second element. Otherwise, we must repeat from the label BB. This test is done with the jump on below or equal instruction. Notice that label BB corresponds to the beginning of the part of the program that compares the elements of the array. Once we fall through the JBE instruction, we have placed the smallest number in the array into the position pointed to by $PNTR_1$. To process the rest of the elements in the array in a similar way, $PNTR_1$ must be moved over the entire range of elements and the foregoing procedure repeated. This can be done by implementing the code that follows:

```
      INC   SI
      INC   SI
      CMP   SI,BX
      JB    AA
      HLT
```

The first two instructions increment pointer $PNTR_1$ such that it points to the next element in the array. The third instruction checks if all the elements have been sorted. The fourth instruction passes control back to the sorting sequence of instructions if $PNTR_1$ does not point to the last element. However, if all elements of the array have been sorted, we come to a halt at the end of the program. The entire program appears in Fig. 8.6(c).

Example 8.8

The sort algorithm developed in Example 8.7 is implemented by the source program in Fig. 8.7(a). This program was assembled and linked to produce a run module in file EX88.EXE. The source listing produced by the assembler during the assembly process is shown in Fig. 8.7(b). Run the program on the IBM PC for an arbitrary set of data points.

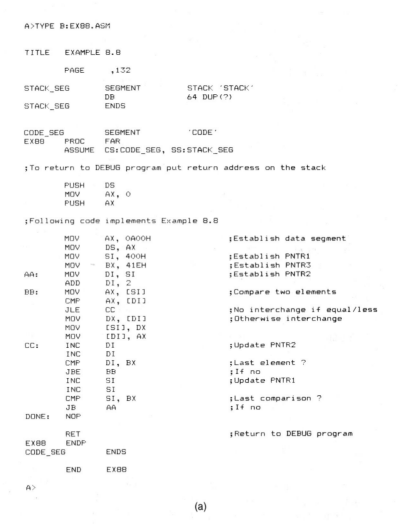

```
A>TYPE B:EX88.ASM


TITLE    EXAMPLE 8.8

         PAGE      ,132

STACK_SEG         SEGMENT         STACK 'STACK'
                  DB              64 DUP(?)
STACK_SEG         ENDS


CODE_SEG          SEGMENT         'CODE'
EX88     PROC     FAR
         ASSUME   CS:CODE_SEG, SS:STACK_SEG

;To return to DEBUG program put return address on the stack

         PUSH     DS
         MOV      AX, 0
         PUSH     AX

;Following code implements Example 8.8

         MOV      AX, 0A00H              ;Establish data segment
         MOV      DS, AX
         MOV      SI, 400H               ;Establish PNTR1
         MOV      BX, 41EH               ;Establish PNTR3
AA:      MOV      DI, SI                 ;Establish PNTR2
         ADD      DI, 2
BB:      MOV      AX, [SI]               ;Compare two elements
         CMP      AX, [DI]
         JLE      CC                     ;No interchange if equal/less
         MOV      DX, [DI]               ;Otherwise interchange
         MOV      [SI], DX
         MOV      [DI], AX
CC:      INC      DI                     ;Update PNTR2
         INC      DI
         CMP      DI, BX                 ;Last element ?
         JBE      BB                     ;If no
         INC      SI                     ;Update PNTR1
         INC      SI
         CMP      SI, BX                 ;Last comparison ?
         JB       AA                     ;If no
DONE:    NOP

         RET                             ;Return to DEBUG program
EX88     ENDP
CODE_SEG          ENDS

         END      EX88

A>
```

(a)

Figure 8.7 (a) Source program for Example 8.8; (b) source listing produced by the assembler; (c) DEBUG sequence.

```
A>TYPE B:EX88.LST
```

```
 The IBM Personal Computer Assembler 04-15-84          PAGE    1-1
 EXAMPLE 8.8
```

```
                              TITLE   EXAMPLE 8.8

                                 PAGE       ,132

0000                          STACK_SEG        SEGMENT         STACK 'STACK'
0000        40 [                              DB              64 DUP(?)
                 ??
                     ]

0040                          STACK_SEG        ENDS


0000                          CODE_SEG         SEGMENT         'CODE'
0000                          EX88    PROC     FAR
                                      ASSUME   CS:CODE_SEG, SS:STACK_SEG

                              ;To return to DEBUG program put return address on the stack

0000  1E                              PUSH     DS
0001  B8 0000                         MOV      AX, 0
0004  50                              PUSH     AX

                              ;Following code implements Example 8.8

0005  B8 0A00                         MOV      AX, 0A00H               ;Establish data segment
0008  8E D8                           MOV      DS, AX
000A  BE 0400                         MOV      SI, 400H                ;Establish PNTR1
000D  BB 041E                         MOV      BX, 41EH                ;Establish PNTR3
0010  8B FE           AA:             MOV      DI, SI                  ;Establish PNTR2
0012  83 C7 02                        ADD      DI, 2
0015  8B 04           BB:             MOV      AX, [SI]                ;Compare two elements
0017  3B 05                           CMP      AX, [DI]
0019  7E 06                           JLE      CC                      ;No interchange if equal/less
001B  8B 15                           MOV      DX, [DI]                ;Otherwise interchange
001D  89 14                           MOV      [SI], DX
001F  89 05                           MOV      [DI], AX
0021  47              CC:             INC      DI                      ;Update PNTR2
0022  47                              INC      DI
0023  3B FB                           CMP      DI, BX                  ;Last element ?
0025  76 EE                           JBE      BB                      ;If no
0027  46                              INC      SI                      ;Update PNTR1
0028  46                              INC      SI
0029  3B F3                           CMP      SI, BX                  ;Last comparison ?
002B  72 E3                           JB       AA                      ;If no
002D  90              DONE:           NOP

                                      RET                              ;Return to DEBUG program
002E  CB              EX88    ENDP
002F                  CODE_SEG        ENDS
002F
                                      END      EX88
```

(b)

Figure 8.7 (continued)

```
The IBM Personal Computer Assembler 04-15-84            PAGE     Symbols-1
EXAMPLE 8.8

Segments and groups:

                N a m e                 Size    align   combine class

CODE_SEG . . . . . . . . . . . .        002F    PARA    NONE    'CODE'
STACK_SEG. . . . . . . . . . . .        0040    PARA    STACK   'STACK'

Symbols:

                N a m e                 Type    Value   Attr

AA . . . . . . . . . . . . . . .        L NEAR  0010    CODE_SEG
BB . . . . . . . . . . . . . . .        L NEAR  0015    CODE_SEG
CC . . . . . . . . . . . . . . .        L NEAR  0021    CODE_SEG
DONE . . . . . . . . . . . . . .        L NEAR  002D    CODE_SEG
EX88 . . . . . . . . . . . . . .        F PROC  0000    CODE_SEG        Length =002F

Warning Severe
Errors  Errors
0       0

A>
```

(b)

```
A>DEBUG B:EX88.EXE
-U
0915:0000 1E           PUSH    DS
0915:0001 B80000       MOV     AX,0000
0915:0004 50           PUSH    AX
0915:0005 B8000A       MOV     AX,0A00
0915:0008 8ED8         MOV     DS,AX
0915:000A BE0004       MOV     SI,0400
0915:000D BB1E04       MOV     BX,041E
0915:0010 8BFE         MOV     DI,SI
0915:0012 83C702       ADD     DI,+02
0915:0015 8B04         MOV     AX,[SI]
0915:0017 3B05         CMP     AX,[DI]
0915:0019 7E06         JLE     0021
0915:001B 8B15         MOV     DX,[DI]
0915:001D 8914         MOV     [SI],DX
0915:001F 8905         MOV     [DI],AX
-U 21 2E
0915:0021 47           INC     DI
0915:0022 47           INC     DI
0915:0023 3BFB         CMP     DI,BX
0915:0025 76EE         JBE     0015
0915:0027 46           INC     SI
0915:0028 46           INC     SI
0915:0029 3BF3         CMP     SI,BX
0915:002B 72E3         JB      0010
0915:002D 90           NOP
0915:002E CB           RETF
-E A00:400 0 1 1 0 5 1 FF FF 7 2 9 8 0 66 89 2 1 DA 00 9A 2 2 3 6 A A 9 7 3 3 3
-D A00:400 420
0A00:0400  00 01 01 00 05 01 FF FF-07 02 09 08 00 66 89 02   ............f..
0A00:0410  01 DA 00 9A 02 02 03 06-0A 0A 09 07 03 03 03 00   .Z..............
0A00:0420  00                                                .
-G 2D

AX=6600  BX=041E  CX=002F  DX=0A0A  SP=003C  BP=0000  SI=041E  DI=0420
DS=0A00  ES=0905  SS=0918  CS=0915  IP=002D   NV UP DI PL ZR NA PE NC
0915:002D 90           NOP
-D A00:400 420
0A00:0400  00 9A 01 DA FF FF 01 00-03 00 00 01 05 01 02 02   ...Z............
0A00:0410  07 02 89 02 03 03 03 06-09 07 09 08 0A 0A 00 66   ...............f
0A00:0420  00                                                .
-G

Program terminated normally
-Q
```

(c)

Figure 8.7 (continued)

Solution:

Looking at Fig. 8.7(c), we see that the program is loaded with the command

$$A > DEBUG \quad B:EX88.EXE \quad (\llcorner)$$

and, as shown, its loading is verified by unassembling the instructions.

Now a table of data is loaded starting at address A00:400 with an E command; its entry is verified with the dump command

$$-D \quad A00:400 \quad 420 \quad (\llcorner)$$

In Fig. 8.7(c), we find that the table contains 16-bit data words arranged in a random order.

The complete program is executed with the command

$$-G \quad 2D \quad (\llcorner)$$

and the sorted table of data is displayed by

$$-D \quad A00:400 \quad 420 \quad (\llcorner)$$

From the displayed information, we see that the information has been correctly sorted. It is important to remember when reading this table that words of data are stored in memory with their least significant byte at the lower address. Therefore, the first three words in the table are read as $9A00_{16}$, $DA01_{16}$, and $FFFF_{16}$. They are negative numbers that are arranged in ascending order.

8.6 GENERATING ELEMENTS FOR A MATHEMATICAL SERIES

One type of operation that can be effectively performed in software is the generation of the numbers for a *mathematical series*. To do this, we must know the relationship among the numbers of the series. This relationship is implemented with a program and when executed, it will generate the numbers of the series.

Many well-known series are in wide use in science and mathematics. One example is the *Fibonacci series*. Here we will write a program for this series and then run it on the PC.

Example 8.9

Write a program to generate the first ten elements of a Fibonacci series. In this series, the first and second elements are zero and one, respectively. Each element that follows is obtained by adding the previous two elements. Use a subroutine to generate the next element from the previous two elements. Store the elements of the series starting at address FIBSER.

Solution:

Our plan for the solution of this problem is shown in Fig. 8.8(a). This flowchart shows the use of a subroutine to generate an element of the series, store it in memory, and prepare for generation of the next element.

The first step in the solution is initialization. It involves setting up a data segment, generating the first two numbers of the series, and storing them at memory locations with offset addresses FIBSER and FIBSER+1. Then a pointer must be established to address the locations for other terms of the series. This address will be held in the DI register. Finally, a counter with initial value equal to eight can be set up in CX to keep track of how many numbers remain to be generated. The instructions needed for initialization are

```
MOV   AX,DATASEGSTART
MOV   DS,AX
MOV   NUM1,0H
MOV   NUM2,1H
MOV   FIBSER,0H
MOV   FIBSER+1,1H
LEA   DI,FIBSER+2
MOV   CX,8H
```

Notice that the data-segment address defined by variable DATASEGSTART is first moved into AX, and then DS is loaded from AX with another MOV operation. Next the memory locations assigned to NUM_1 and NUM_2 are loaded with immediate data 0000_{16} and 0001_{16}, respectively. These same values are then copied into the storage locations for the first two series elements, FIBSER and FIBSER+1. Now DI is loaded with the address of FIBSER+2, which is a pointer to the storage location of the third element of the series. Finally, CX is loaded with 8_{16}.

To generate the next term in the series we call a subroutine. This subroutine generates and stores the elements. Before returning to the main program, it also updates memory locations NUM_1 and NUM_2 with the values of the immediate past two elements. After this, the counter in CX is decremented to record that a series element has been generated and stored. This process must be repeated until the counter becomes equal to zero. This leads to the following assembly language code:

```
NXTNM:   CALL  SBRTF
         DEC   CX
         JNZ   NXTNM
DONE:    NOP
```

The call is to the subroutine labeled SBRTF. After the subroutine runs to completion, program control returns to the DEC CX statement. This statement causes the count in CX to be decremented by one. Next, a conditional jump instruction tests the zero flag to determine if the result after decrementing CX is zero. If CX is

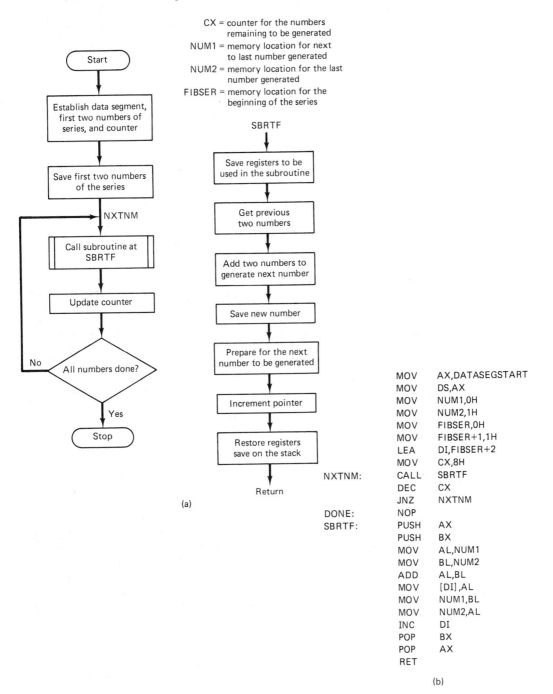

CX = counter for the numbers
remaining to be generated
NUM1 = memory location for next
to last number generated
NUM2 = memory location for the last
number generated
FIBSER = memory location for the
beginning of the series

	MOV	AX,DATASEGSTART
	MOV	DS,AX
	MOV	NUM1,0H
	MOV	NUM2,1H
	MOV	FIBSER,0H
	MOV	FIBSER+1,1H
	LEA	DI,FIBSER+2
	MOV	CX,8H
NXTNM:	CALL	SBRTF
	DEC	CX
	JNZ	NXTNM
DONE:	NOP	
SBRTF:	PUSH	AX
	PUSH	BX
	MOV	AL,NUM1
	MOV	BL,NUM2
	ADD	AL,BL
	MOV	[DI],AL
	MOV	NUM1,BL
	MOV	NUM2,AL
	INC	DI
	POP	BX
	POP	AX
	RET	

(a)

(b)

Figure 8.8 (a) Flowchart for generation of a Fibonacci series; (b) program.

not zero, control is returned to the CALL instruction at NXTNM. If it is zero, the program is complete and execution halts.

The subroutine itself is given next.

```
SBRTF:  PUSH  AX
        PUSH  BX
        MOV   AL,NUM1
        MOV   BL,NUM2
        ADD   AL,BL
        MOV   [DI],AL
        MOV   NUM1,BL
        MOV   NUM2,AL
        INC   DI
        POP   BX
        POP   AX
        RET
```

First we save the contents of AX and BX on the stack. Then NUM_1 and NUM_2 are copied into AL and BL, respectively. They are then added together to form the next element. The resulting sum is produced in AL. Now the new element is stored in memory indirectly through DI. Remember that DI holds a pointer to the storage location of the next element of the series in memory. Then the second element, which is held in BL, becomes the new first element by copying it into NUM_1. The sum, which is in AL, becomes the new second term by copying it into NUM_2. Finally, DI is incremented by one such that it points to the next element of the series. The registers saved on the stack are restored and then we return back to the main program.

Notice that both the subroutine call and its return have Near-proc operands. The entire program is presented in Fig. 8.8(b).

Example 8.10

Figure 8.9(a) shows a source program that implements the Fibonacci series generation routine written in Example 8.9 as a procedure. This program was assembled and linked to produce a run module called EX810.EXE. The source listing produced by the assembler is given in Fig. 8.9(b). Verify the operation of the program by generating the first ten numbers of the series by executing it on the IBM PC.

Solution:

In Fig. 8.9(c) we see that the program is loaded with the DOS command

```
A>DEBUG  B:EX810.EXE  (↵)
```

and then verified with the UNASSEMBLE command.

Now the complete program is executed with the command

```
—G  2C    (↵)
```

```
A>TYPE B:EX810.ASM

TITLE    EXAMPLE 8.10

         PAGE     ,132

STACK_SEG        SEGMENT        STACK 'STACK'
                 DB             64 DUP(?)
STACK_SEG        ENDS


DATASEGMENT      =       0A00H


DATA_SEG         SEGMENT        'DATA'
NUM1             DB             ?
NUM2             DB             ?
FIBSER           DB             10 DUP(?)
DATA_SEG         ENDS


CODE_SEG         SEGMENT        'CODE'
EX810   PROC     FAR
        ASSUME   CS:CODE_SEG, SS:STACK_SEG, DS:DATA_SEG

;To return to DEBUG program put return address on the stack

        PUSH     DS
        MOV      AX, 0
        PUSH     AX

;Following code implements Example 8.10

        MOV      AX, DATASEGMENT       ;Establish data segment
        MOV      DS, AX
        MOV      NUM1, 0               ;Initialize first number
        MOV      NUM2, 1               ;Initialize second number
        MOV      FIBSER, 0             ;First number in series
        MOV      FIBSER+1, 1           ;Second number in series
        LEA      DI, FIBSER+2          ;Pointer to next element
        MOV      CX, 8                 ;Initialize count
NXTNM:  CALL     SBRTF                 ;Generate next element
        DEC      CX
        JNZ      NXTNM                 ;If not done
DONE:   NOP
        RET

SBRTF   PROC     NEAR
        PUSH     AX                    ;Save registers used
        PUSH     BX
        MOV      AL, NUM1              ;Generate next element
        MOV      BL, NUM2
        ADD      AL, BL
        MOV      [DI], AL
        MOV      [DI], AL              ;Save next element
        MOV      NUM1, BL              ;Prepare for next call
        MOV      NUM2, AL
        INC      DI
        POP      BX                    ;Restore registers
        POP      AX
        RET
SBRTF   ENDP

EX810   ENDP
CODE_SEG         ENDS

        END      EX810

A>
```

(a)

Figure 8.9 (a) Source program for Example 8.10; (b) source listing produced by the assembler; (c) DEBUG sequence.

```
A>TYPE B:EX810.LST



The IBM Personal Computer Assembler 04-15-84              PAGE     1-1
EXAMPLE 8.10



                              TITLE    EXAMPLE 8.10

                                   PAGE     ,132
0000                          STACK_SEG       SEGMENT       STACK 'STACK'
0000      40 [                                DB            64 DUP(?)
              ??
                  ]

0040                          STACK_SEG       ENDS


= 0A00                        DATASEGMENT     =        0A00H


0000                          DATA_SEG        SEGMENT       'DATA'
0000   ??                     NUM1            DB            ?
0001   ??                     NUM2            DB            ?
0002      0A [                FIBSER          DB            10 DUP(?)
              ??
                  ]

000C                          DATA_SEG        ENDS


0000                          CODE_SEG        SEGMENT       'CODE'
0000                          EX810   PROC    FAR
                                      ASSUME  CS:CODE_SEG, SS:STACK_SEG, DS:DATA_SEG

                              ;To return to DEBUG program put return address on the stack

0000   1E                             PUSH    DS
0001   B8 0000                        MOV     AX, 0
0004   50                             PUSH    AX

                              ;Following code implements Example 8.10

0005   B8 0A00                        MOV     AX, DATASEGMENT       ;Establish data segment
0008   8E D8                          MOV     DS, AX
000A   C6 06 0000 R 00                MOV     NUM1, 0               ;Initialize first number
000F   C6 06 0001 R 01                MOV     NUM2, 1               ;Initialize second number
0014   C6 06 0002 R 00                MOV     FIBSER, 0             ;First number in series
0019   C6 06 0003 R 01                MOV     FIBSER+1, 1           ;Second number in series
001E   8D 3E 0004 R                   LEA     DI, FIBSER+2          ;Pointer to next element
0022   B9 0008                        MOV     CX, 8                 ;Initialize count
0025   E8 002D R          NXTNM:      CALL    SBRTF                 ;Generate next element
0028   49                             DEC     CX
0029   75 FA                          JNZ     NXTNM                 ;If not done
002B   90                DONE:        NOP
002C   CB                             RET
```

(b)

Figure 8.9 (continued)

```
The IBM Personal Computer Assembler 04-15-84           PAGE   1-2
EXAMPLE 8.10


002D                         SBRTF   PROC    NEAR
002D   50                            PUSH    AX                  ;Save registers used
002E   53                            PUSH    BX
002F   A0 0000 R                     MOV     AL, NUM1            ;Generate next element
0032   8A 1E 0001 R                  MOV     BL, NUM2
0036   02 C3                         ADD     AL, BL
0038   88 05                         MOV     [DI], AL
003A   88 05                         MOV     [DI], AL            ;Save next element
003C   88 1E 0000 R                  MOV     NUM1, BL            ;Prepare for next call
0040   A2 0001 R                     MOV     NUM2, AL
0043   47                            INC     DI
0044   5B                            POP     BX                  ;Restore registers
0045   58                            POP     AX
0046   C3                            RET
0047                         SBRTF   ENDP

0047                         EX810   ENDP
0047                         CODE_SEG        ENDS

                                     END     EX810
```

```
The IBM Personal Computer Assembler 04-15-84           PAGE   Symbols-1
EXAMPLE 8.10


Segments and groups:

                 N a m e              Size   align   combine class

CODE_SEG . . . . . . . . . . . .      0047   PARA    NONE    'CODE'
DATA_SEG . . . . . . . . . . . .      000C   PARA    NONE    'DATA'
STACK_SEG. . . . . . . . . . . .      0040   PARA    STACK   'STACK'

Symbols:

                 N a m e              Type   Value   Attr

DATASEGMENT. . . . . . . . . . .      Number 0A00
DONE . . . . . . . . . . . . . .      L NEAR 002B    CODE_SEG
EX810. . . . . . . . . . . . . .      F PROC 0000    CODE_SEG    Length =0047
FIBSER . . . . . . . . . . . . .      L BYTE 0002    DATA_SEG    Length =000A
NUM1 . . . . . . . . . . . . . .      L BYTE 0000    DATA_SEG
NUM2 . . . . . . . . . . . . . .      L BYTE 0001    DATA_SEG
NXTNM. . . . . . . . . . . . . .      L NEAR 0025    CODE_SEG
SBRTF. . . . . . . . . . . . . .      N PROC 002D    CODE_SEG    Length =001A

Warning Severe
Errors  Errors
0        0

A>
```

(b) (continued)

Figure 8.9 (continued)

```
A>DEBUG B:EX810.EXE
-U
0915:0000 1E              PUSH    DS
0915:0001 B80000          MOV     AX,0000
0915:0004 50              PUSH    AX
0915:0005 B8000A          MOV     AX,0A00
0915:0008 8ED8            MOV     DS,AX
0915:000A C606000000      MOV     BYTE PTR [0000],00
0915:000F C606010001      MOV     BYTE PTR [0001],01
0915:0014 C606020000      MOV     BYTE PTR [0002],00
0915:0019 C606030001      MOV     BYTE PTR [0003],01
0915:001E 8D3E0400        LEA     DI,[0004]
-U
0915:0022 B90800          MOV     CX,0008
0915:0025 E80500          CALL    002D
0915:0028 49              DEC     CX
0915:0029 75FA            JNZ     0025
0915:002B 90              NOP
0915:002C CB              RETF
0915:002D 50              PUSH    AX
0915:002E 53              PUSH    BX
0915:002F A00000          MOV     AL,[0000]
0915:0032 8A1E0100        MOV     BL,[0001]
0915:0036 02C3            ADD     AL,BL
0915:0038 8805            MOV     [DI],AL
0915:003A 8805            MOV     [DI],AL
0915:003C 881E0000        MOV     [0000],BL
0915:0040 A20100          MOV     [0001],AL
-G 2C

AX=0A00  BX=0000  CX=0000  DX=0000  SP=003C  BP=0000  SI=0000  DI=000C
DS=0A00  ES=0905  SS=091B  CS=0915  IP=002C   NV UP DI PL ZR NA PE NC
0915:002C CB              RETF
-D A00:0 C
0A00:0000  15 22 00 01 01 02 03 05-08 0D 15 22 00          ."..........".
-G

Program terminated normally
-Q
```

(c)

Figure 8.9 (continued)

and the execution of the program is verified by dumping memory with the command

$$-D \ \ A00:0 \ \ C \quad (\hookleftarrow)$$

Looking at the displayed memory data in Fig. 8.9(c), we find that the first two
numbers are the final values of variable NUM_1 and NUM_2, respectively. They are
followed by the first ten elements of the Fibonnaci series in data memory locations
0A00:0002 through 0A00:000B.

8.7 CODE CONVERSIONS IN SOFTWARE

Information and data are represented in coded form in computer systems. For
example, in small computers such as the IBM PC, the ASCII code is normally
used. On the other hand, in IBM mainframe computers, information is coded
with EBCDIC instead of ASCII. If we want to communicate between these two

computers, a *code conversion* must take place to convert the transferred information to a compatible code before it can be processed. In older electronic systems, code conversions were performed in hardware; however, today most code conversions are done in software.

One way of implementing a code conversion in software is to define the relationship between the two codes mathematically and then describe this relationship with a program. This technique generally turns out to be very complex. For this reason, it is more common to use a *lookup table technique* to convert between codes. When using the lookup table technique, a table that contains all of the characters of the code that we are to convert to is set up in memory. The different characters of this new code are offset from the beginning of the table by their equivalent values in the original code. For instance, for an EBCDIC-to-ASCII conversion table, the value 37_{16} (number 7 ASCII) is stored at address offset $F7_{16}$ (number 7 EBCDIC). When number 7 is read from a communication buffer for conversion, its EBCDIC value ($F7_{16}$) is combined with an address pointer that points to the beginning of the EBCDIC-to-ASCII conversion table. The address that results points to the location in the table where the ASCII value for number 7 is stored. This value, which is 37_{16}, is read from the table to complete the code-conversion operation.

The 8088 microprocessor's instruction set includes a special instruction, XLAT, that is specifically provided to simplify implementation of lookup tables. In the two examples that follow we will use the XLAT instruction to write a practical program that can be used to convert data coded in EBCDIC to ASCII; then this program is run on the PC.

Example 8.11

Given a string of 100 EBCDIC characters stored starting at offset address EBCDIC_CHAR. Convert them to their equivalent string of ASCII characters and store them at offset address ASCII_CHAR. The translation may be done using a EBCDIC-to-ASCII conversion table that starts at offset memory address EBCDIC_TO_ASCII.

Solution:

The problem to be programmed is illustrated in Fig. 8.10(a). Here we have assumed that the various data elements—the 100 given EBCDIC characters, the conversion table for EBCDIC to ASCII, and the generated ASCII characters—all reside in the same data segment. This data segment starts at the address DATA_SEGMENT. With respect to this data segment, the offset addresses EBCDIC_CHAR, ASCII_CHAR, and EBCDIC_TO_ASCII are as shown in the diagram. Moreover, we are assuming that the string of 100 EBCDIC characters and the EBCDIC-to-ASCII table already exist at the correct locations in memory.

Our solution to the problem is flowcharted in Fig. 8.10(b). We will use the string, translate, and loop instructions to implement the solution. Moreover, we will also use autoincrement mode for the string operations.

The initialization involves setting up the data segment (DS) register to address the area in memory that stores the 100 given EBCDIC characters and the

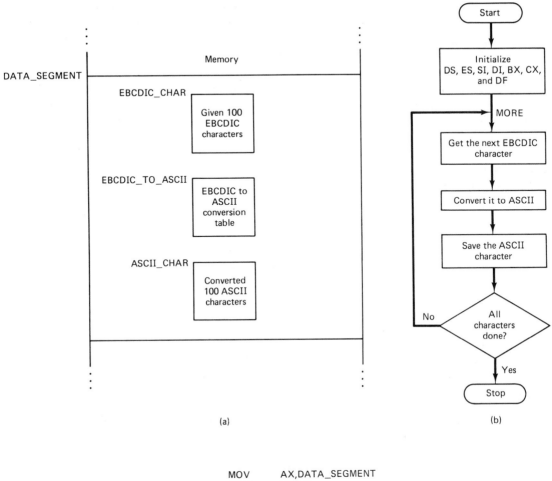

(a)

(b)

```
        MOV      AX,DATA_SEGMENT
        MOV      DS,AX
        MOV      ES,AX
        MOV      SI,OFFSET EBCDIC_CHAR
        MOV      DI,OFFSET ASCII_CHAR
        MOV      BX,OFFSET EBCDIC_TO_ASCII
        MOV      CX,64H
        CLD
MORE:   LODSB
        XLAT     EBCDIC_TO_ASCII
        STOSB
        LOOP     MORE
        HLT
```

(c)

Figure 8.10 (a) EBCDIC to ASCII conversion; (b) flowchart; (c) program.

conversion table. The same memory area will be used to store the converted ASCII characters; therefore, we will make the extra segment, which is needed by the string instructions, overlap the data segment by loading both DS and ES with the same address. This is the value assigned to variable DATA_SEGMENT. Then SI and DI must be loaded with addresses that point to the first characters in the EBCDIC string and the ASCII string, respectively. These addresses are equal to EBCDIC_CHAR and ASCII_CHAR, respectively. The code translation is made using a conversion table and the XLAT instruction. XLAT requires that BX hold a pointer to the beginning of the conversion table. Therefore, BX must be loaded with the address corresponding to EBCDIC_TO_ASCII. To keep track of the number of characters that are converted, CX will be loaded with 100_{10} equal to 64_{16}. Finally, the autoincrement feature is invoked by resetting the direction flag DF. This leads to the following initialization code:

```
MOV   AX,DATA_SEGMENT
MOV   DS,AX
MOV   ES,AX
MOV   SI,OFFSET  EBCDIC_CHAR
MOV   DI,OFFSET  ASCII_CHAR
MOV   BX,OFFSET  EBCDIC_TO_ASCII
MOV   CX,064H
CLD
```

Next, an EBCDIC character can be loaded, translated to its corresponding ASCII character, and stored in the memory area reserved for storage of ASCII characters. This gives us the instructions

```
MORE:  LODSB
       XLAT
       STOSB
```

Execution of the LODS instruction loads the first element of the EBCDIC string into AL. Notice that use of autoincrementing prepares SI to handle the next conversion. Next, the XLAT instruction uses the EBCDIC character code in AL as an offset to address the equivalent ASCII character in the table at EBCDIC_TO_ASCII. This ASCII character is transferred to AL. The translation is now complete; however, the resulting character must be stored in the table defined by the address ASCII_CHAR. This is done with the STOS instruction. During the execution of this instruction, DI is automatically incremented so that it points to the next storage location in the ASCII string.

To repeat the process starting from label MORE, we can use a loop instruction that will decrement CX and jump to MORE as long as the contents of CX are not zero. This assures that translation is repeated for each of the 100 characters in the EBCDIC string. To do this, the instruction is

```
LOOP  MORE
```

To end the program, the halt (HLT) instruction can be executed. The entire program is repeated in Fig. 8.10(c).

Example 8.12

The EBCDIC-to-ASCII code-converter program developed in Example 8.11 is implemented with a procedure in the source program of Fig. 8.11(a). This program was assembled and linked to produce a run module in file EX812.EXE. Figure 8.11(b) is the source listing produced by the assembler during the assembly process. Run the program on the IBM PC.

```
A>TYPE B:EX812.ASM


TITLE    EXAMPLE 8.12

         PAGE     ,132

STACK_SEG        SEGMENT          STACK 'STACK'
                 DB               64 DUP(?)
STACK_SEG        ENDS


DATA_SEG         SEGMENT           'DATA'
EBCDIC_CHAR      DB               0F7H,0C4H, 98 DUP(?)
ASCII_CHAR       DB               100 DUP(?)
EBCDIC_TO_ASCII  DB               193    DUP(?)
                 DB               'ABCDEF'
                 DB               41 DUP(?)
                 DB               '0123456789'
DATA_SEG         ENDS


CODE_SEG         SEGMENT           'CODE'
EX812   PROC     FAR
         ASSUME  CS:CODE_SEG, SS:STACK_SEG, DS:DATA_SEG, ES:DATA_SEG

;To return to DEBUG program put return address on the stack

         PUSH     DS
         MOV      AX, 0
         PUSH     AX

;Following code implements Example 8.12

         MOV      AX, DATA_SEG
         MOV      DS, AX
         MOV      ES, AX
         MOV      SI, OFFSET EBCDIC_CHAR
         MOV      DI, OFFSET ASCII_CHAR
         MOV      BX, OFFSET EBCDIC_TO_ASCII
         MOV      CX, 64H
         CLD
MORE:    LODSB
         XLAT     EBCDIC_TO_ASCII
         STOSB
         LOOP     MORE


         RET                             ;Return to DEBUG program
EX812   ENDP

CODE_SEG         ENDS

         END      EX812

A>
```

(a)

Figure 8.11 (a) Source program for Example 8.12; (b) source listing produced by the assembler; (c) DEBUG sequence.

A>TYPE B:EX812.LST

```
 The IBM Personal Computer Assembler 04-15-84              PAGE    1-1
EXAMPLE 8.12


                        TITLE   EXAMPLE 8.12

                             PAGE    ,132

0000                    STACK_SEG       SEGMENT       STACK 'STACK'
0000      40 [                          DB            64 DUP(?)
             ??
                ]

0040                    STACK_SEG       ENDS


0000                    DATA_SEG        SEGMENT        'DATA'
0000   F7 62 [          EBCDIC_CHAR     DB      0F7H,0C4H, 98 DUP(?)
             ??
                ]

0064      64 [          ASCII_CHAR      DB      100 DUP(?)
             ??
                ]

00C8      C1 [          EBCDIC_TO_ASCII DB      193    DUP(?)
             ??
                ]

0189   41 42 43 44 45 46                DB      'ABCDEF'
018F      29 [                          DB      41 DUP(?)
             ??
                ]

01B8   30 31 32 33 34 35                DB      '0123456789'
       36 37 38 39
01C2                    DATA_SEG        ENDS


0000                    CODE_SEG        SEGMENT        'CODE'
0000                    EX812   PROC    FAR
                             ASSUME  CS:CODE_SEG, SS:STACK_SEG, DS:DATA_SEG, ES:DATA_SEG

                        ;To return to DEBUG program put return address on the stack

0000   1E                               PUSH    DS
0001   B8 0000                          MOV     AX, 0
0004   50                               PUSH    AX

                        ;Following code implements Example 8.12

0005   B8   ---- R                      MOV     AX, DATA_SEG
0008   8E D8                            MOV     DS, AX
000A   8E C0                            MOV     ES, AX
000C   BE 0000 R                        MOV     SI, OFFSET EBCDIC_CHAR
```

(b)

Figure 8.11 (continued)

```
The IBM Personal Computer Assembler 04-15-84                PAGE    1-2
EXAMPLE 8.12


    000F  BF 0064 R                       MOV     DI, OFFSET ASCII_CHAR
    0012  BB 00C8 R                       MOV     BX, OFFSET EBCDIC_TO_ASCII
    0015  B9 0064                         MOV     CX, 64H
    0018  FC                              CLD
    0019  AC                MORE:         LODSB
    001A  D7                              XLAT    EBCDIC_TO_ASCII
    001B  AA                              STOSB
    001C  E2 FB                           LOOP    MORE


    001E  CB                              RET                        ;Return to DEBUG program
    001F                    EX812         ENDP

    001F                  CODE_SEG        ENDS

                                          END     EX812




    The IBM Personal Computer Assembler 04-15-84                PAGE    Symbols-1
EXAMPLE 8.12


Segments and groups:

                N a m e                   Size    align   combine class

CODE_SEG . . . . . . . . . . .            001F    PARA    NONE    'CODE'
DATA_SEG . . . . . . . . . . .            01C2    PARA    NONE    'DATA'
STACK_SEG. . . . . . . . . . .            0040    PARA    STACK   'STACK'

Symbols:

                N a m e                   Type    Value   Attr

ASCII_CHAR . . . . . . . . . .            L BYTE  0064    DATA_SEG     Length =0064
EBCDIC_CHAR. . . . . . . . . .            L BYTE  0000    DATA_SEG
EBCDIC_TO_ASCII. . . . . . . .            L BYTE  00C8    DATA_SEG     Length =00C1
EX812. . . . . . . . . . . . .            F PROC  0000    CODE_SEG     Length =001F
MORE . . . . . . . . . . . . .            L NEAR  0019    CODE_SEG

Warning Severe
Errors  Errors
0       0

A>
```

(b) (continued)

Figure 8.11 (continued)

Solution:

Let us begin by looking at how the data tables are created by the source program. Notice in Fig. 8.11(a) that the tables EBCDIC_CHAR, ASCII_CHAR, and EBCDIC_TO_ASCII are created with define byte (DB) pseudo-op statements. Only two of the byte locations in the EBCDIC_CHAR table are filled with data. They are $F7_{16}$ for the number 7 and $C4_{16}$ for the letter D. Next, the ASCII_CHAR table is defined and its locations are left empty. The last table, EBCDIC-TO-ASCII, is defined with several DB statements. The first 193 locations are allocated but left uninitialized. The next six locations are filled with the ASCII letters A through F.

```
A>DEBUG B:EX812.EXE
-U 0 1E
0915:0000 1E          PUSH    DS
0915:0001 B80000      MOV     AX,0000
0915:0004 50          PUSH    AX
0915:0005 B81709      MOV     AX,0917
0915:0008 8EDB        MOV     DS,AX
0915:000A 8EC0        MOV     ES,AX
0915:000C BE0000      MOV     SI,0000
0915:000F BF6400      MOV     DI,0064
0915:0012 BBC800      MOV     BX,00C8
0915:0015 B96400      MOV     CX,0064
0915:0018 FC          CLD
0915:0019 AC          LODSB
0915:001A D7          XLAT
0915:001B AA          STOSB
0915:001C E2FB        LOOP    0019
0915:001E CB          RETF
-G 1E

AX=0900  BX=00C8  CX=0000  DX=0000  SP=003C  BP=0000  SI=0064  DI=00C8
DS=0917  ES=0917  SS=0934  CS=0915  IP=001E   NV UP DI PL NZ NA PO NC
0915:001E CB          RETF
-D 0 F
0917:0000  F7 C4 00 00 00 00 00 00-00 00 00 00 00 00 00 00    wD............
-D 64 73
0917:0064  37 44 00 00-00 00 00 00 00 00 00 00                7D..........
0917:0070  00 00 00 00                                        ....
-G

Program terminated normally
-Q
```

(c)

Figure 8.11 (continued)

They are followed by 41 more allocated but uninitialized table locations. Finally, the last ten table locations are loaded with values zero through nine.

Now that we know how the data tables are initialized we will look into how the program is loaded. In Fig. 8.11(c), we see that the DOS command

A>DEBUG B:EX812.EXE (↵)

is used to call up the debugger and load the program from file EX812.EXE. Then the loading of the program is verified with an UNASSEMBLE command. By comparing the displayed version of the program in Fig. 8.11(c) to the source listing in Fig. 8.11(b), we find that it has loaded correctly.

Next the program is executed with the GO command

—G 1E   (↵)

To verify that the program has run correctly, we must display the contents of the EBCDIC_CHAR and ASCII_CHAR tables. The EBCDIC for the first 16 characters of the EBCDIC_CHAR table are displayed by the command

—D 0 F   (↵)

In Fig. 8.11(c), we see that the first two locations, as expected, are $F7_{16}$ and $C4_{16}$, respectively. The corresponding elements in the ASCII_CHAR table are displayed with the command

$$-D \ 64 \ 73 \ (\lrcorner)$$

Notice that these values are 37_{16} and 44_{16}. As shown in the ASCII field of the memory dump, these codes represent the number 7 and letter D, respectively. This verifies that the code conversion has been performed correctly.

8.8 SPEAKER CONTROL

The IBM PC has a *speaker* which can be controlled through software to generate tones at various frequencies. It is this speaker that you hear generate a beep whenever DOS is loaded. In this section we will learn how the speaker is controlled through software, and we will write a program that causes it to produce a tone with a specific frequency.

The 8088 microcomputer in the PC controls the speaker through three *I/O ports*, an *8253 timer*, and an *AND gate*. This section of circuitry is shown in Fig. 8.12. Notice that the AND gate has two inputs. They are the pulse output of the 8253 timer and the BIT 1 output of the byte-wide I/O port at I/O address 61_{16}. Looking at this circuit diagram, we see that one way of generating a tone at the speaker is to force the output of the timer to the 1 logic level and then toggling the BIT 1 output of the I/O port at address 61_{16} between the 0 and 1 logic levels. The output of the timer is forced to 1 by setting its BIT 0 input, which is another output on the I/O port at I/O address 61_{16}, to the 0 logic level. The frequency of the tone produced at the speaker is determined by the rate at which the BIT 1 output is switched between the 0 and 1 logic levels.

A second way of controlling the speaker is by setting BIT 1 to the 1 logic level and then using the 8253 timer to generate a *square wave* at its output. This is the type of operation shown in Fig. 8.12. Notice that the timer device accepts a 1.19 MHz clock input. This clock signal is divided within the 8253 by a 16-bit number that is loaded into the timer as two bytes from the 2 DIVISOR BYTEs port at I/O address 42_{16}. A square wave with the frequency

$$f = 1.19 \ \text{MHz}/NNNN$$

is produced at the output. Here NNNN stands for the 16-bit divisor. With BIT 1 set to the 1 logic level, the square-wave output of the timer is supplied to the speaker, where it produces a tone with frequency f.

For the timer to accept the divisor, it must first be put in the proper mode by writing a *mode control byte* to the port at I/O address 43_{16}. For instance, loading MODE CONTROL BYTE $B6_{16}$ sets up the timer to receive the two bytes of the divisor, low byte first, from the port at address 42_{16}.

The three output ports that are used to control the 8253 timer can be loaded by using the *OUT instruction* of the 8088 microprocessor. Moreover, the state of the signals at output port address 61_{16} can also be read with the *IN in-*

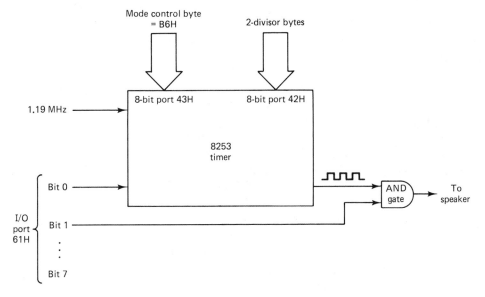

Figure 8.12 Speaker control circuit.

struction. This is important because when outputting to BIT 0 and BIT 1 of this port we must also output to the other six bits at the port. Therefore, we must always first read the contents of the port, modify bits 0 and 1, and then write the modified byte back to the port. In this way the other six bits are not affected.

Example 8.13

Write a program to produce a 1.5 kHz tone for 100 ms with the speaker. Use the 8253 timer to generate the tone signal.

Solution:

A flowchart for a program that will produce this tone at the speaker is shown in Fig. 8.13. Let us first calculate the count that needs to be loaded into the 8253 timer to set the tone frequency to 1.5 kHz. This is done with the expression

$$NNNN = 1.19 \text{ MHz}/f = 1.19 \text{ MHz}/1.5 \text{ kHz}$$
$$= 793$$

Expressing in hexadecimal form, we get

$$NNNN = 319_{16}$$

Thus, to generate the 1.5-kHz tone, we must first load the timer with the divisor 319_{16}. To do this, the mode of 8253 must be first set to accept the divisor. The instructions needed to set the mode are

```
MOV  AL,0B6H
OUT  43H,AL   ; SET MODE TO ACCEPT DIVISOR
```

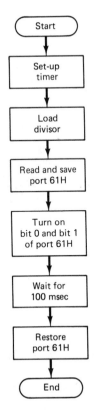

Figure 8.13 Flowchart for tone generation program.

Now the divisor is loaded into the timer with the instructions

```
MOV   AX,319H
OUT   42,AL      ; LOAD  LSBYTE  OF  DIVISOR
MOV   AL,AH
OUT   42H,AL     ; LOAD  MSBYTE  OF  DIVISOR
```

Next we enable both the timer and the AND gate by first reading the state of the output port at address 61_{16}, setting bits 0 and 1 to logic 1, and then writing the byte back to the output port. This is done with the sequence of instructions.

```
IN    AL,61H
MOV   AH,AL
OR    AL,3
OUT   61H,AL
```

Notice that the current value of port 61_{16} has been saved in the AH register.

Now the speaker is turned on and the 1.5-kHz tone is being generated. However, the tone is to be produced for just 100 ms. Therefore, a software delay can be inserted at this point in the program; when the delay is complete, the speaker is to be turned back off. The software delay is produced by the instruction sequence

```
        MOV   CX,5064H  ;  4  CLOCK  CYCLES
DELAY:  NOP             ;  3  CLOCK  CYCLES
        NOP             ;  3  CLOCK  CYCLES
        LOOP  DELAY     ; 17  CLOCK  CYCLES
```

The count loaded into CX by the MOV instruction determines the duration of the time delay. The value 5064_{16} is found from the time it takes to execute the instructions in the loop. The total number of clock cycles in the loop are given by the expression

$$\#CYC = 4 + (X - 1)(3 + 3 + 17) + 12$$

Here the 4 represents the execution of the MOV instruction once; the 12 represents the execution of the instructions that must be executed just after the loop to turn the tone back off; and the expression $(X - 1)(3 + 3 + 17)$ represents the repeated execution of the 3 instruction loop $X - 1$ times. Here X stands for the count loaded into CX. In the IBM PC, each clock cycle has a duration of 210 ns. Thus a 100-ms delay is defined by the expression

$$DELAY = \#CYC \ (CLOCK \ CYCLE \ DURATION)$$

$$100 \ ms \ = (4 + [X - 1][3 + 3 + 17] + 12) \ 210 \ ns$$

Solving this expression for X, we get

$$X \cong 20,708$$

and converting to hexadecimal form gives

$$X = 5064_{16}$$

After the delay is complete, we must turn the speaker back off. This is done by writing the byte saved in AH back to the output port at address 61_{16}. We do this with the instructions

```
        MOV   AL,AH
        OUT   61H,AL
```

Example 8.14

Figure 8.14(a) gives a source program that implements the tone-generation routine written in Example 8.13 as a procedure. This program was assembled and linked to produce a run module in file EX814.EXE. The source listing produced by the assembler is given in Fig. 8.14(b). Run the program on the IBM PC.

Solution:

As shown in the debug sequence in Fig. 8.14(c), the run module for the program is loaded with the command

$$A > DEBUG \quad B{:}EX814.EXE \quad (\dashv)$$

and verified with U commands.
Next it is executed with the command

$$-G \quad (\dashv)$$

As it runs, a short duration 1.5-kHz tone is generated at the speaker.

```
A>TYPE B:EX814.ASM

TITLE    EXAMPLE 8.14

         PAGE      ,132

STACK_SEG        SEGMENT          STACK 'STACK'
                 DB               64 DUP(?)
STACK_SEG        ENDS


CODE_SEG         SEGMENT          'CODE'
EX814    PROC    FAR
         ASSUME  CS:CODE_SEG, SS:STACK_SEG

;To return to DEBUG program put return address on the stack

         PUSH    DS
         MOV     AX, 0
         PUSH    AX

;Following code implements Example 8.14

         MOV     AL, 0B6H                    ;Set up timer
         OUT     43H, AL
         MOV     AX, 319H                    ;Load divisor
         OUT     42H, AL
         MOV     AL, AH
         OUT     42H, AL
         IN      AL, 61H                     ;Read port 61H
         MOV     AH, AL                      ;Save its contents
         OR      AL, 3
         OUT     61H, AL                     ;Enable timer and AND gate
         MOV     CX, 5064H                   ;Delay counter
DELAY:   NOP                                 ;for 25msec delay
         NOP
         LOOP    DELAY
         MOV     AL, AH                      ;Restore port 61H
         OUT     61H, AL
         RET

EX814    ENDP
CODE_SEG         ENDS

         END     EX814

A>
```

(a)

Figure 8.14 (a) Source program for Example 8.14; (b) source listing produced by the assembler; (c) DEBUG sequence.

```
The IBM Personal Computer Assembler 04-15-84          PAGE    1-1
EXAMPLE 8.14


                        TITLE    EXAMPLE 8.14

                        PAGE     ,132

0000                    STACK_SEG      SEGMENT      STACK 'STACK'
0000    40 [                           DB           64 DUP(?)
             ??
          ]

0040                    STACK_SEG      ENDS


0000                    CODE_SEG       SEGMENT      'CODE'
0000                    EX814   PROC   FAR
                                ASSUME  CS:CODE_SEG, SS:STACK_SEG

                        ;To return to DEBUG program put return address on the stack

0000   1E                       PUSH    DS
0001   B8 0000                  MOV     AX, 0
0004   50                       PUSH    AX

                        ;Following code implements Example 8.14

0005   B0 B6                    MOV     AL, 0B6H          ;Set up timer
0007   E6 43                    OUT     43H, AL
0009   B8 0319                  MOV     AX, 319H          ;Load divisor
000C   E6 42                    OUT     42H, AL
000E   8A C4                    MOV     AL, AH
0010   E6 42                    OUT     42H, AL
0012   E4 61                    IN      AL, 61H           ;Read port 61H
0014   8A E0                    MOV     AH, AL            ;Save its contents
0016   0C 03                    OR      AL, 3
0018   E6 61                    OUT     61H, AL           ;Enable timer and AND gate
001A   B9 5064                  MOV     CX, 5064H         ;Delay counter
001D   90              DELAY:   NOP                       ;for 25msec delay
001E   90                       NOP
001F   E2 FC                    LOOP    DELAY
0021   8A C4                    MOV     AL, AH            ;Restore port 61H
0023   E6 61                    OUT     61H, AL
0025   CB                       RET

0026                    EX814   ENDP
0026                    CODE_SEG       ENDS

                        END     EX814



The IBM Personal Computer Assembler 04-15-84          PAGE    Symbols-1
EXAMPLE 8.14


Segments and groups:

              N a m e              Size    align   combine class

CODE_SEG . . . . . . . . . . . .   0026    PARA    NONE    'CODE'
STACK_SEG. . . . . . . . . . . .   0040    PARA    STACK   'STACK'

Symbols:

              N a m e              Type    Value   Attr

DELAY. . . . . . . . . . . . . .   L NEAR  001D    CODE_SEG
EX814. . . . . . . . . . . . . .   F PROC  0000    CODE_SEG        Length =0026

Warning Severe
Errors  Errors
0       0

A>
```

(b)

Figure 8.14 (continued)

```
A>DEBUG B:EX814.EXE
-U
0915:0000 1E          PUSH    DS
0915:0001 B80000      MOV     AX,0000
0915:0004 50          PUSH    AX
0915:0005 B0B6        MOV     AL,B6
0915:0007 E643        OUT     43,AL
0915:0009 B81903      MOV     AX,0319
0915:000C E642        OUT     42,AL
0915:000E 8AC4        MOV     AL,AH
0915:0010 E642        OUT     42,AL
0915:0012 E461        IN      AL,61
0915:0014 8AE0        MOV     AH,AL
0915:0016 0C03        OR      AL,03
0915:0018 E661        OUT     61,AL
0915:001A B96450      MOV     CX,5064
0915:001D 90          NOP
0915:001E 90          NOP
0915:001F E2FC        LOOP    001D
-U 21 25
0915:0021 8AC4        MOV     AL,AH
0915:0023 E661        OUT     61,AL
0915:0025 CB          RETF
-G

Program terminated normally
-Q
```

(c)

Figure 8.14 (continued)

8.9 SEARCHING A DATA STRUCTURE

It is common to store data in memory as a table in a block of consecutive memory locations; however, data can be organized in memory in any manner as long as we can define a way to access it. In earlier examples we examined programs that sorted data that was arranged in a table in memory and also copied blocks of data from one place in memory to another location. We have also found that the machine code for instructions is normally stored in one part of memory at consecutive addresses. In this way, the microprocessor can be given the starting address, and it accesses the next byte of instruction code by just incrementing this address. In all of these cases we are sequentially accessing the elements of a single block of data.

In applications that require a large amount of data, the data may have to be stored in a number of blocks of memory; these blocks can be randomly located in the microprocessor's physical address space. Figure 8.15 shows one such *data structure*. Here we see data that are organized into four blocks called LIST1, LIST2, LIST3, and LIST4. These blocks of data can be located anywhere in the microprocessor's address space. This data structure is known as a *linked list*.

When accessing data that is stored in a linked-list structure, we can still use sequential access methods within a list of data. But to shift from one list of data to the next we need some additional information—for instance, the starting address of the next list. This kind of information can be provided in a number of ways. One common way is to include it as part of the data in the list.

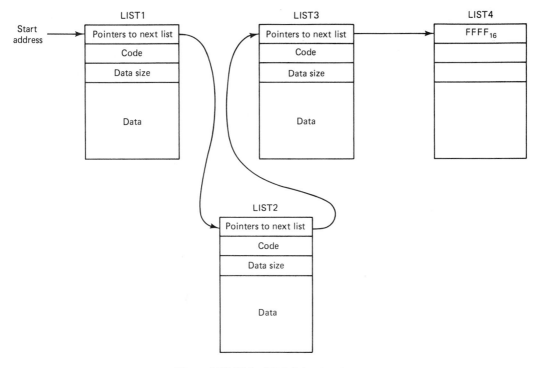

Figure 8.15 Linked list data structure.

For example, in Fig. 8.15 we see that a *pointer address for the next list in the linked list* is stored as the first element in each list. In this way, when we are done searching through the current data list, we can read this address and then use it to go on to the next list. This can be repeated until all data in the linked list has been examined. Notice that the end of data is marked by a special address $FFFF_{16}$ and that this last list does not contain any data. In this way, we see that to access all pieces of data in the linked list all we need to know is the *starting address of LIST1.*

In addition to the address of the next list, a linked list can also include information like a *code number* and *size.* This information can be used when looking for a specific list.

Now we will develop a program that can be used to access data that is stored in a linked list.

Example 8.15

Assume that a linked-list data structure similar to that shown in Fig. 8.15 is provided and that the starting address of the first list is given by the symbol LIST1. Also assume that the last list contains $FFFF_{16}$ in the "pointer to next address" location. Write a program to search this linked-list structure looking for a list with a given code number. If a list with the code number is found, display the contents of the list; otherwise, display a message indicating that the list was not found.

Solution:

Let us begin by establishing a data segment by loading the DS register with data-segment start address (DATA_SEG). Also we will use the DI register as the pointer to the current list; therefore, it must be initialized with the first list start address (LIST1). The instructions needed to do this initialization are:

```
MOV   AX,DATA_SEG
MOV   DS,AX
LEA   DI,LIST1
```

To begin the search, we first compare the contents of DI with the value $FFFF_{16}$ to determine if we are at the end of the linked list. If the answer is no, we compare the given code with the code number for the list. If they are equal, we have found the list we are looking for. If not, then we must advance to the next list by loading the pointer address to the next list into DI. These operations are done with the instructions

```
     CMP   DI,0FFFFH
     JE    NOTFOUND
     CMP   DI,[DI+2]
     JE    FOUND
     MOV   DI,[DI]
JMP  SEARCH
```

To display a message for the case when no list is found to match the code, we load SI with the message address and the CX register with the message size and call the procedure called DISPLAY. This procedure is described in section 8.10. For now it is sufficient to note that by providing the message address and size and calling DISPLAY, we display the message on the screen. The instructions for this are

```
NOTFOUND:
     LEA   SI,MSG_N
     MOV   CX,CNT_N
     CALL  DISPLAY
     JMP   DONE
```

Here MSG_N is the address of the message and CNT_N is its size. Similarly, if a list is found, we can display its contents by using the same procedure. Here the list-contents address needs to be computed. The message is available as part of the list. The instructions to do this are

```
FOUND:
     MOV   AX,5
     ADD   AX,DI
     MOV   SI,AX
     MOV   CX,[DI+3[
     CALL  DISPLAY
```

The complete program is shown in Fig. 8.16.

```
            MOV     AX,DATA_SEG
            MOV     DS,AX
            LEA     DI,LIST1
            CMP     DI,0FFFFH
            JE      NOTFOUND
            CMP     DI,[DI+2]
            JE      FOUND
            MOV     DI,[DI]
            JMP     SEARCH
NOTFOUND:
            LEA     SI,MSG_N
            MOV     CX,CNT_N
            CALL    DISPLAY
            JMP     DONE
FOUND:
            MOV     AX,5
            ADD     AX,DI
            MOV     SI,AX
            MOV     CX,[DI+3]
            CALL    DISPLAY
```

Figure 8.16 Source program for linked-list search.

Example 8.16

A source program for a procedure that includes the linked-list search routine developed in Example 8.15 is shown in Fig. 8.17(a). This program was assembled and linked to produce a run module in file EX816.EXE. The source listing produced as part of the assembly process is given in Fig. 8.17(b). Load this run module with DEBUG and then execute the program for list codes equal to 2, 5, 7, and 3. What gets displayed on the screen?

Solution:

Looking at Fig. 8.17(c), we see that the program is loaded with the DOS command

```
A>DEBUG  B:EX816.EXE  (↵)
```

Next, code number 2 is loaded into DL with the R command

```
—R  DX   (↵)
DX  0000
:2       (↵)
```

Finally, the program is executed with the GO command

```
—G   (↵)
```

Since a list with code number 2 does exist, execution of the program displays the contents of the list on the screen. This is the message "LIST WITH CODE = 2".

```
A>TYPE B:EX816.ASM


TITLE    EXAMPLE 8.16

         PAGE      ,132

STACK_SEG        SEGMENT          STACK 'STACK'
                 DB               64 DUP(?)
STACK_SEG        ENDS


DATA_SEG         SEGMENT          'DATA'
LIST4            DW        0FFFFH
LIST3            DW        OFFSET  LIST4
                 DB        7
                 DW        20
                 DB        ' LIST WITH CODE = 7 '
LIST2            DW        OFFSET  LIST3
                 DB        5
                 DW        20
                 DB        ' LIST WITH CODE = 5 '
LIST1            DW        OFFSET  LIST2
                 DB        2
                 DW        20
                 DB        'LIST WITH CODE = 2 '

MSG_N            DB        ' NO SUCH LIST '
CNT_N            DW        14

DATA_SEG         ENDS


CODE_SEG         SEGMENT          'CODE'
EX818            PROC             FAR
          ASSUME  CS:CODE_SEG, SS:STACK_SEG, DS:DATA_SEG

;To return to DEBUG program put return address on the stack

          PUSH      DS
          MOV       AX, O
          PUSH      AX

;Following code implements Example 8.16

          MOV       AX, DATA_SEG          ;Establish the data segment
          MOV       DS, AX
          LEA       DI, LIST1             ;List1 address
SEARCH:
          CMP       DI, 0FFFFH            ;Is this last empty list
          JE        NOTFOUND              ;If yes display message
          CMP       DL, [DI+2]            ;Match the code
          JE        FOUND                 ;If a match display the list
          MOV       DI, [DI]              ;Try the next list
          JMP       SEARCH

NOTFOUND:
          LEA       SI, MSG_N             ;Message pointer
          MOV       CX, CNT_N             ;Message character count
          CALL      DISPLAY               ;Call display routine
          JMP       DONE

FOUND:
          MOV       AX, 5                 ;Compute list pointer
          ADD       AX, DI
          MOV       SI, AX
          MOV       CX, [DI+3]            ;List character count
          CALL      DISPLAY               ;Call display routine
```

(a)

Figure 8.17 (a) Source program for Example 8.16; (b) source listing produced by the assembler; (c) DEBUG sequence.

```
DONE:    RET                                  ;Return to DEBUG program


DISPLAY        PROC         NEAR
NXT_CHAR:
         MOV     AL, [SI]              ;Get character
         MOV     AH, 14               ;Parameter for INT 10h
         STI                          ;Enable interrupt
         INT     10H                  ;Call service routine
         INC     SI                   ;Point to next character
         LOOP    NXT_CHAR             ;Repeat for next character
         RET
DISPLAY        ENDP

EX818   ENDP
CODE_SEG       ENDS

        END     EX818

A>
```

(a)

```
A>TYPE B:EX816.LST
```

```
The IBM Personal Computer Assembler 05-15-84          PAGE    1-1
EXAMPLE 8.16


                              TITLE    EXAMPLE 8.16

                                      PAGE    ,132

0000                          STACK_SEG      SEGMENT       STACK 'STACK'
0000      40 [               DB            64 DUP(?)
              ??
                  ]

0040                          STACK_SEG      ENDS


0000                          DATA_SEG       SEGMENT      'DATA'
0000  FFFF                    LIST4          DW           0FFFFH
0002  0000 R                  LIST3          DW           OFFSET  LIST4
0004  07                                     DB           7
0005  0014                                   DW           20
0007  20 4C 49 53 54 20                      DB           ' LIST WITH CODE = 7 '
      57 49 54 48 20 43
      4F 44 45 20 3D 20
      37 20
001B  0002 R                  LIST2          DW           OFFSET  LIST3
001D  05                                     DB           5
001E  0014                                   DW           20
0020  20 4C 49 53 54 20                      DB           ' LIST WITH CODE = 5 '
      57 49 54 48 20 43
      4F 44 45 20 3D 20
      35 20
0034  001B R                  LIST1          DW           OFFSET  LIST2
0036  02                                     DB           2
0037  0014                                   DW           20
```

(b)

Figure 8.17 (continued)

```
0039   4C 49 53 54 20 57                    DB         'LIST WITH CODE = 2 '
       49 54 48 20 43 4F
       44 45 20 3D 20 32
       20

004C   20 4E 4F 20 53 55     MSG_N          DB         ' NO SUCH LIST '
       43 48 20 4C 49 53
       54 20
005A   000E                 CNT_N           DW         14

005C                        DATA_SEG        ENDS


0000                        CODE_SEG        SEGMENT          'CODE'
0000                        EX818           PROC             FAR
                              ASSUME   CS:CODE_SEG, SS:STACK_SEG, DS:DATA_SEG

                            ;To return to DEBUG program put return address on the stack

0000   1E                    PUSH       DS
```

The IBM Personal Computer Assembler 05-15-84   PAGE   1-2
EXAMPLE 8.16

```
0001   B8 0000                            MOV        AX, 0
0004   50                                 PUSH       AX

                            ;Following code implements Example 8.16

0005   B8  ---- R                         MOV        AX, DATA_SEG         ;Establish the data segment
0008   8E D8                              MOV        DS, AX
000A   8D 3E 0034 R                       LEA        DI, LIST1            ;List1 address
000E                        SEARCH:
000E   81 FF FFFF                         CMP        DI, 0FFFFH           ;Is this last empty list
0012   74 09                              JE         NOTFOUND             ;If yes display message
0014   3A 55 02                           CMP        DL, [DI+2]           ;Match the code
0017   74 12                              JE         FOUND                ;If a match display the list
0019   8B 3D                              MOV        DI, [DI]             ;Try the next list
001B   EB F1                              JMP        SEARCH

001D                        NOTFOUND:
001D   8D 36 004C R                       LEA        SI, MSG_N            ;Message pointer
0021   8B 0E 005A R                       MOV        CX, CNT_N            ;Message character count
0025   E8 0039 R                          CALL       DISPLAY              ;Call display routine
0028   EB 0E 90                           JMP        DONE

002B                        FOUND:
002B   B8 0005                            MOV        AX, 5                ;Compute list pointer
002E   03 C7                              ADD        AX, DI
0030   8B F0                              MOV        SI, AX
0032   8B 4D 03                           MOV        CX, [DI+3]           ;List character count
0035   E8 0039 R                          CALL       DISPLAY              ;Call display routine

0038   CB                  DONE:   RET                                    ;Return to DEBUG program


0039                        DISPLAY         PROC             NEAR
0039                        NXT_CHAR:
0039   8A 04                              MOV        AL, [SI]             ;Get character
003B   B4 0E                              MOV        AH, 14               ;Parameter for INT 10h
003D   FB                                 STI                             ;Enable interrupt
003E   CD 10                              INT        10H                  ;Call service routine
0040   46                                 INC        SI                   ;Point to next character
0041   E2 F6                              LOOP       NXT_CHAR             ;Repeat for next character
0043   C3                                 RET
0044                        DISPLAY         ENDP

0044                        EX818           ENDP
0044                        CODE_SEG        ENDS

                              END      EX818
```

(b)

Figure 8.17 (continued)

```
  The IBM Personal Computer Assembler 05-15-84          PAGE    Symbols-1
EXAMPLE 8.16


Segments and groups:

                  N a m e               Size   align  combine class

CODE_SEG . . . . . . . . . . . . .      0044   PARA   NONE    'CODE'
DATA_SEG . . . . . . . . . . . .        005C   PARA   NONE    'DATA'
STACK_SEG. . . . . . . . . . . .        0040   PARA   STACK   'STACK'

Symbols:

                  N a m e               Type   Value  Attr

CNT_N. . . . . . . . . . . . . . .      L WORD 005A   DATA_SEG
DISPLAY. . . . . . . . . . . . . .      N PROC 0039   CODE_SEG     Length =000B
DONE . . . . . . . . . . . . . . .      L NEAR 0038   CODE_SEG
EX818. . . . . . . . . . . . . .        F PROC 0000   CODE_SEG     Length =0044
FOUND. . . . . . . . . . . . . .        L NEAR 002B   CODE_SEG
LIST1. . . . . . . . . . . . . .        L WORD 0034   DATA_SEG
LIST2. . . . . . . . . . . . . .        L WORD 001B   DATA_SEG
LIST3. . . . . . . . . . . . . .        L WORD 0002   DATA_SEG
LIST4. . . . . . . . . . . . . .        L WORD 0000   DATA_SEG
MSG_N. . . . . . . . . . . . . .        L BYTE 004C   DATA_SEG
NOTFOUND . . . . . . . . . . . .        L NEAR 001D   CODE_SEG
NXT_CHAR . . . . . . . . . . . .        L NEAR 0039   CODE_SEG
SEARCH . . . . . . . . . . . . .        L NEAR 000E   CODE_SEG

Warning Severe
Errors  Errors
0       0

A>
```

(b)


```
A>DEBUG B:EX816.EXE
-R DX
DX 0000
:2

-G
LIST WITH CODE = 2
Program terminated normally
-R DX
DX 0002
:5
-G
 LIST WITH CODE = 5
Program terminated normally
-R DX
DX 0005
:7
-G
 LIST WITH CODE = 7
Program terminated normally
-R DX
DX 0007
:3
-G
 NO SUCH LIST
Program terminated normally
-Q
```

(c)

Figure 8.17 (continued)

The next three lists are searched for in the same way. Those for code numbers 5 and 7 are found and display the messages "LIST WITH CODE = 5" and "LIST WITH CODE = 7", respectively. On the other hand, no list is found for code number 3; therefore, the "NO SUCH LIST" message is displayed.

8.10 KEYBOARD AND DISPLAY INTERACTION ROUTINES

In section 8.3 we developed a simple program that could be used to run a memory test. This was our first experience in writing software that related to the use of hardware in the PC. Here we will look at a program that uses two more of its hardware units, the *keyboard* and *display*.

The use of the keyboard and display in a program is actually quite easy. This is because DOS 2.1 contains special *device-driver routines* to control them. These routines can be used by simply inserting an appropriate software-interrupt instruction in the program. For example, the *read-keyboard* routine is called by loading 0 into the AH register and then executing the instruction

INT   16H

When this instruction is executed the program waits, looking for a key entry from the keyboard. As a key is depressed, its corresponding ASCII code is placed into AL, and control is returned to the next instruction in the main part of the program. Instructions in the main program can read this ASCII data from AL and process it in the appropriate way.

The second device-driver routine that we will consider at this point is the *display-character* routine. This routine is invoked by loading AL with the ASCII code for the character that is to be displayed, loading AH with 14_{10}, and then executing the software interrupt instruction

INT   10H

Execution of this device driver causes the ASCII code to be read from AL and the corresponding character to be displayed on the screen.

These are not the only device-driver routines provided in DOS 2.1. It also includes routines for control of the *printer, disk drives,* and *cassette.*

These drive-routine instructions are actually what are called *software-interrupt* instructions; for them to be executed, the interrupt interface of the 8088 microprocessor must be enabled. This can be done by executing the *set-interrupts instruction* (STI). For this reason, we should execute the STI instruction before using any of the device-driver routines from DOS 2.1 in a program.

Example 8.17

Write a program that first displays a prompt on the screen to enter either Y or N from the keyboard. If Y is entered, one message is to be displayed; if N is entered, another message is to be displayed; and if a key other than Y or N is entered, a reminder that only Y or N is to be entered is to be displayed.

Solution:

We begin by defining a data segment starting at DATA_SEG. This is done with the instructions

```
MOV   AX,DATA_SEG
MOV   DS,AX
```

Next, we need to write the segment of program that displays the prompt on the screen. To do this, we must define a pointer to the beginning of the message (MSG_P) in memory and a count (PCOUNT) that tells how many characters are in the message. These parameters must be passed to the display routine in registers SI and CX, respectively. This is done with the instructions

```
LEA   SI,MSG_P
MOV   CX,PCOUNT
```

Next we call the DISPLAY procedure that is used to display this message as well as the other messages. This is done with the instruction

```
CALL   DISPLAY
```

where DISPLAY is the name of a procedure that is defined with a pseudo-op. The display routine is as follows:

```
NXT_CHAR:
        MOV   AL,[SI]
        MOV   AH,14
        STI
        INT   10H
        INC   SI
        LOOP  NXT_CHAR
```

This routine starts by loading AL with the first character to be displayed. Then AH is loaded with 14 because the display-character routine is to be used, interrupts are enabled with the STI instruction, and then the display-character routine is called and the character pointed to by the current contents of SI is displayed. This is the first character of the message. After this is done, the INC instruction increments the value in SI so that it points to the next character in the message. Now the LOOP instruction causes the count in CX to be decremented by one and tested for zero. Since CX is not yet zero, the loop is repeated and the next character is displayed. This continues until the complete message is displayed. At this time, CX has decremented to zero and the loop is terminated.

Now that the prompt has been displayed, the program must begin to look for a key entry from the keyboard. This is done with the instruction sequence

```
READ_KEY:
        MOV   AH,0
        INT   16H
```

Here the move instruction loads AH with 0 and then the INT instruction calls the read-keyboard routine. This key entry sequence waits for a key entry to be made and when it is, the ASCII code for the character is loaded into AL.

Now we must test the ASCII code in AL to determine which character was entered, and depending on whether N, Y, or another key was depressed, we display the message starting at MSG_N, MSG_Y, or MSG_X, respectively. After this, control is returned to the point in the program where we look for a key entry. This is done with the sequence of instructions

```
        CMP   AL,'N'
        JE    DSPLY_N
        CMP   AL,'Y'
        JE    DSPLY_Y
        LEA   SI,MSG_X
        MOV   CX,XCOUNT
        CALL  DISPLAY
        JMP   READ_KEY
```

Notice that we first compare the contents of AL to ASCII character N. If it is equal to this character, we jump to the routine DSPLY_N. On the other hand, if it is not equal, the character is compared to ASCII Y and if a match is found, a jump is initiated to the routine DSPLY_Y. However, if the character is also not Y, the pointer to MSG_X is loaded into SI, the count of characters in message X is loaded into CX, and the display routine is called into operation. This causes the message that indicates that the depressed key was not N or Y to be displayed. Then control is returned to the key entry routine with the JMP instructions.

The display sequence that is called for entry of the character N is

```
DSPLY_N:
        LEA   SI,MSG_N
        MOV   CX,NCOUNT
        CALL  DISPLAY
```

where NCOUNT is the length of the message that starts at address MSG_N.

Similarly, for entry of Y, the display routine is entered by the instruction sequence

```
DSPLY_Y:
        LEA   SI,MSG_Y
        MOV   CX,YCOUNT
        CALL  DISPLAY
```

Here YCOUNT is the length of the message that starts at address MSG_Y. The entire program is shown in Fig. 8.18.

```
                        MOV     AX,DATA_SEG
                        MOV     DS,AX
                        LEA     SI,MSG_P
                        MOV     CX,PCOUNT
                        CALL    DISPLAY
            NXT_CHAR:
                        MOV     AL,[SI]
                        MOV     AH,14
                        STI
                        INT     10H
                        INC     SI
                        LOOP    NXT_CHAR
            READ_KEY:
                        MOV     AH,0
                        INT     16H
                        CMP     AL, 'N'
                        JE      DSPLY_N
                        CMP     AL, 'Y'
                        JE      DSPLY_Y
                        LEA     SI,MSG_X
                        MOV     CX,XCOUNT
                        CALL    DISPLAY
                        JMP     READ_KEY
            DSPLY_N:
                        LEA     SI,MSG_N
                        MOV     CX,NCOUNT
                        CALL    DISPLAY
            DSPLY_Y:
                        LEA     SI,MSG_Y
                        MOV     CX,YCOUNT
                        CALL    DISPLAY
```

Figure 8.18 Source program for keyboard and display interaction program.

Example 8.18

Figure 8.19(a) gives a source program that implements the keyboard entry/display routine written in Example 8.17 as a procedure. This program was assembled and linked to produce a run module in file EX818.EXE. The source listing produced by the assembler is given in Fig. 8.19(b). Run the program on the IBM PC.

Solution:

The program is loaded with the DEBUG command

A > DEBUG B:EX818.EXE (↵)

as shown in Fig. 8.19(c). Then it is executed with the command

$$-G \quad (\lrcorner)$$

Notice that this causes the prompt "ENTER N OR Y" to be displayed. The first
time the program was run, the entry was the N key; therefore, the displayed
message is "YOU NEVER SAY YES !". The program was run two more times.
For the second run the entry at the keyboard was Y; for the third run the entry was
an invalid key and this was followed by the N key.

```
A>TYPE B:EX818.ASM


TITLE    EXAMPLE 8.18

        PAGE    ,132

STACK_SEG        SEGMENT          STACK 'STACK'
                 DB               64 DUP(?)
STACK_SEG        ENDS


DATA_SEG         SEGMENT          'DATA'
MSG_P            DB       'ENTER N OR Y '
MSG_Y            DB       '  --- YES MAN ! '
MSG_N            DB       '  --- YOU NEVER SAY YES ! '
MSG_X            DB       '  --- I SAID N OR Y ! '
PCOUNT           DW       13
YCOUNT           DW       16
NCOUNT           DW       26
XCOUNT           DW       22
DATA_SEG         ENDS


CODE_SEG         SEGMENT          'CODE'
EX818            PROC             FAR
        ASSUME  CS:CODE_SEG, SS:STACK_SEG, DS:DATA_SEG

;To return to DEBUG program put return address on the stack

                 PUSH     DS
                 MOV      AX, 0
                 PUSH     AX

;Following code implements Example 8.18

                 MOV      AX, DATA_SEG        ;Establish data segment
                 MOV      DS, AX
                 STI                          ;Enable interrupt
                 LEA      SI, MSG_P           ;Display prompt message
                 MOV      CX, PCOUNT          ;P message length
                 CALL     DISPLAY             ;Call display routine

                 STI                          ;Enable interrupt
READ_KEY:
                 MOV      AH, 0               ;Read a key
                 INT      16H

                 CMP      AL, 'N'             ;Is it N
                 JE       DSPLY_N             ;If yes
                 CMP      AL, 'Y'             ;Is it Y
                 JE       DSPLY_Y             ;If yes display Y message
                 LEA      SI, MSG_X           ;If neither display x message
                 MOV      CX, XCOUNT          ;X message length
                 CALL     DISPLAY             ;Call display routine
                 JMP      READ_KEY
```

(a)

Figure 8.19 (a) Source program for Example 8.18; (b) source listing produced
by the assembler; (c) DEBUG sequence.

```
DSPLY_N:
        LEA     SI, MSG_N           ;Message N address
        MOV     CX, NCOUNT          ;Message N length
        CALL    DISPLAY             ;Call display routine
        JMP     DONE
DSPLY_Y:
        LEA     SI, MSG_Y           ;Message Y address
        MOV     CX, YCOUNT          ;Message Y length
        CALL    DISPLAY             ;Call display routine

DONE:   RET                         ;Return to DEBUG program


DISPLAY         PROC        NEAR
NXT_CHAR:
        MOV     AL, [SI]            ;Get character
        MOV     AH, 14              ;Parameter for INT 10h
        STI                         ;Enable interrupt
        INT     10H                 ;Call service routine
        INC     SI                  ;Point to next character
        LOOP    NXT_CHAR            ;Repeat for next character
        RET
DISPLAY         ENDP

EX818   ENDP
CODE_SEG        ENDS

        END     EX818

A>
```

(a)

```
A>TYPE B:EX818.LST
```

```
The IBM Personal Computer Assembler 05-15-84            PAGE    1-1
EXAMPLE 8.18



                        TITLE   EXAMPLE 8.18

                                PAGE      ,132

0000                    STACK_SEG       SEGMENT         STACK 'STACK'
0000    40 [            DB              64 DUP(?)
              ??
            ]

0040                    STACK_SEG       ENDS


0000                    DATA_SEG        SEGMENT         'DATA'
0000    45 4E 54 45 52 20   MSG_P       DB      'ENTER N OR Y '
        4E 20 4F 52 20 59
        20
000D    20 20 2D 2D 2D 20   MSG_Y       DB      ' --- YES MAN ! '
        59 45 53 20 4D 41
        4E 20 21 20
001D    20 20 2D 2D 2D 20   MSG_N       DB      ' --- YOU NEVER SAY YES ! '
        59 4F 55 20 4E 45
        56 45 52 20 53 41
        59 20 59 45 53 20
        21 20
```

(b)

Figure 8.19 (continued)

```
0037   20 20 2D 2D 2D 20      MSG_X          DB            ' --- I SAID N OR Y ! '
       49 20 53 41 49 44
       20 4E 20 4F 52 20
       59 20 21 20
004D   000D                   PCOUNT         DW            13
004F   0010                   YCOUNT         DW            16
0051   001A                   NCOUNT         DW            26
0053   0016                   XCOUNT         DW            22
0055                          DATA_SEG       ENDS


0000                          CODE_SEG       SEGMENT              'CODE'
0000                          EX818          PROC                 FAR
                                      ASSUME  CS:CODE_SEG, SS:STACK_SEG, DS:DATA_SEG

                              ;To return to DEBUG program put return address on the stack

0000   1E                                    PUSH     DS
0001   B8 0000                               MOV      AX, 0
0004   50                                    PUSH     AX

                              ;Following code implements Example 8.18

0005   B8 ---- R                             MOV      AX, DATA_SEG     ;Establish data segment
0008   8E D8                                 MOV      DS, AX
000A   FB                                    STI                       ;Enable interrupt
000B   8D 36 0000 R                          LEA      SI, MSG_P        ;Display prompt message
```

The IBM Personal Computer Assembler 05-15-84   PAGE   1-2
EXAMPLE 8.18

```
000F   8B 0E 004D R                          MOV      CX, PCOUNT       ;P message length
0013   E8 004A R                             CALL     DISPLAY          ;Call display routine

0016   FB                                    STI                       ;Enable interrupt
0017                          READ_KEY:
0017   B4 00                                 MOV      AH, 0            ;Read a key
0019   CD 16                                 INT      16H

001B   3C 4E                                 CMP      AL, 'N'          ;Is it N
001D   74 11                                 JE       DSPLY_N          ;If yes
001F   3C 59                                 CMP      AL, 'Y'          ;Is it Y
0021   74 1B                                 JE       DSPLY_Y          ;If yes display Y message
0023   8D 36 0037 R                          LEA      SI, MSG_X        ;If neither display x message
0027   8B 0E 0053 R                          MOV      CX, XCOUNT       ;X message length
002B   E8 004A R                             CALL     DISPLAY          ;Call display routine
002E   EB E7                                 JMP      READ_KEY
0030                          DSPLY_N:
0030   8D 36 001D R                          LEA      SI, MSG_N        ;Message N address
0034   8B 0E 0051 R                          MOV      CX, NCOUNT       ;Message N length
0038   E8 004A R                             CALL     DISPLAY          ;Call display routine
003B   EB 0C 90                              JMP      DONE
003E                          DSPLY_Y:
003E   8D 36 000D R                          LEA      SI, MSG_Y        ;Message Y address
0042   8B 0E 004F R                          MOV      CX, YCOUNT       ;Message Y length
0046   E8 004A R                             CALL     DISPLAY          ;Call display routine

0049   CB                    DONE:  RET                                ;Return to DEBUG program


004A                          DISPLAY        PROC                 NEAR
004A                          NXT_CHAR:
004A   8A 04                                 MOV      AL, [SI]         ;Get character
004C   B4 0E                                 MOV      AH, 14           ;Parameter for INT 10h
004E   FB                                    STI                       ;Enable interrupt
004F   CD 10                                 INT      10H              ;Call service routine
```

(b)

Figure 8.19 (continued)

```
0051  46                      INC    SI              ;Point to next character
0052  E2 F6                   LOOP   NXT_CHAR        ;Repeat for next character
0054  C3                      RET
0055              DISPLAY      ENDP

0055              EX818  ENDP
0055              CODE_SEG     ENDS

                  END    EX818
```

The IBM Personal Computer Assembler 05-15-84   PAGE   Symbols-1
EXAMPLE 8.18

Segments and groups:

N a m e	Size	align	combine	class
CODE_SEG	0055	PARA	NONE	'CODE'
DATA_SEG	0055	PARA	NONE	'DATA'
STACK_SEG.	0040	PARA	STACK	'STACK'

Symbols:

N a m e	Type	Value	Attr	
DISPLAY.	N PROC	004A	CODE_SEG	Length =000B
DONE	L NEAR	0049	CODE_SEG	
DSPLY_N.	L NEAR	0030	CODE_SEG	
DSPLY_Y.	L NEAR	003E	CODE_SEG	
EX818.	F PROC	0000	CODE_SEG	Length =0055
MSG_N.	L BYTE	001D	DATA_SEG	
MSG_P.	L BYTE	0000	DATA_SEG	
MSG_X.	L BYTE	0037	DATA_SEG	
MSG_Y.	L BYTE	000D	DATA_SEG	
NCOUNT	L WORD	0051	DATA_SEG	
NXT_CHAR	L NEAR	004A	CODE_SEG	
PCOUNT	L WORD	004D	DATA_SEG	
READ_KEY	L NEAR	0017	CODE_SEG	
XCOUNT	L WORD	0053	DATA_SEG	
YCOUNT	L WORD	004F	DATA_SEG	

Warning Severe
Errors Errors
0   0

A>

(b)

```
A>DEBUG B:EX818.EXE
-G
ENTER N OR Y   --- YOU NEVER SAY YES !
Program terminated normally
-G
ENTER N OR Y   --- YES MAN !
Program terminated normally
-G
ENTER N OR Y   --- I SAID N OR Y !   --- YOU NEVER SAY YES !
Program terminated normally
-Q

A>
```

(c)

Figure 8.19 (continued)

8.11 FLOATING POINT ARITHMETIC CALCULATIONS

In earlier chapters we found that the 8088 can perform arithmetic operations on data expressed as *integer numbers, signed integer numbers, BCD numbers,* and *ASCII numbers.* Moreover, you may have found that this limits the size of numbers that can be processed. For instance, the largest 16-bit integer number is 32,768. Use of *floating point number* representation increases the numerical range for a given number of bits. In this type of representation the number is expressed in two parts, called the *mantissa* and the *exponent.* For example, the number .05 is written as $.5 \times 10^{-1}$ in floating point notation. Here .5 is the mantissa and -1 is the exponent.

The instruction set of the 8088 microprocessor has no instructions that can directly process numbers expressed in floating point notation. Therefore, the available instructions must be used to write software routines to handle arithmetic operations with floating point numbers.

The *floating point multiplication* and *floating point division* operations can be implemented quite easily in software since exponent rules can be used. For example, multiplying two numbers, A and B, represented as

$$A = a \times 10^l$$

$$B = a \times 10^m$$

we get

$$A \times B = (a \times b) \times 10^{l + m}$$

Thus the mantissa of the floating point product is found by simply multiplying the individual matissas; its exponent is formed as the sum of the individual exponents.

For the division operation, an algorithm similar to that for multiplication can be derived. On the other hand, the algorithms for *floating point addition* and *floating point subtraction* are rather complex and require extensive software. To illustrate the implementation of floating point operations in software, we will develop a binary floating point multiplication program and then execute it on the PC in the two examples that follow.

Example 8.19

Write a program that multiplies two numbers A and B in the following form:

$$A = a \times 2^l$$

$$B = b \times 2^m$$

where a and b are fixed-point binary numbers with binary point between the sign bit and the next MSB. Assume that all variables a, b, l, and m are byte-size.

Solution:

The product of A and B will be called C; it is given by the expression

$$C = (a \times b) \times 2^{l+m} = c \times 2^{n}$$

If we obtain c by using the 8088's signed multiplication instructions, the result will be half of what it should be as a fixed-point binary number. This is due to the fact that they perform 2's-complement multiplication, which treats the sign bits just like the other bits. Thus a shift to the left will be required to correct the result. To obtain n, we can use the addition instructions of the 8088 microprocessor. This leads us to the following instruction sequence

```
MOV   AX,DATA_SEG   ; SET UP DATA SEGMENT
MOV   DS,AX
LEA   SI,NUM_A      ; SET POINTERS FOR NUMBERS
LEA   DI,NUM_B
MOV   BL,[SI+1]     ; GET l
ADD   BL,[DI+1]     ; n = l + m
MOV   AL,[SI]       ; GET a
IMUL  BYTE PTR[DI]  ; c = a × b
SHL   AX,1          ; CORRECT FOR DECIMAL MULTIPLY
```

A problem arises due to the size increases that occur when numbers are multiplied. For instance, an 8×8 multiplication yields a 16-bit result. If we multiplied this result by another eight-bit number, the result could be larger than 16 bits. In this case, the most significant bits of the result would be lost. The solution we use for this problem in our program is to just keep the eight most significant bits of the result. That is, the eight least significant bits of the result are just dropped. However, this solution can create another problem when multiplying small numbers. When multiplying two small numbers, most of the more significant bits in the result are zero, and dropping the eight least significant bits may introduce a large percentage of error. This small number problem can be resolved by shifting the result to the left so that the bit after the binary point is a one for positive numbers and zero for negative numbers, and then subtracting the number of shifts from the exponent. Then the eight LSBs are discarded. For positive numbers this can be done with the instruction sequence

```
MORE1:  MOV   DX,4000H  ; MASK FOR MSB
        AND   DX,AX      ; MSB = 1?
        JNZ   DONE1      ; IF YES THEN OUT
        SHL   AX,1       ; OTHERWISE SHIFT LEFT
        SUB   BL,1       ; ACCOUNT FOR SHIFT
        JMP   MORE1
```

A similar instruction sequence can be written to handle negative results.

Example 8.20

A source program for a procedure that includes the floating point multiplication routine developed in Example 8.19 is shown in Fig. 8.20(a). Notice that some instructions have been added to identify whether a number is positive or negative and for correction of small number errors in multiplications with a negative result. This program was assembled and linked to produce a run module in file EX820.EXE. The source listing produced as part of the assembly process is given in Fig. 8.20(b). Load the run module with DEBUG and then execute the program for

$$A = .5 \times 2^{-1}$$
$$B = .5 \times 2^{0}$$

```
A>TYPE B:EX820.ASM

TITLE    EXAMPLE 8.20

        PAGE    ,132

STACK_SEG       SEGMENT         STACK 'STACK'
                DB              64 DUP(?)
STACK_SEG       ENDS

DATA_SEG        SEGMENT         'DATA'
NUM_A           DB              40H, 0FFH
NUM_B           DB              40H, 00H
NUM_C           DB              2 DUP(?)
DATA_SEG        ENDS

CODE_SEG        SEGMENT         'CODE'
EX820           PROC            FAR
        ASSUME  CS:CODE_SEG, SS:STACK_SEG, DS:DATA_SEG

;To return to DEBUG program put return address on the stack

        PUSH    DS
        MOV     AX, 0
        PUSH    AX

;Following code implements Example 8.20

        MOV     AX, DATA_SEG          ;Set up data segment
        MOV     DS, AX

        LEA     SI, NUM_A             ;Set pointers
        LEA     DI, NUM_B

        MOV     BL, [SI+1]            ;Get l
        ADD     BL, [DI+1]            ;n + l + m

        MOV     AL, [SI]              ;Get a
        IMUL    BYTE PTR [DI]         ;c = a*b

        SHL     AX, 1                 ;Correct for decimal multiply
        JS      NEG                   ;If c is negative
        CALL    ADJUST1               ;Correction for positive c
        JMP     AROUND
```

(a)

Figure 8.20 (a) Source program for Example 8.20; (b) source listing produced by the assembler; (c) DEBUG sequence.

```
NEG:      CALL     ADJUST2                  ;Correction for negative c
AROUND:   LEA      SI, NUM_C                ;Save result
          MOV      [SI], AH
          MOV      [SI+1], BL
          RET


ADJUST1            PROC           NEAR
MORE1:    MOV      DX, 4000H                ;Mask for MSB
          AND      DX, AX                   ;MSB = 1 ?
          JNZ      DONE1                    ;If yes
          SHL      AX, 1                    ;Otherwise shift left
          SUB      BL, 1                    ;Account for shift in exponent
          JMP      MORE1
DONE1:    RET
ADJUST1            ENDP


ADJUST2            PROC           NEAR
MORE2:    MOV      DX, 4000H                ;Mask for MSB
          OR       DX, AX                   ;MSB = 0 ?
          JZ       DONE2                    ;If yes
          SHL      AX, 1                    ;Otherwise shift left
          SUB      BL, 1                    ;Account for shift in exponent
          JMP      MORE2
DONE2:    RET
ADJUST2            ENDP

EX820     ENDP
CODE_SEG           ENDS
          END      EX820

A>
```

(a)


```
TYPE B:EX820.LST




The IBM Personal Computer Assembler 06-24-84               PAGE    1-1
EXAMPLE 8.20




                         TITLE    EXAMPLE 8.20

                                  PAGE      ,132

0000                     STACK_SEG        SEGMENT         STACK 'STACK'
0000      40 [           DB               64 DUP(?)
             ??
          ]

0040                     STACK_SEG        ENDS


0000                     DATA_SEG         SEGMENT         'DATA'
0000      40 FF          NUM_A            DB       40H, 0FFH
0002      40 00          NUM_B            DB       40H,00H
0004      02 [           NUM_C            DB       2 DUP(?)
             ??
          ]

0006                     DATA_SEG         ENDS

0000                     CODE_SEG         SEGMENT         'CODE'
0000                     EX820            PROC            FAR
                                  ASSUME  CS:CODE_SEG, SS:STACK_SEG, DS:DATA_SEG
```

(b)

Figure 8.20 (continued)

```
                                        ;To return to DEBUG program put return address on the stack

0000  1E                                PUSH    DS
0001  B8 0000                           MOV     AX, 0
0004  50                                PUSH    AX

                                        ;Following code implements Example 8.20

0005  B8 ---- R                         MOV     AX, DATA_SEG        ;Set up data segment
0008  8E D8                             MOV     DS, AX

000A  8D 36 0000 R                      LEA     SI, NUM_A           ;Set pointers
000E  8D 3E 0002 R                      LEA     DI, NUM_B

0012  8A 5C 01                          MOV     BL, [SI+1]          ;Get 1
0015  02 5D 01                          ADD     BL, [DI+1]          ;n + 1 + m

0018  8A 04                             MOV     AL, [SI]            ;Get a
001A  F6 2D                             IMUL    BYTE PTR [DI]       ;c = a*b

001C  D1 E0                             SHL     AX, 1               ;Correct for decimal multiply
001E  78 06                             JS      NEG                 ;If c is negative
0020  E8 0033 R                         CALL    ADJUST1             ;Correction for positive c
0023  EB 04 90                          JMP     AROUND
```

```
The IBM Personal Computer Assembler 06-24-84                PAGE    1-2
EXAMPLE 8.20

0026  E8 0042 R         NEG:    CALL    ADJUST2                 ;Correction for negative c
0029  8D 36 0004 R      AROUND: LEA     SI, NUM_C               ;Save result
002D  88 24                     MOV     [SI], AH
002F  88 5C 01                  MOV     [SI+1], BL
0032  CB                        RET

0033                    ADJUST1         PROC            NEAR
0033  BA 4000           MORE1:  MOV     DX, 4000H               ;Mask for MSB
0036  23 D0                     AND     DX, AX                  ;MSB = 1 ?
0038  75 07                     JNZ     DONE1                   ;If yes
003A  D1 E0                     SHL     AX, 1                   ;Otherwise shift left
003C  80 EB 01                  SUB     BL, 1                   ;Account for shift in exponent
003F  EB F2                     JMP     MORE1
0041  C3                DONE1:  RET
0042                    ADJUST1         ENDP

0042                    ADJUST2         PROC            NEAR
0042  BA 4000           MORE2:  MOV     DX, 4000H               ;Mask for MSB
0045  0B D0                     OR      DX, AX                  ;MSB = 0 ?
0047  74 07                     JZ      DONE2                   ;If yes
0049  D1 E0                     SHL     AX, 1                   ;Otherwise shift left
004B  80 EB 01                  SUB     BL, 1                   ;Account for shift in exponent
004E  EB F2                     JMP     MORE2
0050  C3                DONE2:  RET
0051                    ADJUST2         ENDP

0051                    EX820   ENDP
0051                    CODE_SEG        ENDS
                                END     EX820
```

```
The IBM Personal Computer Assembler 06-24-84                PAGE    Symbols-1
EXAMPLE 8.20

Segments and groups:

            N a m e                 Size    align   combine class

CODE_SEG . . . . . . . . . . . .    0051    PARA    NONE    'CODE'
DATA_SEG . . . . . . . . . . . .    0006    PARA    NONE    'DATA'
STACK_SEG. . . . . . . . . . . .    0040    PARA    STACK   'STACK'
```

(b)

Figure 8.20 (continued)

Symbols:

Name	Type	Value	Attr	
ADJUST1.	N PROC	0033	CODE_SEG	Length =000F
ADJUST2.	N PROC	0042	CODE_SEG	Length =000F
AROUND	L NEAR	0029	CODE_SEG	
DONE1.	L NEAR	0041	CODE_SEG	
DONE2.	L NEAR	0050	CODE_SEG	
EX820.	F PROC	0000	CODE_SEG	Length =0051
MORE1.	L NEAR	0033	CODE_SEG	
MORE2.	L NEAR	0042	CODE_SEG	
NEG.	L NEAR	0026	CODE_SEG	
NUM_A.	L BYTE	0000	DATA_SEG	
NUM_B.	L BYTE	0002	DATA_SEG	
NUM_C.	L BYTE	0004	DATA_SEG	Length =0002

```
Warning  Severe
Errors   Errors
0        0

A>
```

(b)

```
DEBUG B:EX820.EXE
-U
0915:0000 1E           PUSH    DS
0915:0001 B80000       MOV     AX,0000
0915:0004 50           PUSH    AX
0915:0005 B81B09       MOV     AX,091B
0915:0008 8ED8         MOV     DS,AX
0915:000A 8D360000     LEA     SI,[0000]
0915:000E 8D3E0200     LEA     DI,[0002]
0915:0012 8A5C01       MOV     BL,[SI+01]
0915:0015 025D01       ADD     BL,[DI+01]
0915:0018 8A04         MOV     AL,[SI]
0915:001A F62D         IMUL    BYTE PTR [DI]
0915:001C D1E0         SHL     AX,1
0915:001E 7806         JS      0026
-U
0915:0020 E81000       CALL    0033
0915:0023 EB04         JMP     0029
0915:0025 90           NOP
0915:0026 E81900       CALL    0042
0915:0029 8D360400     LEA     SI,[0004]
0915:002D 8824         MOV     [SI],AH
0915:002F 885C01       MOV     [SI+01],BL
0915:0032 CB           RETF
0915:0033 BA0040       MOV     DX,4000
0915:0036 23D0         AND     DX,AX
0915:0038 7507         JNZ     0041
0915:003A D1E0         SHL     AX,1
0915:003C 80EB01       SUB     BL,01
0915:003F EBF2         JMP     0033
-G 32

AX=4000  BX=00FE  CX=0066  DX=4000  SP=003C  BP=0000  SI=0004  DI=0002
DS=091B  ES=0905  SS=091C  CS=0915  IP=0032   NV UP DI PL NZ NA PE NC
0915:0032 CB           RETF
-D 0 5
091B:0000  40 FF 40 00 40 FE                                  @.@.@~
-G

Program terminated normally
-Q
```

(c)

Solution:

Looking at Fig. 8.19(a), we see that the values of A and B are loaded into memory with DB pseudo-op statements. In these statements the number A is coded as NUM_A with a mantissa value of 40_{16} and exponent value of FF_{16}, and number B is coded as NUM_B with mantissa 40_{16} and exponent 00_{16}. Moreover, space is allocated for storage of the value of C (NUM_C).

This program is loaded at the same time that DEBUG is called up with the command

$$A > DEBUG \quad B:EX820.EXE \quad (\dashv)$$

and then the program is unassembled to verify its loading. Now the program is executed with the command

$$-G \quad 32 \quad (\dashv)$$

Finally, the results of executing the program are displayed with the command

$$-D \quad 0 \quad 5 \quad (\dashv)$$

Here the first two bytes are the mantissa and exponent for A, the next two are the mantissa and exponent for B, and the last two the mantissa and exponent for C. Therefore, the result of the floating point multiply is a mantissa of 40_{16} and an exponent of FE_{16}.

ASSIGNMENT

Section 8.2

1. Implement the expression in Example 8.1 using arithmetic instructions and then run the program on the PC.

2. Write a program to implement the expression

$$\tfrac{1}{8}(AX) + 25(BX) \rightarrow DX$$

Use shift instructions to perform the multiplications and divisions. State any assumption made.

Section 8.3

3. Modify the program in Fig. 8.3(a) so that the pattern $AAAA_{16}$ is used to test memory, and then repeat the debug session performed in Example 8.4.

4. Write a program that can be used to test each memory location in a block of memory alternately with the two patterns 5555_{16} and $AAAA_{16}$.

Section 8.5

5. Modify the program in Fig. 8.7(a) so that when it sorts the array of numbers they end up arranged in descending order, then repeat the debug sequence of Fig. 8.7(c) for this program.
6. Write a program to generate the median of an array of numbers. A median is the middle value(s) above and below which there are an equal number of values.

Section 8.6

7. Write a program to generate the first ten numbers of the series given by the expression

$$N(x) = 5(2^x) \text{ for } x = 0, 1, \ldots\ldots, 9$$

Section 8.7

8. Modify the program in Fig. 8.11(a) so that it can be used to convert ASCII characters to their equivalent EBCDIC characters. Run the program using the DEBUG sequence shown in Fig. 8.11(c).
9. Write a program to convert two digit hexadecimal numbers $> 63_{16}$ to their equivalent decimal numbers.

Section 8.8

10. Change the program in Example 8.13 to produce a 300-ms, 1000-Hz tone with the IBM PC's speaker.

Section 8.9

11. Modify the DATA_SEG in Fig. 8.17(a) such that LIST2 is not part of the linked-list data structure.
12. Modify the DATA_SEG in Fig. 8.17(a) such that a new list LISTN is inserted between LIST1 and LIST2 of the linked-list data structure.

Section 8.10

13. Change the program in Fig. 8.19(a) so that the prompt becomes

ENTER 1 FOR NO AND 2 FOR YES.

Section 8.11

14. Given four fixed-point decimal numbers A, B, C, and D, where the decimal point is between the MSB and the bit next to it. Write a program to compute

$$AB + CD$$

as a fixed-point, byte-size number. Assume that A, B, C, and D are all bytes of data.

SOLUTIONS

CHAPTER 1

Section 1.2

1. A general-purpose computer is a computer designed to run programs for a wide variety of applications; for instance, accounting, word processing, and languages such as BASIC or FORTRAN.
2. Mainframe computer, minicomputer, and microcomputer.
3. The microcomputer is similar to the minicomputer in that it is designed to perform general-purpose data processing; however, it is smaller in size, has reduced capabilities, and is lower in cost than a minicomputer.

Section 1.3

4. Microprocessing unit (MPU).
5. 16-bit microprocessor.
6. Keyboard; mouse and joystick.
7. Video display and printer.
8. Internal and external memory.
9. 320K bytes and 10M bytes.
10. Read-only memory (ROM) and random access read/write memory (RAM).
11. 96K bytes.
12. DOS is loaded from the diskette into RAM. Since RAM is volatile, the operating system is lost whenever power is turned off.

Section 1.4

13. Software.
14. Program.
15. 8088 machine code.
16. Instructions encoded in machine language are coded in 0s and 1s, while assembly language instructions are written in alphanumeric symbols such as MOV, ADD, or SUB.
17. Operation code.
18. The data that is to be processed during execution of an instruction; source operand and destination operand.
19. START.
20. An assembler is a program that is used to convert an assembly language source program to its equivalent program in machine code. A compiler is a program that converts a program written in a high-level language to equivalent machine code.
21. The machine code output of an assembler or compiler is called object code.
22. It takes up less memory and executes faster.
23. A real-time application is one in which the tasks required by the application must be completed before any other input to the program occurs that can alter its operation.
24. Floppy-disk subsystem control and communications to a printer; code-translation and table-sort routines.

CHAPTER 2

Section 2.2

1. 10.
2. 0,1,2,3,4,5,6,7,8,9.
3. Weight.
4. Most significant digit and least significant digit.
5. 9 and 10^{+3}, 8 and 10^{-3}.

Section 2.3

6. 0,1.
7. Bit.
8. MSB and LSB.
9. 2^{-1}
10. 1 and 2^{+5}.

Section 2.4

11.

Decimal	Binary
0	0
1	1
2	10
3	11
4	100
5	101
6	110
7	111
8	1000
9	1001

12. **(a)** 5, **(b)** 11, **(c)** 21, **(d)** 127.
13. 71.
14. **(a)** 101, **(b)** 1001, **(c)** 101010, **(d)** 1100100.
15. 111110100.

Section 2.5

16. 0,1,2,3,4,5,6,7,8,9,A,B,C,D,E,F.
17. 16^{+1}.
18. C and 16^{+2}.

Section 2.6

19. **(a)** 39, **(b)** E2, **(c)** 9A, **(d)** 3A0.
20. F0.
21. **(a)** 1101011, **(b)** 11110011, **(c)** 1000101, **(d)** 1010110000.
22. 101000011011.
23. 0,1,2,3,4,5,6,7,8,9,A,B,C,D,E,F,10,11,12,13,14.

Section 2.7

24. **(a)** 6 bits, **(b)** 8 bits, **(c)** 16 bits.
25. C5.
26. 1E00.
27. **(a)** $+21$, **(b)** -96.

Section 2.8

28. **(a)** 101101, **(b)** 100101011.
29. 110011 and 51.

30. (a) 00011, (b) 10001101.
31. (a) 1101000, (b) 010111111.
32. (a) 0001001, (b) 100010011.
33. (a) 10010, (b) 1011101.
34. (a) 1001, (b) 1101001.
35. 1.
36. 1111.

Section 2.9

37. (a) 9, (b) 39, (c) 870.
38. (a) 00101001, (b) 10011001, (c) 000100000110.
39. (a) 214 and 000100000110, (b) 67 and 01100111.
40. (a) 0110111, (b) 1011001, (c) 0100100.
41. 46
    4F
    52
    20
    49
    3D
    20
    31
    20
    54
    4F
    20
    31
    30.
42. NEXT I.
43. (a) 11110111, (b) 11101000, (c) 01011011.
44. C7
    D6
    E3
    D6
    40
    F1
    F0
    F0.
45. READ N.

Section 2.10

46. For a code to have even parity, each binary combination in the code must have an even number of ones. A code with odd parity has an odd number of ones in each binary combination.

47. Parity bit.

48.

Number	P	b8	b7	b6	b5	b4	b3	b2	b1
0	1	1	1	1	1	0	0	0	0
1	0	1	1	1	1	0	0	0	1
2	0	1	1	1	1	0	0	1	0
3	1	1	1	1	1	0	0	1	1
4	0	1	1	1	1	0	1	0	0
5	1	1	1	1	1	0	1	0	1
6	1	1	1	1	1	0	1	1	0
7	0	1	1	1	1	0	1	1	1
8	0	1	1	1	1	1	0	0	0
9	1	1	1	1	1	1	0	0	1

CHAPTER 3

Section 3.2

1. Aid to the assembly language programmer for understanding the 8088's software operation.
2. Their purpose, function, operating capabilities and limitations.
3. 13.
4. 1,048,576 (1M) bytes.

Section 3.3

5. $FFFFF_{16}$ and 00000_{16}.
6. Bytes.
7. $00FF_{16}$.

8.

Address	Contents
A001	78
A002	56
A003	34
A004	12

Section 3.4

9. 256K bytes.
10. Code-segment (CS) register, stack-segment (SS) register, data-segment (DS) register, and extra-segment (ES) register.
11. 128K bytes.
12. Instructions of the program can be stored anywhere in the memory address space.

Section 3.5

13. Pointers to service routines.
14. Pointer to the power-up initialization software routine.

Section 3.6

15. The instruction pointer is the offset address of the next instruction to be fetched by the 8088 relative to the current value in CS.
16. The instruction is fetched from memory, decoded within the 8088, operands are read from memory or internal registers, the operation specified by the instruction is performed on the data, and results are written back to either memory or an internal register.
17. IP is incremented such that it points to the next sequential instruction.

Section 3.7

18. Accumulator (A) register, base (B) register, count (C) register, and data (D) register.
19. BX.
20. DH and DL.
21. Count for string and multibit shift and rotate instructions.

Section 3.8

22. Addresses.
23. Base pointer (BP) and stack pointer (SP).
24. SS.
25. DS.
26. The address in SI is the offset to a source operand and DI contains the offset to a destination operand.

Section 3.9

27.

Flag	Type
CF	Status
PF	Status
AF	Status
ZF	Status
SF	Status
OF	Status
TF	Control
IF	Control
DF	Control

28. CF = carry-out/borrow-in or no carry-out/no borrow-in for the MSB during an arithmetic instruction.

PF = result produced by executing an instruction has even or odd parity.

AF = carry-out/borrow-in or no carry-out/no borrow-in between the high and low nibble in the lower byte of a word result of an arithmetic instruction.

ZF = result produced by executing an instruction is zero or nonzero.

SF = the result produced by executing an instruction is positive or negative.

OF = an overflow or nonoverflow condition has occurred during the execution of an arithmetic instruction.

29. Instructions can be used to test the state of these flags and, based on their setting, modify the sequence in which instructions of the program are executed.

30. DF.

31. Instructions are provided that can load the complete register or modify specific flag bits.

Section 3.10

32. 16 bits and 20 bits.

33. Offset and base.

34. $021AC_{16}$.

35. $A000_{16}$.

36. 1234_{16}.

Section 3.11

37. The stack is the area of memory that is used to temporarily store information (parameters) that is to be passed to subroutines and other information such as the contents of IP and CS that is needed to return from a called subroutine to the main part of the program.

38. $CFF00_{16}$.

39. 128 words.

40. Contents of address $CFF00_{16}$ equals $11EE_{16}$.

Section 3.12

41. Separate.

42. 64K bytes.

43. Page 0.

Section 3.13

44. Register addressing mode
     Immediate addressing mode
     Direct addressing mode
     Register indirect addressing mode

Based addressing mode
Indexed addressing mode
Based indexed addressing mode
String addressing mode
I/O port addressing mode.

45.

Instruction	Source	Destination
(a)	register	register
(b)	register	immediate
(c)	register indirect	register
(d)	direct	register indirect
(e)	based	register
(f)	indexed	register
(g)	based indexed	register

46. (a) $PA = 0B200_{16}$
(b) $PA = 0B100_{16}$
(c) $PA = 0B700_{16}$
(d) $PA = 0B600_{16}$
(e) $PA = 0B900_{16}$.

CHAPTER 4

Section 4.2

1. $0000001111000010_2 = 03C2H$
2. (a) $1000100100010101_2 = 8915H$,
   (b) $1000100100011000_2 = 8918H$,
   (c) $100010100101011100010000_2 = 8A5710H$.
3. (a) $00011110_2 = 1EH$, (b) $1101001011000011_2 = D2C3H$, (c) $10010001_2 = 91H$.

Section 4.3

4. 3 bytes.
5. 24 bytes.

Section 4.4

6. Supplemental program diskette.
7. ```
A>debug
-
```
8. ```
-R AXBX
      ^ Error
```
9. ```
-R CX
CX 0000
:0010
-
```
```

10. -R F
    NV UP DI PL NZ NA PO NC -PE
    -

11. -R
    AX=0000 BX=0000 CX=0010 DX=0000 SP=70EE BP=0000 SI=0000 DI=0000
    DS=08F1 ES=08F1 SS=08F1 CS=08F1 IP=0100   NV UP DI PL NZ NA PE NC
    08F1:0100 D2C3   ROL   BL,CL
    -

Section 4.5

12. -D CS:0000 000F
    08F1:0000 CD 20 00 10 00 9A EE 6F-0D F9 42 02 00 06 70 02   M ....no.yB...p.
    -

13. -E CS:0000
    08F1:0000 CD.   20.   00.   10.   00.   9A.   EE.   6F.
    08F1:0008 0D.   F9.   42.   02.   00.   06.   70.   02.

14. -E CS:100
    08F1:0100 00.FF 00.FF 00.FF 00.FF 00.FF 00.-
    08F1:0104 FF.-
    08F1:0103 FF.-
    08F1:0102 FF.-
    08F1:0101 FF.-
    08F1:0100 FF.
    -

15. -F SS:70CF 70EE 00
    -D SS:70CF 70EE
    08F1:70CF 00
    08F1:70D0 00 00 00 00 00 00 00 00-00 00 00 00 00 00 00 00   ....
    08F1:70E0 00 00 00 00 00 00 00 00-00 00 00 00 00 00 00   ....

16. -F CS:100 105 11
    -F CS:106 10B 22
    -F CS:10C 111 33
    -F CS:112 117 44
    -F CS:118 11D 55
    -E CS:105
    08F1:0105 11.FF
    -E CS:113
    08F1:0113 44.FF
    -D CS:100 11D
    08F1:0100 11 11 11 11 11 FF 22 22-22 22 22 22 33 33 33 33   ......""""""3333
    08F1:0110 33 33 44 FF 44 44 44 44-55 55 55 55 55 55   33D.DDDDUUUUUU
    -S CS:100 11D FF
    08F1:0105
    08F1:0113
    -

Section 4.6

17. -E CS:100 32 0E 34 12
    -U CS:100 103
    08F1:0100 320E3412   XOR   CL,[1234]
    -W CS:100 1 50 1
    -

18. -E CS:200 03 04
    -D CS:200 201
    08F1:0200 03 04
    -U CS:200 201
    08F1:0200 0304   ADD   AX,[SI]
    -W CS:200 1 10 1

19. -L CS:400 1 10 1
        -U CS:400 401
        08F1:0400 0304   ADD   AX,[SI]
        -

20.

-E CS:100 B8 20 0 8E D8 BE 0 01 BF 20 01 B9 10 0 8A 24 88 25 46 47 49 75 F7 90
-D CS:100 117
08F1:0100   B8 20 00 8E D8 BE 00 01-BF 20 01 B9 10 00 8A 24   8 ..X>..? .9...$
08F1:0110   88 25 46 47 49 75 F7 90   .%FGIuw.
-U CS:100 117
08F1:0100 B82000   MOV   AX,0020
08F1:0103 8ED8   MOV   DS,AX
08F1:0105 BE0001   MOV   SI,0100
08F1:0108 BF2001   MOV   DI,0120
08F1:010B B91000   MOV   CX,0010
08F1:010E 8A24   MOV   AH,[SI]
08F1:0110 8825   MOV   [DI],AH
08F1:0112 46   INC   SI
08F1:0113 47   INC   DI
08F1:0114 49   DEC   CX
08F1:0115 75F7   JNZ   010E
08F1:0117 90   NOP
-W CS:100 1 100 1
-

Section 4.7

21.

(a) -A CS:100
     08F1:0100 MOV [DI],DX
     08F1:0102
     -U CS:100 101
     08F1:0100 8915   MOV   [DI],DX
     -

(b) -A CS:100
     08F1:0100 MOV [BX+SI],BX
     08F1:0102
     -U CS:100 101
     08F1:0100 8918   MOV   [BX+SI],BX
     -

(c) -A CS:100
     08F1:0100 MOV DL,[BX+10]
     08F1:0103
     -U CS:100 102
     08F1:0100 8A5710   MOV   DL,[BX+10]
     -

22.

(a) -A CS:100
     08F1:0100 PUSH DS
     08F1:0101
     -U CS:100 100
     08F1:0100 1E   PUSH   DS
     -

(b) -A CS:100
     08F1:0100 ROL BL,CL
     08F1:0102
     -U CS:100 101
     08F1:0100 D2C3   ROL   BL,CL
     -

(c) ─A CS:100
    08F1:0100 AND AX,[1234]
    08F1:0104
    ─U CS:100 103
    08F1:0100 23063412   AND   AX,[1234]
    ─

Section 4.8

23. ─L CS:300 1 50 1
    ─U CS:300 303
    08F1:0300 320E3412   XOR   CL,[1234]
    ─R CX
    CX 0000
    :000F
    ─E DS:1234 FF
    ─T =CS:300

    AX=0000 BX=0000 CX=00F0 DX=0000 SP=70EE BP=0000 SI=0000 DI=0000
    DS=08F1 ES=08F1 SS=08F1 CS=08F1 IP=0304   NV UP DI NG NZ NA PE NC
    08F1:0304 D8BE0001   FDIVR   DWORD PTR [BP+0100]   SS:0100=32
    ─D DS:1234 1235
    08F1:1234 FF 00   ..

24. ─L CS:200 1 100 1
    ─R DS
    DS 08F1
    :0020
    ─F DS:100 10F FF
    ─F DS:120 12F 00
    ─D DS:100 10F
    0020:0100 FF FF FF FF FF FF FF FF-FF FF FF FF FF FF FF FF   ....
    ─D DS:120 12F
    0020:0120 00 00 00 00 00 00 00 00-00 00 00 00 00 00 00 00   ....
    ─R DS
    DS 0020
    :08F1
    ─R
    AX=0000 BX=0000 CX=00F0 DX=0000 SP=70EE BP=0000 SI=0000 DI=0000
    DS=08F1 ES=08F1 SS=08F1 CS=08F1 IP=0304   NV UP DI NG NZ NA PE NC
    08F1:0304 0000   ADD   [BX+SI],AL   DS:0000=CD
    ─U CS:200 217
    08F1:0200 B82000   MOV   AX,0020
    08F1:0203 8ED8   MOV   DS,AX
    08F1:0205 BE0001   MOV   SI,0100
    08F1:0208 BF2001   MOV   DI,0120
    08F1:020B B91000   MOV   CX,0010
    08F1:020E 8A24   MOV   AH,[SI]
    08F1:0210 8825   MOV   [DI],AH
    08F1:0212 46   INC   SI
    08F1:0213 47   INC   DI
    08F1:0214 49   DEC   CX
    08F1:0215 75F7   JNZ   020E
    08F1:0217 90   NOP
    ─G =CS:200 217

    AX=FF20 BX=0000 CX=0000 DX=0000 SP=70EE BP=0000 SI=0110 DI=0130
    DS=0020 ES=08F1 SS=08F1 CS=08F1 IP=0217   NV UP DI PL ZR NA PE NC
    08F1:0217 90   NOP
    ─D DS:100 10F
    0020:0100 FF FF FF FF FF FF FF FF-FF FF FF FF FF FF FF FF   ....
    ─D DS:120 12F
    0020:0120 FF FF FF FF FF FF FF FF-FF FF FF FF FF FF FF FF   ....
    ─

Section 4.9

25. A syntax error is an error in the rules of coding the program. On the other hand, an execution error is an error in the logic of the planned solution for the problem.

26.
```
-L CS:200 1 100 1
-U CS:200 217
08F1:0200 B82000        MOV     AX,0020
08F1:0203 8ED8          MOV     DS,AX
08F1:0205 BE0001        MOV     SI,0100
08F1:0208 BF2001        MOV     DI,0120
08F1:020B B91000        MOV     CX,0010
08F1:020E 8A24          MOV     AH,[SI]
08F1:0210 8825          MOV     [DI],AH
08F1:0212 46            INC     SI
08F1:0213 47            INC     DI
08F1:0214 49            DEC     CX
08F1:0215 75F7          JNZ     020E
08F1:0217 90            NOP
-R DS
DS 08F1
:0020
-F ds:100 10F FF^G
-F DS:100 10F FF
-F DS:120 12F 00
-R DS
DS 0020
:08F1
-G =CS:200 20E

AX=0020  BX=0000  CX=0010  DX=0000  SP=70EE  BP=0000  SI=0100  DI=0120
DS=0020  ES=08F1  SS=08F1  CS=08F1  IP=020E  NV UP DI PL ZR NA PE NC
08F1:020E 8A24          MOV     AH,[SI]                          DS:0100=FF
-G =CS:20E 215

AX=FF20  BX=0000  CX=000F  DX=0000  SP=70EE  BP=0000  SI=0101  DI=0121
DS=0020  ES=08F1  SS=08F1  CS=08F1  IP=0215  NV UP DI PL NZ AC PE NC
08F1:0215 75F7          JNZ     020E
-G =CS:215 20E

AX=FF20  BX=0000  CX=000F  DX=0000  SP=70EE  BP=0000  SI=0101  DI=0121
DS=0020  ES=08F1  SS=08F1  CS=08F1  IP=020E  NV UP DI PL NZ AC PE NC
08F1:020E 8A24          MOV     AH,[SI]                          DS:0101=FF
-G =CS:20E 215

AX=FF20  BX=0000  CX=000E  DX=0000  SP=70EE  BP=0000  SI=0102  DI=0122
DS=0020  ES=08F1  SS=08F1  CS=08F1  IP=0215  NV UP DI PL NZ NA PO NC
08F1:0215 75F7          JNZ     020E
-G =CS:215 20E

AX=FF20  BX=0000  CX=000E  DX=0000  SP=70EE  BP=0000  SI=0102  DI=0122
DS=0020  ES=08F1  SS=08F1  CS=08F1  IP=020E  NV UP DI PL NZ NA PO NC
08F1:020E 8A24          MOV     AH,[SI]                          DS:0102=FF
-G =CS:20E 217

AX=FF20  BX=0000  CX=0000  DX=0000  SP=70EE  BP=0000  SI=0110  DI=0130
DS=0020  ES=08F1  SS=08F1  CS=08F1  IP=0217  NV UP DI PL ZR NA PE NC
08F1:0217 90            NOP
-D DS:120 12F
0020:0120  FF FF FF FF FF FF FF FF-FF FF FF FF FF FF FF FF  ................
```

CHAPTER 5

Section 5.2

1. A flowchart is a pictorial representation that outlines the solution to a problem.
2. (a) Plan the steps in the solution.
   (b) Implement a flowchart and assembly language program for the solution.
   (c) Create a source file.
   (d) Assemble the source file.
   (e) Link the program into a run module.
   (f) Execute and/or debug the program.
3. (a) Creating a source file.
   (b) Assembling the source file.
   (c) Linking of the object module.
   (d) Executing and debugging the run module.
4. (a) PROG_A.SRC
   (b) PROG_A.LST, PROG_A.OBJ, and PROG_A.CRF
   (c) PROG_A.EXE and PROG_A.MAP

Section 5.3

5. Assembly language statements and pseudo-operation statements.
6. Assembly language instructions tell the 8088 microprocessor what operations to perform.
7. Pseudo-operations give the 8088 macroassembler directions about how to assemble the source program.
8. Label, opcode, operand, and comment.
9. Opcode.
10. (a) Fields must be separated by at least one blank space.
    (b) Statements that do not have a label must have at least one blank space before the opcode.
11. A label gives a symbolic name to an assembly language statement that can be referenced by other instructions.
12. 32.
13. Identifies the operation that must be performed.
14. Operands tell where the data to be accessed resides and how it is to be accessed.
15. The source operand is immediate data FFH, and the destination operand is the CL register.
16. Documents what is done by the instruction; comments are ignored by the assembler.
17. The opcode is replaced by a pseudo-opcode, and there may be more than two operands.
18. MOV AX,[1111111111111111B]; MOV AX,[0FFFFH]
19. JMP 11001B; JMP 19H
20. 0H

Section 5.4

21. Define values for constants, variables, and labels.

22. The symbol SRC_BLOCK is defined equal to 0100H and symbol DEST_BLOCK is defined equal to 0120H.

23. The word-size variable SEG_ADDR is assigned the value 1234_{16}.

24. A block of 128 bytes of memory is allocated to the variable BLOCK_1, and these storage locations are left uninitialized.

25. DATA_SEG SEGMENT WORD COMMON 'DATA'
    DATA_SEG ENDS

26.   PUBLIC BLOCK
    BLOCK PROC   FAR
              •
              •
           RET
    BLOCK ENDP

27. ORG 1000H

28. PAGE 55 80
    TITLE BLOCK-MOVE PROGRAM

Section 5.5

29. Line editor.

30.
```
A>EDLIN EXAMPLE.SRC
New file
*I
    1:*                 MOV     AX, DATASEGADDR
    2:*                 MOV     DS, AX
    3:*                 MOV     SI, BLK1ADDR
    4:*                 MOV     DI, BLK2ADDR
    5:*                 MOV     CX, N
    6:*   NXTPT         MOV     AH, [SI]
    7:*                 MOV     [DI], AH
    8:*                 INC     SI
    9:*                 INC     DI
   10:*                 DEC     CX
   11:*                 JNZ     NXTPT
   12:*^C

  *E

  A>
```

31.
```
A>EDLIN BLOCK.ASM
New file
*I
    1:*
    2:*TITLE    BLOCK MOVE PROGRAM
    3:*
    4:*COMMENT *This program moves a block of specified number of bytes
    5:*from one place to another place*
    6:*
    7:*;Define constants used in program
    8:*
```

```
      9:*          N       =       16
                       .

                       .

                       .

                       .

     52:*CODE_SEG         ENDS
     53:*         END     BLOCK
     54:*^C

   *E
```

Section 5.6

32. Source module.

33. Object module: machine language version of the source program.
    Source listing: listing that includes memory addresses, machine code, source statements, and a symbol table.
    Cross-reference table: tells the number of the line in the source program at which each symbol is defined and the number of each line in which it is referenced.

34.
```
A>MASM BLOCK
The IBM Personal Computer MACRO Assembler
Version 1.00 (C)Copyright IBM Corp 1981

Object filename [BLOCK.OBJ]:
Source listing  [NUL.LST]:
Cross reference [NUL.CRF]:

Warning Severe
Errors  Errors
0       0

A>
```

Section 5.7

35. No, the output of the assembler is not executable by the 8088; it must first be processed with the LINK program to form a run module.

36. (a) Since separate programmers can work on the individual modules, the complete program can be written in a shorter period of time.
    (b) Because of the smaller size of modules, they can be edited and assembled in less time.
    (c) It is easier to reuse old software.

37. Object modules.

38. Run module: executable machine-code version of the source program.
    Link map: table showing the start address, stop address, and length of each memory segment employed by the program that was linked.

39. A>LINK

```
IBM Personal Computer Linker
Version 2.10 (C)Copyright IBM Corp 1981, 1982, 1983

Object Modules [.OBJ]: BLOCK
Run File [BLOCK.EXE]:
List File [NUL.MAP]:
Libraries [.LIB]:

A>
```

Section 5.8

40.
```
A>DEBUG B:BLOCK.EXE
-F 20:100 11F FF
-F 20:120 13F 00
-D 20:100 13F
0020:0100  FF FF FF FF FF FF FF FF-FF FF FF FF FF FF FF FF    ................
0020:0110  FF FF FF FF FF FF FF FF-FF FF FF FF FF FF FF       ................
0020:0120  00 00 00 00 00 00 00 00-00 00 00 00 00 00 00 00    ................
0020:0130  00 00 00 00 00 00 00 00-00 00 00 00 00 00 00 00    ................
-G

Program terminated normally
-D 20:100 13F
0020:0100  FF FF FF FF FF FF FF FF-FF FF FF FF FF FF FF FF    ................
0020:0110  FF FF FF FF FF FF FF FF-FF FF FF FF FF FF FF FF    ................
0020:0120  FF FF FF FF FF FF FF FF-FF FF FF FF FF FF FF FF    ................
0020:0130  00 00 00 00 00 00 00 00-00 00 00 00 00 00 00 00    ................
```

CHAPTER 6

Section 6.3

1. **(a)** Loads SI with the contents of the memory location with address $(DS)0 + 0ABC_{16}$.

(b) Stores the number $ABCD_{16}$ at the location in memory corresponding to the address $(DS)0 + (SI)$.

2.
```
A>DEBUG
-A
08F1:0100        MOV SI, [0ABC]
08F1:0104
-E 0ABC FF FF
-D 0ABC 0ABD
08F1:0ABC  FF FF                                              ..
-R SI
SI 0000
:
-T

AX=0000  BX=0000  CX=0000  DX=0000  SP=FFEE  BP=0000  SI=FFFF  DI=0000
DS=08F1  ES=08F1  SS=08F1  CS=08F1  IP=0104  NV UP DI PL NZ NA PO NC
08F1:0104 0000         ADD      [BX+SI],AL                       DS:FFFF=00
-Q
```

3.
```
A>DEBUG
-A
08F1:0100        MOV WORD PTR [SI], ABCD
08F1:0104
-R SI
SI 0000
```

```
:OABC
-E OABC 00 00
-D OABC OABD
08F1:OABC  00 00                                                      ..
-T

AX=0000  BX=0000  CX=0000  DX=0000  SP=FFEE  BP=0000  SI=OABC  DI=0000
DS=08F1  ES=08F1  SS=08F1  CS=08F1  IP=0104    NV UP DI PL NZ NA PO NC
08F1:0104 0000          ADD    [BX+SI],AL                        DS:OABC=CD
-D OABC OABD
08F1:OABC  CD AB                                                  M+
-Q
```

4. Instruction sequence:

```
MOV  DX,AX

MOV  AX,BX

MOV  BX,DX
```

Debug sequence

```
A>DEBUG
-A 100
08F1:0100     MOV DX, AX
08F1:0102     MOV AX, BX
08F1:0104     MOV BX, DX
08F1:0106
-R AX
AX 0000
:1111
-R BX
BX 0000
:2222
-G 106

AX=2222  BX=1111  CX=0000  DX=1111  SP=FFEE  BP=0000  SI=0000  DI=0000
DS=08F1  ES=08F1  SS=08F1  CS=08F1  IP=0106    NV UP DI PL NZ NA PO NC
08F1:0106 0000          ADD    [BX+SI],AL                        DS:1111=00
-Q
```

5. The byte from memory location

$$10000_{16} + 0100_{16} + 0010_{16} = 10110_{16}$$

is loaded into AL.

6. A>TYPE B:EXER66.ASM

```
    TITLE    EXERCISE 6 ( SECTION 6.3 )

         PAGE       ,132

    STACK_SEG      SEGMENT         STACK 'STACK'
                   DB              64 DUP(?)
    STACK_SEG      ENDS


    DATA_SEG       SEGMENT         'DATA'
    TABL1          DB      OFFH,OFEH,OFDH,OFCH,OFBH,OFAH,OF9H,OF8H
    TABL2          DB      OAH,OBH,OCH,ODH,OEH,OFH,10H,11H
    MEM1           DB      ?
    MEM2           DB      ?
    DATA_SEG       ENDS


    CODE_SEG       SEGMENT         'CODE'
    EXER66         PROC    FAR
           ASSUME  CS:CODE_SEG, SS:STACK_SEG, DS:DATA_SEG
```

```
                ;To return to DEBUG program put return address on the stack

                        PUSH    DS
                        MOV     AX, 0
                        PUSH    AX

                ;Following code implements Exercise 6 Section 6.3

                        MOV     AX, DATA_SEG            ;Establish data segment
                        MOV     DS, AX
                        MOV     AL, MEM1                ;Get the given code
                        MOV     BX, OFFSET TABL1
                        XLAT    TABL1                   ;Translate
                        MOV     MEM1, AL                ;Save new code
                        MOV     AL, MEM2                ;Repeat for 2nd code
                        MOV     BX, OFFSET TABL2
                        XLAT    TABL2
                        MOV     MEM2, AL
                        RET                             ;Return to DEBUG program
                EXER66  ENDP
                CODE_SEG        ENDS

                        END     EXER66

            A>
```

```
A>TYPE B:EXER66.LST
```

```
 The IBM Personal Computer Assembler 06-28-84                PAGE    1-1
EXERCISE 6 ( SECTION 6.3 )



                                TITLE   EXERCISE 6 ( SECTION 6.3 )

                                        PAGE    ,132

0000                            STACK_SEG       SEGMENT         STACK 'STACK'
0000    40 [                                    DB              64 DUP(?)
              ??
                    ]

0040                            STACK_SEG       ENDS


0000                            DATA_SEG        SEGMENT         'DATA'
0000    FF FE FD FC FB FA       TABL1           DB              0FFH,0FEH,0FDH,0FCH,0FBH,0FAH,0F9H,0F8H
        F9 F8
0008    0A 0B 0C 0D 0E 0F       TABL2           DB              0AH,0BH,0CH,0DH,0EH,0FH,10H,11H
        10 11
0010    ??                      MEM1            DB              ?
0011    ??                      MEM2            DB              ?
0012                            DATA_SEG        ENDS


0000                            CODE_SEG        SEGMENT         'CODE'
0000                            EXER66          PROC    FAR
                                        ASSUME  CS:CODE_SEG, SS:STACK_SEG, DS:DATA_SEG
```

```
                                ;To return to DEBUG program put return address on the stack

0000  1E                              PUSH    DS
0001  B8 0000                         MOV     AX, 0
0004  50                              PUSH    AX

                                ;Following code implements Exercise 6 Section 6.3

0005  B8  ---- R                      MOV     AX, DATA_SEG           ;Establish data segment
0008  BE D8                           MOV     DS, AX
000A  A0 0010 R                       MOV     AL, MEM1               ;Get the given code
000D  BB 0000 R                       MOV     BX, OFFSET TABL1
0010  D7                              XLAT    TABL1                  ;Translate
0011  A2 0010 R                       MOV     MEM1, AL               ;Save new code
0014  A0 0011 R                       MOV     AL, MEM2               ;Repeat for 2nd code
0017  BB 0008 R                       MOV     BX, OFFSET TABL2
001A  D7                              XLAT    TABL2
001B  A2 0011 R                       MOV     MEM2, AL
001E  CB                              RET                            ;Return to DEBUG program
001F                         EXER66   ENDP
001F                         CODE_SEG          ENDS

                                      END     EXER66
```

```
      The IBM Personal Computer Assembler 06-28-84          PAGE    Symbols-1
      EXERCISE 6 ( SECTION 6.3 )


      Segments and groups:

                          N a m e              Size   align   combine class

          CODE_SEG . . . . . . . . . . . .     001F   PARA    NONE    'CODE'
          DATA_SEG . . . . . . . . . . . .     0012   PARA    NONE    'DATA'
          STACK_SEG. . . . . . . . . . . .     0040   PARA    STACK   'STACK'

      Symbols:

                          N a m e              Type   Value   Attr

          EXER66 . . . . . . . . . . . . .     F PROC 0000    CODE_SEG       Length =001F
          MEM1 . . . . . . . . . . . . . .     L BYTE 0010    DATA_SEG
          MEM2 . . . . . . . . . . . . . .     L BYTE 0011    DATA_SEG
          TABL1. . . . . . . . . . . . . .     L BYTE 0000    DATA_SEG
          TABL2. . . . . . . . . . . . . .     L BYTE 0008    DATA_SEG

      Warning Severe
      Errors  Errors
      0       0

      A>
```

```
      A>DEBUG B:EXER66.EXE
      -U 0 1E
      0915:0000 1E              PUSH    DS
      0915:0001 B80000          MOV     AX,0000
      0915:0004 50              PUSH    AX
      0915:0005 B81709          MOV     AX,0917
      0915:0008 8ED8            MOV     DS,AX
```

```
0915:000A A01000          MOV      AL,[0010]
0915:000D BB0000          MOV      BX,0000
0915:0010 D7              XLAT
0915:0011 A21000          MOV      [0010],AL
0915:0014 A01100          MOV      AL,[0011]
0915:0017 BB0800          MOV      BX,0008
0915:001A D7              XLAT
0915:001B A21100          MOV      [0011],AL
0915:001E CB              RETF
-G A

AX=0917  BX=0000 CX=0032 DX=0000 SP=003C BP=0000 SI=0000 DI=0000
DS=0917  ES=0905 SS=0919 CS=0915 IP=000A  NV UP DI PL NZ NA PO NC
0915:000A A01000          MOV      AL,[0010]                       DS:0010=00
-E 10 5 3
-G 1E

AX=090D  BX=0008 CX=0032 DX=0000 SP=003C BP=0000 SI=0000 DI=0000
DS=0917  ES=0905 SS=0919 CS=0915 IP=001E  NV UP DI PL NZ NA PO NC
0915:001E CB              RETF
-D 10 11
0917:0010  FA 0D                                                  z.
-G

Program terminated normally
-Q
```

7. LDS AX,[0200]

```
A>DEBUG
-A
08F1:0100          LDS AX, [0200]
08F1:0104
-E 200 30 00 40 00
-T

AX=0030  BX=0000 CX=0000 DX=0000 SP=FFEE BP=0000 SI=0000 DI=0000
DS=0040  ES=08F1 SS=08F1 CS=08F1 IP=0104  NV UP DI PL NZ NA PO NC
08F1:0104 89D3          MOV      BX,DX
-Q
```

Section 6.4

8. MOV   DS,0

    MOV   BX,0A10H   ; Pointer for results

    MOV   DX,[0A00H]

    ADD   DX,[0A02H]   ; Generate the sum

    MOV   [BX],DX   ; Save the sum

    MOV   DX,[0A00H]

    SUB   DX,[0A02H]   ; Generate the difference

    MOV   [BX+2],DX   ; Save the difference

    MOV   AX,[0A00H]

    MOV   CX,[0A02H]

    MUL   CX   ; Generate the product

    MOV   [BX+4],AX   ; Save LS part of product

    MOV   [BX+6],DX   ; Save MS part of product

```
        MOV   AX,[0A00H]

        DIV   CX              ; Generate the quotient

        MOV   [BX+8],AX       ; Save the quotient
```

9.
```
    A>DEBUG
    -A
    08F1:0100        DIV BL
    08F1:0102
    -R AX
    AX 0000
    :0123
    -R BX
    BX 0000
    :0010
    -T

    AX=0312  BX=0010  CX=0000  DX=0000  SP=FFEE  BP=0000  SI=0000  DI=0000
    DS=08F1  ES=08F1  SS=08F1  CS=08F1  IP=0102   NV UP DI NG NZ NA PE CY
    08F1:0102 0002         ADD    [BP+SI],AL                       SS:0000=CD
    -Q
```

10. `A>TYPE B:EXER610.ASM`

```
    TITLE   EXERCISE 10 ( SECTION 6.4 )

            PAGE        ,132

    STACK_SEG        SEGMENT         STACK 'STACK'
                     DB              64 DUP(?)
    STACK_SEG        ENDS


    DATA_SEG         SEGMENT         'DATA'
    NUM1             DB       45H
    NUM2             DB       72H
    NUM3             DB       ?
    DATA_SEG         ENDS


    CODE_SEG         SEGMENT         'CODE'
    EXER610          PROC    FAR
            ASSUME  CS:CODE_SEG, SS:STACK_SEG, DS:DATA_SEG

    ;To return to DEBUG program put return address on the stack

            PUSH    DS
            MOV     AX, 0
            PUSH    AX

    ;Following code implements Exercise 10 Section 6.4

            MOV     AX, DATA_SEG         ;Establish data segment
            MOV     DS, AX
            MOV     AL, NUM2             ;Get the 2nd number
            SUB     AL, NUM1             ;Subtract the binary way
            DAS                          ;Apply decimal adjustment
            MOV     NUM3, AL             ;Save the result

            RET                          ;Return to DEBUG program
    EXER610 ENDP
    CODE_SEG         ENDS

            END     EXER610

    A>
```

```
    A>TYPE B:EXER610.LST
```

```
                                    TITLE    EXERCISE 10 ( SECTION 6.4 )

                                        PAGE    ,132

0000                                STACK_SEG      SEGMENT        STACK 'STACK'
0000    40 [                                       DB             64 DUP(?)
                ??
                    ]

0040                                STACK_SEG      ENDS


0000                                DATA_SEG       SEGMENT        'DATA'
0000    45                          NUM1           DB     45H
0001    72                          NUM2           DB     72H
0002    ??                          NUM3           DB     ?
0003                                DATA_SEG       ENDS


0000                                CODE_SEG       SEGMENT        'CODE'
0000                                EXER610        PROC    FAR
                                        ASSUME  CS:CODE_SEG, SS:STACK_SEG, DS:DATA_SEG

                                    ;To return to DEBUG program put return address on the stack

0000    1E                                  PUSH    DS
0001    B8 0000                             MOV     AX, 0
0004    50                                  PUSH    AX

                                    ;Following code implements Exercise 10 Section 6.4

0005    B8  ---- R                          MOV     AX, DATA_SEG        ;Establish data segment
0008    8E D8                               MOV     DS, AX
000A    A0 0001 R                           MOV     AL, NUM2            ;Get the 2nd number
000D    2A 06 0000 R                        SUB     AL, NUM1            ;Subtract the binary way
0011    2F                                  DAS                        ;Apply decimal adjustment
0012    A2 0002 R                           MOV     NUM3, AL            ;Save the result

0015    CB                                  RET                        ;Return to DEBUG program
0016                                EXER610 ENDP
0016                                CODE_SEG       ENDS

                                        END     EXER610
```

Segments and groups:

N a m e	Size	align	combine	class	
CODE_SEG	0016	PARA	NONE	'CODE'	
DATA_SEG	0003	PARA	NONE	'DATA'	
STACK_SEG.	0040	PARA	STACK	'STACK'	

Symbols:

N a m e	Type	Value	Attr	
EXER610.	F PROC	0000	CODE_SEG	Length =0016
NUM1	L BYTE	0000	DATA_SEG	
NUM2	L BYTE	0001	DATA_SEG	
NUM3	L BYTE	0002	DATA_SEG	

Warning Severe
Errors Errors
0   0

A>

```
-DEBUG B:EXER610.EXE
-U 0 15
0915:0000 1E              PUSH    DS
0915:0001 B80000          MOV     AX,0000
0915:0004 50              PUSH    AX
0915:0005 B81709          MOV     AX,0917
0915:0008 8ED8            MOV     DS,AX
0915:000A A00100          MOV     AL,[0001]
0915:000D 2A060000        SUB     AL,[0000]
0915:0011 2F              DAS
0915:0012 A20200          MOV     [0002],AL
0915:0015 CB              RETF
-G 15

AX=0927  BX=0000  CX=0023  DX=0000  SP=003C  BP=0000  SI=0000  DI=0000
DS=0917  ES=0905  SS=0918  CS=0915  IP=0015   NV UP DI PL NZ AC PE NC
0915:0015 CB              RETF
-D DS:0 2
0917:0000  45 72 27                                                  Er'
-G

Program terminated normally
-Q
```

Section 6.5

11. The new contents of AX are the 2's complement of the old contents.

```
A>DEBUG
-A
08F1:0100          NOT AX
08F1:0102          ADD AX, 1
08F1:0105
-R AX
AX 0000
:FFFF
-T

AX=0000  BX=0000  CX=0000  DX=0000  SP=FFEE  BP=0000  SI=0000  DI=0000
DS=08F1  ES=08F1  SS=08F1  CS=08F1  IP=0102   NV UP DI PL NZ NA PO NC
08F1:0102 050100          ADD     AX,0001
-T

AX=0001  BX=0000  CX=0000  DX=0000  SP=FFEE  BP=0000  SI=0000  DI=0000
DS=08F1  ES=08F1  SS=08F1  CS=08F1  IP=0105   NV UP DI PL NZ NA PO NC
08F1:0105 D300            ROL     WORD PTR [BX+SI],CL          DS:0000=20CD
-Q
```

12.   NOT   NUM2

    MOV   CL,AL

    AND   AL,NUM2

    OR   AL,BL

    AND   CL,NUM1

    OR   AL,CL

Section 6.6

13. Condition: $(AX) <$ or $= 0FFF_{16}$ (positive numbers)

```
A>DEBUG
-A
08F1:0100          MOV CL, 4
08F1:0102          SHL AX, CL
08F1:0104          SHR AX, CL
08F1:0106
```

```
-R AX
AX 0000
:1F00
-G 106

AX=0F00  BX=0000  CX=0004  DX=0000  SP=FFEE  BP=0000  SI=0000  DI=0000
DS=08F1  ES=08F1  SS=08F1  CS=08F1  IP=0106  NV UP DI PL NZ NA PE NC
08F1:0106 0000          ADD    [BX+SI],AL                  DS:0000=CD
-R IP
IP 0106
:0100
-R AX
AX 0F00
:0F12
-G 106

AX=0F12  BX=0000  CX=0004  DX=0000  SP=FFEE  BP=0000  SI=0000  DI=0000
DS=08F1  ES=08F1  SS=08F1  CS=08F1  IP=0106  NV UP DI PL NZ NA PE NC
08F1:0106 0000          ADD    [BX+SI],AL                  DS:0000=CD
-Q
```

Section 6.7

14. `A>TYPE B:EXER614.ASM`

```
TITLE    EXERCISE 14 ( SECTION 6.7 )

        PAGE     ,132

STACK_SEG       SEGMENT         STACK 'STACK'
                DB              64 DUP(?)
STACK_SEG       ENDS


CODE_SEG        SEGMENT         'CODE'
EXER614         PROC    FAR
        ASSUME  CS:CODE_SEG, SS:STACK_SEG

;To return to DEBUG program put return address on the stack

        PUSH    DS
        MOV     AX, 0
        PUSH    AX

;Following code implements Exercise 14 Section 6.7

        MOV     BL, AL
        MOV     CL, 5
        SHR     BX, CL
        AND     BX, 1

        RET                             ;Return to DEBUG program
EXER614 ENDP
CODE_SEG        ENDS

        END     EXER614

A>




A>TYPE B:EXER614.LST
```

```
                                    TITLE   EXERCISE 14 ( SECTION 6.7 )

                                    PAGE      ,132

0000                        STACK_SEG        SEGMENT        STACK 'STACK'
0000      40 [                                DB             64 DUP(?)
              ??
                  ]

0040                        STACK_SEG        ENDS


0000                        CODE_SEG         SEGMENT        'CODE'
0000                        EXER614          PROC      FAR
                                    ASSUME  CS:CODE_SEG, SS:STACK_SEG

                            ;To return to DEBUG program put return address on the stack

0000  1E                                PUSH     DS
0001  B8 0000                           MOV      AX, 0
0004  50                                PUSH     AX

                            ;Following code implements Exercise 14 Section 6.7

0005  8A D8                             MOV      BL, AL
0007  B1 05                             MOV      CL, 5
0009  D3 EB                             SHR      BX, CL
000B  81 E3 0001                        AND      BX, 1

000F  CB                                RET                        ;Return to DEBUG program
0010                        EXER614 ENDP
0010                        CODE_SEG         ENDS

                                    END     EXER614
```

Segments and groups:

N a m e	Size	align	combine	class
CODE_SEG	0010	PARA	NONE	'CODE'
STACK_SEG.	0040	PARA	STACK	'STACK'

Symbols:

N a m e	Type	Value	Attr	
EXER614.	F PROC	0000	CODE_SEG	Length =0010

```
Warning Severe
Errors  Errors
0       0

A>
```

```
A>DEBUG B:EXER614.EXE
-U O F
0915:0000 1E            PUSH    DS
0915:0001 B80000        MOV     AX,0000
0915:0004 50            PUSH    AX
0915:0005 8AD8          MOV     BL,AL
0915:0007 B105          MOV     CL,05
0915:0009 D3EB          SHR     BX,CL
0915:000B 81E30100      AND     BX,0001
0915:000F CB            RETF
-G 5

AX=0000  BX=0000  CX=0010  DX=0000  SP=003C  BP=0000  SI=0000  DI=0000
DS=0905  ES=0905  SS=0916  CS=0915  IP=0005   NV UP DI PL NZ NA PO NC
0915:0005 8AD8          MOV     BL,AL
-R AX
AX 0000
:1234
-G F

AX=1234  BX=0001  CX=0005  DX=0000  SP=003C  BP=0000  SI=0000  DI=0000
DS=0905  ES=0905  SS=0916  CS=0915  IP=000F   NV UP DI PL NZ NA PO NC
0915:000F CB            RETF
-G

Program terminated normally
-Q
```

CHAPTER 7

Section 7.2

1. CLI

    LAHF

    MOV   DS,0

    MOV   [A000H],AH

    CLC

Section 7.3

2. Both instructions subtract the operands and change flags as per the result. In a compare instruction the result of the subtraction does not affect either operand. However, in a subtract instruction, the result of the subtraction is saved in the destination operand.

3. The ZF and CF flags are affected as follows:

Instruction	ZF CF
Initial state	NZ NC
MOV BX,1111H	NZ NC
MOV BX,0BBBBH	NZ NC
CMP BX,AX	NZ CY

```
A>DEBUG
-A
08F1:0100          MOV BX, 1111
08F1:0103          MOV AX, BBBB
08F1:0106          CMP BX, AX
08F1:0108
-R F
NV UP DI PL NZ NA PO NC -
-T

AX=0000  BX=1111  CX=0000  DX=0000  SP=FFEE  BP=0000  SI=0000  DI=0000
DS=08F1  ES=08F1  SS=08F1  CS=08F1  IP=0103   NV UP DI PL NZ NA PO NC
08F1:0103 B8BBBB         MOV      AX,BBBB
-T

AX=BBBB  BX=1111  CX=0000  DX=0000  SP=FFEE  BP=0000  SI=0000  DI=0000
DS=08F1  ES=08F1  SS=08F1  CS=08F1  IP=0106   NV UP DI PL NZ NA PO NC
08F1:0106 39C3           CMP      BX,AX
-T

AX=BBBB  BX=1111  CX=0000  DX=0000  SP=FFEE  BP=0000  SI=0000  DI=0000
DS=08F1  ES=08F1  SS=08F1  CS=08F1  IP=0108   NV UP DI PL NZ AC PE CY
08F1:0108 0000           ADD      [BX+SI],AL                    DS:1111=00
-Q
```

Section 7.4

4. (a) $1000_{16} = 16^3 = 4096$ times

   (b)   MOV AX,0
      DLY1: MOV CX,0
      DLY: DEC CX
            JNZ DLY
            DEC AX
            JNZ DLY1
      NXT: NOP

5. A>TYPE B:EXER75.ASM

```
TITLE    EXERCISE 5 ( SECTION 7.4 )

        PAGE      ,132

STACK_SEG        SEGMENT          STACK 'STACK'
                 DB               64 DUP(?)
STACK_SEG        ENDS


DATA_SEG         SEGMENT          'DATA'
FACT             DB        ?
DATA_SEG         ENDS


CODE_SEG         SEGMENT          'CODE'
EXER75           PROC      FAR
        ASSUME   CS:CODE_SEG, SS:STACK_SEG, DS:DATA_SEG

;To return to DEBUG program put return address on the stack

        PUSH      DS
        MOV       AX, 0
        PUSH      AX
```

```
;Following code implements Exercise 10 Section 6.4

          MOV     AX, DATA_SEG              ;Establish data segment
          MOV     DS, AX
          MOV     AL,1
          MOV     CL, 0
NXT:      CMP     CL, DL                    ;All numbers multiplied ?
          JE      DONE                      ;If done, exit
          INC     CL                        ;If not, do next
          MUL     CL
          JMP     NXT
DONE:     MOV     FACT, AL                   ;Save the result

          RET                                ;Return to DEBUG program
EXER75    ENDP
CODE_SEG          ENDS

          END     EXER75

A>
```

A>TYPE B:EXER75.LST

```
 The IBM Personal Computer Assembler 06-28-84              PAGE     1-1
EXERCISE 5 ( SECTION 7.4 )



                         TITLE   EXERCISE 5 ( SECTION 7.4 )

                              PAGE      ,132

 0000                    STACK_SEG       SEGMENT       STACK 'STACK'
 0000     40 [           DB              64 DUP(?)
              ??
                  ]

 0040                    STACK_SEG       ENDS


 0000                    DATA_SEG        SEGMENT       'DATA'
 0000     ??             FACT            DB       ?
 0001                    DATA_SEG        ENDS


 0000                    CODE_SEG        SEGMENT       'CODE'
 0000                    EXER75          PROC     FAR
                              ASSUME   CS:CODE_SEG, SS:STACK_SEG, DS:DATA_SEG

                         ;To return to DEBUG program put return address on the stack

 0000     1E                     PUSH     DS
 0001     B8 0000                MOV      AX, 0
 0004     50                     PUSH     AX
```

```
                              ;Following code implements Exercise 10 Section 6.4

0005  B8  ---- R              MOV     AX, DATA_SEG        ;Establish data segment
0008  8E D8                   MOV     DS, AX
000A  B0 01                   MOV     AL,1
000C  B1 00                   MOV     CL, 0
000E  3A CA        NXT:       CMP     CL, DL              ;All numbers multiplied ?
0010  74 06                   JE      DONE                ;If done, exit
0012  FE C1                   INC     CL                  ;If not, do next
0014  F6 E1                   MUL     CL
0016  EB F6                   JMP     NXT
0018  A2 0000 R    DONE:      MOV     FACT, AL            ;Save the result

001B  CB                      RET                         ;Return to DEBUG program
001C                 EXER75   ENDP
001C                 CODE_SEG          ENDS

                              END     EXER75
```

```
     The IBM Personal Computer Assembler 06-28-84          PAGE    Symbols-1
     EXERCISE 5 ( SECTION 7.4 )


     Segments and groups:

                     N a m e                Size    align   combine class

     CODE_SEG . . . . . . . . . . . .       001C    PARA    NONE    'CODE'
     DATA_SEG . . . . . . . . . . . .       0001    PARA    NONE    'DATA'
     STACK_SEG. . . . . . . . . . . .       0040    PARA    STACK   'STACK'

     Symbols:

                     N a m e                Type    Value   Attr

     DONE . . . . . . . . . . . . . .       L NEAR  0018    CODE_SEG
     EXER75 . . . . . . . . . . . . .       F PROC  0000    CODE_SEG        Length =001C
     FACT . . . . . . . . . . . . . .       L BYTE  0000    DATA_SEG
     NXT. . . . . . . . . . . . . . .       L NEAR  000E    CODE_SEG

     Warning Severe
     Errors  Errors
     0       0

     A>
```

```
     A> DEBUG B:EXER75.EXE
     -U 0 1B
     0915:0000 1E            PUSH    DS
     0915:0001 B80000        MOV     AX,0000
     0915:0004 50            PUSH    AX
     0915:0005 B81709        MOV     AX,0917
     0915:0008 8ED8          MOV     DS,AX
     0915:000A B001          MOV     AL,01
     0915:000C B100          MOV     CL,00
     0915:000E 3ACA          CMP     CL,DL
     0915:0010 7406          JZ      0018
```

```
0915:0012 FEC1              INC    CL
0915:0014 F6E1              MUL    CL
0915:0016 EBF6              JMP    000E
0915:0018 A20000            MOV    [0000],AL
0915:001B CB                RETF
-G 5


AX=0000  BX=0000  CX=0021  DX=0000  SP=003C  BP=0000  SI=0000  DI=0000
DS=0905  ES=0905  SS=0918  CS=0915  IP=0005   NV UP DI PL NZ NA PO NC
0915:0005 B81709            MOV    AX,0917
-R DX
DX 0000
:5
-G 1B


AX=0078  BX=0000  CX=0005  DX=0005  SP=003C  BP=0000  SI=0000  DI=0000
DS=0917  ES=0905  SS=0918  CS=0915  IP=001B   NV UP DI PL ZR NA PE NC
0915:001B CB                RETF
-D DS:0 0
0917:0000  78                                                          x
-G

Program terminated normally
-Q
```

Section 7.5

6. Add the instruction

$$\text{ADD DX,CX}$$

just before the RET instruction in the subroutine SUM. For execution see the debug sequence for Problem 7.

7.
```
A>TYPE B:EXER77.ASM


TITLE    EXERCISE 7 ( SECTION 7.5 )

         PAGE       ,132

STACK_SEG          SEGMENT         STACK 'STACK'
                   DB              64 DUP(?)
STACK_SEG          ENDS


CODE_SEG           SEGMENT         'CODE'
EXER77  PROC       FAR
        ASSUME  CS:CODE_SEG, SS:STACK_SEG

;To return to DEBUG program put return address on the stack

        PUSH      DS
        MOV       AX, 0
        PUSH      AX

;Following code implements Exercise 7 ( Section 7.5 )

        CALL      SUM
        RET

SUM     PROC      NEAR
        PUSH      DX
        MOV       DX, AX
        ADD       DX, BX        ; DX = AX + BX
```

```
                        ADD      DX, CX           ; DX = AX + BX + CX
                        POP      DX
                        RET
            SUM         ENDP

            EXER77  ENDP
            CODE_SEG          ENDS

                        END      EXER77

        A>
```

A>TYPE B:EXER77.LST

```
 The IBM Personal Computer Assembler 06-28-84              PAGE     1-1
 EXERCISE 7 ( SECTION 7.5 )



                        TITLE    EXERCISE 7 ( SECTION 7.5 )

                                 PAGE        ,132

0000                    STACK_SEG        SEGMENT          STACK 'STACK'
0000      40 [                           DB               64 DUP(?)
               ??
                    ]

0040                    STACK_SEG        ENDS


0000                    CODE_SEG         SEGMENT          'CODE'
0000                    EXER77  PROC     FAR
                                 ASSUME  CS:CODE_SEG, SS:STACK_SEG

                        ;To return to DEBUG program put return address on the stack

0000   1E                        PUSH     DS
0001   B8 0000                   MOV      AX, 0
0004   50                        PUSH     AX

                        ;Following code implements Exercise 7 ( Section 7.5 )

0005   E8 0009 R                 CALL     SUM
0008   CB                        RET

0009                    SUM      PROC     NEAR
0009   52                        PUSH     DX
000A   8B D0                     MOV      DX, AX
000C   03 D3                     ADD      DX, BX           ; DX = AX + BX
000E   03 D1                     ADD      DX, CX           ; DX = AX + BX + CX
0010   5A                        POP      DX
0011   C3                        RET
0012                    SUM      ENDP

0012                    EXER77  ENDP
0012                    CODE_SEG          ENDS

                        END      EXER77
```

```
    The IBM Personal Computer Assembler 06-28-84          PAGE    Symbols-1
    EXERCISE 7 ( SECTION 7.5 )


    Segments and groups:

                N a m e                     Size    align   combine class

    CODE_SEG . . . . . . . . . . . . .      0012    PARA    NONE   'CODE'
    STACK_SEG. . . . . . . . . . . .        0040    PARA    STACK  'STACK'

    Symbols:

                N a m e                     Type    Value   Attr

    EXER77 . . . . . . . . . . . . .        F PROC  0000    CODE_SEG      Length =0012
    SUM. . . . . . . . . . . . . . .        N PROC  0009    CODE_SEG      Length =0009

    Warning Severe
    Errors  Errors
    0       0

    A>
```

```
    A>DEBUG B:EXER77.EXE
    -U 0 11
    0915:0000 1E              PUSH     DS
    0915:0001 B80000          MOV      AX,0000
    0915:0004 50              PUSH     AX
    0915:0005 E80100          CALL     0009
    0915:0008 CB              RETF
    0915:0009 52              PUSH     DX
    0915:000A 8BD0            MOV      DX,AX
    0915:000C 03D3            ADD      DX,BX
    0915:000E 03D1            ADD      DX,CX
    0915:0010 5A              POP      DX
    0915:0011 C3              RET
    -G 5

    AX=0000  BX=0000  CX=0012  DX=0000  SP=003C  BP=0000  SI=0000  DI=0000
    DS=0905  ES=0905  SS=0917  CS=0915  IP=0005   NV UP DI PL NZ NA PO NC
    0915:0005 E80100          CALL     0009
    -R AX
    AX 0000
    :FFE0
    -R BX
    BX 0000
    :1B
    -R CX
    CX 0012
    :A
    -G 10

    AX=FFE0  BX=001B  CX=000A  DX=0005  SP=0038  BP=0000  SI=0000  DI=0000
    DS=0905  ES=0905  SS=0917  CS=0915  IP=0010   NV UP DI PL NZ AC PE CY
    0915:0010 5A              POP      DX
    -G

    Program terminated normally
    -Q
```

8. BCD2BIN: .

     PUSH CX   ; Save registers on the stack

     PUSH AX

     MOV   CH,10   ; (CH)=10, decimal base

```
        MOV     CL,4        ; (CL)=4, shift count

        MOV     AL,DL       ; (AL)=(DL)=BCD number

        SHR     AL,CL       ; Extract MSD

        AND     AL,OFH

        MUL     AL,CH       ; (AL)=MSD*10

        AND     DL,OFH      ; (DL)=LSD

        ADD     DL,AL       ; (DL) = LSD+MSD*10

        POP     AX          ; Restore registers

        POP     CX

        RET
```

Section 7.6

```
  9.                        TITLE    EXERCISE 9 ( SECTION 7.6 )

                            PAGE       ,132

0000                        STACK_SEG        SEGMENT       STACK 'STACK'
0000    40 [                                 DB            64 DUP(?)
            ??
                  ]

0040                        STACK_SEG        ENDS


0000                        CODE_SEG         SEGMENT       'CODE'
0000                        EXER77  PROC     FAR
                            ASSUME  CS:CODE_SEG, SS:STACK_SEG

                            ;To return to DEBUG program put return address on the stack

0000    1E                          PUSH     DS
0001    B8 0000                     MOV      AX, O
0004    50                          PUSH     AX

                            ;Following code implements Exercise 9 ( Section 7.6 )

0005    B2 AB                       MOV      DL, OABH
0007    B8 OB00                     MOV      AX, OB00H
000A    8E D8                       MOV      DS, AX
000C    BE 0010                     MOV      SI, 10H
000F    B9 00A0                     MOV      CX, OAOH
0012    46              AGAIN:      INC      SI
0013    38 14                       CMP      [SI], DL
0015    EO FB                       LOOPNE   AGAIN

0017    CB                          RET                     ;Return to DEBUG program
0018                        EXER77  ENDP
0018                        CODE_SEG         ENDS

                            END      EXER77
```

```
                                    TITLE   EXERCISE 9 ( SECTION 7.6 )

                                            PAGE    ,132

0000                     STACK_SEG          SEGMENT        STACK 'STACK'
0000      40 [          DB             64 DUP(?)
              ??
                  ]

0040                     STACK_SEG          ENDS


0000                     CODE_SEG           SEGMENT        'CODE'
0000                     EXER77  PROC       FAR
                                 ASSUME   CS:CODE_SEG, SS:STACK_SEG

                         ;To return to DEBUG program put return address on the stack

0000  1E                         PUSH       DS
0001  B8 0000                    MOV        AX, 0
0004  50                         PUSH       AX

                         ;Following code implements Exercise 9 ( Section 7.6 )

0005  B2 AB                      MOV        DL, 0ABH
0007  B8 0B00                    MOV        AX, 0B00H
000A  8E D8                      MOV        DS, AX
000C  BE 0010                    MOV        SI, 10H
000F  B9 00A0                    MOV        CX, 0A0H
0012  46             AGAIN:      INC        SI
0013  38 14                      CMP        [SI], DL
0015  E0 FB                      LOOPNE     AGAIN

0017  CB                         RET                      ;Return to DEBUG program
0018                     EXER77  ENDP
0018                     CODE_SEG           ENDS

                                 END        EXER77
```

Segments and groups:

Name	Size	align	combine	class
CODE_SEG	0018	PARA	NONE	'CODE'
STACK_SEG.	0040	PARA	STACK	'STACK'

Symbols:

Name	Type	Value	Attr	
AGAIN.	L NEAR	0012	CODE_SEG	
EXER77	F PROC	0000	CODE_SEG	Length =0018

Warning Severe
Errors Errors
0   0

A>

```
A>DEBUG B:EXER79.EXE
-U 0 17
0915:0000 1E              PUSH    DS
0915:0001 B80000          MOV     AX,0000
0915:0004 50              PUSH    AX
0915:0005 B2AB            MOV     DL,AB
0915:0007 B8000B          MOV     AX,0B00
0915:000A 8ED8            MOV     DS,AX
0915:000C BE1000          MOV     SI,0010
0915:000F B9A000          MOV     CX,00A0
0915:0012 46              INC     SI
0915:0013 3814            CMP     [SI],DL
0915:0015 E0FB            LOOPNZ  0012
0915:0017 CB              RETF
-G 12


AX=0B00   BX=0000   CX=00A0   DX=00AB   SP=003C   BP=0000   SI=0010   DI=0000
DS=0B00   ES=0905   SS=0917   CS=0915   IP=0012       NV UP DI PL NZ NA PO NC
0915:0012 46              INC     SI
-G 17


AX=0B00   BX=0000   CX=0000   DX=00AB   SP=003C   BP=0000   SI=00B0   DI=0000
DS=0B00   ES=0905   SS=0917   CS=0915   IP=0017       NV UP DI PL NZ AC PE CY
0915:0017 CB              RETF
-D 10 AF
0B00:0010  00 00 00 00 00 00 00 00-00 00 00 00 00 00 00 00   ................
0B00:0020  00 00 00 00 00 00 00 00-00 00 00 00 00 00 00 00   ................
0B00:0030  00 00 00 00 00 00 00 00-00 00 00 00 00 00 00 00   ................
0B00:0040  00 00 00 00 00 00 00 00-00 00 00 00 00 00 00 00   ................
0B00:0050  00 00 00 00 00 00 00 00-00 00 00 00 00 00 00 00   ................
0B00:0060  00 00 00 00 00 00 00 00-00 00 00 00 00 00 00 00   ................
0B00:0070  00 00 00 00 00 00 00 00-00 00 00 00 00 00 00 00   ................
0B00:0080  00 00 00 00 00 00 00 00-00 00 00 00 00 00 00 00   ................
0B00:0090  00 00 00 00 00 00 00 00-00 00 00 00 00 00 00 00   ................
0B00:00A0  00 00 00 00 00 00 00 00-00 00 00 00 00 00 00 00   ................
-G

Program terminated normally
-Q
```

10.
```
                              MOV   CX,1000H
              DLY:  LOOP DLY
              NEXT: NOP
```

Notice that in terms of real time, this delay loop is not exactly the same as that in Problem 4. This is due to the reason that execution of the LOOP instruction takes less clock cycles as compared to the DEC CX and JNZ instructions in the earlier example.

11.
```
                              MOV   AX,0
              DLY1: MOV   CX,0
              DLY:  LOOP DLY
                    DEC   AX
                    JNZ   DLY1
              NXT:  NOP
```

Section 7.7

12. A>TYPE B:EXER712.ASM

```
TITLE   EXERCISE 12 ( SECTION 7.7 )

        PAGE    ,132

STACK_SEG       SEGMENT         STACK 'STACK'
                DB              64 DUP(?)
STACK_SEG       ENDS
```

```
DATA_SEG        SEGMENT        'DATA'
MASTER          DW             100 DUP(?)
COPY            DW             100 DUP(?)
DATA_SEG        ENDS


CODE_SEG        SEGMENT        'CODE'
EXER712 PROC    FAR
        ASSUME  CS:CODE_SEG, SS:STACK_SEG, DS:DATA_SEG, ES:DATA_SEG

;To return to DEBUG program put return address on the stack

        PUSH    DS
        MOV     AX, 0
        PUSH    AX

;Following code implements Exercise 12 ( Section 7.7 )

        MOV     AX, DATA_SEG
        MOV     DS, AX
        MOV     ES, AX
        CLD
        MOV     CX, 100
        MOV     SI, OFFSET MASTER
        MOV     DI, OFFSET COPY
REPNE   CMPS    MASTER, COPY

        RET                         ;Return to DEBUG program
EXER712 ENDP
CODE_SEG        ENDS

        END     EXER712

A>
```

```
A>TYPE B:EXER712.LST




 The IBM Personal Computer Assembler 06-28-84          PAGE   1-1
EXERCISE 12 ( SECTION 7.7 )




                              TITLE   EXERCISE 12 ( SECTION 7.7 )

                                  PAGE      ,132

0000                          STACK_SEG     SEGMENT        STACK 'STACK'
0000        40 [              DB             64 DUP(?)
                ??
                      ]

0040                          STACK_SEG     ENDS


0000                          DATA_SEG      SEGMENT        'DATA'
0000        64 [              MASTER        DW             100 DUP(?)
                ????
                      ]

00C8        64 [              COPY          DW             100 DUP(?)
                ????
                      ]

0190                          DATA_SEG      ENDS
```

```
0000                          CODE_SEG      SEGMENT        'CODE'
0000                          EXER712 PROC  FAR
                              ASSUME  CS:CODE_SEG, SS:STACK_SEG, DS:DATA_SEG, ES:DATA_SEG

                              ;To return to DEBUG program put return address on the stack

0000  1E                          PUSH      DS
0001  B8 0000                     MOV       AX, 0
0004  50                          PUSH      AX

                              ;Following code implements Exercise 12 ( Section 7.7 )

0005  B8  ---- R                  MOV       AX, DATA_SEG
0008  8E D8                       MOV       DS, AX
000A  8E C0                       MOV       ES, AX
000C  FC                          CLD
000D  B9 0064                     MOV       CX, 100
0010  BE 0000 R                   MOV       SI, OFFSET MASTER
0013  BF 00C8 R                   MOV       DI, OFFSET COPY
0016  F2/ A7              REPNE    CMPS      MASTER, COPY

0018  CB                          RET                       ;Return to DEBUG program
0019                          EXER712 ENDP
0019                          CODE_SEG      ENDS

                              END      EXER712
```

```
        The IBM Personal Computer Assembler 06-28-84            PAGE    Symbols-1
        EXERCISE 12 ( SECTION 7.7 )


        Segments and groups:

                        N a m e                 Size   align   combine class

        CODE_SEG . . . . . . . . . . . .        0019   PARA    NONE    'CODE'
        DATA_SEG . . . . . . . . . . . .        0190   PARA    NONE    'DATA'
        STACK_SEG. . . . . . . . . . . .        0040   PARA    STACK   'STACK'

        Symbols:

                        N a m e                 Type   Value   Attr

        COPY . . . . . . . . . . . . . .        L WORD  00C8   DATA_SEG       Length =0064
        EXER712. . . . . . . . . . . . .        F PROC  0000   CODE_SEG       Length =0019
        MASTER . . . . . . . . . . . . .        L WORD  0000   DATA_SEG       Length =0064

        Warning Severe
        Errors  Errors
        0       0

        A>
```

```
        A>DEBUG B:EXER712.EXE
        -U 0 18
        0915:0000 1E              PUSH    DS
        0915:0001 B80000          MOV     AX,0000
        0915:0004 50              PUSH    AX
        0915:0005 B81709          MOV     AX,0917
        0915:0008 8ED8            MOV     DS,AX
        0915:000A 8EC0            MOV     ES,AX
        0915:000C FC              CLD
        0915:000D B96400          MOV     CX,0064
        0915:0010 BE0000          MOV     SI,0000
        0915:0013 BFC800          MOV     DI,00C8
        0915:0016 F2              REPNZ
```

```
0915:0017 A7              CMPSW
0915:0018 CB              RETF
-G 18


AX=0917  BX=0000  CX=005A  DX=0000  SP=003C  BP=0000  SI=0014  DI=00DC
DS=0917  ES=0917  SS=0930  CS=0915  IP=0018    NV UP DI PL ZR NA PE NC
0915:0018 CB              RETF
-D 0
0917:0000  78 72 27 FC FB FA F9 F8-0A 0B 0C 0D 0E 0F 10 11   xr'{zyx........
0917:0010  FA 0D 00 00 00 00 2E 0B-01 00 42 02 05 00 00 00   z.........B.....
0917:0020  00 00 00 00 00 00 2E 0B-01 00 42 02 00 00 AB 00   ..........B...+.
0917:0030  B0 00 00 00 00 00 00 0B-00 06 02 00 05 09 16 F0   0..............p
0917:0040  00 00 00 00 00 00 17 09-00 06 02 00 05 09 46 F0   ..............Fp
0917:0050  00 00 00 00 00 00 17 09-00 06 02 00 05 09 02 F0   ..............p
0917:0060  00 00 00 00 00 00 00 00-00 00 00 00 00 00 00 00   ................
0917:0070  00 00 00 00 00 00 00 00-00 00 00 00 00 00 00 00   ................
-D C8
0917:00C8  00 00 00 00 00 00 00 00 00                        .........
0917:00D0  00 00 00 00 00 00 00 00-00 00 00 00 00 00 00 00   ................
0917:00E0  00 00 00 00 00 00 00 00-00 00 00 00 00 00 00 00   ................
0917:00F0  00 00 00 00 00 00 00 00-00 00 00 00 00 00 00 00   ................
0917:0100  00 00 00 00 00 00 00 00-00 00 00 00 00 00 00 00   ................
0917:0110  00 00 00 00 00 00 00 00-00 00 00 00 00 00 00 00   ................
0917:0120  00 00 00 00 00 00 00 00-00 00 00 00 00 00 00 00   ................
0917:0130  00 00 00 00 00 00 00 00-00 00 00 00 00 00 00 00   ................
0917:0140  00 00 00 00 00 00 00 00                           ........
-G

Program terminated normally
-Q
```

CHAPTER 8

Section 8.2

1. A>TYPE B:EXER81.ASM

```
TITLE    EXERCISE 1 ( SECTION 8.2 )

         PAGE      ,132

STACK_SEG        SEGMENT        STACK 'STACK'
                 DB             64 DUP(?)
STACK_SEG        ENDS


CODE_SEG         SEGMENT        'CODE'
EXER81  PROC     FAR
        ASSUME   CS:CODE_SEG, SS:STACK_SEG

;To return to DEBUG program put return address on the stack

        PUSH     DS
        MOV      AX, 0
        PUSH     AX

;Following code implements Exercise 1 ( Section 8.2 )

        MOV      CX, 3         ;Form 3(AX)
        IMUL     CX
        MOV      DI, AX        ;(DI) = 3(AX)
        MOV      CX, 7         ;Form 7(BX)
        MOV      AX, BX
        IMUL     CX
        MOV      DX, DI        ;(DX) = 3(AX)
        ADD      DX, AX        ;(DX) = 3(AX) + 7(BX)
```

```
            RET                              ;Return to DEBUG program
EXER81   ENDP
CODE_SEG         ENDS

         END    EXER81

A>


A>DEBUG B:EXER81.EXE
-U 0 17
0915:0000 1E              PUSH    DS
0915:0001 B80000          MOV     AX,0000
0915:0004 50              PUSH    AX
0915:0005 B90300          MOV     CX,0003
0915:0008 F7E9            IMUL    CX
0915:000A 8BF8            MOV     DI,AX
0915:000C B90700          MOV     CX,0007
0915:000F 8BC3            MOV     AX,BX
0915:0011 F7E9            IMUL    CX
0915:0013 8BD7            MOV     DX,DI
0915:0015 03D0            ADD     DX,AX
0915:0017 CB              RETF
-G 5

AX=0000  BX=0000  CX=0018  DX=0000  SP=003C  BP=0000  SI=0000  DI=0000
DS=0905  ES=0905  SS=0917  CS=0915  IP=0005   NV UP DI PL NZ NA PO NC
0915:0005 B90300          MOV     CX,0003
-R AX
AX 0000
:FFFF
-R BX
BX 0000
:3
-G 17

AX=0015  BX=0003  CX=0007  DX=0012  SP=003C  BP=0000  SI=0000  DI=FFFD
DS=0905  ES=0905  SS=0917  CS=0915  IP=0017   NV UP DI PL NZ AC PE CY
0915:0017 CB              RETF
-G

Program terminated normally
-Q
```

2. In the program that follows, it was assumed that the intermediate and final results do not exceed 16 bits.

```
A>TYPE B:EXER82.ASM


TITLE    EXERCISE 2 ( SECTION 8.2 )

         PAGE    ,132

STACK_SEG        SEGMENT         STACK 'STACK'
                 DB              64 DUP(?)
STACK_SEG        ENDS


CODE_SEG         SEGMENT         'CODE'
EXER82   PROC    FAR
         ASSUME  CS:CODE_SEG, SS:STACK_SEG

;To return to DEBUG program put return address on the stack

         PUSH    DS
         MOV     AX, 0
         PUSH    AX
```

```
;Following code implements Exercise 2 ( Section 8.2 )

        MOV     CL, 3           ;Form 1/8(AX)
        SAR     AX, CL
        MOV     DX, AX          ; (DX) = 1/8(AX)
        ADD     DX, BX          ; (DX) = 1/8(AX) + (BX)
        SHL     BX, CL          ;Form 8(BX)
        ADD     DX, BX          ; (DX) = 1/8(AX) + 9(BX)
        SHL     BX, 1           ;Form 16(BX)
        ADD     DX, BX          ; (DX) = 1/8(AX) + 25(BX)

        RET                     ;Return to DEBUG program
EXER82  ENDP
CODE_SEG        ENDS

        END     EXER82

A>


A>DEBUG B:EXER82.EXE
-U 0 15
0915:0000 1E            PUSH    DS
0915:0001 B80000        MOV     AX,0000
0915:0004 50            PUSH    AX
0915:0005 B103          MOV     CL,03
0915:0007 D3F8          SAR     AX,CL
0915:0009 8BD0          MOV     DX,AX
0915:000B 03D3          ADD     DX,BX
0915:000D D3E3          SHL     BX,CL
0915:000F 03D3          ADD     DX,BX
0915:0011 D1E3          SHL     BX,1
0915:0013 03D3          ADD     DX,BX
0915:0015 CB            RETF
-G 5

AX=0000  BX=0000  CX=0016  DX=0000  SP=003C  BP=0000  SI=0000  DI=0000
DS=0905  ES=0905  SS=0917  CS=0915  IP=0005    NV UP DI PL NZ NA PO NC
0915:0005 B103          MOV     CL,03
-R AX
AX 0000
:10
-R BX
BX 0000
:1
-G 15

AX=0002  BX=0010  CX=0003  DX=001B  SP=003C  BP=0000  SI=0000  DI=0000
DS=0905  ES=0905  SS=0917  CS=0915  IP=0015    NV UP DI PL NZ NA PE NC
0915:0015 CB            RETF
-G

Program terminated normally
-Q
```

Section 8.3

3. In the program of Fig. 8.3(a), replace the statement

$$PATTERN = 5555H$$

with

$$PATTERN = 0AAAAH$$

For the DEBUG operation, follow the sequence in Fig. 8.3(c). The DUMP command will show AA_{16} as the contents of memory locations 1000_{16} through $107F_{16}$.

4. A>TYPE B:EXER84.ASM

```
TITLE   EXERCISE 4 ( SECTION 8.4 )

        PAGE    ,132

STACK_SEG       SEGMENT         STACK 'STACK'
                DB              64 DUP(?)
STACK_SEG       ENDS


PATTERN         =       5555H
PATT2           =       0AAAAH
MEM_START       =       1000H
MEM_STOP        =       107FH
DSEG_ADDR       =       0H


CODE_SEG        SEGMENT         'CODE'
EX84    PROC    FAR
        ASSUME  CS:CODE_SEG, SS:STACK_SEG

;To return to DEBUG program put return address on the stack

        PUSH    DS
        MOV     AX, 0
        PUSH    AX

;Following code implements Exercise 4 ( Section 8.3 )

        MOV     AX, DSEG_ADDR           ;Establish data segment
        MOV     DS, AX
        MOV     SI, MEM_START           ;Next memory address
        MOV     CX, (MEM_STOP-MEM_START+1)/2   ;No of locations
AGAIN:  MOV     WORD PTR [SI], PATTERN  ;Write the pattern
        MOV     AX, [SI]                ;Read it back
        CMP     AX, PATTERN             ;Same ?
        JNE     BADMEM
        MOV     WORD PTR [SI], PATT2    ;Repeat for the other pattern
        MOV     AX, [SI]
        CMP     AX, PATT2
        JNE     BADMEM
        INC     SI                      ;Repeat for next location
        INC     SI
        LOOP    AGAIN
        MOV     DX, 1234H               ;Code for test passed
        JMP     DONE
BADMEM: MOV     DX, 0BADH               ;Code for test failed
DONE:   NOP

        RET                             ;Return to DEBUG program
EX84    ENDP
CODE_SEG        ENDS

        END     EX84

A>


A>DEBUG B:EXER84.EXE
-U
0915:0000 1E              PUSH    DS
0915:0001 B80000          MOV     AX,0000
0915:0004 50              PUSH    AX
0915:0005 B80000          MOV     AX,0000
0915:0008 8ED8            MOV     DS,AX
0915:000A BE0010          MOV     SI,1000
0915:000D B94000          MOV     CX,0040
0915:0010 C7045555        MOV     WORD PTR [SI],5555
0915:0014 8B04            MOV     AX,[SI]
0915:0016 3D5555          CMP     AX,5555
0915:0019 7515            JNZ     0030
```

```
0915:001B C704AAAA    MOV     WORD PTR [SI],AAAA
0915:001F 8B04        MOV     AX,[SI]
-U 22 34
0915:0022 AA          STOSB
0915:0023 AA          STOSB
0915:0024 750A        JNZ     0030
0915:0026 46          INC     SI
0915:0027 46          INC     SI
0915:0028 E2E6        LOOP    0010
0915:002A BA3412      MOV     DX,1234
0915:002D EB04        JMP     0033
0915:002F 90          NOP
0915:0030 BAAD0B      MOV     DX,0BAD
0915:0033 90          NOP
0915:0034 CB          RETF
-G 34

AX=AAAA  BX=0000  CX=0000  DX=1234  SP=003C  BP=0000  SI=1080  DI=0000
DS=0000  ES=0905  SS=0919  CS=0915  IP=0034   NV UP DI PL NZ AC PO NC
0915:0034 CB          RETF
-D 100- 107F
0000:1000  AA AA AA AA AA AA AA AA-AA AA AA AA AA AA AA AA  ****************
0000:1010  AA AA AA AA AA AA AA AA-AA AA AA AA AA AA AA AA  ****************
0000:1020  AA AA AA AA AA AA AA AA-AA AA AA AA AA AA AA AA  ****************
0000:1030  AA AA AA AA AA AA AA AA-AA AA AA AA AA AA AA AA  ****************
0000:1040  AA AA AA AA AA AA AA AA-AA AA AA AA AA AA AA AA  ****************
0000:1050  AA AA AA AA AA AA AA AA-AA AA AA AA AA AA AA AA  ****************
0000:1060  AA AA AA AA AA AA AA AA-AA AA AA AA AA AA AA AA  ****************
0000:1070  AA AA AA AA AA AA AA AA-AA AA AA AA AA AA AA AA  ****************
-G

Program terminated normally
-Q
```

Section 8.5

5. In the program of Fig. 8.7(a), replace the statement

$$\text{JLE CC}$$

by

$$\text{JGE CC}$$

For the DEBUG operation, follow the sequence in Fig. 8.7(c). The DUMP command will show that the numbers are arranged in descending order.

6. The program in Fig. 8.7(a) sorts an array located from address $A400_{16}$ through $A41F_{16}$. Thus the median word will be at locations $A40E_{16}$ and $A410_{16}$. If both these words are not the same, we may take their average. On the other hand, if the program in Fig. 8.7(a) is changed to sort an array with an odd number of elements, there is only one median value. For the case in Example 8.8, we can use the same program to find the median value. The two median words can be averaged by adding the following instructions before the RET instruction

```
MOV AX,[0A0E]
ADD AX,[0A10]
SAR AX,1
```

Section 8.6

7. A>TYPE B:EXER87.ASM

```
    TITLE    EXERCISE 7 ( SECTION 8.6 )

             PAGE      ,132

    STACK_SEG          SEGMENT        STACK 'STACK'
                       DB             64 DUP(?)
    STACK_SEG          ENDS


    DATA_SEG           SEGMENT        'DATA'
    SERIES             DW             10 DUP(?)
    DATA_SEG           ENDS


    CODE_SEG           SEGMENT        'CODE'
    EXER87  PROC       FAR
            ASSUME  CS:CODE_SEG, SS:STACK_SEG, DS:DATA_SEG

    ;To return to DEBUG program put return address on the stack

            PUSH       DS
            MOV        AX, 0
            PUSH       AX

    ;Following code implements Exercise 7 ( Section 8.6 )

            MOV        AX, DATA_SEG          ;Establish data segment
            MOV        DS, AX
            LEA        DI, SERIES            ;Pointer to next element
            MOV        CX, 10               ;Initialize count
            MOV        AX, 5                ;First element
    NXTNM:  MOV        [DI], AX             ;Save next element
            SHL        AX, 1                ;Generate next element
            INC        DI                   ;Point to next element
            INC        DI
            LOOP       NXTNM                ;If not done, go back
            RET

    EXER87  ENDP
    CODE_SEG           ENDS

            END        EXER87

    A>
```

```
A>DEBUG B:EXER87.EXE
-U 0 1C
0915:0000 1E         PUSH     DS
0915:0001 B80000     MOV      AX,0000
0915:0004 50         PUSH     AX
0915:0005 B81709     MOV      AX,0917
0915:0008 8ED8       MOV      DS,AX
0915:000A 8D3E0000   LEA      DI,[0000]
0915:000E B90A00     MOV      CX,000A
0915:0011 B80500     MOV      AX,0005
0915:0014 8905       MOV      [DI],AX
0915:0016 D1E0       SHL      AX,1
0915:0018 47         INC      DI
0915:0019 47         INC      DI
0915:001A E2F8       LOOP     0014
0915:001C CB         RETF
-G 1C
```

```
AX=1400  BX=0000  CX=0000  DX=0000  SP=003C  BP=0000  SI=0000  DI=0014
DS=0917  ES=0905  SS=0919  CS=0915  IP=001C   NV UP DI PL NZ NA PE NC
0915:001C CB          RETF
-D DS:0 10
0917:0000  05 00 0A 00 14 00 28 00-50 00 A0 00 40 01 80 02   ......(.P. .@...
0917:0010  00                                                .
-G

Program terminated normally
-Q
```

Section 8.7

8. The program in Fig. 8.11(a) must be modified as follows: change EBCDIC to ASCII and ASCII to EBCDIC; change the entries in the new ASCII_CHAR table to valid ASCII characters; change the entries in the new ASCII_TO_EBCDIC conversion table so that an entry at an offset address equal to an ASCII value is the corresponding EBCDIC code.

9. The source program and debug sequence (for hexadecimal number 63) are as follows:

```
A>TYPE B:EXER89.ASM

TITLE    EXERCISE 9 ( SECTION 8.7 )

         PAGE    ,132

STACK_SEG       SEGMENT         STACK 'STACK'
                DB              64 DUP(?)
STACK_SEG       ENDS


DATA_SEG        SEGMENT         'DATA'
HEXNUM          DB              ?
DECNUM          DB              ?
DATA_SEG        ENDS


CODE_SEG        SEGMENT         'CODE'
EXER89  PROC    FAR
        ASSUME  CS:CODE_SEG, SS:STACK_SEG, DS:DATA_SEG

;To return to DEBUG program put return address on the stack

        PUSH    DS
        MOV     AX, 0
        PUSH    AX

;Following code implements Exercise 9 ( Section 8.7)

        MOV     AX, DATA_SEG    ;Establish data segment
        MOV     DS, AX
        MOV     AL, 0           ;DECNUM = 0
        MOV     CX, 8           ;Count = 8
        MOV     DL, HEXNUM      ;Get the Hex number
NXTBIT:
        SHL     AL, 1           ;DECNUM = DECNUM*2
        DAA                     ;Convert to Decimal
        SHL     DL, 1           ;Extract MSB
        ADC     AL, 0           ;DECNUM = DECNUM + MSB
        DAA                     ;Convert to Decimal
        LOOP    NXTBIT          ;Repeat for next bit
        MOV     DECNUM, AL      ;Save Decimal number

        RET                     ;Return to DEBUG program
EXER89  ENDP
CODE_SEG        ENDS

        END     EXER89

A>
```

```
A>DEBUG B:EXER89.EXE
-U 0 20
0915:0000 1E            PUSH    DS
0915:0001 B80000        MOV     AX,0000
0915:0004 50            PUSH    AX
0915:0005 B81809        MOV     AX,0918
0915:0008 8ED8          MOV     DS,AX
0915:000A B000          MOV     AL,00
0915:000C B90800        MOV     CX,0008
0915:000F 8A160000      MOV     DL,[0000]
0915:0013 D0E0          SHL     AL,1
0915:0015 27            DAA
0915:0016 D0E2          SHL     DL,1
0915:0018 1400          ADC     AL,00
0915:001A 27            DAA
0915:001B E2F6          LOOP    0013
0915:001D A20100        MOV     [0001],AL
0915:0020 CB            RETF
-G F

AX=0900  BX=0000  CX=0008  DX=0000  SP=003C  BP=0000  SI=0000  DI=0000
DS=0918  ES=0905  SS=0919  CS=0915  IP=000F   NV UP DI PL NZ NA PO NC
0915:000F 8A160000      MOV     DL,[0000]                          DS:0000=00
-E 0 63
-D 0 1
0918:0000  63 00                                               c.
-G 20

AX=0999  BX=0000  CX=0000  DX=0000  SP=003C  BP=0000  SI=0000  DI=0000
DS=0918  ES=0905  SS=0919  CS=0915  IP=0020   NV UP DI NG NZ NA PE NC
0915:0020 CB            RETF
-D 0 1
0918:0000  63 99                                               c.
-G

Program terminated normally
-Q
```

Section 8.8

10. For a 1000 Hz tone, the divisor is given as

$$NNNN = 1.19 \text{ MHz}/1000 \text{ Hz} = 1190$$

Thus in Fig. 8.14(a), change the instruction

```
            MOV  AX,319H
```

to

```
            MOV  AX,1190
```

Next for 300 ms duration, the delay constant X is given as

$$X = 3_{10} \times 5064_{16} = F12C_{16}$$

Thus in Fig. 8.14(a), change the instruction

```
            MOV  CX,5064H
```

to

```
            MOV  CX,0F12CH
```

Section 8.9

11. Change the first line in LIST1 to read

$$\text{LIST1 DW OFFSET LIST3}$$

12. Change the first line of LIST1 to

$$\text{LIST1 DW OFFSET LISTN}$$

and the first line in LISTN should be

$$\text{LISTN DW OFFSET LIST2}$$

The second line in LISTN can specify its code, the third line its size, and the lines that follow its contents.

Section 8.10

13. The following statements need to be changed in the program of Fig. 8.19(a).

Current statement	New statement
MSG_P DB 'ENTER N OR Y'	MSG_P DB 'ENTER 1 FOR NO AND 2 FOR YES'
PCOUNT DW 13	PCOUNT DW 29
CMP AL,'N'	CMP AL,1
CMP AL,'Y'	CMP AL,2

Section 8.11

14. A>TYPE B:EXER814.ASM

```
TITLE   EXERCISE 14  SECTION 8.11 )

STACK_SEG          SEGMENT          STACK 'STACK'
                   DB               64 DUP(?)
STACK_SEG          ENDS


DATA_SEG           SEGMENT          'DATA'
NUM_A              DB      ?
NUM_B              DB      ?
NUM_C              DB      ?
NUM_D              DB      ?
RESULT             DB      ?
DATA_SEG           ENDS


CODE_SEG           SEGMENT          'CODE'
EXER814            PROC             FAR
          ASSUME  CS:CODE_SEG, SS:STACK_SEG, DS:DATA_SEG
```

```
        ;To return to DEBUG program put return address on the stack

                PUSH    DS
                MOV     AX, O
                PUSH    AX

        ;Following code implements Exercise 14 ( Section 8.11 )


                MOV     AX, DATA_SEG            ;Set up data segment
                MOV     DS, AX

                LEA     SI, NUM_A               ;Set pointer
                MOV     AL, [SI]                ;Get A
                IMUL    BYTE PTR [SI+1]         ;A*B*.5
                MOV     BL, AH
                MOV     AL, [SI+2]              ;Get C
                IMUL    BYTE PTR [SI+3]         ;C*D*.5
                MOV     AL, AH
                ADD     AL, BL                  ;Add up partial products
                SHL     AL, 1                   ;A*B + C*D
                MOV     RESULT, AL              ;Save the result

                RET                             ;Return to DEBUG
        EXER814         ENDP
        CODE_SEG        ENDS
                        END     EXER814

        A>


        A>DEBUG B:EXER814.EXE
        -U 0 24
        0915:0000 1E            PUSH    DS
        0915:0001 B80000        MOV     AX,0000
        0915:0004 50            PUSH    AX
        0915:0005 B81809        MOV     AX,0918
        0915:0008 8ED8          MOV     DS,AX
        0915:000A 8D360000      LEA     SI,[0000]
        0915:000E 8A04          MOV     AL,[SI]
        0915:0010 F66C01        IMUL    BYTE PTR [SI+01]
        0915:0013 8ADC          MOV     BL,AH
        0915:0015 8A4402        MOV     AL,[SI+02]
        0915:0018 F66C03        IMUL    BYTE PTR [SI+03]
        0915:001B 8AC4          MOV     AL,AH
        0915:001D 02C3          ADD     AL,BL
        0915:001F D0E0          SHL     AL,1
        0915:0021 A20400        MOV     [0004],AL
        0915:0024 CB            RETF
        -G A

        AX=0918  BX=0000  CX=0035  DX=0000  SP=003C  BP=0000  SI=0000  DI=0000
        DS=0918  ES=0905  SS=0919  CS=0915  IP=000A  NV UP DI PL NZ NA PO NC
        0915:000A 8D360000      LEA     SI,[0000]                      DS:0000=0000
        -E 0 40 40 40 20
        -G 24

        AX=0830  BX=0010  CX=0035  DX=0000  SP=003C  BP=0000  SI=0000  DI=0000
        DS=0918  ES=0905  SS=0919  CS=0915  IP=0024  NV UP DI PL NZ AC PE NC
        0915:0024 CB            RETF
        -D 0 4
        0918:0000  40 40 40 20 30                              @@@ 0
        -G

        Program terminated normally
        -Q
```

BIBLIOGRAPHY

Bradley, David J., *Assembly Language Programming for the IBM Personal Computer*. Englewood Cliffs, N.J.: Prentice-Hall, Inc., 1984.

Ciarcia, Steven, "The Intel 8086," *Byte,* Nov. 1979.

Coffron, James W., *Programming the 8086/8088*. Berkeley, Calif.: Sybex Inc., 1983.

Intel Corporation, *Components Data Catalog*. Santa Clara, Calif.: Intel Corporation, 1980.

Intel Corporation, *iAPX86,88 User's Manual*. Santa Clara, Calif.: Intel Corporation, July 1981.

Intel Corporation, *MCS-86^{tm} User's Manual*. Santa Clara, Calif.: Intel Corporation, Feb. 1979.

Intel Corporation, *Peripheral Design Handbook*. Santa Clara, Calif.: Intel Corporation, April 1978.

Lemair, Ian, and Robert Nobis, *Electronic Design 19,* Sept. 1, 1978.

Morse, Stephen P., *The 8086 Primer,* Rochelle Park, N.J.: Hayden Book Company, Inc., 1978.

Norton, Peter, *Inside the IBM PC,* Bowie, Md.: Robert J. Brady Co., 1983.

Rector, Russell, and George Alexy, *The 8086 Book,* Berkeley Calif.: Osborne/McGraw-Hill, 1980.

Scanlon, Leo J., *IBM PC Assembly Language,* Bowie, Md.: Robert J. Brady Co., 1983.

Schneider, Al, *Fundamentals of IBM PC Assembly Language*. Blue Ridge Summit, Pa.: Tab Books Inc., 1984.

Triebel, Walter A., *Integrated Digital Electronics*. Englewood Cliffs, N.J.: Prentice-Hall, Inc., 1979.

Triebel, Walter A., and Alfred E. Chu, *Handbook of Semiconductor and Bubble Memories.* Englewood Cliffs, N.J.: Prentice-Hall, Inc., 1982.

Triebel, Walter A., and Avtar Singh, *The 8086 Microprocessor: Architecture, Software, and Interface Techniques.* Englewood Cliffs, N.J.: Prentice-Hall, Inc., 1985.

Willen, David C., and Jeffrey I. Krantz, *8088 Assembler Language Programming: the IBM PC.* Indianapolis, Ind.: Howard W. Sams & Co., Inc., 1983.

TO ORDER YOUR DISKETTE

A diskette, containing the programs listed in this book, is available from Prentice-Hall for $24.95.

To order, mail your check to

    Book Distribution Center
    Route 59 at Brook Hill Drive
    West Nyack, NY 10995

IBM PC/8088 Assembly Language Programming (diskette) 44831-6

INDEX

Prog1.ASM **1. Editing**

Creat & modify Source Code <u>EDLIN</u>

IN
Prog1.ASM **2. Assembling**
OUT
Prog1.OBS   <u>MASM</u>

.LST File — Mostly
Translated code

IN: XX.OBJ **3. Linking**
OUT: XX.EXE

    <u>LINK</u>

4. Running

    <u>DeBug</u>

Display command to list prog.
in M.L. (can be transported to
SDK - 86)

<u>Source Program</u>

1st line

   Page 60,132   Tells assembler that the printer can displa
                 132 cols (otherwise, 80 cols. is limit)

Program on DOS

   Mode   LPT 1: 132

   Basic: LPrint chr$(15)
     (commpressed print mode)